In *Quebec National Cinema* Bill Marshall tackles the question of the role cinema plays in Quebec's view of itself as a nation. Surveying mostly fictional feature films, Marshall demonstrates how Quebec cinema has evolved from the innovative direct cinema of the early 1960s into the diverse canvas of popular comedies, glossy co-productions, and reworked *auteur* cinema of the postmodern 1990s. He explores the faultlines of Quebec identity – its problematic and contradictory relationship with France, the question of native peoples, the influence of the cosmopolitan and pluralist city of Montreal, and the encounters between sexuality, gender, and nation traced and critiqued in women's and queer cinemas.

In the first comprehensive, theoretically informed work in English on Quebec cinema, Marshall views his subject as neither the assertion of some unproblematic national wholeness nor a random collection of disparate voices that drown out or invalidate the question of nation. Instead, he shows that while the allegory of nation marks Quebec film production, it also leads to a tension between textual and contextual forces, between homogeneity and heterogeneity, and between major and minor modes of being and identity.

Drawing on a broad framework of theory and particularly indebted to the work of Gilles Deleuze and Félix Guattari, *Quebec National Cinema* makes a valuable contribution to debates in film studies on national cinemas and to the burgeoning interest in French studies in the culture and politics of *la francophonie*.

BILL MARSHALL is professor of modern French studies at the University of Glasgow. He has written several books and numerous articles on film and francophone culture.

Quebec National Cinema

Bill Marshall

McGill-Queen's University Press
Montreal & Kingston • London • Ithaca

ISBN 0-7735-2103-8 (cloth)
ISBN 0-7735-2116-X (paper)

Legal deposit first quarter 2001
Bibliothèque nationale du Québec

Printed in Canada on acid-free paper

Publication of this book has been made possible by
grants from the University of Glascow and the
International Council for Canadian Studies through
their publication fund.

McGill-Queen's University Press acknowledges the
financial support of the Government of Canada through
the Book Publishing Industry Development Program
(BPIDP) for its activities. It also acknowledges the support
of the Canada Council for the Arts for its publishing
program.

Canadian Cataloguing in Publication Data

Marshall, Bill
    Quebec national cinema
    Includes bibliographical references and index.
    ISBN 0-7735-2103-8 (bound)
    ISBN 0-7735-2116-X (pbk.)
    1. Motion pictures – Social aspects – Quebec (Province)
    2. Nationalism in motion pictures. 3. Motion pictures –
    Quebec (Province) – History. I. Title.
    PN1993.5.C32Q8 2001   791.43'09714   C00-900557-9

This book was typeset by Typo Litho Composition Inc.
in 10/12 Baskerville.

Contents

For Eric, Rex, and Martha-Marie

Preface

Any work on "national cinema" has to justify its boundaries and exclusions, even and especially if it aims to address several disciplines and potential readerships. The richness and diversity of Quebec cinema deserve wider recognition beyond the tiny corpus of films distributed beyond its frontiers. Those qualities, and the debates they generate, need to be put more fully on the map of French studies and film studies in the anglophone world and beyond. So this book aims for a certain comprehensiveness, and may help as a reference work, but it also seeks to explore Quebec cinema via a variety of theoretical approaches which have helped me disentangle some of the currently compelling issues around cultural identity and identities. The work thus contains broad histories and summaries of Quebec film production, but is also keen to explore the faultlines of the national idea and project. Indeed, as well as the interest I have had in Quebec since my first visit there in 1979, I initiated this project partly out of work I was doing on Europe and cultural studies. The resonances back and forth across the Atlantic of the debates around global, national, regional, local, and sexual identities have generated for me a stimulating intellectual commerce, one of the best kinds there can be.

Inevitably, given the size of this project, I have had to make certain difficult decisions. Thus the book is heavily weighted towards discussion of fictional feature films, for the reasons discussed in chapter 1 and particularly because they represent the main cinematic site in which the imagined (but no less "real") community of the nation is constructed and constituted. (Animation seems to me to involve distinct methodologies and is not included here.)[1] In addition, my understanding of "Quebec national cinema" is that it is francophone, since it is above all the French language which represents the distinctness of Quebec. (Even so, I have been unable and unwilling to fit in discussion of every production, and discussion is sometimes unevenly shared between films according to their representativeness, relevance to my argument, and, dare I say, interest. On the other hand, a test of any book's success is to leave author and reader wanting more.)

The borders implied in any answer to the question "What is a Quebec film?" are of course porous, and this is not just about the frequent cross-fertilization of documentary and fictional categories. Fundamentally, we can say it is any film made in French in Quebec with majority or significant Quebec funding and personnel. And yet any discussion of Quebec cinema must take into account the gaps in that definition opened up by the cinematic relationships with the rest of Canada (especially neighbouring Ontario), Hollywood (personnel who end up or spend time there, the preferences of Quebec audiences, the "American" dimension of Quebec identity), and France.

Nonetheless, as one of the threads of argument in the book insists, defence of certain provisional "solidities" by which we live is often necessary, because at their most productive they undermine master narratives and positions. The sympathy towards Quebec's "nationhood" in this book is based on its pluralizing, anti-hegemonic potential. For example, there exists an important anglophone Quebec cinema, partly because of the location of the National Film Board in Montreal. But to place it on an equivalent footing with "Quebec national cinema" as object of analysis would in my view be a conceptual error, one complicit with the political project of certain federalists of denying the status of nationhood to Quebec by drowning it in a set of multicultural and liberal-individualist equivalences. I would here follow Michel Seymour in arguing that Quebec's anglophones are, of course, an integral part of the socio-political community that is the Quebec nation, but that they form part of a "national minority" rather than being assimilated to the "national majority" on which the Quebec nation is based (but to which is not reduced).[2]

To take another example, the idea of this book was rejected by another publisher's series on national cinemas on the grounds that Quebec "is not a nation," whereas "Canada is" (in the singular). In Canada and Quebec, this represents a loaded political statement which immediately takes sides in the ongoing controversy about Quebec's status. My argument, that Quebec certainly is a nation and has a national cinema, and that these terms are still useful, whatever or rather because of the problematizing gloss I give them, does not, however, lead to any conclusion for or against the sovereignty project. Supporters of either side of that debate may find comfort from what is written here. "Quebec national cinema" needs to be posited and then immediately called into question. In any case, while culture is always bound up with politics, no cultural artefacts or analyses worth their salt can really be summed up by a political choice or option.

Many thanks are called for, to both individuals and institutions who have provided support, advice, information, and/or hospitality. This book would not have been completed without them (and in particular those Québécois of all persuasions and positions who have made researching on this topic a real pleasure): José Arroyo, Jody Berland, Aubin Boudreau, Peter Brown, Michel Coulombe, Kevin Crombie, Mireille Dansereau, Eric Darier, Jill Forbes, Rex Fyles, Ivan Gekoff, Peter Harcourt, Sue Harper, Ken Hirschkop, Emmanuel Kattan, Martha-Marie Kleinhans, Michel Larouche, Jim Leach, Jocelyn Létourneau, Yves Lever, Ian Lockerbie, Eric Paquin, Christian Poirier, Bruce Robbins, Robert Schwartzwald, Sherry Simon, Christina Stojanova, James Tully, and Tom Waugh. All the mistakes are mine, as well as the translations unless otherwise stated. Many thanks also to the staff of the Bibliothèque nationale du Québec and the Cinémathèque québécoise, and to numerous production and distribution companies in Montreal for arranging viewings and lending video copies. The British Academy, the British Association of Canadian Studies, the Canadian High Commission in London, the Faculty of Arts of the University of Southampton, and the Nuffield Foundation were also very generous in their financial support of my research activities. Publication of this book was made possible by a grant from the International Association for Canadian Studies.

Bill Marshall
London and Southampton,
March 2000

Down but not out: Dominique Michel as the spunky heroine of
Tiens-toi bien aux oreilles à papa.
Courtesy Cinémathèque québécoise

The Metro as antechamber to death and redemption:
Catherine Wilkening, Lothaire Bluteau and
Johanne-Marie Tremblay in *Jésus de Montréal*.
Courtesy Cinémathèque québécoise

Cross-language liaisons in an English-looking Montreal:
Suzanne Grossman and Marcel Sabourin in
Il ne faut pas mourir pour ça.
Courtesy Cinémathèque québécoise

The Metro as alienation: Marcia Pilote and Pascale Bussières in *Sonatine*.
Courtesy Cinémathèque québécoise

Mature and anti-conformist: Geneviève Bujold in *Les Noces de papier*.
Courtesy Cinémathèque québécoise

Before the catastrophe: Robert Gravel and Jacques Lussier as the lovers in *Pouvoir intime*.
Courtesy Cinémathèque québécoise

Picking ways through a world of images: Véronique Le Flaguais in *La Vie Rêvée*.
Courtesy Cinémathèque québécoise

Minor dalliances and transversal liaisons: Claude Jutra and Johanne Harelle in
À tout prendre.
Courtesy Cinémathèque québécoise

The open mouth of Roy Dupuis.
Courtesy Cinémathèque québécoise

1 Producing and Envisioning the Nation

During the course of 1998, a site appeared on the World Wide Web (www) announcing a forthcoming Quebec film, *Québec Jour J*, in effect a war film, with the largest budget of any Quebec film so far, about the consequences of a successful "yes" vote in a Quebec referendum on independence. In response, Canada, or rather "la fédération," launches "a military repression on a scale never imagined," but the heroic "Quebec forces" fight back, and deal the federation "a bloody good hiding." Two sequels were also announced: *La Fédération contre-attaque* and *La Reconquista*.

This book is in part about the impossibility of such a film. Canadian and Quebec cinema rely to a large part on public money, federal and provincial, for their existence. None would be available for such an inflammatory piece as *Québec Jour J*, let alone a high-budget combination of *The Battle of Algiers* and the *Star Wars* series, and the private sources the www site refers to would not be able to fill the gap. However, the spoof at least offers a caricature, and an interesting limit case because of its very impossibility, of what "national cinema" might be. To go to the other extreme, another electronic source, Microsoft Cinemania, describes *Cinéma québécois*, in its section on "Canada," as "the most highly developed *regional* cinema in the world"[1] (as well as misspelling the names of two of its key directors).

Quebec cinema is most certainly a "national cinema," but this latter phrase and concept, far from designating a stable object of investigation, let alone a master category grounding interpretations and analysis, represents a significant problem. "Nation" and "identity" are ever provisional, historically contingent, ceaselessly elaborated constructions, and yet at some level they are inescapable. The world cinema industry, with the heterogeneity of its texts' modes of address and audiences, and the cross-border flows of its capitalization and personnel, seems to lend itself with ever greater difficulty to nation-centred readings, even if certain groups, particularly but not exclusively national cultural élites, maintain an interest in polarizing the relationship with "Hollywood" or "American" mass culture. Why, then, continue to choose "the national" as (master) reading of film texts, and how to do so? Why "Quebec cinema," that is, why Quebec and why its cinema as fruitful objects of cultural investigation of this kind? And how to theorize in this context the relationship between text and context, between meaning or symbolic production and material practice or production?

Fredric Jameson's argument concerning "Third-World" literature is that its specificity lies in the national allegories it tends to embody; "the story of the private individual destiny is always an allegory of the embattled situation of the public third-world culture and society,"[2] whereas in the developed world, the political is recontained and psychologized or subjectivized by way of the private/public split. This line has been critiqued for the binary opposition it creates between First and Third Worlds,[3] but it and the debate provoked shed much light on the case of Quebec, where since the 1960s ideologies of nation-building have been hegemonic, sometimes drawing on totalizing Third World models of subalternity and self-assertion but more recently seeking to reconcile Quebec sovereignty with contemporary globalization. The domination of the world audio-visual industry by the United States, able to amortize production costs in its immense home market and to capitalize on the commercial and cultural historical advantages entrenched since 1914, has made national allegorical readings possible of other film and television production, be it from the First or the Third world.

These readings, as Jameson correctly and subtly points out, will not be one-to-one homologies of, say, nation and individual protagonist (we shall see that this has been one approach to Quebec cinema) but will be "profoundly discontinuous, a matter of breaks and heterogeneities, of the multiple polysemia of the dream rather than the homogeneous representation of the symbol."[4] This language renders the reading of the "national" in, say, film texts, analogous with the dream work in Freud or the labour performed upon ideology as described by Pierre Macherey in *Pour une théorie de la production littéraire* of 1967 and taken up by Terry Eagleton at his most Althusserean in *Criticism and Ideology* of 1976. Its advantage is to preserve the inescapability of politics in the text and yet to respect the specifically aesthetic procedures of meaning production. Since Quebec film texts tend to be vehicles for competing (as opposed to totalizing) discourses of the nation, this methodology of plurality within an anchoring framework is quite a boon. And yet it may be possible to go farther down the road of "polysemia" while preserving the rootedness in history and politics. One of the contradictions of nationalism, as we shall see, lies in the way it both asserts the nation (vis-à-vis an Other or Others) and at the same time proclaims the nation's equality within a community, or world system, of nation-states. (This is the sense of the moment in his victory speech in September 1994 when Parti Québécois leader Jacques Parizeau wanted the Québécois[5] to become "a *normal* people in a country to which it belongs.") Thus the "national" in terms of the "normal" might be read according to more elusive discourses, of the banal, of the non-assertion or at least non-foregrounding of the nation, of the representation of Quebec reality in terms of its non-specificity as opposed to its specificity. The "national" may then quite easily tip over into a non-differentiation, in which other allegorical discourses begin to apply, as when a film may be seen to allegorize modernity or postmodernity, Jameson's "geopolitical aesthetic," as we shall see. "National" film texts are thus always inevitably pluralized and even destabilized by the competing discourses of and on the nation that exist in the culture and polity, the work of aesthetic form on non-aesthetic (ideological) discourses, and the contradictions and paradoxes inherent in the idea of the nation itself. We must imagine, therefore, a constant tension between forces of homogeneity and heterogeneity, between the centripetal and centrifugal. (I am drawing here on Mikhail Bakhtin's description of the forces in language between an inert unitary form and the plurality and movement of "heteroglossia": "Every concrete utterance of a speaking subject serves as a point where centrifugal as well as centripetal forces are brought to bear.")[6] It is this tension that creates and that is the "national allegory." There is no master hermeneutic of "the nation" for decoding the films of a "national cinema." Rather, the nation is unfixed, not one reference point, not a refuge of stability faced with globalization,[7] but a very mobile spiral.

However, this tension is not to be seen as some feeble halfway compromise, nor this spiral as a chain of signifiers in which meaning is endlessly deferred. For contacts, exchanges, and negotiations to be made between cultures, for borders to be crossed, even for new becomings to occur, there has to be something we call a culture, an identity, "Quebec," on which the signifiers so provisionally alight. This is not an essay that deconstructs that notion out of existence. Rather, that national-allegorical tension is positive and productive, for it makes national cinema or any other manifestation of national culture possible.

This is why the case of Quebec is so interesting. The "national" is inescapable because of unsettled political questions. However, the "ground" of the Quebec national idea is a shifting one. Quebec national culture and identity are simultaneously naturalized (as for "a normal people") and non-naturalized. Many Franco-Québécois, arguably most of those who voted "yes" to *souveraineté-partenariat* in the October 1995 referendum, claim a double allegiance to Quebec and Canada. The "no" votes were concentrated in the Montreal region, where nearly half of Quebec's population lives, indicating a spatial split in the territory itself constructed by differentiated insertions into the Canadian, North American, and world systems as well as by larger concentrations of anglophones and ethnic minorities (Montreal is 63 per cent francophone, Quebec as a whole 82 per cent). The Franco-Québécois are a majority in Quebec, a minority in Canada, where 24 per cent of the population is francophone. Canada is a nation whose size, diversity, and relatively weak symbolic investments are creating centrifugal forces that threaten its long-term viability. At the same time, sections of the population, and especially the elites of southern Ontario, faced with the possible non-differentiation from and assimilation to the United States, make Canada's defence a priority. (This was most evident in the then opposition Liberal Party's resistance to the North American Free Trade Agreement at the 1988 elections.) The construction and development of a Quebec national cinema has therefore included aspects of assertion but also contestation (not only of Canadian federalism but also of the pre-1960 social and political order and its technocratic successor).

"National cinema" is therefore not a master hermeneutic but a master problematic for this study, since it constantly returns, as in a spiral, to undermine its own so provisional categories. I have chosen Quebec cinema, as opposed to Quebec television, theatre, or literature, for three reasons. First, of these cultural forms, cinema is the most hybrid and communicates the most with the others. Secondly, it is the form that embodies in the most comprehensive manner "high" and "low," legitimate and popular, cultural practices. In these ways it is the most representative practice, that which contains the most dialogue with other cultural forms (although of course it is not the most popular, in the sense of audience figures or time spent consuming it: that belongs to television). Thirdly, it is the most exportable cultural artefact, that which possesses the most significant interface with the world industry of production and consumption of images. Or rather, given the relative paucity of Quebec films consumed outside Quebec itself, it best exemplifies the criteria of exportability or inexportability.[8] It seems to me that these are especially characteristics of fictional feature films rather than documentary, where distinct patterns of exhibition and consumption apply. However, we shall see that in Quebec fictional features have engaged in close dialogue and even osmosis with the documentary form and tradition.

The national-allegorical tension can be explored further by making links between the case of Quebec, national cinema, and four key elements that are also potential faultlines in the elaboration of national identity: recognition, space, time, and ontology/identity.

Benedict Anderson's oft-quoted work on the nation as "imagined community" stresses above all the conditions of possibility for the emergence of the national idea and of nations themselves. These lie in the development of capitalism, particularly print capitalism with its attendant validation of vernacular languages, its products consumed by the literate audience of the growing bourgeoisie. National bourgeoisies require, therefore, the existence of institutions of mass media to create the sense of community in a territory "covered" by those institutions. This community is necessarily imagined because, unlike in, for example, traditional village life, any individual will never meet the vast majority of its members: "All communities larger than primordial villages of face-to-face contact ... are imagined. Communities are to be distinguished, not by their falsity/genuineness, but by the style in which they are imagined."[9] The sociologist Fernand Dumont has traced how this was true for the "French-Canadians" as much as for any other territorialized linguistic group,[10] but with certain peculiarities: the conquest of 1759 meant they missed that paroxysm of the nation-state, the French Revolution, but those (professional) élites that remained nonetheless benefited from the creation of parliamentary institutions in Lower Canada in 1791 and the attendant explosion of newspapers and of discourse on their society. The failure of the Patriotes' rebellion of 1837–38, and the dominance of an anglophone business class in Quebec, meant a long retreat, within the Canadian Confederation established in 1867, into a defensive, clerical nationalism, and an identification of the nation with the people rather than with its élites. It was only in the post-Second World War era, and especially after 1960, that a francophone business class and technocracy gained hegemony in (now Quebec, as opposed to French-Canadian) society, and here the new mass media, beginning with radio and then television and cinema, played a crucial role.

This role was one of constructing recognition, which can be understood as a visual and aural process that is ideological, in the sense of reproducing what are accepted as social "norms" such as national belonging, but that also contributes to the construction of subjectivity itself. As Althusser points out in his 1969 essay "Ideology and Ideological State Apparatuses,"[11] social reproduction works through the interpellation or hailing ("Vous," for example, in the mode of address of television news) of subjects by discourses in institutions. Instead of bumping into someone familiar in the village street, we recognize others in our community, and ourselves, through these processes. Whereas Althusser admits that this must be constantly repeated, he neglects somewhat the instabilities inherent in the process, as identities change over time and new "norms" have to be negotiated. In addition, the workings of imagination, and of desire, in this imagined community are likely to produce surprises and lines of flight, to use a Deleuzean term, beyond these codings. Nevertheless, recognition is a useful category for the way it links identity, the senses, the media, and the importance of others (as when members of the community recognize me, or even when the international community of nations "recognizes" one of its own).

Indeed, the desire for "recognition" was put forward by many Québécois supporting sovereignty in the referendum. It is also at the centre of Charles Taylor's conceptualization of the politics of identity, which, in common with other commentators such as Anthony Giddens and Alasdair Macintyre, he places in the context of modernity and the passing of hierarchical societies. "Recognition" can thus no longer be socially derived but must be "inwardly generated": "What has come about in the modern age is not the need for recognition but the conditions in which the attempt to be recognized can fail."[12] It is to the failure of recognition that Taylor ascribes the contemporary impasses of the Canada/Quebec relationship. (Taylor's location in Quebec, and specifically as a bilingual anglophone Montrealer, is one that informs not only his engagement in Canadian political questions – his activism in the 1960s and 1970s in the left-wing New Democratic Party, his support for the Meech Lake Accord and an asymmetric federalism which would respond to Quebec's aspirations[13] – but also, in less well-known ways, his wider thought. The limitations of working in basically liberal paradigms, which we shall discuss in a moment, are tempered in Taylor by an awareness of dialogism and an engagement with difference that are obvious to any thinking denizen of Montreal. Drawing on Gadamer's notion of "the fusion of horizons," he writes of "learning to move in a broader horizon, where what we once took for granted as the background to valuation can be situated as one possibility alongside the different background of the unfamiliar culture.")[14]

The imagined community of the nation is also one that is spatially organized, projected, and represented on physical and mental maps. This includes the delineation of borders to mark what is inside or outside the territory of the community; the differentiation of space within those borders (the distinction between Montreal and other parts of Quebec, for example, or between the sedentary *habitant*'s agricultural community in New France and the frontiers traversed by the emblematic and supremely gendered fur-trapper, the *coureur de bois*); the nature of the relationship (for example, proximity or distance) with other spaces, such as France, Britain, and the United States; and the relationship between the official, bureaucratic, or technocratic mapping of, for example, the city, and the creative, alternative mappings of the inhabitants of its *quartiers*. Space plays a crucial role in Quebec politics and culture, examples being the discussions concerning the possible partition of a sovereign Quebec to take account of the preferences of certain anglophones and native groups;[15] the questioning of provincial borders supposedly settled in 1912 with the allocation of the Arctic and subarctic territories of the Hudson's Bay Company; the dispute with Newfoundland over the ownership of Labrador; and the post-1960 territorial delineation "Quebec" as the homeland of the francophones of North America, as opposed to the more dispersed notion of "French-Canadians." This latter term once included the *francophones hors Québec*, notably the important adjacent minorities of New Brunswick and Ontario, numbering 250,000 and 700,000 respectively, who now count for little in the Quebec national project. (They have their own national organization that lobbies the federal government, the Association des communautés francophones et acadiennes.) Jean Morisset, for example, was one of the few Québécois intellectuals to break with the nationalist consensus around the 1980 referendum. His work, *L'Identité usurpée: L'Amérique écartée* of 1985, invokes the alternative mapping of *Américanité*, of the vast spaces of hybridity traversed by the original, non-territorial, racially "impure" *canadien*, who, crucially for Morisset's argument, was bereft of a state, escaping as he did the hierarchies and boundaries of French absolutism. We shall see how this figure returns in various cultural configurations within the modern Quebec state.

Any identity or identities contained in the national-allegorical tension are temporally as well as spatially arranged. This takes the form of myths of origins, of often competing national narratives teleologically organized from a present, completed standpoint[16] but also projections into a possible future. This utopian or rather uchronic strain is present from an early stage in the history of the French Canadians, for example, in the fascination with the native peoples and the *pays d'en haut*, but the absence of political utopianism meant that New France developed differently and suffered a different fate from the English colonies. It persists in some discourses today in the notion of "just one more referendum" and the victory for sovereignty that surely lies beyond. However, both the myths of origin and the uchronic strain suggest a lack or an incompleteness located at the heart of even the most totalizing nationalist discourse.

The time of the nation is closely connected to the concept of recognition, not just because the advent of modernity meant the establishment of shared national as opposed to local time zones (often as local as the church clock), but also because the secularized nation-states and the new media became vehicles for a new apprehension, that of "homogeneous empty time." Just as identity based on personal biography relies on a narrative moving through time, so do nations come to be conceived "as a solid community moving steadily down (or up) history," a movement measured by clock and calendar, a simultaneity of temporal coincidence which finds its expression in those forms that grew out of eighteenth-century nation-building, the novel and the newspaper, and that is to be distinguished from medieval and religious notions of time vertically linked to divine Providence, past, present, and future as a simultaneous instant. This "complex gloss upon the word 'meanwhile'"[17] connects with the national subject's sense of the simultaneous activity of the unseen members of the national community. It finds its contemporary expression in television news bulletins, and also in film.

However, the text of the nation, in its allegorical tension and play of deterritorialization and reterritorialization, is riven with temporal discontinuities and problems. Historical and cultural memory is always a question of selection and therefore of forgetting. Its activation is often dependent on the existence of rituals, sites, or *lieux de mémoire* ("realms of memory") whose meanings in turn depend on the shifting consensus of present-day national signification. The idea of the nation appeals to far-off origins, but at the same time the modern nation is unquestionably a product of the Enlightenment and the American and European bourgeois revolutions, its timeworn traditions – the ice hockey league, for example – often very recent inventions. The temporal schemes involved include a teleology of progress but also the persistence of tradition, even irrational atemporalities: a realism and a romanticism. As Homi Bhabha has argued from a post-colonial perspective of migration and hybridity, the relationship between the origins and the present of the "national people" is problematic.

The people of the origins are "us" and "not us." The national "we" is temporally split:

> The people are the historical "objects" of a nationalist pedagogy, giving the discourse an authority that is based on the pre-given or constituted historical origin or event; the people are also the "subjects" of a process of signification that must erase any prior or originary presence of the nation-people to demonstrate the prodigious, living principle of the people as that continual process by which the national life is redeemed and signified as a repeating and reproductive process ... In the production of the nation as narration there is a split between the continuist, accumulative temporality of the pedagogical, and the repetitious, recursive strategy of the performance.[18]

The nation can even be considered to be a site of conflicting or at least plural temporalities, marked by class, ethnicity, gender. Indeed, Julia Kristeva's famous essay on "Women's Time"[19] differentiates between the *linear* time of the modern nation-state's logic of rationalism, progressivism, and teleology (the time of history) and those perceptions of time that are *cyclical* (involving the repetitions of biology) and *monumental* (involving notions of, for example, maternity which go well beyond the particular historical sediments of particular cultures and nations). Fortunately, Kristeva realizes that these different perceptions of time, while gendered, relate in mobile, gender-non-specific ways within given individuals and societies. She uses them, however, to introduce a politically informed notion of difference into the supposedly homogeneous temporality of the nation.

Clearly, as we have seen, whereas nationalist discourse would seek to pass off the nation as natural and inevitable, it is in fact a construction and a fiction, and this is much like personal identity. Stuart Hall summarizes a sophisticated version of that first position, which

> defines "cultural identity" in terms of the idea of one, shared culture, a sort of collective "one true self," hiding inside the many other, more superficial or artificially imposed "selves," which people with a shared history and ancestry hold in common. Within the terms of this definition, our cultural identities reflect the common historical experiences and shared cultural codes which provide us, as "one people," with stable, unchanging and continuous frames of reference and meaning, beneath the shifting divisions and vicissitudes of our actual history.[20]

Just as the delineation of a nation's borders, of outside and inside, parallels the ontological (that is, philosophical) distinction of self and other, of that which is not me and that which is me, so can the individual self construct a view of its sameness, its oneness, its identity (a cultural term), across the chronologies, spaces, and experiences it traverses. There are numerous theoretical arguments to choose from in order to refute that particular position. Althusser's emphasis on ideological interpellation to explain "identity," for example, draws on Lacan's idea of the subject caught in the signifying chains of language and perpetually seeking but failing to achieve the illusory oneness or plenitude of self associated with the infant's relationship with the mother's body in the Imaginary before its entry into the Symbolic Order. Identity is assigned by the Other (parents and indeed whole symbolic order) to produce the subject, that is, one is looked at from somewhere other than the position from which one sees; there is a split between the eye of the subject and the gaze of the other. As in language, the sign is split, the symbolic order dividing subject between S_1 (signifier of subject) and S_2 (sign that would give it its value), and thus producing non-coincidence, alienation, between the subject of the enounced and the subject of the enunciation. This separation of the subject in language from living being means no more *jouissance* as in the Imaginary, just lack. Fantasies remain about seeking the lost *objet a*, that which goes missing when the subject enters the symbolic order (and which can never be regained and which, in a sense, is always already lost). This is the trace of *la chose/Das Ding*, which is the originary and fundamental lack, the primordial mother who nonetheless is lacking but who gives rise to the myth of lost paradise, a promise of absolute plenitude and, when encountered, the experience of its lack. The subject is the phallus (enunciator) for the Other, but for itself is castrated (alienated, split in language).

However, this is partly to anticipate debates later in this work concerning sexuality, the unconscious, and national identity. In this current consideration of the ontology of the self, questions of identity, and the self/other, same/difference split, it is the work of Deleuze and Guattari that seems the most pertinent to the Quebec situation and its paradoxes, especially their notions of territorialization and deterritorialization and the very particular distinction they make between majority and minority discourse.

In the article quoted above (on Caribbean cultures, in fact), Stuart Hall outlines the alternative position, that of process and the unfinished self, to one that emphasizes fixity of being: "As well as the many points of similarity, there are also critical points of deep and significant *difference* which constitute 'what we really are' and what we have *become*."[21] Becoming, *le devenir*, as opposed to being, *l'être*, is at the core of Gilles Deleuze's philosophy, and it is to be understood in not only temporal terms but also spatially. In his work with the radical psycho-analyst Félix Guattari, Deleuze dispenses with identity and sees the self or the nation as a historically contingent organization of flows. The machine which connects, directs, or arrests flows is not a metaphor but a model for all such arrangements: flows of blood or fluids in bio-logical systems, of energy in engineering and technology, of desire or language in human societies, of capital in the world economy. Having abandoned the Cartesian notion of the self, the distinction with the Other can also be jettisoned, and this is the point of becoming rather than being: "Starting from the forms one has, the subject one is, the organs one has, or the functions one fulfills, becoming is to extract particles between which one establishes the relations of movement and rest, speed and slowness that are *closest* to which one is becoming, and through which one becomes. This is the sense in which becoming is the process of desire."[22] The emphasis is therefore on movement, process and multiplicity, rather than fixity and identity: "The proper name does not designate an individual: it is on the contrary when the individual opens up to the multiplicities pervading him or her, at the outcome of the most severe operation of depersonalization, that he or she acquires his or her true proper name. The proper name is the instantaneous apprehension of a multiplicity."[23]

However, this does not mean that the "proper name," as in "Québé-cois," is to be dismissed as fiction. Rather, it is always already plu-ralized, its bits, components, particles, and molecules arranged and organized according to bigger, molar, structures but at the same time potentially taking off in new directions: "Signs are not signs of a thing; they are signs of deterritorialization and reterritorialization, they mark a certain threshold crossed in the course of these movements."[24] The most useful categories within this theoretical work for our pur-poses are those of territorialization/deterritorialization, and the very particular sense of majority/minority, major/minor.

It is through territorialization, the code of grounding, that the flows of meaning and desire are checked, and through deterritorialization, a process of decoding or unfixing, that they are relaunched, perhaps to be reterritorialized. To take one example from *A Thousand Plateaus*, hyperinflation can be said to deterritorialize the money supply, but the introduction of a new currency, a semiotic transformation in this case, makes reterritorialization possible. These are to be seen not as binary oppositions but as processes in interaction: coding and decoding are inseparable, just as, for example, the genetic code always includes an element of genetic drift. In industrial capitalism, the territorializations of earlier, sedentary, and agricultural societies are replaced by a more groundless "axiomatic" of profit and accumulation. The nation is

constituted on the deterritorialized remainders of previous societies –
administrative units, an abstract "people" – and gives them new consistencies, compensatory reterritorializations.

The Quebec national project is riven with the tension between territorialization and deterritorialization because of the competing discourses of *Québécité* and *Américanité,* the migrant flows of globalized
capital into which it is unevenly inserted, and the different relationships lived with Canada. These Deleuzean paradigms seem to offer a
way out of some of the quandaries generated by notions of identity
associated with Hegelian and Kantian traditions, such as to be found in
Charles Taylor, who is hostile to the Nietzscheanism of much contemporary French theory, which he equates with an abdication of evaluation (an attitude perhaps overdetermined by the uses to which Derrida
and Foucault have been put in American identity politics). In Taylor,
there is a tension between his concepts of the "self" (a stable if evolving entity) and of the fundamentally dialogical, indeed Bakhtinian
reality of social existence. The question arises of the relationship between the two, given the slippage that recurs in his writing between the
individual and collective self. As we see, Deleuze and Guattari take the
radical step of dispensing with these binary oppositions – between self
and other, individual and collective – in favour of flows and codes.

However, this does not mean an abandonment of "evaluation," even
if the objects (and subjects) of such evaluation can no longer be understood as discrete and stable entities. Charles Taylor's prioritizing of
"value" is often predicated on encounters between "whole" cultures,
across what is for him the fundamental dilemma of a "difference-
blind" universalism and the equally risky fostering of particularity.
Deleuze and Guattari have a concept that, in its simultaneous evocation of identity and negativity, speaks to the tensions of the Canadian
and Quebec contexts and the shifting categories of majority and
minority. Deleuze and Guattari conceive the "minor" not in terms of
numbers but in terms of the relationship between becoming and the
territorialization/deterritorialization process. The writings of Kafka, or
of African-Americans, or of the Irish, all possess an ambiguous relationship to the "major" language in which they write, language that
they affect with "a high coefficient of deterritorialization."[25] Kafka, for
example, wrote German as a Jew excluded from the German-speaking
minority in a peripheral city of an empire in which German was a lin-
gua franca in the marketplace but not "at home." Quebec artists of the
1960s, to take another example, were conscious that their language
was not only "minor" in relation to the language of the vast North
American and Canadian anglophone majority but was peripheral and

relatively deterritorialized vis-à-vis the "major" language that is standard metropolitan French. This implies, as when Jameson writes of national allegory, that any individual utterance is always already in this context magnified to embrace politically the whole collectivity. (Indeed, for Deleuze and Guattari, "there is no individual enunciation," since enunciation always implies "collective assemblages" and we all speak in indirect discourse.)[26] The point is not to talk about Quebec French as a particular dialect, but to realize that "minor" and "major" attitudes can be adopted towards this language and culture. One may fall back on a new territorialization: "The Canadian singer can also bring about the most reactionary, the most Oedipal of reterritorializations, oh mama, oh my native land, my cabin, olé, olé."[27] Or one may follow the logic of the "minor" status, with its capacity for proliferation and innovation (becoming), its antithesis therefore to the rank of master, and its undermining of the "major" culture's pretensions to the natural, normal, and universal: "It is a question not of reterritorializing oneself on a dialect or patois but of deterritorializing the major language."[28] Minorities have their own territorialities but must also be considered as "seeds, crystals of becoming whose value is to trigger uncontrollable movements and deterritorializations of the mean or majority."[29] The "minor" languages and cultures that emerge may be completely innovative. We shall see how different tendencies in Quebec cinema have run the gamut of responses to this question.[30] Not only, as Deleuze argues in *The Time-Image*, did the dominated status of the Québécois make them into an absent people to be invented, typical of what he calls "modern" cinema bereft of the certainties of the pre-war era, but their status of "perpetual minorities, in a collective identity crisis,"[31] I argue, continues in effect throughout the forty-year history of their national cinema. The multiple, relational reality of Quebec cultural identity means that to inhabit that cultural space is always to be becoming something else.

Andrew Higson has described the mistakes often made in talk about "national cinema": "To *identify* a national cinema is first of all to specify a coherence and a unity; it is to proclaim a unique *identity* and a stable set of meanings. The process of *identification* is thus invariably a hegemonizing, mythologizing process, involving both the production and assignation of a particular set of meanings, and the attempt to contain or prevent the potential proliferation of other meanings."[32]

Given the complexities (but inescapability) of the national-allegorical tension and the peculiarities of the Quebec context, this study will seek to grapple with Quebec cinema not as coherence but as patterns of incoherence: to explore the ways in which a national hegemony may be constructed, but also how it is made constantly provisional; to examine its relationship with both the rest of Quebec culture and the international film industry; and to investigate the relationships among production, text, and audiences.

The four key elements or faultlines of the nation can thus be applied to specifically cinematic practices (taking place as they do within specifically cinematic institutions), and represent an avenue of inquiry running parallel to the sections of this book arranged by historical period, genre, or subject-matter.

Recognition includes a film's mode of address and its interpellation of audiences in shared (as in "nous les Québécois") or differentiated (as by gender) subject position(s). The literal audiences themselves are to be problematized, as in, for example, the distinction between art and popular cinema. Recognition works through aural and visual repetition, and we shall see how Quebec cinema produces a repertory of images and voices. Cinematic realism relies on the representation of the national landscapes, and, joined to it, a star or, more accurately, celebrity system which provides a repertory of faces for repeated close-ups. This is itself a form of territorialization, or rather reterritorialization, for, as Deleuze and Guattari argue, the face, a culture of the face, marks a deterritorialization, part of a move away from the body or organism – ever since humanity has walked upright – towards regimes of significance and subjectivation.[33] These repetitions partake of those other practices of repetition and difference that have characterized mass-movie going, namely, stars and genre. In addition, language, Québécois French, is one of the most fundamental modes of recognition, and its importance in Quebec cinema can be inscribed in a whole history of sound cinema, its introduction throughout the world in the 1920s and 1930s marking a certain (but incomplete) falling back on national cultural modes, a kind of 1789 or 1848 of cinema.

Questions of space arise obviously in connection with cinematic space, that created by the camera and editing in realist cinema. Classical realist cinema attempts to create a coherent space (and time) and, combined with the inclusiveness of realism itself, raises questions about what kind of national space, or rather organization as opposed to content of space, is being figured, including the relationship between the frame and what is implied off frame. In addition, space is important for the way borders of cinematic practice may be constructed or overcome: the relationship, in terms of production, finance, and cultural reference, with other cinemas. In this connection, the role of exhibition practices in Quebec is relevant for the way in which anglophone and francophone cinemas are zoned and market differentiations mapped out.

The notion of time is thus important cinematically not just for the representations of the past (or future) to be found in historical costume genres but for the novelistic totalizing grand national "meanwhile" a film may set up. Classical forms of narration developed in early Hollywood cinema by Griffith emerge from the temporal conventions of the nineteenth-century novel. For example, montage is figured as concurrent or convergent, alternating the moments of two actions or plotlines which then join up, and this contributes to the organic unity or wholeness of the text. In addition, the organization of narrative and narration is dependent on time: the handling of contradictions, the degrees of closure, the position of the narrative voice and its relation to the nation's plural temporalities. The institution of "Quebec cinema" is also dependent on histories and historiography.

The vicissitudes of ontology and identity translate into cinematic practices primarily around debates concerning Oedipal or anti-Oedipal readings of film's processes of subjectivation. What can be termed "1970s gaze theory" was preoccupied with the ways in which mainstream film constructs a stable (dominant) subject position for the spectator across the movements and scissions of the text. Our task is not only to incorporate national hegemonies into those heterosexual and masculinized processes, and investigate the extent to which they confirm or undermine the dominant discourses, but also to analyse desire in the film text in terms of the processes of deterritorialization and reterritorialization, the flows of possibilities beyond Oedipal fixities, for which it is a conduit. Key questions will be the ways in which the film text articulates the process of becoming, in the identities it constructs, in the narratives it sets in motion.

Production of feature films in Quebec has not been even since 1960: one or two films per year in the early 1960s, a sizeable increase after the creation of the Canadian Film Development Corporation (CFDC)/Société de développement de l'industrie cinématographique canadienne (SDICC) in 1967, a low dip of one film in 1981, and since then an average of ten features per annum. Quebec, with seven million people, has a per capita film production less than that of France (141 films produced in 1995). The 1997 audience share of Quebec films in Quebec was 3.7 per cent, of Canadian films excluding Quebec 0.3 per cent, of French films 4.9 per cent, and of American films 84.1 per cent. (In Canada as a whole, Canadian films capture 2–3 per cent of the box office.) Including video rental, the figures are roughly the same for share of receipts. "Quebec national cinema" means, therefore, a share, but a marginal one, of a market massively dominated by Hollywood. That indigenous market share is obviously lower than that of countries such as France (37.3 per cent) or even Britain

(6.6 per cent), but the comparison with countries more similar to Quebec in terms of population size and minority-language status is also unfavourable: Denmark 17 per cent (twenty feature films produced), Netherlands 5.4 per cent (eighteen), Sweden 18 per cent (twenty-seven) (all 1996 figures). However, Quebec audiences often express preferences for "Québécois" television programs. Only 2 per cent of English Canadians' viewing of television drama is of Canadian product, whereas for the Québécois the figure is 20 per cent, and some programs can reach massive audiences, even half the population (*Les Filles de Caleb*, 3.7 million on 31 January 1991). This factor plays a major role in the continuance of a Quebec popular cinema, as we shall see.

The average low figure for audience share of Quebec films needs to be placed in context, for a particular success can have a massive effect. Since 1980, Quebec films have managed in some years to generate nearly a 10 per cent total audience share. The biggest-grossing Quebec film in Quebec in the 1980s, and in the world in absolute terms, was *Le Déclin de l'empire américain* (Denys Arcand, 1986), followed by the popular comedy *Cruising Bar* (Robert Ménard, 1989). In the first half of the 1990s, only three Quebec films figured in the top fifty list of takings (*Jurassic Park* was at number one): the highest, at number twenty-six, was *Louis 19, le roi des ondes* (1994), which had a total audience of 332,292 and box-office receipts of $1,669,376. And then *Les Boys* (Louis Saïa, 1997), a popular comedy about a hockey team, managed to pulverize all records, taking $6 million with an audience of 3.5 million, second only to *Titanic*. (Even though it was released at the end of 1997, it still managed to boost the audience share of all Quebec films that year by 1 per cent of the total.) The problems for Quebec production lie in the small home audience, the small number of French speakers in the world relative to, among others, English, Spanish, and speakers of the major Asian languages, and difficulties of exportability to the main existing market, France, as we shall see.

In addition, film distribution in Canada and Quebec is a major issue. Famous Players and Odeon between them control 40 per cent of all screens in Canada, account for over 50 per cent of all revenues, and command all first-run films from the American majors and even some independents. (In 1984 Odeon was taken over by a Canadian firm, Cineplex, which then merged with MCA and was later bought by Loew's in 1998. Despite the fact that the distribution-arm is Canadian-owned, Loew's is under no obligation to show Alliance's Canadian productions.) Canada is thus for all intents and purposes an extension of the American home market, representing 10 per cent of such, the third-largest "foreign" market after Japan and France. In Quebec, the importance of the francophone market had led historically to the emergence of specialist distributors, notably France Film, which dominated this activity from the 1930s to the 1960s, and by the late 1970s a host of others, notably Cinépix and Films Mutuels. However, in the early 1980s the American majors expanded heavily into non-American film distribution, and this was perceived by industry professionals, particularly in Quebec, as a threat to their profitability and even existence. The Parti Québécois (PQ) government at the time also perceived a cultural and linguistic threat in the delays in releasing French versions of American films. The result was Bill 109, passed unanimously by the Quebec National Assembly in June 1983, which attempted to create a market share for Canadian and Québécois distributors and to oblige them all to invest part of their income in Quebec productions. These provisions were either never applied or watered down through lobbying by the Motion Picture Association of America (MPAA) before the electoral defeat of the PQ government in 1985.[34] The Québécois distributors were saved, however, by the financial failure of the majors' distribution of foreign films, the development of new markets such as video and pay-TV, the box-office success of several Quebec films including *Le Déclin de l'empire américain*, and the creation by Telefilm Canada, successor to the CFDC, of a *Fonds d'aide à la distribution des longs métrages*. Indeed, the very possibility of a Quebec cinema is dependent on television and on state aid from provincial or federal sources. While 54.2 per cent of the finance for the production of fictional Quebec features in 1996–97 came from pre-sales (and 21.6 per cent from coproduction money), a third came from public-sector investments: 16.1 per cent from provincial tax credits, 2.5 per cent from the provincial Société de développement des entreprises culturelles (SODEC), and 9.4 per cent from Telefilm Canada, a peak sum of $62 million ($147.6 million for audiovisual production as a whole). At both the federal and the provincial level, efforts continued in the late 1990s to render indigenous filmmaking more competitive with other cinemas in terms of both production (the average budget dropped from $2.9 million to $1.5 million in the first half of the decade) and marketing (average spending was $150,000). Louise Beaudoin, minister of culture in the PQ government re-elected in 1998, announced increased annual resources of $10 million for the film industry in November that year.

The outline just given serves to remind us of the material context of Quebec film culture, its shaping of the parameters of production, and its location of production in a history that is both general and specific.

What follows is an account of the emergence of a Quebec national cinema in the early 1960s, to be followed in the next chapter by an analysis of two pairs of key films from different historical conjunctures.

The emergence of narrative feature films is closely bound up with two pre-existing contexts: documentary production and television. In one sense, however, the history of this cinema could begin slightly earlier. Fifteen feature films were made in French between 1944 and 1954, that is, during the peak period of cinema attendance in Quebec, and indeed in the rest of the industrialized world, before or just at the beginning of the television era. CBC/SRC (Société Radio Canada) began broadcasting in 1952, the year of the highest cinema attendance on record in Canada: 58.76 million. (In 1953, 9.7 per cent of Canadian households had a television set, in 1956 66.2 per cent, in 1962 90.8 per cent.) Those fifteen French-speaking films were in some respects a false start and are to be distinguished in most ways from the post-1960 production associated with the new national assertion of "Quebec," in contrast to the defensive cultural identity of "French Canada." (However, the most significant films of that epoch, such as *La Petite Aurore l'enfant martyre*, directed by Jean-Yves Bigras in 1951, form part of Quebec's film memory, as we shall see. The fact that their fundamentally melodramatic mode and popular-cultural origins in theatre and radio were of little interest to the filmmakers of ten years later says much about the agenda, priorities, and limitations of the cultural practitioners of the Quiet Revolution.)

The Quebec of 1945–60 can be understood as experiencing increasingly blatant disjunctures between its social, cultural, economic, and official realities. The Union nationale government of the autocratic Maurice Duplessis had been, since its first period in power in the 1930s, the ideological vehicle for the clerical-nationalist élites that had dominated Quebec since the Rebellion of 1837–8. Its brand of nationalism combined the defensive myth of a Catholic francophone Quebec, wedded to traditional values of family and rural life, with an openness to foreign or English-Canadian companies seeking to develop the economy. At the same time, the increased role of the federal government in the Second World War had led to Ottawa's adoption in the post-war period of Keynesian, interventionist policies – in health, education, and other areas – which accompanied the nationwide phenomena of high economic growth and robust consumerism.

It is within these tensions that the conditions of possibility for the emergence of a Quebec national cinema can be discerned. It is difficult, however, to disentangle those conditions from the teleological historiographies of the period that have been hegemonic in Quebec society since 1960. As with accounts of the Quiet Revolution (to be discussed in chapter 3), myth can become reality, and narrativization of this kind itself becomes part of nationalist self-image: If the majority of present-day Québécois believe that 1960 marks a new departure in their history, much of the film-making world concurs with Marcel Jean's assertion that the short documentary *Les Raquetteurs* of 1958 defines "a new aesthetic" and makes plain "a new relation to the real."[35] Such discourses, even the existence of this book, stress the performative aspect of constructing the national.

Suffice it to say that the conditions of possibility are at once political and economic, as indicated, but also technological (the development of television and 16 mm., for example) and cultural-aesthetic: most notably, the waning of traditional élite discourses in Quebec, and the interplay in the 1950s between the two leading ideas in non-Hollywood film-making, namely, auteurism and realism, the latter in Canada particularly understood as documentary realism. It was that unique institution, the National Film Board of Canada (NFB)/Office national du film (ONF), which was the crucible for Quebec national cinema but also the site of its emerging, competing, and ongoing contradictions. (Not for the last time was a federal institution to play such a role.) The NFB is world-renowned, largely for its astute and strategic cultivation of the twin specializations of documentary and animation in the face of the Hollywood-dominated world film industry. The origins, however, of the institution and its practices lie in wartime and in the imported British (Scottish) managers and personnel. John Grierson (1898–1972) was its first commissioner during the war years, having initially been invited from the General Post Office film unit by the Canadian government to report on the state of the film industry in this country. Grierson in turn invited to the NFB in 1941 the animator Norman McLaren (1914–87), with whom he had worked at the GPO film unit.

These origins provide a context and point of departure to be later imitated and challenged in terms of both aesthetic practice and national identity. For Grierson, documentary was both a "creative treatment of actuality"[36] and a sociological public-education text, particularly in the Canada of the early 1940s. The creation of patriotic wartime propaganda, however artfully achieved, would adjust in peacetime to aims made explicit in clause 9a of the 1950 National Film Act: "The Board is established to initiate and promote the production and distribution of films in the national interest and in particular to produce and distribute and to promote the production and distribution of films designed to *interpret Canada to Canadians and to other nations*."[37] This voluntarism – and the very existence of the NFB – therefore goes beyond the daily ideological work that constructs "the nation" in the media and underscores the insecure nature of Canadian identity, along with the problematic status of the French speakers. The standard NFB documentary was bound up with authority: that of the "truth" of the film (exemplified in a preconceived script and a voice-over commentary), that of the pseudo-neutral film-maker, and that of "Canada."

The status of French in the NFB progressed in fits and starts. Grierson was initially unsympathetic to the claims of francophones, and the reigning belief was that the board should simply make French versions of films already shot in English. However, by the mid-1950s there had been significant developments. The beginnings of national television service in Canada, with the CBC/Radio Canada providing separate anglophone and francophone channels from 1952, saved the NFB by creating a demand for films in both languages, and more francophone personnel were recruited. The NFB moved from Ottawa to Montreal in 1956 and could thus draw on a large pool of both anglophone and francophone personnel. A separate studio was created for making the French versions. While a press campaign in the Montreal daily *Le Devoir* in January 1957 demanded a distinct French section within the NFB, a francophone, Guy Roberge (1915–91), was appointed commissioner. It was at this time that a new generation of francophone technicians and film-makers could be appointed, notably, for these first two chapters, Michel Brault (b. 1928), Gilles Groulx (1931–94), and, on a freelance basis, Claude Jutra (1930–86). It should be noted that, despite the earlier unevenness of support within the NFB for francophone productions, the institution could be turned into a resource for progressive film-makers from Quebec critical of the Duplessis government, which, given its hostility not only to federalist intervention but also to trades unionism, for example, considered the NFB to be a nest of communists.

Documentary film practice was also evolving. Anglophone film-makers in Unit B had created a series, *Candid Eye* (1958–60), which sought to renew documentary film-making at the NFB and to get round the problem of authority, supposedly by employing hidden cameras and telephoto lenses. Brault had participated in some of these as cinematographer and camera operator. The series *Panoramique* (1956–57) and *Temps présent* (1968–64), half-hour documentaries for broadcast by Radio Canada in prime time, explored, in terms of content, new economic and social realities in Quebec. The new documentaries represented a significant step forward for the francophone film-makers, because all that was needed to negotiate a film was a scenario of a page or so, as opposed to the previous practice of getting an entire screenplay translated into English and then sending it to a producer who read it and criticized it in English, the critique afterwards being translated into French before being sent back to the director.[38]

Les Raquetteurs is important because it combines innovation in terms of both form and content. A fourteen-minute black-and-white documentary, directed by Michel Brault and Gilles Groulx, about the annual snowshoe festival in Sherbrooke, it is generally considered to mark the birth of direct cinema, *le direct*. The precarious and historically limited definitions of this term, and its theoretical weaknesses, are partly bound up with the fact that *le direct* was a reactive form of film practice. It sought to break with the didacticism and pseudo-objectivity of much documentary film-making, dealing with the problem of the power relationship between the film-maker and the subject of the film through participation, or rather the creation of a communicative relationship between them. Direct cinema would aim to minimize (abolition being impossible) the mediating work of film-maker and camera on "the real," while at the same time rejecting the conventions that in classic documentary or even dominant Hollywood practices seek to disguise that mediation:

As its name indicates, it therefore designates a cinema which directly captures ("on the ground" – outside the studio) words and gestures by means of material (camera and tape recorder) that is synchronous, light and easy to handle, it is in other words a cinema which establishes "direct" contact with man, which attempts to "cling to the real" as far as it can (given the mediation involved in the enterprise). This new cinema does not claim to present truth on a silver platter, but it aims to pose the problem of truth on the level of human relationships. It is above all a cinema of communication.[39]

For example, Brault presented *Les Raquetteurs* to a Flaherty seminar in California in 1959. The work of Robert Flaherty (1884–1951), director of *Nanook of the North* (1920) and *Man of Aran* (1934), had been characterized by the replacement of pre-written scripts with the filming of events and rituals suggested and provoked by the film-maker's presence in the lives of his subjects.

Le direct also depended on technological changes and on dialogue with events in world cinema, notably France. The importance of 16 mm. had been magnified by its use in television news reporting and in the demand for documentary films by the CBC. Technicians at the NFB had made changes to the German-made Arriflex camera to make it lighter and able both to be shoulder-held and to handle synchronous sound-recording; cameras were "blimped" to make them less noisy; faster film stock was used. The influence and prestige of Italian neo-realism of a decade earlier, of the recent British Free Cinema movement, and especially of developments in France also made themselves felt. The French documentary, partly protected by a law which until 1953 prevented double features in French cinema, had been characterized in the ten years after the Second World War by a degree of authorship and/or political commitment that ran counter to the Anglo-Saxon tradition of "objectivity." Jean Rouch (b. 1917) had studied anthropology and went to West Africa to make films such as *Les Maîtres fous* (1955) and *Moi, un noir* (1957), which combine an anticolonialist perspective with the provocation and even fictionalization of scenes by the director himself, all in the name of an engaged "truth" to be communicated. As an example of the exchanges impelled by the emerging Canadian *direct*, Rouch invited Brault to participate in the making of subsequent films in France such as *Chronique d'un été* (1961: co-directed Edgar Morin).

Les Raquetteurs is indeed film-making in the thick of its subject. In one of cinema's most dazzling examples of its mobility, the camera dives into the crowds, films them from within with wide-angle lenses, pans across rooms. The soundtrack – synchronous in fact only for part of the mayor's speech, and that is interrupted – energetically blasts out band music and the cacophony of the crowd. Total absence of commentary means that the "truth" of the film must be sought elsewhere. However, the main thrust of the film is a carnivalesque humour which renders anything as grave as "truth" as slippery as the snow and ice on which the *raquetteurs* frequently tumble. For this is a popular *fête*, in which, in Bakhtinian terms, social categories and hierarchies are disrupted and confused. The film plays on boundaries being transgressed, even and at the same time as the camera crosses the line separating it from its subject: the sound of the snowshoes is confused with that of a dog's paws; the races, their semblance of order epitomized by the lanes in which they are "run," are memorable for participants falling over, or, in the case of a woman "runner," failing to start at all; bodies fill the screen in an excess of enjoyment and drink; a carnival "queen" is crowned. To the carnivalesque humour evoked by Bakhtin in his work on Rabelais[40] can be added Bergson's theory of laughter as the revenge of spontaneous and non-linear interiority on the mechanically ordered and rigidified external. The crowd's takeover of the main street, the progress of the procession, is only briefly interrupted during the film by a train moving horizontally across frame at the level crossing. However, at the end, even as the title "Fin" appears, the motor cars have reoccupied the space: the carnival is over.

The "truth" of *Les Raquetteurs* seems therefore to be in a sense a negative one, one of anti-authority. However, in its carnivalesque portrayal of the festival and its resolute refusal to concentrate on élite discourses (the interruption of the mayor's speech exemplifies this) or film practices, a "people" is constituted. *Les Raquetteurs* is a film of landscape, cityscape, and faces. The town, Sherbrooke, is hosting a festival based on a largely rural practice. The snow is not only iconic of the national landscape and climate, it manages to elide many differences between urban and rural. Faces in close-up are not individuated as for celebrities, but rather form a collective panorama and in this way are not constituted as "citizens" but as "people."

"The real" is therefore not, of course, transparently relayed via the film-making practice, and never can be. *Les Raquetteurs* mediates its reality to the same extent as a Hollywood movie or standard NFB documentary, but differently. The moment of *Les Raquetteurs* is one of competing claims on the real, and so we are dealing in cultural texts with competing "reality effects," to quote Roland Barthes.[41] The ambiguity of the photographic or cinematographic image's powerful claims on the "real" (this image is what was there), along with the mediating force of cinematic language, is a constant of film criticism and practice: we need only look at the work of André Bazin. The theoretical weaknesses of *le direct* are less important than the fact that its time had come. The determinants of its emergence outlined above point to the way in which at this specific cultural moment a certain rhetoric of "the real," of the real as shock, research, invention, could be the most effective mobilizing strategy against the complacencies of 1950s North America, the Duplessis regime, or the NFB.

But what kind of "Québécois" people or identity is being articulated? Who is included? There are no non-white faces in the crowd. This is not surprising for Sherbrooke in 1958, but the *raquettes*, invoked here as a great popular tradition, are, of course, Amerindian in origin. If in terms of space the film seeks to federate the rural and urban, in terms of time it seems to look both backwards and forwards. The festival is a *tradition* that risks dying out – the closing "Fin" has this connotation, too – but the "people" are constituted via the technical virtuosity of the movie camera and the supremely *modern* modes of film spectatorship. What becomes of that "people" outside the carnivalesque moments of festival and film? Significantly, the people are portrayed in terms of pleasure and consumption, and these will take, are taking, very non-traditional forms with the advance of consumerism. Finally, this invocation of "the people," running counter to the mystifications of English Canada and the Duplessis regime, implies a unity, a people-as-one, a notion exemplified in Marsolais's account, despite his qualification: "[Francophone] Quebec society is indeed living at this time decisive years in the course of which *it* is resolving to take *its* destiny into its own hands on all levels."[42]

The effects of *le direct* are both profound and diffuse. In his study of the cinema of the Quiet Revolution period, Yves Lever argues[43] that *le direct* remained a marginal current in documentary film-making. However, its influence loosened up much filmmaking practice, in fiction as well as documentary. So broad indeed is this influence that the opposition between fiction and documentary begins to unravel. Writing in the aftermath of May 1968 in France, and seeking to explore creatively political film practices, Jean-Louis Comolli was interested in asserting this disruptive potential of *le direct*, which is not about "representing or reproducing life" but about a reciprocal production, "the intermodification of cinema and world." For one thing, the practice of synchronous sound had crucial political consequences, completing in a sense the sound revolution of the late 1920s by democratizing it: "With the coming of sound, cinema was conquered by *the language of the class in power* and of dominant ideologies; whilst with synchronous sound, it is *cinema itself which conquers* language, all of language, that of everyone, that of the workers as well as the bosses."[44] Allowing for the hyperboles of post-68 discourse, this point is supremely relevant to the constitution of a Quebec national cinema. What is more, for Comolli, in *le direct* the truth of the film's spectacle lies not only in displaying the facticity of representation but in producing a film event: "In direct cinema, if you like, the filmed event does not pre-exist the film or the shoot, but is produced by them. We can no longer speak of an outside 'reality' of which the film makes the image, but merely of filmed material which is the entire reality the film has to deal with."[45] Just as no unmediated documentary purchase on "the real" can exist, so neither, in much subsequent Quebec cinema, can there be a "fiction" from which culturally agreed notions of "the real" are completely banished. Indeed, some of the characteristics of *le direct* (a rhetoric of the relatively unmediated "real" and of spontaneity, populism, a sense of the collective, mobile camera, irreverence, naturalistic treatment of human physicality) as well as its contradictions (a problematic unanimity, ambiguous attitudes to tradition and to social and cultural change) are among the most enduring in Quebec cinema. Along with auteurism, the documentary-realist tradition in general has since 1960 dominated élite discourses on film. All these factors feed into our first analysis of two other "foundational" films.

2 Foundational Fictions

Two feature films of the early 1960s, *Pour la suite du monde*, directed by Pierre Perrault and Michel Brault, and *À tout prendre*, directed by Claude Jutra, serve to illustrate and develop both the problematic nature of "national cinema" in general and the ambiguities of Quebec cinema as it emerges within a particular material, ideological, and aesthetic context.

Pour la suite du monde, shot in 1962 and released in 1963, seems at first sight to be easily categorized within *le direct*, with the qualifier that Perrault (1927–99) and Brault instigate and participate in the event they film. They encourage the inhabitants of the Île aux coudres on the lower St Lawrence to revive the tradition, abandoned in 1924, of capturing the beluga whale by creating an enclosure of tall saplings (*harts*) which, planted in the river at low tide, at high tide confuses the creature into believing it is trapped. Backed by the NFB, the project had its gestation in Perrault's series on the region, *Au pays de Neufve-France*, made for radio in the early 1950s and for television in 1959–60. Brault and Perrault seek to minimize the mediation between "reality" and representation, eschew commentary in favour of the inhabitants' own words, and develop strategies for making the presence of the noisy Arriflex equipment as unobtrusive as possible (covering it with blankets, using minimal lighting in the one interior night scene, the mid-Lent carnivalesque equivalent of Halloween "trick or treat").

However, something new in the method is also occurring, and it has profound implications for Quebec identity construction. The "reality" represented in the film is one provoked by the film-makers, and is the film's solution to the problem of representation itself. If representation always implies a loss of the direct relationship to "reality" because of the selections and combinations it involves, then the action deemed appropriate here is to produce rather than record reality and to blur the distinction between documentary and fiction, or, more accurately, reality and "fabulation," in the name of a higher reality, an "authenticity." The complicity between film-makers and the characters filmed, within the project of a "cinéma du vécu/cinema of the lived," "makes the real character into an actor and the film crew into a participant."[1] Having been prompted to revive this form of hunt, the islanders then have the initiative to a certain extent, leading their "observers" to key sites of action (for example, Perrault recounts the way they rushed ahead to see the captured whale) and creating their own *mise en scène*: "Alexis, the central character of the film, directs the film and his addressee, through gesture and language, acquires an 'identity' which makes him a contemporary of the event, and an accomplice, in his turn, of those producing it."[2]

So, while *Pour la suite du monde* continues *le direct*'s concern to film "the people" from within, the processes of identification and recognition in the film come to depend not only on (considerable) use of close-ups, wide-angle landscape shots, and a rich rendition of the islanders' French on the soundtrack, but on a transformative process of dialogue (between spectator, film-maker and islanders) and creation (the *mise en scène* of the hunt and the myths and stories surrounding it). What is crucial to the interpretation of the film is the relationship between this procedure and the question of truth and authenticity. Are truth and authenticity given categories in the film? Does *Pour la suite du monde* look backward or forward?

"Fabulation" was preferred to "fiction" above because, for Perrault, "fiction" implies the alienations and falsities of contemporary mass culture and especially Hollywood:

All the room is taken up by the image of the empire. Like idols. And turns us away from ourselves. It takes up all the room, invests it. It leaves no room any more for meaning, for dreams, for hope. I am no longer free to dream. The imaginary of the commodity represents a prohibition to dream.[3] ... I couldn't recognize myself in the writing. To take myself for Yves Montand or James Dean. To navigate my still wild and rebellious river, in the ships and mythologies of Ulysses.[4]

Pour la suite du monde validates the islanders' identity, and by extension that of the Québécois, for they are afforded recognition from outside when they travel to New York to deliver the beluga to a zoo.

Perrault thus sets up a homology between "real life," the islanders and their culture, and those aspects of "Quebec" and the "Québécois" untainted by capitalism and mass society. Clearly, problems lie in the relationship with the emerging Quiet Revolution in Quebec. While the film appears to offer a plenitudinous national identity via the technology of a mass medium, it does so seemingly outside modernity. Also, Perrault's delineation of the "real" and "authentic" obviously recall the Frankfurt School's rejection of, for example, "Hollywood" as an extension of the reign of the object or commodity into cultural life and as an alienation both from a critical, dialectical relationship with the world and from nature. Where Ulysses represents for Adorno and Horkheimer the prototype of Enlightenment man manipulating nature, for Perrault he is simply an example of a character from someone else's story. *Pour la suite du monde* may be read as a rendition of Adorno and Horkheimer's valorization of "the capacity for reflection as the penetration of receptivity and imagination,"[5] but it is grounded in terms of the "people" and of "Quebec" and of a renewed ownership.

Pour la suite du monde successfully avoids some of the totalizing excesses of this position, first because of its plurality of discourses, in particular that of "poetry." (As Yves Lever points out, many Quebec film-makers of the 1960s had begun their careers elsewhere – Perrault had practised law – and were published poets.)[6] The rediscovery of Quebec's oral tradition, spurred on by Perrault's radio work, is one of the major themes of the film. However, the film's "poetic" mode also introduces ambivalences, appropriately enough, between the denotative documentary mode and a connotative mode that is present throughout. Much of the latter is linked to the discrepancies between tradition and modernity we shall discuss in a moment. However, it is also present in the polysemy of Michel Brault's images. Let us take, for example, the *harts* planted in the water. Barthes's distinction between denotation and connotation is useful for the way it explains the legitimizing power of realist cinema to represent what *is there*, to convey a *being-there* beyond the codings of culture. At the same time, these denotations ground and connect the scattered and multiple connotations. In advertising or other mass-media texts, this connecting is a process of naturalization, an address to "common sense."[7] In the national art cinema that Perrault and Brault partly inaugurate, the polysemy of the image partakes of the play of homogenizing and heterogenizing discourses that characterizes the national-allegorical tension. Thus, to take an obvious example, if the St Lawrence river is a metonym of Quebec itself (one nationalist group of the 1960s proposed the name "Laurentie" for a new francophone nation), its connotations do not end there. For one thing, Perrault himself, of course, does not refrain from writing metaphorically of such a scene in his résumé of the film: "A panoramic image of the *harts*, side by side, like an immense barricade, a crowd huddled in impatience, a network of agitation, a deliberate manoeuvre accomplishing a project for the future ... The image of the *harts* and of their reflections in the water which enjoy torturing them to give us the chance of looking upon the illusory. Water dreams the image of fishing by distorting it."[8] However, before we can develop further the ways in which the film pulls against the totalizations of the "authentic," it is necessary to explore further the relationships it constructs between time, the image, identity, and truth.

Pour la suite du monde, and the work of Perrault in general, are the only Quebec films discussed by Gilles Deleuze in his two volumes on cinema, *L'Image-Mouvement* and *L'Image-Temps*. Deleuze's project is to describe two kinds of cinema and the philosophical assumptions and consequences of their attitudes towards the image. For Deleuze, cinema always deterritorializes, because the cinematic frame and screen construct a common measure for spaces as diverse as landscapes and faces. But in the movement-image, which characterizes mainstream and even avant-garde cinemas until the 1940s, those deterritorializations, which could take off into abstract movement with the universe as sole limit, are held in check by relative movement organized around "centres of indetermination" (usually, the protagonists) operating in closed sets, empirical succession, and organic narrative totalizations achieved through rational divisions. In contrast, the time-image, inaugurated by Orson Welles and Italian neo-realism, and continued by the French New Wave and New German Cinema, offers, through "irrational" cuts and discrepancies between sound and image, a new kind of image which offers "a receptivity to the multiple, the diverse, and the nonidentical."[9] This is because of the way Deleuze draws on Bergson's theories of time and Nietzsche's idea of eternal recurrence. Bergson emphasized the way in which time does not operate spatially and cannot be mapped by successive, separate divisions like the hands on a clock. On the contrary, each moment is swollen with the past and with the next. Because each moment of time is divided simultaneously into a launch towards an indeterminate future and a falling away into the past, we may speak of "points of the present": those of the present of the past, present, and future. The past, the whole of the past, exists as a virtual archive of discontinuous and non-chronological layers or sheets. This means that the "self" is also always fundamentally split (this introduction of time upsets Cartesian boundaries and certainties). The coexistence of the virtual and actual (like two sides of a piece of paper or two facets of a crystal) means that there is no "identity" in the sense of the return of the same. Rather, it is difference that returns, and it is only in this dynamic becoming – as opposed to stasis – that thinking is possible. The cinema of this view of time must therefore "include the before and the after."[10]

For Deleuze, this is what Perrault achieves in his use of fabulation, which is future-directed and quite different from the unearthing of the myths of a *past* people. Whereas Flaherty and the ethnographic documentary-makers that followed him were bedevilled by the relationship between subject and object (themselves, the camera, and the communities they filmed), Perrault and Brault are involved in a double becoming. The peoples of the island are "intercessors," real but engaged in creating fictions and legends, and a reciprocal communication and transformation characterize their relationship with the film-makers. Time is the force that puts truth in crisis. Through fabulation, Perrault and Brault are freed from a model of truth, and what Deleuze, drawing on Nietzsche, calls the "power of the false" breaks the repetition of the past and provokes, not a recalling, but a calling forth. As with the (other) Third World film-makers he examines, such as Ousmane Sembene and Glauber Rocha, Deleuze sees *Pour la suite du monde* as an example of "minor" cinema in which "the people" are perceived as "lacking" rather than offering a full identity or presence.

What cinema must grasp is not the identity of a character, whether real *or* fictional, through his objective and subjective aspects. It is the becoming of the real character when he himself starts to "make fiction," when he enters into "the flagrant offence of making up legends" and so contributes to the invention of his people. The character is inseparable from a before and an after, but he reunites these in the passage from one state to the other. He himself becomes another, when he begins to tell stories without ever being fictional. And the film-maker for his part becomes another when there are "interposed," in this way, real characters who wholly replace his own fictions by his own story-telling.[11]

This is what makes post-war cinema different from Eisenstein's revolutionary masses, or, say, Capra's democratic people, in which a fundamentally homogeneous force is seen as awakening to collective power. In this "becoming-other" of a people in minor mode, there is no fixed and finished outcome that the people "become."

However, *Pour la suite du monde* was always going to be a somewhat paradoxical choice for the kind of Nietzschean reading to which Deleuze subjects it. This is not to say that Perrault's work shies away from challenging received myths; witness his problematizing examination of the French ancestry of the Québécois in the third film in the

Île aux coudres trilogy, *Le Règne du jour* (1967: to be discussed in chapter 4), or the similar "in-between-ness" and disorientation of the urban intellectual participating in the hunt in *La Bête lumineuse* (1982). But Perrault is not Jean Rouch, whose *Moi, un noir* (1957) had his black African protagonists "fabulating" as characters and stars from Western films and Rouch himself "becoming-other" in the process. Deleuze realizes that through these "intercessions" Perrault is joining his "own" people, and at one point he slips into a surprising essentialism: "The concern is to belong to his dominated people, and to rediscover a lost and repressed collective identity."[12]

This is why it seems more fruitful to see *Pour la suite du monde* as a site of contestation between different forces and tendencies configuring the nation, and for this we need to return to the image of the river, which is crucial to the different understandings of the national time and space. These relations play on the oppositions between flowing and fixed, nature and culture. The harnessing of the river's resources implies an arresting or rather territorialization of its flows, which are not only physical but economic and demographic, so that territorialization is in tension with the deterritorializing flows of capitalism (the links with the North American interior and Atlantic commerce). The vertical axes of the *harts* imply a settlement, an organized community, in Deleuze and Guattari's terms a striated space as opposed to the smooth space of the stateless nomad.[13] For the islanders, the enclosure is not only a spatial (re)conquest of the river, an extension, it is also bound up with time. The traces of past enclosures unite space and time in a single image. Flowing water is a standard metaphor for the passage of time, but for the islanders, and by extension the Québécois, it has connotations both of the past (a return to a traditional practice, but also a harking back to Jacques Cartier's 1534–35 voyage in which their island is named and described and the hunting of beluga evoked) and of the future (the enterprise as situated in the film's unfolding narrative, a definitive revival, a transformation or becoming that their fable or adventure provokes). The *harts* stand out as a manifestation of human labour within nature and therefore provoke a whole set of other questions.

If the *harts* in the river connote time, what narrative and what "mapping" of time are to be inferred? These questions have crucial implications for Québécois identity. On the one hand, the film proposes a founding myth, the voyage of Jacques Cartier, and a re-founding myth, the rediscovery and promotion of an "authentic" Québécois identity. On the other, just as the individual memories of the islanders are both a resource and possess their fair share of fantasy, so are the historical accounts open to debate. Crucially, there is considerable debate in the film as to whether this particular hunting practice is native or French/ Breton in origin. The appeal to "tradition" also implies a problem with the contemporary world, with modernity itself, a reading of time far away from the linear and teleological progressivism of the nation-state, and yet that appeal is constructed through technology and a federal institution. The potential is there in Perrault's work for a masculinized, totalized, and highly territorialized notion of the nation. In a recent interview conducted by the semiologists at the Université du Québec à Montréal (UQAM) Perrault draws analogies between the defence of Quebec and the buffalo (filmed for his 1993 short L'Oumigmag) defending his own territory. He acknowledges the almost total silence of the women in Pour la suite du monde but fails to analyse the social and cultural reasons why it was the men and not the women who had the sufficient "personnalité" and "force" to assert themselves.[14] The world of the hunt in Pour la suite du monde is profoundly homosocial, and very sexualized, and this is made explicit in the "sequence of the cock who breeds the whole year."

There are two connotations here of the word dépayser. For Perrault, it is associated with that loss of place provoked by, above all, the United States ("you empty yourself of your substance and your strength [force], money is strength, you'll take it to the Americans").[15] However, in the same volume as that quotation, an article that, like Deleuze, attempts to rescue Perrault for Nietzsche and a certain postmodern theory argues for the emancipatory nature of the dépaysement, created by the proliferation of cultures (and perspectives, in Nietzsche's sense of the lack of groundedness of values in modernity): "The media who allow 'local rationalities' and 'dialects' ... to express themselves, prevent, because of this multiplicity, the return of a hegemonic reason."[16] The reinvestment of the "local" in Pour la suite du monde gives voice, with considerable effectiveness and beauty, to a community and culture bypassed by the hegemonies of North America. The film is therefore a site of struggle between a "minor" use of that culture, challenging the dominant and revelling in its contradictions, and a "major" one which founds new exclusions and which is unable to break out of the historical loop it constructs.

The construction of the canon of directors in Deleuze's cinema books is open to some questioning. As far as Third World figures are concerned, his choices are somewhat limited to those (usually one per country) adopted by Cahiers du cinéma in the 1960s, hence the choice of Perrault as representative of Quebec. He might instead have alighted upon À tout prendre, shot in 1961–63 and released in 1964, which revels in "the minor," but, paradoxically, a minor mode constructed from within the urban bourgeoisie (and whose main protagonist speaks impeccable metropolitan French). This quasi-autobiographical piece, produced in the private sector, portrays the affair between film-maker Claude (Claude Jutra) and a black model, Johanne (Johanne Harelle), who is still living with her (estranged and unseen) husband. The vicissitudes of the relationship – first encounter, obsession, other dalliances, Johanne's pregnancy, subsequent rejection by Claude, and miscarriage – are less important than the way the film combines formal experimentation with a sustained problematization of identity itself. Where *Pour la suite du monde*, in one reading at least, seemed to be producing a "truth" and seeking to uncover an "authenticity" beyond the world of appearances, *À tout prendre* joyously undercuts the "self" on which the film would seem narcissistically to centre. At the time, however, the film was largely greeted with incomprehension and seen as having little to do with the emerging assertion of Quebec identity associated with the Quiet Revolution.[17]

From the opening scene in which Claude gets ready for the party, the spectator is confronted with the fragility of the "self." The "realism" of body details in the shower (such as washing feet) combines with a montage of shots of Claude in various guises in front of the mirror, ending with him firing a gun so that it shatters and fragments. The self-proclaimed "quest" of the film is to "get rid of my youth and of the characters [*personnages*] inside me." The film proceeds to address this longing, but ultimately Claude discovers that there is no unified identity for him to step into. In fact, "Je est un autre," "I is another" (the quotation from Rimbaud's *Lettre du voyant* of 1871 which Deleuze uses to describe the non-identical in time and the non-identity of image and concept, and which he sees manifesting itself in Rouch's practice in *Moi, un noir*). The way forward is through fabulation.

The style of *À tout prendre*, and the combination of cultural inputs it contains, testifies to that play of instability, plurality, and difference. The film is dedicated to two men. One is Jean Rouch, and indeed the film owes much to *le direct* (mobile camera, lack of aestheticism in the shots, sense of immediacy). The other is Norman McLaren. Jutra had worked with McLaren at the NFB on the short *A Chairy Tale* of 1957, with its use of stop-action animation; the representation of the guns firing in Claude's fantasies in *À tout prendre* obviously recall McLaren's animation technique of scratching directly on the celluloid. Jutra had first met François Truffaut, who makes a cameo appearance in *À tout prendre*, at a film festival in Tours in 1957 in which both *A Chairy Tale* and Truffaut's *Les Mistons* were entered. They made a short film together, *Anna la bonne*, in 1959, based on a theatrical poem by Cocteau. We shall discuss subsequently the relations between early Quebec cinema and the French *nouvelle vague*. Suffice it to say here that aspects of

À tout prendre are reminiscent of both *Les Quatre Cents Coups* (Claude's problems are those of a man in his early 30s still negotiating the identity crises of adolescence, bereft of a solid place in a society he can believe in) and *À bout de souffle* (for its formal playfulness). For Deleuze, the *nouvelle vague* was a key expression in cinema of "the power of the false," in which the "form of truth" was replaced by forces and powers, of life and of cinema.

À tout prendre combines immediacy and self-reflexivity, and so a promise of "truth" or "the real," of the "authority" of the "author," is constantly undermined by a dazzling array of rapid camera movements, rapid montage, extensive use of zoom, freeze frame and slow motion, discontinuous interruptions from Claude's fantasy life, a soundtrack that veers from synchronous dialogue to music to Claude's stream of consciousness and his ironic voice-over commentary, and, of course the film within the film, the love story Claude is shooting. Plot – the anecdotal "real" of the film – is periodically suspended in favour of falsifying narration and sequences of "pure" spectacle, in particular what Deleuze calls a *gestus*[18] of Claude's body (a sequence has him performing various gaits, and then a return to "the true" is announced – in fact to his film shoot). The formal and thematic strategy is dovetailed in, for example, the scene of Claude and Johanne's first encounter. Longer takes than average for the film are used to portray Johanne's rendition at the party of the Creole song "Choucoune." (The scene is an unused sequence from the student film by Denys Arcand, Denis Héroux, and Stéphane Venne, *Seul ou avec d'autres*). This contrast, along with that struck with the chatter of the (white, middle-class) gathering, suggests an "authenticity" which is undermined not only by its status as performance but by the cut (Claude's point of view?) of an increasingly out-of-focus female figure, who may or may not be Johanne, standing up to sway to the music. This is preceded and followed by shots of Claude looking at her. Significantly, he asks a partygoer what her name is: "Johanne" flashes up twice on a blank screen. That particular question thus provides an unambiguous answer, but *who she is* is a quite different matter. Johanne will prove to be, in a familiar treatment in Western culture, ungraspable as love object, but her identity is also a performance. She confesses later to Claude that her status as "Haitian" is a fiction, a performance she has learned, for she is in fact an orphan from Quebec. The cuts in that first scene to Claude looking, the last in extreme close-up, establish an equivalence in ambiguity of the two individuals and their interaction to come.

The gaze of Claude upon Johanne is thus not to be characterized as the standard male heterosexual gaze of mainstream Hollywood and even art cinema, fixing the threatening female body as an object of voyeurism or fetishism. Claude's position is continuously undermined by what we might term the apprenticeship of difference that Johanne forces him to experience. This is the case in terms of race (she explicitly refuses to be exoticized), her own identity masquerade, in the troubling scenes when Claude's gaze is returned (notably by Johanne and Barbara [Monique Mercure]), and most notably in the acknowledgement of his own homosexual inclinations that she in fact provokes. She renders visible Claude's "identity" or rather *plurality* of identit*ies*, which is thus predicated on a dialogue with otherness, a becoming-other. This becoming the Other can lead Jutra/the film to embrace the process of decolonization, as in his documentary *Le Niger jeune république* of 1961, shots of which are inserted into *À tout prendre*. However, the lessons for Quebec are that any national struggle must be predicated on provisional and not full or unified notions of identity. This is the point missed by contemporary commentators such as Denys Arcand, who identified national maturity with heterosexual relations with "one's own", "women of the real, of the everyday": "There we find, I think, an unconscious refusal to coincide with one's collective self."[19] At the end of the film, Claude walks past graffiti for "Québec libre," with the preceding voice-over, at the end of the affair with Johanne, suggesting, "Il faut penser à autre chose/We have to think about something else." The implication is that such a project is worth pursuing, especially since, as Jim Leach points out, there is a politics of language in the film, with English figured as the language of cultural authority (in the opening scene with *Life* magazine, at the bank, and in the fashion shoot juxtaposed with Claude's love-making).[20] However, the nationalist project is qualified and tempered by what occurs in the film. Notably, *À tout prendre* ends not with that shot but with a gag sequence fantasizing about Claude's possible suicide and representing his departure for elsewhere. In an interview later in the decade, Jutra made explicit his attitude to any kind of committed cinema: "I believe in ideas: the right of a people to self-government, each person's need for a national and cultural identity. But, as I get carried away with enthusiasm, I can't help thinking that the worst collective crimes were committed in the name of nationalism. This contradiction tortures me and it is to this contradiction that I am committed." His project is thus to "define the contradictions, and share the anguish."[21]

The fact that *À tout prendre* can be co-opted only with considerable difficulty for a political project extends also to identity politics. The refreshing – and astonishing for 1963 – treatment of homosexuality is far from constituting an "identity" (Johanne's phrase, "do you like boys?" is based on *acts*). It prompts Claude to *act*, by, it is heavily implied, seducing the lead actor of his film, but the fact that gay assertion goes no further is attributable not only to the historical context.[22] As we have seen, the film cannot be read as a straightforward assertion of "Quebec" either. Its treatment of its identity position(s) is decidedly, and triumphantly, "minor."

The criticism of the film's "narcissism" is also somewhat misplaced.[23] The equation of homosexuality and narcissism is a highly debatable amalgamation of Freud and the "common-sense" view that since lesbians and gay men desire the same sex they must be narcissistic. As I have argued, far from being a withdrawal into the self, reminiscent, in the Quiet Revolution narrative, of the defensiveness and impotence of the Duplessis era, the film's preoccupation with self is based on a fragmentation and disintegration of that self, a provisionality born out of an encounter with difference. The "selfishness" of Claude is constantly undermined; his "self" cannot be taken entirely seriously, form and content combining here in the ludic nature of the film. Claude and Johanne circle each other in the photography scene not in some closed repetition but in a relationship of mutual dependency and attraction: they consist of bits, fragments, atoms, rather than complete and finished persons or identities (although Johanne ultimately turns out to be trapped within the desire for wholeness predicated on heterosexual romance). Narcissism is self-consciously an issue in the film, and "narcissism" itself is an extremely complex phenomenon. There are arguments to be made that it can represent a way of reducing, not affirming, rigidity of self. It looks back to the polymorphous perverse before the entry into Oedipal identifications.[24] The plenitude of the Lacanian mirror stage is a misrecognition and can never be attained, so the self desired as object is in a sense other and not the self.[25]

À tout prendre is noteworthy for its preoccupation with death mediated by ultimately French cultural references. Claude's fantasies of being shot need to be placed in the context of the other references to death in the film: the death-like mask Claude and Johanne see in the city streets; his constant references to ageing and lost youth; the fantasy "suicide" at the end (anticipating Jutra's own death in 1986 when he threw himself into the St Lawrence after having been diagnosed with Alzheimer's); and, of course, the X-ray sequence which exposes another hidden but insufficient "truth" of the self while at the same time displaying his future bare skeleton. It is this obsession and perspective which qualify the theme of birth: his drawing of the pregnant Johanne which points to himself as the foetus; and the extraordinary scene when he visits his mother to discuss the possibility of his marriage to Johanne. Yves Lever has criticized Jutra for an insufficient critique of the bourgeoisie, but this scene subtly combines social, filmic, and metaphysical anxieties. Claude approaches his mother's bedroom like a furtive burglar but also like a devout worshipper. The tempo of the editing slows radically; the house is seemingly empty except for the dogs; the usually cacophonous soundtrack reproduces a ticking clock only; the camera follows Claude, in slow motion, climbing the stairs; his hand, in extreme close-up, is seen to turn the handle of his mother's bedroom. His mother (the splendid Tania Fédor), propped up in her bed and stroking a dog's head, is calm and authoritative; there is no reverse shot, her face and upper body fill the screen. The scene connotes both birth (the mother's body, the womb, attained via a long series of "passages") and death (the frozen, interminable time of the bourgeoisie). Incidentally, the sceptical mother formulates Claude's dilemma in the very Québécois or French-Canadian terms of that between the "voyageur" and the "sédentaire."

À tout prendre is thus marked by a certain existential and even existentialist attitude which juxtaposes the search for meaning in life with the proximity and inevitability of death. This is the implication of the visit to the (rather unusually free-thinking) priest, rather than Claude's unwillingness to break away from past sources of authority in Quebec society. In addition, the debt to the nouvelle vague, and the rather Cocteau-ish "solution" to sexual and metaphysical preoccupations to be found in the aesthetic, make the film an open and porous example of "national cinema." It is certainly much more individualist than Pour la suite du monde, but that individualism is very modern and at the same time not based on a fixed and complete identity. Claude's disarray is bound up with history and society and is also a source of enjoyment for him and for the audience. It is a film very much of its time, with its portrayal of the decay of older certainties, but it also looks ahead, even far ahead, as it faces the possibility but also questionability of new ones emerging. The tension in the film is between an aspiration to identity and wholeness and a falling away or flight from it. For D.N. Rodowick, in his lucid summary of Deleuze's film writings, this is what characterizes "becoming other":

Rather than identity, becoming-other is driven by a tension between power and evasion. Power articulates itself as a socially managed force that limits the body's range of dynamic affects; becoming-other emerges from a countervailing desire to evade those limits, to find lines of flight wherein new potentialities for desire and identity can be expressed. This process is a double movement from both the side of I and the other.[26]

The "people" in Quebec in 1963 are also in a process of "becoming." À tout prendre suggests that that process must be one that never stops, that there is no fixity, no "sameness" which they eventually "become."

Founding cinematic fictions such as *À tout prendre* and *Pour la suite du monde* have been seen to inaugurate, not a wholeness, but founding problematics and ambivalences. But in fact any reference back to a founding moment, a golden age, a discovery, victory, or settlement, involves a highly paradoxical relationship between "then" and "now," the moment and its re-enactment. It can only be a relationship of lack. This can be illustrated by looking not at the foundation of Quebec feature film-making, but rather at an historical event – then represented cinematically – widely considered to be central to the formation of Quebec nationhood.

Along with de Gaulle's declaration of 1967 and the two sovereignty referenda, the crisis of October 1970 is one of the events that brought the Quebec question to international attention. Beginning with the kidnapping of British diplomat James Cross by the Front de libération du Québec (FLQ) on 5 October, the crisis escalated with the seizure by another FLQ cell of the Quebec government's employment minister, Pierre Laporte, on the 10th, and then, most dramatically, with the Canadian government's proclamation of the War Measures Act on the 16th. With the Canadian army in control of the province and civil liberties suspended, more than 500 people – including the nationalist poet Gaston Miron – were interned without trial as suspected "FLQ sympathizers"; some, such as the trades unionist Michel Chartrand, remained in custody for several months. Laporte's body was discovered on 17 October; Cross was released unharmed on 3 December.

The ramifications of the crisis were many and operated on different levels. On the one hand, this paroxysm of the FLQ's near decade-long campaign can be seen to mark its defeat, both militarily and politically, for its actions engendered in the vast majority of the Quebec population, nationalists and others, a strong distaste for violence; on the other, the excessive force deployed by the Canadian government, with Quebec effectively occupied by the federal army, provoked widespread sympathy for the nationalist cause. The combination of these two points, nationalism and non-violent politics, played into the hands of the Parti Québécois and contributed to its election victory of November 1976. However, the crisis can also be seen in symbolic terms. For one thing, one of its elements was certainly a battle for symbols and for the manipulation of symbols: the FLQ manifesto read out on CBC/Radio Canada as part of its demands, the sheer visibility of the army presence, guarding, among other places, that very TV headquarters. In addition, the crisis can also be seen as performative, as actually constructing the scenario (of national emergency and identity) of which it claimed to be the result. On both the Canadian and Quebec side of the national equation, the crisis offered a way of reaffirming and *staging* the nation through a drama played out in the mass media.

The crisis can thus be seen as foundational, not simply because it marks an important stage in the development of what is to become PQ hegemony, nor, as Heinz Weinmann argues, because it offers a sacrificial moment.[27] Rather, in this outburst of "major" constructions of the nation, the fundamental reality of identity and nation as lack, and the specific twists the case of Quebec offers that reality, can be discerned. Régis Debray's argument in *Critique of Political Reason* is that the constitution of any political community necessarily involves an illusion, an appeal to an element or elements (God, the proletariat, a lost golden age) which are outside the enclosures of the system. This incompleteness (Debray says *incomplétude*) or lack marks the "trou fondateur" or "basic [foundational] hole" which organizes a relationship between fixity or place "down here" and "e-motion" or projection "up there."[28] Examples would include the connection between nationalism and sacrifice, certainly, but also the nostalgia for an ethnic past. The polarizations of the October crisis intensified both Canadian and Quebec nationalisms, but in both cases the intensified sense of "us" depended on an "elsewhere," the process as a whole depending on an investment in representation.

Of course, these arguments can take on a highly universalist inflection, and the notion of identity as lack is a commonplace in contemporary theory influenced by French post-structuralism. The most notable example of this for our purposes is the Slovenian school, which uses Hegel and Lacan to understand the relationship between identity and non-identity in the constitution of political communities. The relationship between what the state is ("Subject": negatively related to its particular content) and what it ought to be ("Substance," positive mediation of its content: "a sovereign Quebec," "a strong and united Canada") is in fact what constitutes the state's identity: their non-identity is, in Slavoj Žižek's words, "strictly correlative" to the inherent non-identity, or split, of the content of that "ought" itself, namely, a totalization or plenitude which can never, by definition, be achieved or grasped.[29] The reason for this is that it depends on a symbolic system or order. The national Substance needs to display, to fascinate the gaze of its subjects, in order to exist and function, and this in itself epitomizes its inherent lack. And language itself, French or English, is a circular system of signifiers without external support and which can never achieve a consistent Whole. The *boundaries* of national identification (its external limitations, everything that is not "Canadian" or "Québécois") have to be understood as being reflected in the nation's internal *limits*, the unattainability of being "fully," purely, and unproblematically "Canadian" and "Québécois."

The analysis of identity as lack is particularly telling in the Canadian context, in that both Canada and Quebec live explicitly the tension between "major" and "minor" modalities of nation-ness (the October crisis, indeed Trudeau's whole stewardship, understood as Canada in attempted "major" mode, spectacularly disavowing its constitutive lack), and both invest heavily in the performativity of symbolic systems (media, language) in order to ground its identifications in a fascination and display constructed as "not American." Quebec films on the October crisis therefore have to deal with these paradoxes within the national-allegorical tensions of "Quebec cinema." Diachronically, they approach the events in different ways depending on the historical context of their production. They also represent spaces in which the national idea is asserted but its content also contested. In addition, however, their use of the crisis as foundational for different perspectives on Quebec nation-building means that their take on the events is centrally and problematically marked by their messy, theatricalized, and "negative" symbolism.

In fact, a number of Quebec films deal with the October crisis, either directly or indirectly.[30] In documentary, Robin Spry's *Action: The October Crisis of 1970* (1973) is significant for several reasons. Made by an anglophone at the NFB at a time when censorship prevented a francophone view of the crisis, the film is an exercise in montage of archive material which, within the limits of NFB "objectivity," has the merit of delving well beyond 1970 to explore the historical roots of the crisis in the Duplessis era and the ferment of the 1960s. This contextualization was itself provoked by Spry's realization of the limitations of his medium-length film of the same year, *Reaction: A Portrait of a Society in Crisis*. However, the use of archive material that ends with the *dénouement* of the crisis itself means that, apart from the manifesto read out on Radio Canada, the FLQ discourse is absent.

At the popular end of Quebec cinema, *Bingo* (Jean-Claude Lord, 1974) was the first to turn the crisis, or a transposition of it, into drama (or melodrama). As we shall see in subsequent chapters, Lord (b. 1943) was at the forefront of attempts from the 1960s onwards to construct a Quebec popular cinema. In what is basically an Oedipal drama, an initially apolitical young working-class man, François (Réjean Guénette), becomes involved with a group of strikers at the factory from which his broken father (Jean Duceppe) has lost his job. Egged on by Pierre (Gilles Pelletier), an activist who is in fact in the pay of the political Right (the context is that of an election campaign, reminiscent of that won by Montreal mayor Jean Drapeau during and after the October crisis), the group engage in kidnapping and other radical acts. The enterprise ends in disaster with the killing by the police of François and his girlfriend, Geneviève (Anne-Marie Provencher), his whereabouts given away by his bingo-obsessed grandmother (Manda Parent). Whereas it could be argued that the film is ultimately depoliticizing in its equation of "terrorism" and right-wing manipulation, former FLQ militant Pierre Vallières and others were relatively kind about it, mainly criticizing its lack of analysis of the shadowy workings of state and political power.[31] Another family drama of self-destruction is recounted in Jean-Claude Labrecque's *Les Années de rêves* (1984), an ambitious and rather heavy-handed historical fresco which tells the tale of Louis and Claudette Pelletier (Gilbert Sicotte and Anne-Marie Provencher) as they traverse the 1960s from their (church) wedding in Quebec City in 1964 through their move to Montreal in 1967 (cue de Gaulle's "Vive le Québec libre" speech, around which Labrecque at the time had made a short documentary) and Louis's involvement with the FLQ. It ends in October 1970 with Louis and his son injured by the bomb he had been carrying, his passage to hospital impeded by army trucks. The catalogue of events and references (the Beatles, American hippies ...) which cram the film forms a rather crass "background," with the possible exception of the changes in women's condition, which disrupt the central relationship and add to Louis's uncertainties. Pierre Véronneau suggests that the final disillusionment has more to do with the context of the 1980 referendum defeat and its aftermath than with the actual events portrayed.[32]

The two fiction films of substance on October are Michel Brault's *Les Ordres* (1974), which won the director's prize at Cannes, and Pierre Falardeau's *Octobre* (1994). *Les Ordres* concentrates on the state repression following the promulgation of the War Measures Act on the night of 15–16 October. It was made in the private sector with some help from the Canadian Film Development Corporation, and had to compromise on means: it mixes black-and-white and colour footage because money was not available for a complete colour feature, but the complete black-and-white option was rejected because of its potential to discourage audiences. Based on the testimony of some of the arrestees and filmed from their point of view, the film recounts the detention of trades unionist Clermont Boudreau (Jean Lapointe) and also his wife, Marie (Hélène Loiselle); of unemployed father Richard Lavoie (Claude Gauthier), socialist doctor Jean-Marie Beauchemin (Guy Provost), and social worker Claudette Dusseault (Louise Forestier).

As Gilles Marsolais points out,[33] *Les Ordres* can be related to the direct cinema tradition and the way in which in the 1970s it took hybrid, fictionalized forms. As well as the credentials of the "authentic" testimonies, the film opens with the actors explaining their roles and then slipping into character for "interview" sequences. This technique allows the film apparently to compromise between the two tendencies of 1970s political cinema, realism and form, identification and distance. However, it must be said that after these opening scenes the film tips over entirely into identificatory strategies in which the interpellated spectator's point of view is reproduced by the camera and protagonists. In fact, the "compromise" or relationship is really one with "objectivity."

Indeed, this – the privileging of emotion over political analysis – was the major criticism of the film in 1974–75. Pierre Vallières, so gentle with *Bingo*, largely lambasts *Les Ordres* for its depiction of passive and resigned arrestees as opposed to passionate and politicized militants and individuals. Its emphasis on "innocent," even third-party points of view therefore contributes to the naturalization of apoliticism and is a reflection more of the political atmosphere of 1974 and of the long aftermath of the events than of the events themselves.[34]

However, it is important not to underestimate the politics of *Les Ordres*, nor its overall reach. The film does engage with economic interests and their relationship with state power, as in the factory's restrictions on Clermont's union activities and the eviction, witnessed by Claudette, of a family from their apartment. Beauchemin is a doctor active in socially deprived districts of the city, and he offers analyses of the system – fairly timidly, it is true – while in prison. The film's ambitions go beyond a chronicling of historical events. A pro-civil liberties quotation from Trudeau in the 1950s is used as an ironic but nominative comment on the action. *Les Ordres* also contains references to previous Quebec films on which Brault worked. Most notably, *Les Raquetteurs* is quoted in the close-ups of faces in crowds, now alienated instead of constituting a national "people" (but a community is momentarily recreated among the women prisoners when Hélène is released), and in the depiction of a majorette band rehearsing, seen from Clermont's point of view through a wire mesh. And the presence of Claude Gauthier as Richard refers to, not only his own persona as one of Quebec's main *chansonniers*, but also his role as the country boy coming to town in Brault's main Quiet Revolution film, *Entre la mer et l'eau douce* of 1966 (to be discussed in the next chapter).

Moreover, the film's abstractions that so displeased Vallières – he called it "un mélodrame kafkaïen" – in fact open out its significance beyond the contexts of 1970 and 1974 and construct productive tensions with its documentary ambitions. After the introductory interviews, the film's first procedure is to create dramatic confrontations around the signifier "home," *chez nous*, with the series of police raids on the protagonists' apartments (preceded by the eviction). The inside/outside binary is both established and disrupted through visual (shots through windows and curtains) and auditory (banging on doors) effects. That disruption is completed when a parent is removed from the home, the family thus shattered. However, this crisis of the categories of inside/outside, home/not home, "us"/"them" is producing something more complex than a confrontation around totalized notions of "Quebec"/"Canada." Although the latter's state power is implicated, the arrests and other oppressive procedures are conducted in French by Québécois, and two small but revealing elements in the film contribute to an apprehension of "cracks" on either side of the divide. The first is in the raid on the Boudreau household (with Clermont absent driving his taxi). A voice-over by Marie coincides with a close-up of a "nice" policeman, and she comments on his visible unease. The second is in a later snatch of "interview" material which reveals something about the workings of the Boudreau "home," in which it is made clear that, especially for Clermont, Hélène's only notion of politics was to agree with her husband.

The abstractions of *Les Ordres* in fact have profound implications for an understanding of the workings of power and national identity. The main damage of the October crisis is seen to be a kind of national self-surveillance for Quebec, in the sense in which Foucault argues in *Surveiller et punir/Discipline and Punish* (1975) that men and women in modernity wander around with internalized notions of always being watched and therefore of watching themselves, what Foucault calls panopticism. Clermont declares at the end of the film, "We'll never again have the same freedom," and certainly the film emphasizes in great detail the effects of the "legal" and prison apparatus on the bodies (nakedness, intimate searches) and minds (a mock execution, metaphors of "amputation") of the arrestees. On the other hand, these processes also illustrate the inadequacies inherent to the federal/Canadian/social order. Here Kafka is not so removed from Vallières's critiques of the system. As Žižek points out, in *The Trial*, Kafka's "man from the country" (Subject) "finds himself impotent and null in front of the impenetrable Palace of Law (Substance)." But this disparity is in fact inherent to the Substance itself (Palace of Law, Canada) which does not and can never correspond to its own notion: "Its entire spectacle is staged in order to fascinate the gaze of those who endeavour in vain to penetrate its mystery – the horrifying and imposing edifice of Power, totally indifferent towards the miserable individual, *feigns this indifference in order to attract its gaze.*"[35]

This seems a very apt description of the "theatre" of the October crisis, a theatricality acknowledged even in the NFB's *Action*. In the context of this study, however, it must be recalled that such internal disparity and lack in the Substance of the nation applies also to "Quebec." This helps to explain further the impossibility of *Québec Jour J* (even sovereign and "major" nations contain these incoherences). But what happens when a more totalizing and nationalist cinematic gaze is turned on the October crisis?

Pierre Falardeau (b. 1946) can be seen as one of the main representatives of a militant, nationalist cinema in Quebec. Opposed to the soft consensus of Quebec society in the 1980s and 1990s, he has produced a cinematic *oeuvre* which has often collided with the institutional structures of the industry and which has also run the risk of a certain machismo. In 1980, along with the actor Julien Poulin, he directed *Speak White*, a short montage film inspired by Michèle Lalonde's poem denouncing American imperialism. The comedy *Elvis Gratton* (1981–85) will be analysed in chapter 7 on popular cinema. His first fictional feature per se, *Le Party* (1990), is set in a prison. Including a distasteful rape scene, the film denounces the system via encounters among the prisoners, a woman journalist, and a cabaret troupe.

Falardeau's script collaborator on *Le Party* was Francis Simard, jailed for his part in the kidnapping and murder of Pierre Laporte in 1970. Falardeau's project of making a film on the October crisis in collaboration with Simard dated back to 1981 on his release from prison (Falardeau had first met him there, by chance, for a film screening in 1977). In 1994 *Octobre* was released, coproduced by ACPAV (Association coopérative de productions audio-visuelles) and the NFB and with money from Telefilm Canada, but not from the Quebec provincial agency SODEC. The story of the film's financing and production is a chequered one and includes a campaign against it by Senator Philippe Gigantès, who was leaked the script.[36] The unified action of *Octobre* takes place among the four members (unnamed during the film) of the Chénier cell of the FLQ, between the decision taken on 9 October to kidnap Laporte (Serge Houde) and his killing on the 17th. Most of the dialogues are set in the bungalow on the rue Armstrong in which Laporte was held, with the exceptions of the kidnapping itself, the story of one of the gang who is tailed by police after leaving a communiqué in a Metro bin and who has to disguise himself in a safe house (to rendezvous later with the cell that kidnapped James Cross), and the dumping of the body (recounted at the start of the film).

Philosophically, the film's evaluation of the murder of Laporte is based on the oxymoronic quotation from Camus, "necessary and unjustifiable," which announces the "flashback" to the day before the kidnapping early in the film.[37] Politically, the killing is placed in the twin contexts of that week's dramatic confrontation with the provincial and federal governments and of Quebec's historical "defeats" in 1760 and 1837–38. The argument put forward is that the War Measures Act was promulgated as a response to popular support in Quebec for the FLQ's manifesto. Faced with Laporte's severe injuries from an escape attempt, the two remaining *felquistes* had to choose between freeing or killing him, or, in their and the film's terms, surrendering yet again or fighting back. The choice itself of violence and kidnapping for political ends is articulated when the youngest *felquiste* (Pierre Rivard) responds to Laporte's arguments about democracy with a very class-based discourse.

The fears of Senator Gigantes or even the negative judgments of the film by critics such as Yves Lever – about, respectively, the glorification or banalization of killing and the limitations of such a "univocal intimist drama" – are, however, not fully borne out on closer examination.[38] *Octobre* both knowingly and unknowingly articulates elements that pull against the militant, totalizing potential of its stance. The film is self-conscious about its theatricality and, implicitly, about the theatricality of its politics and the identities it constructs. This boys' film, in its preoccupation with disguise (two sequences present *felquistes* in this way, in the kidnapping scene – in which one is dressed as a woman – and when "Le Gros" [Hugo Dubé] leaves the safe house as an old man), dissimulation, seeing and not seeing (the faces hidden from Laporte through blindfold and masks) – in fact suggests the fragility rather than solidity of identities. This could be read as a symptom of Quebec's colonized status, but it meshes with the whole political strategy, if it can be called that, of not "losing face," in which appearances count a great deal. The faces of the *felquistes* crack as the tension of their situation increases, to a point where the youngest has to leave; it is no accident that the strongest arguments for the murder come from "Le Gros," disembodied and faceless over the telephone. In addition, and despite the condemnation of American culture to be found in *Elvis Gratton*, both the *mise en scène* and the soundtrack at times recall Hollywood cop or suspense movies, notably in the drive back to the bungalow with the kidnapped Laporte and the encounter with a police car, and in the failure to start the car immediately when his body is dumped.

Most of the action takes place in the claustrophobic set representing the bungalow, its space dominated by the curtained window opening on to the *outside*. As in *Les Ordres*, this inside/outside distinction is the crucial boundary of the film. Its tension is emphasized by the scenes with the food-delivery man on the liminal space of the doorstep; the trope is repeated as "Le Gros" sits in a café with soldiers seen in the background through the window. However, internal limits are also being suggested. The group have, after all, kidnapped a francophone Québécois, and half their battle is against the Quebec government itself, albeit located in the federal Canadian system. Moreover, the compassion for Laporte, particularly felt by the youngest, recalls those scenes in the first half of *The Crying Game* (Jordan, 1992) when the political solidities and certainties of the IRA man begin to collapse when confronted with his captive. Thus the tendentiousness of the film breaks down at points when Laporte's position is granted viewpoint and voice, notably in his moving letter to Premier Bourassa and the shot of light, from his point of view, through the front window, anticipating a later shot of birds and clouds seen by a *felquiste* (Luc Picard), implying that they are all captives. The psychological ambiguity so inherent in the art movie,[39] here needed if the film is not to be a totalized piece of propaganda, is now working to problematize some of its very premises. The external boundaries (the federal army, the Canadian system, everything that is not "Quebec") are also reflections of the internal limits of "Quebec." The reading of the poem "l'Octobre" from Gaston Miron's *L'Homme rapaillé* here functions as any reference to the transcendent would in this context, as an absence that structures and constitutes "the group." Notably, the killing of Laporte is filmed as an absence or gap in the action, as the two remaining *felquistes* move out of frame to do the deed and the camera lingers silently on a shot of the front window. This procedure is consistent with the cell members' refusal since 1970 to name names in the affair, but also with the centrality of lack to the whole enterprise. To its credit, *Octobre* thus refuses the temptation of a "major" film-making which would render unproblematic any divisions between self and other, inside and outside.

For Falardeau, the project of *Octobre* was about continuity and memory.[40] However, the film can also claim to be a "foundational fiction" in that the past, rather than being reconstituted (there is little attempt at period detail), is set up as an absence or lack which can structure current and future struggles for the group, the Québécois. It momentarily renders that absence present, just as the (anachronistic) clips from Spry's *Action* serve in *Octobre* to contextualize the present for the 1970 protagonists and 1970 for the 1990s spectators. Significantly, after years of rejections and negotiations similar to the *Octobre* saga, Falardeau in March 1999 received approval for $500,000 of Telefilm Canada funding for his project on the Patriotes' Rebellion, *15 février 1839*.

3 The Cinema of Modernization

The term "Quiet Revolution" or *révolution tranquille* has come to designate that period of reform in Quebec economic and political affairs that began in 1960 with the provincial election victory, after a fifteen-year gap, of the Liberal Party led by Jean Lesage under the slogan "maîtres chez nous"/"masters in our own house." A Ministry of Education was created, with control of the system transferred from the Roman Catholic Church to the provincial government, which also took over health and welfare. A number of companies were nationalized, the most important of which was Hydro Quebec. There was also an expansion of francophone private capital invested in francophone firms. (The number of financial institutions controlled by francophones increased from 25.8 per cent to 44.8 per cent between 1961 and 1978.) The Quebec government set up its own delegations abroad. As a consequence, the number of civil servants rose by 43 per cent. Between 1960 and 1966, there was a vast increase in provincial public expenditure, from $598 million in 1959 to $30 billion by the late 1980s. (Between 1939 and 1952, it had actually dropped from 13.9 per cent to 8.9 per cent of GDP.) These developments meant a rapid expansion of the professional and administrative middle classes, as well as an advancement of the francophone working class, owing to "catching up" economic growth rates above European and Canadian averages in the 1960s and 1970s.

However, a discussion of "what happened" in the 1960s is complicated by questions of periodization and ideology. As Jocelyn Létourneau has argued in several articles,[1] the cultural and intellectual leadership of the technocracy since 1960 has promoted a historical narrative of "before" and "after," "lack" and "plenitude," that obscures the long processes of change which were in motion after 1945 and even 1900 (with urbanization and industrialization). What is more, there is the vexed question of when the Quiet Revolution ended: 1966, with the return to power (with a lower share of the vote than the Liberals, because of the vagaries of the electoral system) of the Union nationale under Daniel Johnson, who nonetheless continued the revolution's modernizing trajectory; 1973, with the first oil shock and first economic recession since the war; or 1980, with the first accomplishments of the Parti Québécois government elected in 1976 punctured by the defeated sovereignty-association referendum. These questions suggest that the 1960s, far from being a decade of seamless unanimity in Quebec, in fact contained its own contradictions, was a contested time and space, with the transmission belt of history bringing problems from the past as well as recasting future dilemmas. The most obvious examples are the split over the national issue in the provincial Liberal Party in 1967 and the foundation in 1968 by René Lévesque, the minister who had nationalized the electricity industry in 1963, of the Parti Québécois. This chapter will seek to analyse and conceptualize what a surprised Yves Lever sees as films that are in fact antagonistic to their historical context, in that they are vehicles for "a lack of fighting spirit" and "inaction" faced with the momentous transformations in progress,[2] devoid of representations of politicians or technocrats.[3] The two most useful concepts for this purpose are modernization and hegemony.

I take modernization to designate that process by which an economy and society are aligned to the demands of capital, a process characterized by the supplanting of traditional practices, communities, beliefs, identities, and hierarchies and their rapid transformation. In Marx's words, "all fixed, fast-frozen relations, with their train of ancient and venerable prejudices and opinions are swept away, all new-formed ones become antiquated before they can ossify. All that is solid melts into air, all that is holy is profaned, and man is at last compelled to face with sober senses, his real conditions of life, and his relations with his kind."[4]

What was true of much of Europe in the 1840s and after can be applied to the Quebec experience of the 1960s, as religious belief and practice collapsed (in 1955 there had been 58,000 clergy in Quebec, one for every hundred inhabitants), sexual attitudes and practices altered, and the relentless pace of modernity transformed the physical face of Montreal and consolidated the way of life of the vast majority of Québécois according to the norms of consumption, suburbanization, tertiary-sector growth, and mass media.

In Quebec these changes were compounded by their particularly accelerated nature and, as elsewhere in the western world, by the large proportion of baby boomers and the cultural and ideological contestation which they articulated. In 1961, 44.2 per cent of the population was aged nineteen or less, although, because of the collapse of the birth rate after 1965, by the mid-1980s the proportion was down to 28.3 per cent. Quebec, therefore, partakes both of a general Western phenomenon in the 1960s and a particular experience due to its own peculiar context. The comparison with France is illuminating. In both France and Quebec, the state played a leading role in the modernization process, which in turn tended to produce a middle class coterminous with the nation itself, naturalizing its order and seeking to evacuate class conflict. But, while France existed as the model of the modern and modernizing francophone nation for some Québécois elites, a parallel echoed by de Gaulle as he triumphantly crossed Quebec on his way to the famous proclamation of "Vive le Québec libre" from the balcony of Montreal's City Hall in 1967, the fact of radically different histories remained. Whereas Gaullism, at least until 1968, was effective in providing a transmission belt between old and new ideologies, conservative and technocratic France, no such "solution" was available in Quebec because there was no "old" "Quebec" as there was an "old" France. The year 1960 had to be represented as a founding myth, a break from an alienated past: "The Quiet Revolution sanctions the reconciliation between the community and its historical consciousness; in other words, from the very start of the Quiet Revolution in 1960 we witness a community burning with the desire to overcome its former condition, its course set on progress, its situation one of catching up and emancipation; a community, in other words, which is leaving behind its incapacities and incompetence, and emerging from its 'accumulated silences.'"[5]

The Quebec "nation" is therefore, unlike France, still to be elaborated, and the fact that its emergence coincides with its modernization produces a tense relationship with the past and an uncertain future. In these historical circumstances, how to reconcile the "people," and its roots, with the technocracy? What is more, both Quebec and France have to face the implications of the possible homology between "modernization" and "Americanization," which does much to explain de Gaulle's nationalist posturings. As Kristin Ross has argued, France's nervousness on this score, its fear of being colonized, is intensified by its experience as colonizer, and indeed French modernization must always be understood in relation to its experience of decolonization.[6] For Quebec and its inchoate "nationhood," "America" represents a possible identity, a possible extension of itself in space ("Américanité" as opposed to identities centred on Quebec), and in time ("rattrapage"/"catching up"), a leap-frogging over the restrictive and limiting Canadian state. In addition, the fate of the million Québécois emigrants to the textile towns of New England in the later nineteenth century suggests the ultimate dread, that of assimilation to an overwhelmingly anglophone continent. Rather than a foil compensating a developing but established national culture for the headlong rush of modernization, "America" is part of Quebec's identity crisis, or rather is one of its possible destinies. At the same time, Quebec's history as "colonized" meant for some that the process of modernization-Americanization had itself to be challenged, now not from the position of Catholicism and traditionalism but in a dialectical surpassing that would embrace Third World revolution and identify with the marginalized of the continent (Pierre Vallières's *Nègres blancs d'Amérique* of 1965.) Thus for Quebec, modernization, destabilizing in itself, is closely bound up with an identity to be built and fought over. It is an uneven, incomplete process.

This cultural and ideological churning, these competing discourses over what is to constitute the national "we," are best understood in terms of Gramsci's notion of hegemony. Cultural artefacts such as films do not "reflect" the economic base or even the wider society. Within Marxism's intricate debates over the relationship between economy, society, and culture, Gramsci offers an account of lived feeling which is not totalized, as in Lucien Goldmann's work, into a mapping of homologies between class situations, world-views, and artistic forms but which is rendered in all its complexity. Hegemony refers to the values and ideas of the dominant class or group in society. The latter are in a position of intellectual and moral leadership, and their beliefs permeate the rest of the population as the common sense or horizon of their world. Domination is achieved not by state coercion nor by the imposition of an ideology, but by complex processes of negotiation and consent taking place in civil society. Examples of hegemonic ideas would be welfare capitalism in Britain from 1945 to 1979, entrepreneurial individualism and economic liberalism from 1979 to 1997 (roughly), new formulations ("New Labour") beyond that; Gaullism in France from 1958 to 1968, a combination of statism and liberal modernization in the 1980s around "republican humanism," and so on.

The fundamental hegemonic idea in modern societies is the nation, the basic social glue, but its definition may be a site of contestation. This is obviously the case in Quebec, and in the 1960s we witness a hegemonic shift, a reworking and reformulation of ideas that constitute the national "we." The Quiet Revolution can be read in this straightforwardly Gramscian way:

the phase in which previously germinated ideologies become "party," come into confrontation and conflict, until one of them, or at least a single combination of them, comes to prevail, to gain the upper hand, to propagate itself throughout society – bringing about not only a unison of economic and political aims, but also intellectual and moral unity, posing all the questions around which the struggle rages not on a corporate but on a "universal" plane, and thus creating the hegemony of a fundamental social group over a series of subordinate groups ... the development and expansion of the particular group are conceived of, and presented, as being the motor force of a universal expansion, of a development of all the "national" energies.

There thus takes place "a continuous process of formation and superseding of unstable equilibria ... in which the interests of the dominant group prevail, but only up to a certain point."[7] What must be stressed is that this is therefore a highly active and dynamic process, never at rest. In a sense we are always living in an "interregnum" (the term Gramsci uses to describe post-First World War Italian society),[8] between a dying old order and a new struggling to be born, and this is nowhere more true than in 1960s Quebec (as it had been in the 1950s and before). The Quiet Revolution is not a final or originary point, but part of a never-ending flux of contestation, definition, shifting social meaning, becoming. For Gramsci, the individual subject is multiple and composite: "It contains Stone Age elements and principles of a more advanced science, prejudices from all past phases of history at the local level and intuitions of a future philosophy which will be that of a human race united the world over."[9] In the same way, a given society will always sit astride past and present beliefs and future possibilities. At any given moment, that society will contain, beside its hegemonic formations, residual and emergent values, beliefs, and significances, that is, those that are lived and practised on the basis of the residue of some previous social formation and those that are in the process of being created. As Raymond Williams points out, the cultural analyst must be attentive to, and cannot know definitively, the extent to which these cultures are incorporated into hegemony or the extent to which they are simply alternative or oppositional to that hegemony.[10]

Quebec films of the 1960s are not direct expressions of a particular social class, the hegemonizing technocracy, but partake of this complex flux of meaning that is dominant or contested and that is profoundly marked by the links between past, present, and future. We saw, for example, how both *À tout prendre* and *Pour la suite du monde* were contested sites of meaning in relation to residual and emergent beliefs. A clue to the significance of the 1960s films lies in their abundant representation of intellectuals and cultural practitioners. In this national cinema that explores and questions a "national" that is still in the process of elaboration, the protagonists are uncertain as to the nature of the society that surrounds them and the future that faces them. They are in interregnum. Moreover, they are uncertain as to the status of the ideas they articulate: residual? emergent? oppositional? alternative to be incorporated in the new hegemonic formation? And they are therefore uncertain as to their own status as intellectuals. Gramsci distinguishes between "common sense" and "good sense." "Common sense" is that fragmented jumble of beliefs we possess that is naturalized into the horizon of our significant world. "Good sense" would mean to have passed to a different level, that of the coherence which makes criticism possible: "The starting-point of critical elaboration is the consciousness of what one really is, and is 'knowing thyself' as a product of the historical processes to date which has deposited in you an infinity of traces, without leaving an inventory. The first thing to do is to make such an inventory."[11]

There would then be the possibility of leaving behind the artificial stasis of the "traditional" intellectual (who purports autonomously to float free of social and other determinants) and of becoming that "organic" intellectual who "must have a critical consciousness of the world, a desire to question and to change existing conditions, and a sense of collectivity with others in working to restructure society."[12] Protagonists of Quebec films of the 1960s draw up the inventory (we saw the fragmented Claude's ludic pleasure with this in À tout prendre), but, because of the unfinished and contradictory nature of the Quiet Revolution, they encounter terrible obstacles to advancing further.

This incompleteness manifests itself both in politics and in the emerging film industry. In a sense the Quiet Revolution is indeed an originary moment, but it founds conflict rather than wholeness, providing the discursive and other battlelines for Quebec and Canada in the decades ahead. The new aspirations of Quebec, prolonged by René Lévesque's new Parti Québécois, are matched by developments on the federal level, with the creation in 1963 by Lester Pearson's Liberal government of the Laurendeau-Dunton Royal Commission on Bilingualism and Biculturalism and the adoption in 1969 of the Official Languages Act extending the use of English and French to all federal institutions. Pearson's successor, the Québécois Pierre Elliott Trudeau, was thus offering a new definition of Canada, a cosmopolitan, liberal, bilingual, and multicultural vision that situated itself at opposite poles from Quebec nationalism and that was consistent with the "emergent" arguments of the review *Cité libre* that he had founded in Quebec in the 1940s with his now fellow minister Gérard Pelletier.

Film is both marked by the discourses competing for hegemony in this climate and distinguished by the specificity of its practices. The 1960s as a whole do not represent a sudden boom in Canadian or Quebec film-making. The context was one of a precipitous drop in cinema-going among the general public since the 1950s – 60 million tickets sold in Quebec in 1952, 19 million in 1969 – although this had stabilized from 1962 onwards and had been very partially compensated for by increases in ticket prices. The emerging cinema had to contend with uncertainty both as to its potential audience(s) and as to funding and government policy. Nevertheless, thirty-seven narrative features were produced in Quebec during the 1960s. There was an expansion of film culture in the shape of the Montreal International Film Festival after 1960 and the Festival of Canadian Cinema after 1963; the continuation of the review *Séquences* (founded 1955), with its connections to the church and the moral agenda; the foundation in 1960 of *Objectif*, interested in formal issues and influenced by *Cahiers du cinéma*; and the foundation in 1963 of the Association professionnelle des cinéastes which, among other activities, lobbied for official support and funding. Of the thirty-seven films, twenty were from the new private sector, operating in artisanal conditions, as with *À tout prendre*, but also representing a first attempt to create a commercial Quebec cinema with the production company Coopératio, founded in 1963 by Pierre Patry, a refugee from the NFB, and France Film, the main distributor of French films in the province. Its first production, *Trouble-fête* of 1964, achieved a highly creditable 300,000 spectators and was thus one of the few films of the decade to recoup its costs. Thirteen of the films were produced at the NFB, nine after 1966 when it embarked on an ambitious policy of narrative feature film-making. (The rest were made by the Association générale des étudiants de l'Université de Montréal – notably the decade's first feature, *Seul ou avec d'autres* of 1962 – and the Office du Film du Québec.)

The rules of the game in which Canadian and Quebec film-making would henceforth operate are to be found in developments at the NFB, the creation of a federal funding body in 1967, and the relaxation of the censorship laws in 1968. Out of this would emerge a fully fledged film industry but also an uncertain relationship between its two tendencies, auteur and popular cinema.

In the atmosphere of the new Pearson Liberal government and the new stress on biculturalism, a separate French production unit was set up at the NFB early in 1964, with a separate budget (one-third of the

NFB's production total), and Pierre Juneau became its first director. However, the NFB still proceeded uncertainly in its attitude to features, notably narrative features; the first in French, the historical drama *Le Festin des morts*,[13] directed by Juneau's deputy Fernand Dansereau in 1965, followed the first English feature, *Drylanders*, in 1963. Consistent with the incomprehension of English Canada and other federal institutions to the new Quebec nationalism and the turbulence in the province, the NFB, having been the catalyst of the new Quebec cinema, now assumed a rather less organic role. Most notably, in the spring of 1964, at the same time as Pierre Elliott Trudeau in *Cité libre* was lambasting the "separatist counter-revolutionaries" who swarmed at the NFB and CBC, the journal of the left-wing nationalist intelligentsia, *Parti pris*, published four critical articles by NFB employees. The film-makers – Jacques Godbout (b. 1933), Gilles Carle (b. 1929), Clément Perron (1929–1999), Denys Arcand (b. 1941), and Gilles Groulx – basically made in their different ways a plea for a Quebec national cinema in the sense of narrative features with a passionate personal vision, as opposed to documentary with its abstract "objectivity" taking priority over myth and commitment. At the NFB, they were both free and unfree. The journal's editor, Pierre Maheu, went farther and labelled the NFB a colonial institution. Arcand, Groulx, and Michel Brault would seek work in the private sector in 1966, when they founded the production company Cinéastes associés. Juneau and the commissioner, Guy Roberge, left their posts for less troubled waters that same year.

The latter part of the 1960s found the NFB struggling with budget restrictions after 1967 and with the redefining of its priorities in the new political and industrial context. With more feature films, the new auteurism was thus breaking yet farther away from Griersonian educational priorities. Jacques Godbout's *Kid Sentiment* (1968) and Claude Jutra's *Wow* (1969) are docu-fictions about (bourgeois) youth, the first emphasizing the impact of consumer culture via a procedure similar to Perrault's in *Pour la suite du monde*, but with a more interventionist and indeed appalled director, the second more influenced by American counter-culture and ultimately more sympathetic to the young people's rebellion, dreams, and fantasies. A new mission was also beginning for socially engaged documentaries at the NFB, partly a response on the part of film-makers to the politically charged climate of the late 1960s, and partly a federal government-led initiative seeking educational films relevant to departments such as health, agriculture, and so on[14] in the context of rapid social transformation. Thus in early 1967 was born *Challenge for Change*, in French *Société nouvelle*, building on the already existing Groupe de recherches sociales, an example of whose film-making was the short *La P'tite Bourgogne*, directed by Maurice Bulbulian, about a citizens' committee participating in the revitalization of their district of Montreal.

The year 1967 also saw the creation of the first Canadian state aid for the private sector, in the form of the CFDC/SDICC. The origins of the idea are to be found at the NFB in the early 1960s, when Guy Roberge proposed feature-film production as more appropriate to a state-aided private sector than the NFB, and had rejected quotas because of an unwillingness to take on the Hollywood majors that dominated Canadian distribution. Under Communications Minister Maurice Lamontagne, the CFDC received $10 million over five years to invest in productions in exchange for a share of the profits, to make loans with interest to producers, to make awards to Canadian films, and to assist in the distribution of the films it funded. Applicants had to be Canadian companies, and the film supported had to have "a significant Canadian creative, artistic, and technical content."[15] The organization thus attempted a balancing act between laissez-faire (a reluctance to offend the Hollywood majors or to set up an alternative distribution network) and national voluntarism. Nonetheless, the impact of the CFDC in the 1970s was considerable, as we shall see.

Since the beginnings of cinema in the province, censorship (a provincial, not federal jurisdiction) in Quebec had been severe, with a Bureau de censure des vues animées zealous in the banning and cutting of films and in interference with film posters and publicity. For the church, cinema was anathema until Pope Pius XI's more tolerant encyclical of 1936. A fire at a Montreal cinema in 1927 that killed seventy-eight children resulted in a law banning movie theatres to those under sixteen. Even *Les Enfants du paradis* (Marcel Carné, 1945) was banned on the explicit instructions of Premier Duplessis. It is not therefore surprising that a relaxation and indeed disappearance of censorship other than the establishment of age categories was part of the Quiet Revolution. The cutting of *Hiroshima mon amour* (Alain Resnais, 1958) for commercial distribution after its full version had been shown at the Montreal Film Festival in 1960 provoked outrage and led to the setting up of a commission which recommended the abolition of censorship, a move that took effect in 1967 although the climate had relaxed considerably before then. These events were to have as profound an influence on Quebec cinema as the CFDC did, since they would lead to an explosion of erotic films, beginning with *Valérie* (Denis Héroux, 1968).

The 1960s are thus transitional as far as the Canadian/Quebec film industry, the political debates, and hence the ongoing elaborations of hegemony are concerned. These factors are all evident in the major films of the decade.

Le Chat dans le sac (Groulx, 1964) was shot on a $75,000 budget and represented a hijacking, for auteurist purposes, of what was originally an NFB documentary project. Like *À tout prendre*, the film recounts the dying affair of a "cross-community" urban heterosexual couple and combines techniques from *le direct* (synchronous sound, "interviews" to camera, hand-held mobile shots following characters in the street) with montage and voice-over. Claude (Claude Godbout) is a twenty-three-year-old francophone Québécois would-be journalist, Barbara (Barbara Ulrich), a twenty-year-old anglophone Jewish aspiring actress. The film largely consists of conversations between the two on national and sexual political issues. Its intellectual ambitions are signalled from the start, as Claude holds up to the camera books on the black American revolt, the Cuban revolution, Jean Vigo, and the battle against censorship; copies of Frantz Fanon and *Parti pris*; and the Larousse *Dictionnaire des proverbes, sentences et maximes*. Links between Quebec politics and anti-colonial revolution are made with Vigo's French-but-transnational youth-anarchism, but they coexist uneasily with the Larousse tome connoting tradition and Claude's desire for a mapping or guidance that make sense to him. Similarly, his "Je suis canadien-français donc je me cherche"/"I am French-Canadian and therefore trying to find myself" reinforces both this disarray (he sticks to the old name for his nationality rather than the emerging "Québécois") and a desire for a fixity and certainty of identity which is far from being realized (the insistence on "je," the reversal and adaptation of that older, and French, Cartesian proverb, sentence, and maxim). The "identity" at stake in the film is thus as yet ungraspable, since it is in the throes of contradiction, emergence, and elaboration. Thus Claude seeks work and advice, unsatisfactorily for him, from the real-life editors of *Parti pris*, *Objectif*, and the francophone version of the pan-Canadian news weekly, *Maclean's*. He goes off to a house in the countryside to think and read, and his relationship with Barbara peters out.

However, the film attempts to establish parameters for this elaboration of the hegemony to come, so that Claude and his debates do not dissipate into some random flux. There is a "we," even if it is unformed, and this was acknowledged both by contemporary commentators and by Groulx himself. Robert Daudelin, co-founder of *Objectif* and author of the first monograph on Quebec cinema (published by the Quebec Ministry of Culture in 1967), wrote a paean to the film's national modes of recognition: "At least we had a film before us which was really our own, in which we happily recognized ourselves and saw ourselves up close."[16] Interviewed in *Cahiers du cinéma* in July 1965, Groulx made the following paradoxical remarks:

We bear testimony to a reality which is still very obscure and very difficult to determine. We find it very difficult to extract the essence of it, because this reality is being lived out at an accelerated rhythm, it is changing a lot; so much so that a situation which might have been true three years ago would now seem false. … Besides it's the only way we can end up with a national cinema, not only in the sense of the state or economy, but with a character and psychology specific to a nation.[17]

There is a tension here between the shifting sands of modernization and the certainty attached to the use of the singular "character" and "psychology" of the nation. *Le Chat dans le sac* is a film about the elaboration of hegemony, but at the same time a film about lack, since the contemporary outlets for Claude's expression – the new technocracy of the Quebec state or the political violence of the FLQ – are intellectually and temperamentally unacceptable (although, as in other films of the decade, the potential or latent violence within Quebec society is hinted at, an example being the final section of the film when Claude watches the children playing with toy guns). And yet the film also steers some sort of path for the (interpellated, nation-recognizing) spectator, primarily through its attempt to privilege the discourse of Claude over that of Barbara.

Claude is the social critic; his perception of lack creates a sentiment of, but also a belief in, alienation. The consumerism of the modern city is rejected for its falsity and distortion of, it is implied, the "authentic" individual or nation. His reportage on a festival of majorettes describes the event – worlds away from the authenticities of the "people" constituted in *Les Raquetteurs* – as "a new folklore of alienation." This is bound up with the status of Quebec, colonized by American culture, peripheral to a Parisian centre (he admonishes Barbara for wanting to go to Paris, and in general those anglophone Canadians who learn French to go to France), with a lower standard of living than Ontario's. This alienation, this lack, prevent him from acting. He says to the camera at the beginning of the film: "The society I was born into doesn't give me what I need to live an intelligent life"; to Barbara, in the countryside towards the end of their affair: "It is difficult to exist when you're not given the means to act." The ending is ambiguous. The "countryside" connotes that cult of the rural which was the hallmark of the Duplessis regime and clerical nationalism, the retreat to it a confession of impotence. Or it could be read as a holding operation, as a suspension of identity and agency, temporarily deep frozen in the Quebec winter. It should also be stressed that the journeys to the country house are just as important, for the new perceptions associated with travelling by car are part of the transforming maelstrom of the identities of modernization. The countryside is emerging as an extension of leisure and consumerism, as well as residually representing the traditional past. The city/country contrast is rendered in the soundtrack of the film, with Coltrane for the city sequences (North America, modernity, hybridity), Vivaldi but also Couperin (contemporaneous with the New France period) for the countryside.

Most contemporary commentators underplay the role of Barbara. If she scores any points at all in the discussions with Claude, it is as a foil or else as a result of Claude's disabling historical and social position. The early sequences code Barbara as "frivolous." To camera, her equivalent profession of identity to that of Claude is: "I'm Jewish. I was born under the sign of Libra," no self-analysis, at ease with unproblematic combinations of identity, either believing in horoscopes or confident enough to be able to joke about her self. While Claude holds up his books, she is making herself up in the mirror. "I'm doing up my hair, undoing it, putting on my make-up," which she does frequently throughout the film. She is happy to embrace the pleasures of consumerism; her acting is to be understood as imitation and inauthenticity.

However, as soon as we start to problematize gender and its relationship to Claude's quest for (national) identity, and in the process denaturalize heterosexuality, the figure of Barbara comes to represent yet another (emergent) seam of hegemonic potential. Kristin Ross has argued, in her stimulating study of the culture of French modernization, that the young heterosexual couple in the city came to offer a new compensatory myth for a society faced with the loss of traditional familial ties.[18] In addition, "youth" became a sounding board for the anxieties associated with a rapidly modernizing culture. Claude and Barbara markedly fail to achieve this compensation, and it is noteworthy that their relationship finally ends outside the city; moreover, the end occurs in a blank countryside in which tradition no longer seems to operate. The fact that any future fails to include Barbara is, of course, bound up with the complicating factor of Quebec nationalism. If the formation of a middle class coterminous with the French nation was central to modernization there, the question mark over what constitutes Quebec national identity severely damages the relationship between Claude and Barbara and underlines all the more the link between personal and collective destinies, since the French modernization myth of the autonomous private and domestic domain is seen as unsustainable here. Claude cannot deal with the Otherness of Barbara, either as femininity or as anglophone Jew. He is disappointed, for example, that, given the history of her own "people," she has little sympathy for the Québécois as oppressed and colonized. She is an *étrangère* for him, but he is "étranger à moi-même/a stranger to myself." In other words, he could relate to her only as she might incarnate the Same. Unlike the Claude of *À tout prendre* who could oxymoronically live with fragmentation and unity, accepting the provisionality of its achievement, the Claude of *Le Chat dans le sac* is strikingly "homo" in his heterosexuality, as he seeks a oneness and unity in similarity rather than in a dialogue with heterogeneity that would include his own "identity" or "identities." This is a result of the "wholeness" associated with his own masculinity; the way that the lack characterizing his own predicament thus represents gender as well as national insecurity. Claude's inertia is a manifestation of machismo, or at the least a reluctance to question masculine identity, but with an inferiority complex. He is given a goal-oriented narrative ("Je me cherche"), as in genre action movies, but he fails to achieve the goal. This is also because the Oedipal identifications he entertains prove inadequate to him also, as his very 1960s "youth revolt" has him rejecting the complacency of his elders: "It's when you're 40 and no longer feel like struggling that you have the right to speak."

Against Claude's masculinist and modernist reading of his situation, Barbara can be understood as offering an alternative hegemonic arrangement. She is able to get beyond binary categories. Jewish and anglophone, she nonetheless acts in French and seeks to improve her linguistic skills further so that, by losing her accent, she can get bigger roles. Her Jewishness is an identity she claims but it is a very secular version of it, "non-Jewish Jewishness," in Isaac Deutscher's terms.[19] Living on the borderlines of cultures that are both major and minor gives her an advantage Claude does not possess but does not fully recognize, in that she is able to play with the relativities of position. Her claim to an astrological as well as Jewish identity, far from denoting emptyheaded frivolity, shows her willingness to entertain fictions and by so doing to allegorize her life. She is more at ease in consumerism because she realizes that identity, rather than grounded in nature, is to do with a play of surfaces and a performance of artifices and disguises. In this way, Barbara can be read as possessing privileges of relativity that are not, as yet, available to Claude or the Québécois in general. The mirror for her represents surface rather than depth: in the final sequences, putting on her make-up does not prevent her from lucidly analysing her relationship and engaging in dialogue, in glances away from her own reflection, with an interviewer as if in *le direct*; this is followed by Claude peering into his mirror in the morning as if a truth might lie beyond his image, and also as if to investigate the passage of time which is ineluctably taking him to the age of forty. Barbara pursues not just any acting project but a production of Brecht, whose whole aesthetic strategy was based on displaying the artifice and avoiding the naturalization of "the real," but to highly political and, for the audience, empowering purposes. (Claude takes no interest in this and, according to Barbara, refuses to see that theatre in Quebec has changed.) These attitudes permit Barbara to travel both physically and metaphorically, to contemplate utopias (her fascination for the *Nord*, the Arctic), to admit their utopianism, and therefore to act in the general sense, to make choices. While she is caught for much of the film in the traps of heterosexual romance, quoting Simone de Beauvoir but arguing that men are superior to women and that she only wants a man to love her, she actually emancipates herself by the film's close and precipitates the end of the affair as much as if not more than Claude.

At one point, as in a dressing room full of costumes, Barbara puts a top hat on Claude as he reads *La Presse*, a dressing-up which momentarily undermines his solemn analysis of a political story. Claude is a straight boy who takes himself seriously, already naturalizes his masculine identity, and seeks to endow his nationality with the same wholeness and certainty. The question arises as to what extent the film *Le Chat dans le sac* is aware of these ambiguities even as it articulates the notion of a lack at the heart of its subject. Claude's body, for example, is actually eroticized more than that of Barbara, an eroticization that breaks with dominant representations of masculinity but that is probably inadvertent. The point is that the film embodies, in its two protagonists, fundamental dilemmas of Quebec or any other national cinema: identity as naturalized unity or identity as artifice. It cannot come to a conclusion and is less self-conscious of the problem than *À tout prendre*, but it points to the complexities of locating the 1960s in relation to what came before and after. Yves Lever argues that the twenty-three-year-old Claude actually stands in for the anxieties of the generation of thirty- to thirty-five-year-olds, such as Groulx, who suffered the full brunt of Catholic education and were historically disabled by it.[20] But the film also looks to the future, as the depthless consumer culture, and its consequences for identity and politics, took over North America in the following decades and as the contradictions of the Quiet Revolution took subjects such as Claude beyond the opposition between the technocrats and the FLQ.

Preoccupation with the mass media and the new cultural industries of sound and image informs the content and form of Groulx's other two 1960s films, *Où êtes-vous donc?* (1968) and *Entre tu et vous* (1969). Like his first feature, the former is a hijacking of a NFB project, this time on Quebec song, then at the forefront of national cultural self-definition, with Robert Charlebois and Claude Gauthier building on the rural imaginings of Félix Leclerc and Gilles Vigneault. Opening with an Indian chant and a Quebec folk song with its rhythm banged out on spoons, *Où êtes-vous donc?* turns into a film narrative that traces the respective destinies of two young men newly arrived in Montreal from the Côte-Nord, Christian (Christian Bernard), a lorry driver and budding musician, and Georges (Georges Dor) a Maoist ex-factory worker who befriend Mouffe (Claudine Monfette), a budding singer. Through the use of montage, scenes in television shops, and images of other screens portraying "degraded" images (the cartoon Indian), the film satirizes the Montreal of Expo 1967, the big city linked to the tourist, consumer, and image flows of North America, counterposed to the discourses of national liberation to be found in Vietnam. Christian ends up in a pop group that is a kind of Québécois Monkees, while Mouffe succeeds in her singing ambitions but, similarly, loses control over her life. Only Georges is left at the end to proclaim, "Où êtes-vous donc, bande de câlisses?" *Entre tu et vous* radicalizes the use of montage, downgrading its narrative of the decay of a heterosexual relationship with a collage of intertitles, contradictory voice-over, and quotations from the audiovisual media (the couple at one point recite the day's TV schedules) which, in typical 1960s avant-garde fashion, denounces the alienating and flattening effects of mass culture. As in Godard's *Le Gai savoir* (1968), Groulx's procedure is that of montage and distanciation, in which the avoidance of the cosy subject position provided by narrative pleasure and the defamiliarization of colliding, decontextualized images serve to induce critical reflection on the part of the spectator.

This 1960s modernism, confident in the position ("authenticity," "national liberation") from which it issues its denunciations, was valuable for its scepticism with regard to the triumphalism of the Quiet Revolution technocracy and its belief in linear progress, to the inequalities the new society brought in its wake, and to the euphoria in North American and especially Canadian media "analysis" (McLuhan) concerning the creation of the new communicative sphere of the global village. Battle will be joined later in this book concerning the theoretical assumptions of this in fact totalizing criticism of the mass media. Suffice it to say for now that Western capitalism, ever adaptable, was able to use 1960s dissent to renew itself by the 1980s and 1990s. Groulx represents one strand of film-making which seeks to present itself as irrecuperable in relation to that process, and this position can be read either as a dead end or as a resource.[21] The tension in his films is located in that national space which he seeks to make autonomous from the media flows of North America, a space which is neither that past authenticity articulated by Perrault nor the modernization of the Quiet Revolution, and whose audience is by definition elusive.

The 1960s films of Jean Pierre Lefebvre (b. 1941) share Groulx's cultural pessimism about the mass media but in so doing seek to create a more sustainable if artisanal space for alternative kinds of production (the creation of Les Films J.P. Lefebvre and then in 1969 Cinak, with his wife Marguerite Duparc). A former critic for *Objectif*, Lefebvre succeeded in setting up his own auteurist cinematic practice, sharing characteristics with the early *nouvelle vague* but with its own consistent traits. Whether in those films that privilege Godardian montage or those that emphasize long takes around some sort of journey or romance and the experiences and impressions around them ("narrative" would be too strong a word), Lefebvre combines an eye for the detail of social interaction and position which makes his films highly permeable to the collective reality of Quebec society ("the personal apprehension of a collective experience," writes Barrowclough),[22] although they invariably do so in a highly oblique manner: "For me an individual in my films is never just an individual, but a sign, a symbol, an image, an allegory of many people – our society exists through its signs and its images of itself." A character thus becomes "a dictionary of attitudes, of mores, of taboos in our society."[23]

Le Révolutionnaire (1965) and *Jusqu'au coeur* (1968 – one of two films made by Lefebvre at the NFB) exemplify similar strategies of Godardian alienation and distantiation, Bressonian silences, and a certain dose of sentimentality. *Le Révolutionnaire* is basically an experimental film which places a group of young male "revolutionaries" in a country farmhouse as they train for the "revolution" under an autocratic leader ("I forbid you to dream"). The precise aims and agenda of this revolution are never made clear, but since the men parade below a Quebec flag it can be assumed that the film is a satire of those Québécois intellectuals attracted by the idea of importing Cuban or other Third World strategies, in the manner of the FLQ. The arrival of a young woman fleeing her violent husband disrupts the authoritarian discourse, as the leader forms a romantic liaison with her and a series of mishaps wipes out the whole group. The film plays humorously on the incongruities of the revolutionary paraphernalia and the resources available (the Volkswagen dressed up like a tank, the queue in snowshoes for the outside toilet), and it contains one montage sequence in which the young men play out the history of Canada, including 1534 and the Confederation of 1867, with the embellishment of Pierre Hébert's scratch animation.

Jusqu'au coeur relies to a greater extent on montage, the parallel montage between the urban couple formed by Garou (Robert Charlebois) and Monfette (Claudine Monfette/Mouffe) and images of violence, war, and the indoctrination Garou is subjected to in a science-fiction setting. Here the negatively charged "system" is associated not with national but with global and especially American power structures, most notably those associated with the Vietnam War and the fear of nuclear holocaust. The heterosexual couple and the desire to have a child ("un Québécois") is posited against, not only aggression in general, but what seem to be coded as less life-affirming practices such as homosexuality and abortion (Mouffe's song "Of what do aborted children dream?"). Lefebvre employs Godardian strategies in *Jusqu'au coeur*, but to different ends and with different results. The critical distance constructed in the latter film is limited to one side of a binary opposition between "violence/structure/system/US mass media" and categories such as "the imaginary," "dreaming," and especially "l'amour" – in the very specific form of the urban heterosexual couple – which are not deemed to partake themselves of the flow of image and meaning construction. However valid or interesting these categories may be, they are still, like their opposites, constructed out of texts, of those cultures in our heads, but Lefebvre suggests a transcendence that recalls the Catholic discourses of pre-1960 Quebec. This is confirmed by the motif in the film of Martians coming to Earth with a new look on things. The problem in this and other Lefebvre films extends to that of the people, or rather their absence. Whereas Godard was operating in a context in which, momentarily at least, the avant-garde of youth-leftist politics and the mass of workers might conceivably or momentarily coincide (the problematics around May 1968, the ambiguities of *La Chinoise*, but the successful juxtaposition of mass and élite discourses in *Tout va bien*), Lefebvre is operating in a 1960s Quebec in which, as we have seen, the "national people" is still in the process of political formation. Moreover, the masses are to be perceived as equally alienated and befuddled as their pseudo-representatives. The building workers in *Jusqu'au coeur* are more interested in wolf-whistling a woman than in listening to their worker priest talking about Quebec. The closing text of *Q-Bec My Love*, Lefebvre's 1969 satire on the emerging and, for him, pornographic state of politics and film-making, contains the following lines: "How far will the hypocrisy go of those who think for other people, and those who let other people think for them. How far will the hypocrisy go of those who despise man by reducing him to the single function of passive spectator ..."[24]

The least that can be said is that such a description of ideology at work is profoundly undialectical, with the masses or the spectator deemed to be passive objects of manipulation rather than active, resistant entities engaging with dominant but not necessarily totalizing discourses. In this context, it is illuminating to examine why Lefebvre disliked À *tout prendre* so much and the vocabulary he uses to express this. For him, the work is, among other things, "molle/soft" and lacking in "stability": "It's the idea which is confused in him, it's the idea which fails to achieve plenitude and thus borrows superficial and bastard forms, and also dons an experimental guise which is just an excuse, a pretext to hide an incapacity [*impuissance*] to master thought."[25] Lack of "plenitude" is opposed to "bastard" and "impuissance," indicating a nostalgia for or aspiration to transcendent categories that are in fact full of social and sexual connotations.

It is in the more intimist films that Lefebvre is far more successful in articulating the personal and collective. As he put it in his admiring pronouncement on *Le Chat dans le sac*, such films represent "a work created entirely at the level of the self but at the same time a social testimony which joins the human by passing through the consciousness of a creator."[26] Lefebvre is a film-maker of Quebec in a minor key, that is, his work never becomes a molar entity (or "structure" as he puts it), but the rather traditional and humanist assumptions of his discourse on marriage and the heterosexual couple risk creating other totalities and plenitudes. In fact, *Il ne faut pas mourir pour ça* (1967), his first film on 35 mm., is a kind of variation on À *tout prendre*, taking as its subject a lost but playful male protagonist with a dominant mother and contradictory relationships with women. Abel, unforgettably played by Marcel Sabourin, lives an eccentric existence, collecting insects, model planes (kept in a birdcage), and jars of sweets, and creating rituals involving toothbrushes and dressing gowns in the act of getting up. His day, which begins with him writing on a blackboard "Aujourd'hui je voudrais transformer le cours des choses/Today I'd like to transform the course of things," is punctuated by a series of comic vignettes (including the equivalent of a custard pie in the face at a bakery in response to his sexual innuendo) and by encounters with his current lover, Madeleine (Claudine Monfette/Mouffe), for whom he buys a dress she already owns, and with his former lover, Mary (Suzanne Grossmann). It ends with the death of his mother (Monique Champagne).

Abel has been read as a retarded adolescent "whose development has been stunted by his milieu and who is sleep-walking through his own life ... incapable of decision, choice and action and infantilized by a matriarchal society."[27] He would thus be an example of a homology, frequent in critical discourse as we shall see in chapter 5, between failed masculinity and a failed or incomplete national project. Abel's father has been absent in Brazil for many years. The minoritization of the French language and therefore of Quebec "identity" are foregrounded in the film in the relationship between Abel and Mary. One of their scenes takes place in a Montreal café where, typically (this is well before the PQ's 1977 language law 101), all the signs and menus are very visibly in English. When Abel encourages her to switch to French, she replies, "This isn't the Republic of Quebec yet." However, a concrete state beyond that minoritization is not envisaged in the film, and this can be read as Abel's failure but also as his perspicacity, since his own "project" is not to produce a new phallic or paternal ("national") position but to concentrate on that "yet," that state of being in between, in interregnum, which he manages through "minor" acts of becoming, of fantasy, humour, affection, and resistance. The movement and dialogue these entail are what "fill" – but so provisionally – the still and spartan space of Lefebvre's very long takes. Lefebvre produces a film which obviously resembles *Le Chat dans le sac* (the anglophone lover, the literal cat taken out of a bag) but also, more paradoxically, *À tout prendre*, despite his own evaluation of that film. While Jutra goes farther in the analysis and disruption of identity, both films alight upon provisionality and fantasy as central to the individual and collective self, eschewing closures or plenitudes (hence the quotation from Brassens ["Il est idiot de mourir pour des idées"] in *Il ne faut pas mourir pour ça*, reworked of course in the title). But, whereas Jutra achieves his effects with montage and a crammed frame and soundtrack, Lefebvre's equally "minor" cinema opts for the pro-filmic, a *mise en scène* pared down to the austere, in which objects and the spatial relations established between them acquire disproportionate significance.

In complete contrast, the 1960s also saw the beginnings of the quest for a Quebec popular cinema. In *Trouble-fête*, Pierre Patry's strategy lies in a rewriting of Quebec identity through the modern, the American, and the homosocial, but with an inferiority complex. The film centres on young and handsome Lucien (Lucien Hamelin), who attends an all-male *collège classique* (high school run by the Catholic Church) and rebels, in a manner more structured than that of his rambunctious colleagues, against its regulations and incompetence. In a sexual relationship with Lise (Louise Rémy), with whom he does theatre work, but in a dysfunctional relationship with his parents, Louis has his downfall when he rejects a gay man's advances and provokes his death in a car accident. Returning to the scene, he is recognized and confronted by the crowd and the police.

Trouble-fête navigates between an anachronistic (even for 1964) scenario of revolt against the power of the church as source of Quebec's backwardness and impotence, and an aspiration to an American individualism and hedonism without really believing in its capacity for success. The ambiance is very American, with free-thinking youth, cars, rapid editing pace, and even the presence at the end of a black policeman (rare in Montreal at the time: he is played by Percy Rodrigues, later the first male black lead on the American prime-time soap opera *Peyton Place*). Lucien is defeated partly out of (Catholic?) guilt and partly out of a homophobia the source of which is his own uneasy personal, sexual, and national identity. The film thus has to underline the internalized reasons for Lucien's act: an earlier sequence in a bar has him responding ambiguously to the man's gaze. This, however, gives the game away: the Other that Lucien (and masculinist accounts of Quebec's national problems) construct is in fact within.

Given the impasses of Quebec masculinity, it is significant that the most successful Quebec film of the decade in terms of box-office revenue places a woman at the centre of a project of reconciliation, hegemony, modernity, and pleasure (but, decisively, a woman to be looked at). The eponymous heroine of *Valérie* (Danielle Ouimet) is a young woman who escapes from an orphanage run by nuns and establishes herself in Montreal first as a topless dancer and later as a high-class prostitute but then finds true love with an artist, Patrick (Guy Godin) and his young son. The film marked the beginning of a Quebec popular cinema, with vast returns being made on its $99,000 budget both in Quebec and in France (the post-synchronized voices reveal few traces of a Quebec accent). Its director, Denis Héroux (b. 1940), had, after *Seul ou avec d'autres*, graduated to commercial film-making with Onyx Films, directing company films but also the first attempt at a commercial success, *Pas de vacances pour les idoles* (1965), which drew on the popularity of a number of television and musical celebrities. After *Valérie*, he was to make several more popular successes in the early 1970s before concentrating on production, becoming a major player in Alliance-Vivafilm in the 1980s and Astral Bellevue Pathé in the 1990s. However, *Valérie* lives in legend (see the reference to it in *L'Escorte*, 1996) as the first Québécois pornographic film. Indeed, many of the scenes, including the very first, and much of the narrative (Valérie poses in the artist's studio) are constructed around the baring of Danielle Ouimet's breasts and can be seen to partake of those very 1960s constructions of sexual liberation as a greater availability of stimulation and relief for heterosexual men, and of Quebec nationalism as a male plenitude based on the historically deferred undressing of *la petite Québécoise* (see chapter 5). The film is thus structured like much soft porn, to the point of soft focus photography when Valérie at last loses her virginity, the reaction shots are on her pleasure and not the client's, and the representation of prostitution is highly sanitized. On the other hand, the film has been widely analysed as a moral tale,[28] in that Valérie returns to the fold of marriage and maternity: woman as whore or mother/angel.

In fact, the film is of interest because of what we might call its kaleidoscopic articulation of hegemony in the making, the juxtaposition and juggling around of social discourses pertaining to identity, pleasure, and morality for which Valérie herself is a vehicle. She is first looked at by a man through a kaleidoscope, emphasizing her subordination to a regime of looking and to a thematics of hegemonic process, but she is also a subject of the look, in, for example, the relationship with Patrick and the abuse she suffers from the final (wealthy and repulsive) client. Valérie is thus part of a whole lineage of melodramatic media texts which seek to restate new hegemonies by charting a woman's social progress/process (*Chateauvallon, Dynasty*). That mode – melodrama – is one that relocates the sacred (decisively rejected at the beginning of the film and by the *mise en scène* of rebirth which immediately follows the title sequence), and with it polarities of "good" and "bad," within personal relations. In *Valérie*, the ending, with all its paraphernalia of Quebec flags on the belvedere overlooking Montreal, does not mark a return to the Catholic values and morality of the orphanage. Valérie loves sex, and the marriage with Patrick will not mean a renunciation of her enjoyment. Moreover, through his painting – and his open-air artistic practice – Patrick belongs to the worlds, seen as non-contradictory, of both modernity and nature which have been a source of enjoyment for Valérie. She is not François's natural mother, so to an extent the "family" (re)constituted is not a traditional one but one based on choice: critics have noted François's statement that he wants Valérie to be his "maman" and the supposedly traditional consequences for her rather than the innovation such autonomy represents for him. The "family" comes into being as a symbol for the wider society (in contrast with the orphaned alienation that had previously reigned), but it is a family that is able to offer at least something to women.

It is through modernity and pleasure that the film is able to articulate its version of the emergence of the new. Valérie's gaze into the mirror at the beginning, the close-up of the eye both looking and looked at, is qualitatively different from the depths being sought by Claude or the multiplicity of performances foreseen by Barbara in *Le Chat dans le sac*. It denotes a narcissism that emphasizes sensual pleasure and an ease with the body, an attitude of consumerism and individual autonomy. Valérie's education in the city is one that will seek to manage that attitude by reconciling it with the demands of social order, namely, marriage. However, it is made clear throughout the film that this social order is itself a newness, a modernity that addresses Valérie's agenda. The city is triumphantly entered, and its spaces are extensions of Valérie's bodily pleasures: the shopping malls where she buys her clothes, and the Metro, where, in one extraordinary scene, she caresses the outside of the trains and uses the central metal pole as a potential dancing prop. *Valérie* is a film about the new shocks and stimuli of modernity which serve to reconstruct the self, its perception and pleasures. It is not too outlandish to evoke here Walter Benjamin's analyses of nineteenth-century Paris as rendered by Baudelaire. That culture is seen to be very double-edged: the sacred, the unique "aura" traditionally associated with art, has gone; its loss is perceived but new possibilities for poetry are unearthed; memories are liquidated, but mechanical reproduction such as photography shows the triumph of volitional remembrance; the new rhythms and subjectivities are consistent with the mechanization and segmentation of industrial labour, but the "luster of a crowd with a motion and soul of its own"[29] is one that can dazzle the *flâneur*, that leisured wanderer of the city, poised for new experiences and the unearthing of new treasures. The film has Valérie herself, "a kaleidoscope equipped with consciousness,"[30] to quote Baudelaire on one who plunges into a crowd, supposedly reconciling these aspects of modernity: astonishingly, her availability (for prostitution) becomes a kind of *flânerie*, her labour a form of sexual fulfilment. Throughout the film, it is emphasized that the transformations of Valérie and of "Quebec," unlike, needless to say, those to be found in *Les Fleurs du mal*, do not constitute a crisis.

In the scene in the Metro carriage, a montage shows different images of women in advertising. In a procedure at opposite poles from that of Groulx, these are to be understood in the film as modern examples of traditional ways in which women have been represented in art. Later, Valérie is seen to flick through an art-history book (of which her apartment is full) and a montage shows her in poses from Rubens and others. This is a standard alibi in pornography, of course, but here it is harnessed to a discourse that seeks to proclaim the aesthetic as non-religious and as continuous with the aestheticizations and sexualizations of consumer society. Thus the artefacts of the orphanage are replaced by the art objects of her apartment. At the same time, Valérie is presented as a reconciling or non-excessive figure, defying the nuns' severity but also mocking a "repressed" intellectual woman and, moreover, resisting the lesbian advances of her flatmate and drawing the line at a physically repulsive client, despite his pecuniary offers (high-class prostitution indeed, and an indication that at least some of this film's "pornographic" effects depend on the presentability of the men, too). The film's sanitization of the worlds it depicts underlines the class basis of this new hegemony in the making: the universalization of a consuming, secular middle class that values most highly individual choice and the aesthetic.[31] Much of the Quebec cinema that followed in the 1970s would explore these avenues but qualify them from the point of view of a national "people" and the complex needs and positions of its women protagonists.

Gilles Carle's two feature films released in the 1960s contain in embryo the directions the national cinema might take. They paint, however, a less than dynamic portrait of the new Quebec. Like *Le Chat dans le sac*, *La Vie heureuse de Léopold Z.* started off as an NFB documentary – on snow-clearing in Montreal – but was surreptitiously transformed into a narrative feature. It recounts the Christmas Eve spent by Léopold (Guy L'Écuyer), a rotund thirty-two-year-old snow-plough operator employed by the city, between his work in the snowstorm and his familial duties such as buying presents for his wife, Catherine (Monique Joly), and his son, Jacques, collecting at the station his wife's cousin Josette (Suzanne Valéry), a jazz singer, and fetching furniture for his superintendant and friend Théo (Paul Hébert). Léopold is finally able to attend midnight Mass at the Oratoire Saint-Joseph, hear Jacques sing in the choir, and give his wife her fur coat.

La Vie heureuse de Léopold Z. is another film concerned with questions of identity and power. An early montage in the film provides, with voice-over third-person narration, an autobiographical summary of Léopold, with his birthplace in the working-class east of the city, stills of the school where he learned little, the presence of the church, the self-conscious development of his signature, even the contents of his wallet. The photographs of him that hint at multiple identities through performance, such as dressed as a knowing businessman, comment on his disempowerment rather than his ability to exploit, like Barbara in *Le Chat dans le sac*, those provisionalities. A product of the materially and culturally dispossessed francophone working class, and the ninth of eleven children, "Léo has never been able to express himself in the first person." He is on the receiving end of hierarchies, including with Théo, and is largely incapable of self-assertion or meaningful agency, except in connection with the struggle to make it to midnight Mass on time. The social portrait of this quintessential Québécois "little man," endowed with the commonest surname of all, is played out against a backdrop of the characteristically "national" landscape of winter and its attendant rituals and practices.

From this it is but a short leap to portraying the film as another negative critique of Quebec society from the point of view of some nationalist-intellectual "truth." Gilles Carle himself described Léopold as "a pre-revolutionary character, who goes round in circles."[32] Michel Houle, in his 1976 study of Carle, reproached the film for its mere description of a state of affairs: "Léopold's lack of awareness is total and unfailing ... not the slightest glimmer of understanding of the forces ranged against him. Nor really for the spectator any way of identifying, of recognizing the interests which manipulate these forces and profit from them."[33] However, the importance of *La Vie heureuse de Léopold Z.* lies in its attempt to construct the possibility of a popular national cinema. The dialogue with fellow-intellectuals that characterized *À tout prendre* and *Le Chat dans le sac* gives way here to at least an attempt to address the need Gramsci perceived for the organic intellectual to engage with the "feeling" of the people. For Gramsci, the intellectual could not be an intellectual, but would merely be a pedant, if he or she were "distinct and separate from the people-nation, that is, without feeling the elementary passions of the people, understanding them and therefore explaining and justifying them in the particular historical situation." Representation is possible only if there is this organic link between "feeling-passion," understanding and knowledge.[34] In *La Vie heureuse de Léopold Z.*, the feeling-passion is pleasure, the pleasures Léopold takes in his life and those offered by a film whose comedy relies on an interplay for the spectator between identification (with Léopold and, through the processes of recognition, with "Quebec") and distance. Léopold is to be figured as "one of us," but that "us" is complex, for it contains contradictory elements of similarity and difference, past and present.

Léopold's pleasures are associated with consumerism, the figure of Josette, and the reconciling final rituals. However, like Homer Simpson, Léopold is bewildered by modernity. As the film takes us through landscapes of shopping and transactions, Léopold is often on the receiving end of sight gags, such as his antics with a pen attached to a desk at the loan company, or of others' greater fluency with the language of consumerism, as when he pays too much for the fur coat or cannot cope with the choice of goods at the department store. He is therefore to be distinguished from those characters, equally Québécois, who deal with the contemporary world more confidently, such as the upwardly mobile Théo or Catherine (although even she finds herself wishing "Joyeux Noël" to a recorded message). The sexually alluring Josette is multilingual, unlike Léopold, and this produces a verbal gag:

Josette: Vous parlez anglais, Léo?
Léopold: Yes, very much.

But, through the variety of her musical styles, Josette suggests a less parochial Quebec, and via her travels she even seems able to co-opt Léopold – "my gaucho of the snows" – to a potentially more multidimensional figure. Midnight Mass at the Oratoire may be read as some residual cultural element that Léopold fails to question. However, the event is coded not as something excessively religious but rather as the achievement of that goal – reconciliation – which the narrative of Léopold's day had set up. Contradictions are thus reconciled in community and family, tenacious factors for the vast majority of Québécois in the 1960s. However, even this ritual is detotalized by two elements. The radio announces that will this be not only a *Noël blanc* but also a "White Christmas," which, rather than some American colonization, is to be read in a more sanguine way to signify the porousness of this "people" and culture, open to the outside. The Oratory's religious significance is undermined by Léopold's presentation of the fur coat to Catherine, a manifestation simultaneously of contemporary consumerism but also a whole economic history of Montreal, Quebec, and Canada.

However, the scene involves one more element that proves excessive, as Catherine strokes the fur in the last shot of the film, in extreme close-up of her hand with wedding ring. This mild hint of perversion is significant because it goes beyond the "realism" of her pleasure in acquisition to embrace a fetishism that destabilizes the avowed meaning of the scene. The fur coat forms part of the final ritual of reconciliation. However, it also suggests a trouble at the heart of that supposed unity. Clearly, part of that trouble is to be located in consumerism itself, in that the coat is part of that commodity fetishism that Marx denounced in the pages of *Capital.* In this analysis, the circulation of goods for exchange disguises the relations between people, and the input of labour power, as unalterable relations between things: "The objective conditions essential to the realization of labour are alienated from the worker and become manifest as fetishes endowed with a will and a soul of their own. Commodities, in short, appear as the purchasers of persons."[35] Léopold is caught within that circulation, in his ineptitude as shopper (these things to purchase are alien) but also in the emphasis in the film on his labour time. Léopold's time is devoted to earning enough to buy into the consumer society, but that time is disrupted in the film by three events – Josette, Théo, and the snowstorm – which possess a different, more traditional logic bound up with family ties, an almost feudal relationship of hierarchy and mutual dependency, and the extremes of Quebec "nature" and the collective effort needed to combat it. The film's final reconciliation is in this way a reconciliation of different time-frames belonging to different strata of Quebec's history. *Valérie* operates a similar reconciliation but via an allegorical narrative of change and transformation.

The coalition of tradition and modernity represented in the final scene of *La Vie heureuse de Léopold Z.* is, however, extremely fragile, since beneath the good humour there lie histories of alienation, dispossession, and lack of autonomy. It is here that the Freudian rather than Marxist meaning of fetishism comes to the rescue for Léopold's subject position. It could be argued, of course, that the fetishistic pleasure is that of Catherine. However, throughout the film the dominant gaze has been that of heterosexual masculinity. Josette's performance is a clear example of the fetishistic, as opposed to voyeuristic, representation of women in cinema, for she is the object of the gaze of Léopold and Théo, and her over-evaluated allure comfortingly places her beyond the film's processes of narrative and identification. The comfort of the fetish for men is, of course, according to Freud, that it permits a disavowal of castration, of the memory of perceiving women as lacking a penis.[36] The resort to the fetish is a logical continuation of much of the humour of the film, which depends on a lack or gap between Léopold's aspirations and his achievement and which is often coded in gender terms. Théo is full of marriage advice and macho bravado as Léopold drives him around, but his appeal to nature, couched in modern terms after all ("It's the law of nature ... You can't fight against nature"; "Chromosomes are stronger than men"), is undermined by the very trappings of modernity, technology, and science that form the basis of his job, namely, the collective enterprise of snow-clearing but also the new consumer world in which Catherine is able to cover her Christmas tree with "snow" from an aerosol; by the decidedly unglamorous and non-fetishistic vehicle, the ungainly snow-plough; and by the tawdriness of his own fantasy scene with Josette, conducted in English. On occasions there is a cut to a woman's (controlling) gaze: the still of a model winking to camera that follows the scene in which Léopold and Théo buy perfume in the department store; and the moment in Théo's fantasy when the camera tracks up a tropical fern to frame a bauble on Catherine's Christmas tree which reflects her face. The film mocks the men's machismo because it is inappropriate in their case, not because of a desire to move beyond dominant gender roles and identities. The implication is that the malaise lies in not possessing a phallic wholeness, and thus an identification is made between nationhood and phallic maturity: Léopold's expression for being overcharged for his house purchase is, "Je me suis fait fourrer là/I got screwed." We shall see later how Carle's often fetishistic *mise en scène* develops in his *oeuvre*, and how it affects his representation of women.

Le Viol d'une jeune fille douce (1968) is to be distinguished from Carle's first feature in that its central protagonist is a woman and it was made in the private sector, although still on 16 mm. and on a restricted budget ($45,000). Onyx Films had been founded by the brothers André (b. 1932) (later to become NFB commissioner, 1975–79) and Pierre

Lamy (1926–98) in 1962 and had since taken over the production company founded by Denis Héroux. The film recounts the pregnancy of Julie, a young technical draughtsman (Julie Lachapelle). She makes an appointment for a clandestine abortion but chooses not to turn up. A Moroccan Jewish lover, Jacques (Jacques Cohen) moves in for a short while. Her next-door neighbour, Suzan (Suzan Kay), an eccentric French-speaking anglophone, commits suicide. Her three brothers, with their angelic names Raphaël, Gabriel, and Joachim (played by André Gagnon and Daniel and Donald Pilon), seek to avenge the "dishonour" caused to their sister and, with the vaguest of clues from Julie, beat up a Frenchman in a country chalet. On their journey they rape a hitch-hiker. When Julie's baby is born, she hesitates as to whether to put it up for adoption or abandon it. In the end she keeps it and moves into a new apartment.

The film is in keeping with Quebec's cinema of modernization, combined with an emerging authorial style from Carle. Post-traditional sexual values, consumerism, fast cars, a passive protagonist, and a highly uncertain and uninspiring future are here rendered in a distant and ironic style. Frequent long takes and static panoramas, such as the rape scene, filmed in extreme long shot with no gesture to titillation, are interrupted by the occasional home-movie-like montage of street scenes. Perhaps the most interesting element is the portrayal of Jacques, who offers the potential of dialogue with the Other, in his preoccupation with the complexities of identity (he is composing his autobiography in Arabic), his anti-Americanism and references to the Vietnam War, his invocation of the anti-Semitism of the Pétain regime, and the parallels between his home town of Meknès, with its juxtaposition of cultures, and Montreal.

However, the film takes risks with the character of Julie. Her passivity (Jacques is better informed than her about the Quebec political situation) and final acquiescence to patterns of consumerism built around the albeit fatherless family (her decorating the new apartment) invite a general identification with "Quebec" but at the expense of neglecting the specificity of her gender and even of denying her a voice. Just as masculine identity is an issue for Claude in *Le Chat dans le sac* and Léopold in *La Vie heureuse de Léopold Z.* to be articulated with the national question, so must Julie's femininity. It is true that the violence of her brothers is represented as closely bound up with masculinity, or rather its masquerade, a pseudo-feudal question of "honour" dressed up in stetsons from a fantasy western and myth of conquest. However, the fact that Julie can be seen to stand in for the whole culture (with the rape symbolically applying to her too) seems to be complicit with her own silence, women used for symbolic purposes rather than given voice. This process is compounded by Carle's ironic *mise en scène*, so that Julie becomes a blank canvas for the would-be auteur's preoccupations. At the same time, the film, with its provocative title and brief scenes of female nudity (the bare breasts of the corrupt police chief's wife bedded by the brothers), is clearly taking advantage of the new climate following the abolition of censorship and, like *Valérie*, seeking to establish a basis for a popular cinema on a certain erotic promise that is overwhelmingly for a heterosexual male gaze. The ambiguities of Carle in the 1970s are closely bound up with these twin, very gendered cinematic legacies of the 1960s, auteurism and the popular-erotic.

It is useful finally to look at what is one of the most accomplished feature films of the decade, Michel Brault's *Entre la mer et l'eau douce* (1967), for its qualities and also its production details offer a kind of résumé or balance sheet of the period. It tells the story of Claude Tremblay, played by the singer Claude Gauthier, who leaves his village in the Lower St Lawrence to seek upward mobility in the city. The film is narrated in flashback from the position of his success as a singer, playing at the Place des Arts, the vast arts complex, Montreal's Lincoln Center or South Bank, built in the 1960s in the francophone part of the city. With a script by Brault, Denys Arcand, Claude Jutra, the playwright Marcel Dubé, and the poet and nationalist politician Gérald Godin, the film combines two cultural fields. One is the standard modern narrative of the (male) arriviste or parvenu, who descends on the city from outside and whose experiences as liberal, mobile individual represent a kind of apprenticeship of modernity. In Quebec, of course, this narrative combines with a sense of the collective entry of a "people" into this generalized modernity: indeed, the title of one of Gauthier's most famous songs, performed by Claude in the film, shifts in the decade from "Je suis de nationalité canadienne-française" to "Je suis de nationalité québécoise-française." *Entre la mer et l'eau douce* extends, comments on, and, to a certain extent, critiques a version of the nation presented in *Pour la suite du monde*, for which Brault had shared directorial credits with Pierre Perrault. The title of the 1967 film is a quotation from Jacques Cartier that is already alluded to in *Pour la suite du monde.*[37] Claude hails from Saint-Irénée, in Charlevoix just opposite the Île aux coudres. In *Entre la mer et l'eau douce*, the emphasis is on the ambiguities of the spatial and temporal structures traced out by Claude's journeys. He leaves behind a lover, a Montagnais Indian, who is thus a – rather enigmatic – element within his "origins." Halfway to Montreal, he sleeps with a prostitute in Trois-Rivières: there follows an immediate cut to him leaving a confession box the next day. In the city, he drifts through casual and marginal jobs, including that of refuse collector. He has an affair with a waitress, Geneviève (Geneviève Bujold), but she breaks it off. Returning to Saint-Irénée, he seeks to reconnect with its myth of origins but finds the mid-Lent carnival (as featured in *Pour la suite*) sabotaged by the discovery of his sister Aude in bed with his best friend (Robert Charlebois). The landscape there is represented not by tradition but is criss-crossed by those noisy symbols of modernity (and of Québécois engineering via the Bombardier company), skidoos.

Brault employs many of the techniques of *le direct* but in a fictional context. The camera is in the thick of the action for the rural carnival. The long scene in which Claude and Geneviève split up is conducted like an interview *en direct*, and Claude and his brother are indeed "filmed" in the street by a television reporter. However, their remarks illustrate one of the dangers of the totalizations which the film is seeking to problematize, when they blame "immigrants" for taking the jobs of "Québécois." An anglophone black in the restaurant voices doubts about Quebec's ability to achieve independence. (He is played by the boxer Ronald Jones from the 1961 NFB documentary Brault had worked on for Groulx, *Golden Gloves*). As the title suggests, the film is about the "in-betweenness" of identity and place, but also of time. This is a Gramscian interregnum indeed, and one intensified by the inarticulate way (apart from his music) in which Claude experiences his destiny. As Lever puts it, the polysemic title can mean "between the past and the present, between two value systems, between two symbolic worlds, faced with a collection of ideologies which he has difficulty in understanding and can't master."[38] This is because he himself embodies those contradictions, in his guilt and expectations in relations to women, and in his musical career which combines the mass media and evocations of rural "authenticity." "Between the sea and freshwater" emphasizes also in spatial terms the contradictions of the Quebec national project, torn and potentially dispersed between a native past and a multiracial present and future. The metaphor of fluidity is perfect, and it is conveyed both through fictional and documentary modes and in dialogue with other texts of this young cinema. Brault's film is able to articulate individual and collective "structures of feeling" precisely because it is in tune not only with the social and ideological contradictions of the time but also with the fact that contemporary nation-building is and will be characterized by tension.

"From Expo '67 to the October Crisis" would be a similarly structured title. The decade of the Quiet Revolution was ending in not a little political turbulence in Quebec: the *nuit de la matraque* on 24 June 1968, when demonstrators at the Saint-Jean Baptiste national day were attacked by police on the eve of Pierre Trudeau's election as Canadian prime minister; the continuing activity of the FLQ; the colossal uncertainty over whether the marshalling of pro-sovereignty forces could achieve power. An interregnum by definition never loses its capacity for crisis.

4 Quebec/France

The abundance of references to France in Quebec popular culture emphasizes the pervasive presence of the "mother country" but also a tension. Often the butt of humour, French culture can be portrayed as a beacon of taste and manners to be undermined by the quintessentially *quétaine* (naff or kitsch) Québécois couple in the television sitcom *La Petite Vie*, or as backwardly lacking in the (especially sanitary) comforts North Americans such as the Québécois might expect; on the latter point, witness the comedienne Dominique Michel's cameo as the travel agent in *Le Crime d'Ovide Plouffe* (Arcand, 1984; set in the 1940s); or Léopold Tremblay's description of toilets in French cafés to his fellow farmers on the Île-aux-coudres in *Le Règne du jour* (Perrault, 1967); or the plumbing in the hotel the hockey players stay at in *Les Boys II* (Saia, 1998). These ambivalences extend, of course, to political debates in the public sphere, with the invocation of "France" (which France? clerical or republican? Gaullist or socialist?) serving at different times to position a discourse in different ways vis-à-vis debates on the church in Quebec or on Quebec's relationship to the rest of the North American continent. There is no better example of the national-allegorical tension than "Quebec/France," because "France" becomes a cipher to be used in different, fluctuating ways; because it is a site whose meaning is constantly to be contested; and because it mobilizes different spatial and temporal definitions of the Quebec nation. Before we examine in more specific terms the consequences of this tension for film production (and co-production), the attempted construction of a transatlantic francophone film audience, and the cultural translation of certain film-making practices, it is necessary to examine more closely the contested sites involved.

First of all, there is the question of history and the interpretations of the conquest and its consequences for French/Quebec relations. There is a strong argument, articulated, for example, by the historian Laurier L. Lapierre in Jacques Godbout's documentary *Le Sort de l'Amérique* (1996), in favour of making a clear distinction in 1759 between the French and the *canadiens*. The relatively neglected backwater that was New France contained an élite (which, other than the clergy, fled after the conquest) but also a medley of other people (*habitants* farming under the feudal system, *coureurs de bois* seeking to escape it, indifferent urban citizenry) who identified with *le Canada* rather than the colonial power and *ancien régime*. The Radio Canada *téléroman Marguerite Volant* (1996–97) emphasized the contradictions of the post-conquest period, in which the victorious British eventually sought, with the Quebec Act of 1774, to safeguard the "distinctness" of French-Canadian society in order to forestall any sympathy for the rebellious colonists in British America. So, although powerful discourses persist in stressing the continuity of the terms "French" – "French-Canadian" – "Québécois," revisionist histories are available to argue for the discontinuities.

Nowhere is this tension played out with greater psychic potential than in familial discourses relating to the "mother country." We shall see in the next chapter how the loss of 1759 can be figured as the "orphaning" of Quebec. In addition, the narrative of origins implied in the fixation on France can dovetail into a vertical, hierarchical mapping, or, alternatively, one that emphasizes the central position of France (that is, Paris) and the peripherality of Quebec. These arguments in turn depend on the historical context and social position of the enunciator. That hierarchical mapping was sustained in the nineteenth century by the clerical-nationalist élites in Quebec, although for them the origin was the pre-revolutionary *ancien régime* and the dialogue was mainly with traditionalist and monarchist sectors of French society.[1] High culture in Quebec tended to rely on the centre/periphery model. Indeed, the literary syllabus or *cours classique* devoted in schools to the canonical authors and texts of French literature persisted into the 1960s. But popular discourses and those of many post-Quiet Revolution nationalists sought to undermine that hierarchy in favour of an identity centred on Quebec. This undermining was often translated in terms of gender, with the maternal or feminine France inappropriate to, or indeed holding back, the full development of a Quebec national plenitude read as masculine.

De Gaulle's visit to Quebec in 1967 is so significant because it both crystallizes a tradition of discourses circulating around "Quebec/ France" and reinvents that tradition for modernity. If certain French élites nearly a century earlier began to be interested in French Canada because of its resonance for the creation of a new colonial empire, particularly in Algeria, in the 1960s attention to Quebec takes place in the context of the end of empire and is in part a compensation for its loss. (De Gaulle had visited Canada in 1960 with far less fracas, not being in a position to admonish the Québécois on self-determination while the Algerian war still raged.) Much more than the cliché of de Gaulle's long-held resentment against the Anglo-Saxon powers, the Second World War is important here for the Gaullist narrative imposed afterwards of a straightforward (and majority) resistance against an occupier. Indeed, the president's triumphal progress through Quebec[2] is said to have reminded him of his entry into Paris and other liberated French cities in 1944.[3] Typically, the Gaullist discourse combines the old and the new. His notion of filiation is less familial than corporeal and organic: in his radio appeal of August 1940, the French Canadians were "an old French branch which became a magnificent tree"; in 1967 they are "a part of the French people,"[4] A tree is certainly hierarchical if we recall Deleuze and Guattari, but this less emotionally and sexually charged language permits a nationalism which, in the 1960s, can be harnessed to pluralist ends, hence the Phnom Penh speech of 1966 and the attempts to bypass Cold War polarities and counterbalance American hegemony. In turn, this nationalism is one based on modernization rather than colonization, and in this way the technological and industrial assertionism of the Quiet Revolution could be read both by de Gaulle and by Quebec nationalist politicians as paralleling the triumphalist heyday of the Fifth Republic before 1968. De Gaulle and France thus offered a French rather than American model of modernization, all the more so in that the rhetoric of Gaullism was able successfully, for a while, to minimize the perception in France that modernization meant Americanization (an outcome that haunts French élites to this day). However, many cultural comparisons between France and Quebec, and not only those relating to sanitation, turn on the comparative experience of modernization and the waning of tradition.

A Quebec could be envisaged that was modern and autonomous on this French model, part of an international community of francophone states. La francophonie obviously emphasizes language above other affiliations and assignments of identity, and therefore, as we shall see in chapter 10, is potentially more inclusive. Quite apart from the persistent tendency of the term to peripheralize that which is not France (perhaps unavoidable given the fact that, unlike Britain, Spain, and Portugal, France was never surpassed in terms of population and power by any of its former colonies), it also serves both to redefine Quebec's relationship to France and to create a potential outflow, a language-based market for Quebec industrial but especially cultural products. The fact that this has worked so well for popular song (Céline Dion, of course, and also Diane Dufresne, Félix Leclerc, Robert Charlebois, Gilles Vigneault, Richard Desjardins, the Acadian Roch Voisine) but not for film will be explored further.

The complicating factor is America. The current state of play of global capital and cultural flows, including "globalization" and the North American Free Trade Agreement, will be explored fully in chapter 11. Quebec has always had a continental as well as Atlantic vocation. Commenting on the "tension" that is the "very motor of our survival" between the two unattainable poles of France and the United States, Gilles Thérien considers the transatlantic, east-west direction as based on time and vertical relations (tradition, hierarchies), the north-south, continental direction as based on space and horizontal relations.[5] While concurring with his valorization of the tension at the heart of Quebec's hybridity, I would also argue that France and America present two models, not so much of modernization as of polities and nations within modernization. Both constituted in the eighteenth century rival models of the republic, and it is fair to say that the impact of globalization, of immigration, but also arguably of the AIDS crisis has rendered more fragile the French model of abstract citizenship and national oneness than the American model of individual rights and identity coalitions.[6] This rivalry informs debates in Quebec concerning ethnicity and citizenship but also has wide repercussions within popular and consumer culture. The sheer exportability of American mass-cultural products is due not to historical and economic factors alone but also to their inclusive address to a variety of groups (especially youth) and their combinations of pleasure and mobility. If French youth, faced with catastrophic levels of unemployment and an inflexible labour market centred on the rigidities of the bureaucratic-state apparatus, looks so often and so much to America, then the hybridities of Quebec cultural identity and of its cinematic products create both misrecognitions and great opportunities, as we shall see.

In his otherwise perceptive article, Thérien laments the fact that Quebec films deal so much with the American "pole" (in terms of both content and style) but not with the French: "On the other hand, there are no novels and films which problematize our relations with France. These relations are always examined in terms of the continuity and tradition of a strong, unproblematic link. From here, it always seems that it is more natural for us to be French than American." The rest of this chapter seeks to explore the ways in which Quebec cinema has indeed looked at "Quebec/France" in highly problematizing ways.

First, key examples can be taken from the art cinema of the 1960s and 1970s. *Le Règne du jour* (1966) is the second part of Pierre Perrault's trilogy on the Île-aux-Coudres, after *Pour la suite du monde* (1963) and before *Les Voitures d'eau* (1968). The film takes members of the Tremblay family who "starred" in the first work (the octogenarian Alexis, his wife Marie, son Léopold, and his wife Marie-Paule) to France in a quest for origins and ancestry. However, the unanimity associated with ethnic nationalism, complicated by the polysemy of *Pour la suite du monde*, is undermined by several factors. The masculine discourse of the islanders, dominant up to this point, is contradicted by the much greater voice given to Marie. Alexis is the one who emphasizes historical continuity, as he seeks to trace ancestral identity through the name of the father and husband, the original Tremblay who left for New France in the seventeenth century. At the end he has, to some disagreement from his family, brought back a grandfather clock, and he wants France to come back and take Canada. In contrast, it is clear that, for Marie, this visit to France, her first outside North America, represents less a reconnection with patriarchal time but a welcome relief from a lifetime of domestic labour: "Je m'occupais pas de la vie, je vivais pour vivre/I wasn't busy with life, I lived in order to live," a contradiction that the closing shot of the film, showing the old couple sitting on either side of the grandfather clock, fails to overcome. In addition, Perrault's parallel editing, as, for example, when comparing how a pig is slaughtered in the two societies, concentrates on the fact that the populations being represented are peasants. The film thus portrays a "France" that is historically both continuous (the cultural memory of the peasantry, as in *Pour la suite du monde*, recalled in this film in the visit to the beluga whale in New York) and discontinuous, in that it refers to a very particular relationship to the nation and to the modern. The peasants of the Perche region between Paris and Normandy speak non-standard French in a manner analogous to the Québécois. The connection being made in the film is one that leapfrogs over the French Revolution and the creation of a modern, centralized French nation state. It is a discussion between two peripheries.

Moreover, unanimity is undermined not only by gender and region but also by historical change. The discussions in the film turn not only on comparative farming customs or the difference between the tenant farmers of western France and landowning farmers of Quebec, but also on the different experiences of modernization on the land as well as in terms of consumerism and fashion. Other differences underlined include the portrayal of the French aristocracy in the *chasse à l'épouvante* sequence, and the recent French experience of war and occupation, which, unlike in the Gaullist discourse invoked above, does not provide any point of comparison with Quebec. Finally, the film throws up as many if not more differences between Quebec and France than similarities, and they are articulated between two unstable peripheries rather than between two plenitudes or centres.

The Quebec-France relationship has been a preoccupation of Jean-Pierre Lefebvre. His *Patricia et Jean-Baptiste* of 1966 cast himself as a young Québécois cabinet maker, a passive "little man" with no ambition. His overbearing employer of French origin (who hires mainly anglophone Italians) tells him to help the new secretary, Patricia (Patricia Lacroix), newly arrived from France (in fact Courbevoie, a dull suburb of Paris), to find an apartment. The film follows their fruitless peregrinations through a grey, wintry Montreal; at one point at a hockey game, Jean-Baptiste makes a half-hearted pass at Patricia. Lefebvre's playful and "minor" procedure (the last scene has Jean-Baptiste presenting Patricia with flowers that spray water) undoes any grand narratives or sexual/romantic fantasms of the Quebec-France relationship, both in its emphasis on inaction rather than action and its refusal to fulfil the promise of a "truth" which Lefebvre saw as a fault of direct cinema. *Le Vieux pays où Rimbaud est mort*, which he directed in 1977, takes up the story of Abel, again played by Marcel Sabourin, from *Il ne faut pas mourir pour ça* ten years earlier. The three sequences of Abel's visit to France correspond to the places where, in order, Rimbaud lived, was born, and died. In the first, he is in Paris, where among other vignettes, he is subjected to a diatribe on the state of the country from a taxi-driver (Jean-François Stévenin) and assailed in a café by various French stereotypes (a policeman, minister, priest, "reactionary" and "revolutionary"). He travels to Charleville in the north and visits his friend Jeanne (Myriam Boyer), who is suffering from the death of her husband in an industrial accident, the more recent death of her mother, the drunkenness and violence of her father, and the problems of her younger brother Yves, just released from youth detention. In Provence, Abel takes up briefly with Anne (Anouk Ferjac), who is visiting her mother and who turns out to be Yves's lawyer.

As Susan Barrowclough points out, the Quebec/France relationship turns out to be all a question of representations, and not only because of the Rimbaud connection. Lefebvre's use of colour enables him to photograph the three French locations in different tones and to exploit other cultural modes and references: Zola for the industrial north, Cézanne for Provence.[7] The slow pace, attention to detail, and humour that placed "Quebec" in a minor key in *Il ne faut pas mourir pour ça*, as well as the play of chance in the film, now undercut any master narrative of the Quebec-France relationship, in turn plunging the characters' personal relationships into a contingency framed by their maturity, self-consciousness, and awareness that the flux of images and representations cannot be disentangled from their identities: Abel, at a moment of "truth," communication, and intimacy in the film, says to Anne, "I see us on a huge postcard." The Quebec-France relationship is mediated not only by representation but also by misapprehension and stereotype, the first of which is linguistic. In a reference to Hollywood constructions of "Paris" in films such as *Moulin Rouge* (Huston, 1952) or *An American in Paris* (Minnelli, 1951) (Abel also has a poster of Batman in his room and has chalked on his blackboard "Paris ne dort pas/Paris isn't sleeping," an allusion, of course, to René Clair's 1924 film), the Montmartre portrait painter fails to identify Abel's accent and thinks he's from either Belgium or Provence (Abel's reply: "Je suis d'ailleurs, tabarnak/I'm from somewhere else, for fuck's sake"). The posh friends of his father condescendingly refer to Voltaire's "arpents de neige" but also imitate Abel's accent when giving orders to the maid. Linguistic differences (the pronunciation of "hait") serve, however, to propel the first conversation with Anne, which turns out to be a relationship in which the flux of similarity and difference can be managed and even contribute to its enhancement.

So Abel's quest, articulated to Yves, that he had come to France to see if the French were still like "us" after they came to Canada 300 years ago only to forget "us" with the conquest of 1759, is one that clearly cannot end in any of the major inscriptions of "France" into Quebec identity, including that of modernization in a shared language. One reason for this, other than Abel's indifference to "the modern," is the shadowy presence in all three sections of the film of a third entity, Algeria. The wealthy friends knew Abel's peripatetic father in Algiers. Jeanne's father fought there in the French army. Anne grew up there and recalls "the stupid force of the crowd, injustice and fascism."

As we saw earlier, the attraction of Gaullism for some Quebec nationalists in 1967 was made possible by its resolution of the Algerian question in 1962 and the parallels with Quebec's own modernization. However, this attitude always sat uneasily with identifications with Third World nationalism, and after 1968 the fixation on France as fellow modernizer begins to unravel. The events of May 1968 in France not only discredited de Gaulle but could be perceived as a delayed consequence of the mobilizations against French involvement in Algeria, with "workers" and "students" replacing "Algerians" as subjects to be freed and empowered.[8] For a while at least, French capitalism and bourgeois society would be perceived by many on the Left in Quebec as no different from that represented by the United States. The year 1968 also saw in Quebec a radicalization of certain forms of Quebec nationalism, as well as certain forms of Quebec culture that represent a break with the legitimacy conferred by the Frenchness of France, for example, the first performance of *Les Belles-sœurs*, Michel Tremblay's play in Montreal dialect, *le joual*.

The presence of the Algerian conflict in the lives of the protagonists of *Le Vieux Pays où Rimbaud est mort*, and the fact that their personal lives are deeply affected by it, suggest a more general difference between Quebec and France which the film seeks to emphasize. The opening and closing shots of winter landscape that coincide with Abel's departure and return speak not only of different spaces and climates but of different relationships to space. France comes to be identified with time (Anne: "I feel old like my old country"), Quebec with space (Abel – to camera: "I'm a guy without a history, Anne, I've just got landscapes in my heart and head, excessive landscapes which bring me down because of their grandeur and excess"). Thus the canvas in Abel's Paris flat which he takes home – a black rectangle containing white space and entitled KEBEC – assumes all the significance of a space to be filled up with time, with history. The binary opposition set up here between France/Quebec, Europe/America is partly undermined by Abel's enigmatic words to Anne, "I'm without history, but your Algeria is a little bit my Quebec," indicating the intractability of the past, and especially of childhood, in the formation of identities, however provisional.

Largely through the concept and experience of modernization, the previous chapter hinted on various occasions at the links between the emerging Quebec cinema of the 1960s and the French *nouvelle vague*. The play of similarities and difference can be elaborated further with reference to Terry Lovell's delineation of aesthetic, technological, and political factors.[9]

There is much in common between the whole of the *nouvelle vague* and Canadian/Quebec direct cinema: the technological shift to lightweight cameras, synchronous sound, and fast-film stock which in turn impelled the escape to location shooting from the studio-bound *tradition de qualité* lambasted by Truffaut in 1954 and from both the dialogue-led French-Canadian cinema of 1944–52 and the script-led documentary practices at the NFB. There was a certain homology between the filmmakers, the protagonists of the films, and the (youngish, male, secular, modern, middle-class intellectual or student) audience that both cinemas addressed. Both, as we have seen, produced films symptomatic of the process of modernization going on around them, often centring on the urban heterosexual couple as new locus of meaning. In both cases, auteurism, though tempered in Quebec by the role of teams of directors and cinematographers, was encouraged by the private means available to some film-makers such as Chabrol and Jutra. Both the French and the Québécois film-makers used language as a kind of national affirmation, as in the slang of *À bout de souffle* or, quite simply, the French of the new Quebec cinema. Both cinemas roughly coincided with new political orders for which the question of national assertion was central, and they in different ways participated in redefinitions of national identity that accompanied the new regimes while also containing avant-garde elements that would question both. Here, 1968 represents that moment when any ideological consensus around both Gaullism and the Quiet Revolution visibly collapses, and is preceded and accompanied by some of the film-makers (Godard, Groulx, Lefebvre) radicalizing their social and political critiques.[10]

Of course, there are crucial differences, partly to do with the time-lag in the development of Quebec cinema in relation to French, partly to do with more profound questions of cultural difference. One of the historical tasks of the *nouvelle vague* was to help constitute a new art-house film audience in the context of the decline of total box-office receipts in France in the years 1957–60, due to suburbanization rather than television. This would, incidentally, become the audience for Quebec and other emerging national cinemas in the 1960s. In Quebec, *le direct* and the feature films that followed were less important than the *nouvelle vague* itself (and the likes of Antonioni and Bergman) in constituting that audience, through the Festival des films du monde and other institutions. The new Quebec production, as we saw in the previous chapter, took place in the context of declining but stabilizing audiences (although from a much bigger per capita base than in France and with higher ticket prices providing some consistency in receipts) and, potentially at least, a less antagonistic relationship to television (where the French *tradition de qualité* had fled). However, the crucial differences between the two cultures lay in relation to Hollywood and their own respective national cinemas.

In France, a national cinema already existed, even if its world position had been fatally undermined by the First World War and the establishment of Hollywood's hegemony. And the French popular audience in the 1950s and 1960s vastly preferred French cinematic production, while much of the intellectual audience was watching American cinema, especially that which could be co-opted to the *politique des auteurs*; witness the *Cahiers du cinéma* group's affection for Ford, Hawks, Hitchcock, Ray, Welles, and, slightly later and somewhat notoriously, Jerry Lewis. In Quebec, the situation was the reverse. The popular audience, while entranced by indigenous radio and then television representations of Quebec culture, vastly preferred American cinematic product, a result of Canada's long infeodation to North American distribution and exhibition structures. The arthouse audience looked to Europe and especially France. The emergence of Quebec cinema in the 1960s is riven by these two tendencies, on the one hand a debt to French cinematic models, and on the other the developing quest for a national-popular audience that is yet to be constructed. The situation is compounded by the dilemma that, even restricted to an arthouse audience, the new Quebec cinema had to appeal to the notion of a "people" to legitimate its national project. In France, this element – as well as the role of Hollywood in the French film market as a whole – was studiously ignored by the practitioners of the *nouvelle vague*.

The paradox is, of course, that the *nouvelle vague* itself represents a Franco-American hybridization and could not have come about, or at least not in the same form, without the *Cahiers* groups' fascination for Hollywood "B" pictures or the success of Marcel Duhamel's *Série noire* list at Gallimard. As Ginette Vincendeau has pointed out,[11] the *policier* was the terrain in France on which the popular and arthouse audience could meet. Indeed, *À bout de souffle* remains Godard's biggest box-office success in France. Engagement with American mass culture comes later in France than in Quebec, where, despite the admonitions of the church in the period between the Patriotes' revolt and the Quiet Revolution, the United States has had a profound influence, reflected in the emigrations to New England of the late nineteenth century, in the cultural openness of Montreal, and, of course, in the frequentation of Hollywood films. The recuperation of national "authenticity" in the early 1960s thus involved for Quebec film-makers the construction of a francophone cinema distinct and even antagonistic to Hollywood, hence the influence of France. However, that French cinema was already marked by Hollywood, so the circuit of cultural exchange is profoundly hybrid. Indeed, it could be argued that the origins of the *policier* lie in nineteenth-century France, with Eugène Sue and Victor Hugo, so the movement goes from France to Hollywood to France to Quebec. Moreover, the *cinéphile* Quebec audience of the 1960s, like their French equivalents, took no interest in genre cinema in France such as comedy which actually engaged quite profoundly with questions of national identity, and so the pole "France" in Quebec culture continued to function as high cultural, learned legitimacy, with the risk, as in France itself, of a real schism between art and popular films and audiences, as we shall see. The common language meant that Quebec film-makers were drawn to French product, with the risk of underestimating the ever shifting complexity of that relationship.

Cinematic relations between France and Quebec are predicated on the wider cultural terrain outlined above, but they also possess a history. As far as critical reception in general is concerned, in France the image of Quebec cinema has moved from a certain attention in the 1960s that coincided with, for example, *Cahiers du cinéma*'s fascination with new emerging national cinemas, to a banalization of Quebec after about 1976, with the perception that Quebec's difference has been erased and its cinema flattened out along with most of the rest of the Hollywood-dominated world film industry. As far as audiences are concerned, Québécois films in France have met with relatively little success, only thirteen ever achieving more than 100,000 tickets sold at the box office. In fact, language is one of the main problems rather than an advantage: Quebec cinema is often perceived in France as "no longer really exotic, not really commercial, not really arthouse either, it talks French but with *a funny accent.*"[12] An audience study carried out at the Quebec Film Festival held in Blois in 1992 and 1993 showed that, when asked about their comprehension of four feature films, an average of 22 per cent found the films "difficult" or "very difficult" to understand, but this varied widely. *Les Bons Débarras* (Mankiewicz, 1980), one of the most lauded films in the Canadian pantheon, was found difficult to understand by 48 per cent of respondents.[13] The linguistic relationship between France and Quebec is therefore not analogous with that between Britain and the United States, where different dialects are arguably much more mutually incomprehensible, although even this is rather one-sided, with the overwhelming flow of twentieth-century mass culture bringing familiarity with many American accents to Britain, rather less in the reverse direction (the subtitling of Ken Loach's *Kes* [1970], for example). If linguistic comprehensibility is the prime factor of exportability, and if French audiences frequently demand subtitles to understand Québécois dialogue, then Quebec cinema in France ends up in the position of having to compete for a place in the small and shrinking market segment of non-French and non-American cinema in France. This diminished from 14.2 to 2 million spectators between 1982 and 1991.

The thirteen most successful Quebec films in France, those that managed at least 100,000 spectators, are:

Le Déclin de l'empire américain (Arcand, 1986)	1,236,322
Les Mâles (Carle, 1971)	302,950
La Vraie Nature de Bernadette (Carle, 1972)	282,992
J'ai mon voyage! (Héroux, 1973)	214,239
Les Plouffe (Carle, 1981)	191,294
Pour le meilleur et pour le pire (Jutra, 1975)	188,579
La Mort d'un bûcheron (Carle, 1973)	188,372
Jésus de Montréal (Arcand, 1989)	187,827
Valérie (Héroux, 1968)	153,734
Comment faire l'amour avec un nègre sans se fatiguer (Benoît, 1989)	128,006
Maria Chapdelaine (Carle, 1983)	127,003
Fantastica (Carle, 1980)	116,885
J.A. Martin photographe (Beaudin, 1976)	103,880[14]

Certain questions immediately arise, some of which can be answered more easily than others. Sex sells (*Le Déclin* even if it's all talk, but aided by a summer advertising campaign which stressed this aspect of the film; *Valérie*; *Comment faire l'amour*; most of Carle's films). Ease of linguistic comprehension helps, hence the success of those films which for the most part reproduce a bourgeois or middlebrow quasi-international French (*Le Déclin*, *Pour le meilleur et pour le pire*, *J.A. Martin photographe*, co-productions such as *Les Plouffe* and *Maria Chapdelaine*). Publicity achieved because of the presence of a star (Carole Laure in the latter three Carle films, although her presence was no guarantee of success) or because of a prize at Cannes (*Jésus de Montréal*, *J.A. Martin photographe*) is also useful. To understand more fully this top thirteen, it is necessary to investigate in detail the history of the reception of Quebec cinema in France and of some *auteurs* in particular: why, for example, the dominant presence of Gilles Carle?

It is, first of all, Pierre Perrault who is taken up by French critics in the 1960s, notably *Cahiers du cinéma*. More critical articles are written about him than any other aspect of Quebec cinema. Perrault is seen as responding to certain French agendas: the adjacency of the *nouvelle vague* and *le direct*, the latter's capacity for short-circuiting dominant Hollywood structures (Comolli's article of 1969), the interest in emerging national and third cinemas, and a reaction to the processes of modernization and urbanization, with the denizens of the Île aux coudres recalling vanishing communities and oral cultures that would come to be associated with emerging Breton and Occitan regionalisms.[15] But the emergence of a Quebec film industry in the 1970s, along with the vogue for co-productions, and the banalization/Americanization of the image of Quebec invoked earlier, suggest that the importance of Perrault was very contingent, bound up with a certain historical moment. Indeed, the critical attention in France led to paltry box-office success, and his position has come under increasing criticism in Quebec itself for its perceived archaism.

It has been argued that an additional reason for the interest in Quebec cinema in the 1960s, and then its possible decline, was its auteurism and consequent lack of interest in marketing.[16] However, a close look at practices surrounding Gilles Carle's early films reveals otherwise. René Prédal argues, for example,[17] that Carle's presentational skills, as he accompanied *La Vie heureuse de Léopold Z*. and his later films to festivals in France, were a major factor in his being taken up by certain networks in the late 1960s and early 1970s. He adroitly inserted himself in a niche of left-wing film-makers embraced by *L'Humanité* and *Le Nouvel Observateur*. In March 1969 he came to present *Le Viol d'une jeune fille douce* at a festival organized by the Nice *ciné-club*, and subsequently his films were promoted by the two main *ciné-club* networks in France and by their journals *Cinéma* and the *Revue de cinéma*. The politics and personalization of French film criticism also played a role (factors not totally absent from Prédal's article), in that these journals were thus asserting their autonomy vis-à-vis *Cahiers du cinéma* and *Positif*, which ignored Carle (indeed, *Cahiers*, as we have seen, tended to privilege one *auteur* from the emerging cinema of its choice, although Lefebvre received some attention in addition to Perrault). These factors must be added to the sex and Carole Laure after 1973 to explain the persistence of Carle's success, but even they could not shore up his support as the quality of his production entered terminal decline.

Quebec films in France thus face certain cultural and economic problems. Linguistic commonality and community of taste cannot be assumed. French colonial history and cultural protectionism impel critical discourses that place France at the centre, Quebec at the periphery, of francophone cinema: Perrault is the Québécois Rouch, Lefebvre and Groulx the Québécois Godard, for example. Currently, Quebec cinema occupies the place of any other non-Hollywood, non-French, or non-European cinema in French film distribution, competing for a shrinking share (about 5 per cent) of a shrinking market. *Le Déclin de l'empire américain* was distributed by UGC, one of the "big three" along with Gaumont and Pathé, but most Quebec films would have to deal with smaller distributors and miniscule promotional budgets because only French films are entitled to governmental promotion-aid programs (promotion being crucial to a film's success in that it enables word-of-mouth attendance to take off).[18] With the importance of television deals for theatrical distribution, Quebec films hit the obstacle of the government's quotas on French (50 per cent) and European (10 per cent) films broadcast on the networks. (The divisive common language also rears its head in the political economy of dubbing non-French language films into French, where a highly protectionist law stipulates that all such films circulating in France must have been dubbed in a studio in France. Dubbing in Quebec has 58 per cent of the market there because of a 1985 law insisting that a French version must be released within forty-five days of an English-language film, and because of the greater popularity of locally dubbed films – publicized as such in listings publications such as the Montreal freesheet *Voir*. But it currently has no outlet in France.)[19]

The solution would seem to lie in Franco-Québécois co-productions, which also provide the opportunity for larger budgets and for taking advantage of public grants in more than one country since such films are considered to be "national" ones by each signatory country. There is a history here, accompanying and conditioning the history of the emergence of the Quebec film industry. In 1963 the impulsion of Guy Roberge at the NFB saw the first treaty between Canada and France relative to co-production, but the outcome in terms of features was limited[20] until the establishment of the CFDC in 1967 and the expansion of the private sector. (Treaties are needed for co-productions for legal reasons because certain immigration and fiscal restrictions have to be lifted.) The first majority Canadian participation was *Kamouraska* (Jutra, 1971), the most expensive Quebec film to that date, with Geneviève Bujold but also a French star, Philippe Léotard. It failed dismally at the French box office. The main pattern was set by Denis Héroux, who had directed (and produced, with John Kemeny) the first majority coproduction with Israel, a sex film called *Sept fois par jour* in 1970, as well as, with France, *J'ai mon voyage!* (1973), with 80 per cent Canadian participation. In 1974 the co-production accords were strengthened, the result being, with the exception of *Le Vieux Pays où Rimbaud est mort*, bigger-budget films mostly directed by French nationals (*La Menace*, 1977, directed by Alain Corneau, starring Yves Montand and Carole Laure, shot partly in British Columbia; *Violette Nozière*, 1977, directed by Claude Chabrol), sometimes in English (*Atlantic City USA*, 1979, directed by Louis Malle). By this time the administration of the accords had been taken over from the NFB and the Federal Department of Communications by the CFDC. What is more, although these co-productions provided work for Canadian film personnel, they contributed to the inflation of film production and promotion costs in Quebec in the late 1970s and had little effect on the creation of "national" texts mobilizing the cultural symbols of Quebec. There was also a perceived imbalance in what Canada was getting out of the arrangement: from 1963 to 1982, it was the main producer in a minority (39 per cent) of projects and only 24 per cent of films were directed by Canadians while Canada was contributing 47 per cent of the money.[21] Nevertheless, the Franco-Québécois arrangement was reinforced in 1983, with both the PQ government and the Socialist French Culture Minister Jack Lang at that time seeking to give a new impetus to francophone "resistance" to American mass culture (the context is that of Lang's famous speech to UNESCO in 1982 denouncing American "cultural imperialism" and the Quebec government's tense disagreements with the MPAA). After 1983, the proportion of Canadian personnel working on co-productions with France increased to more than half (although Quebec "content" remained in the minority), the accord was extended to television series, and a high proportion, 30 per cent, of "Franco-Québécois" films were made in English. Indeed, the most successful "Quebec" film in France (in the sense of majority participation) is, strictly speaking, not *Le Déclin de l'empire américain* but *Quest for Fire* (Annaud, 1980), whose language was invented by Anthony Burgess. Co-produced by Héroux and Kemeny, it sold nearly five million tickets at the French box office.

The French government lays down strict rules as to what constitutes a "French film" or *oeuvre d'expression originale française*, namely, that shooting, script, and dialogues should be in French, and this now favours

Quebec over English Canada. Before 1991 a film could be "French" even if it were in English as long as its majority financing and personnel were French, but this is no longer the case.

The question of co-productions therefore raises several questions for Quebec national cinema, and in particular its relationship with France. At best, co-productions have provided employment for film personnel based in Montreal and a supplement to the overall total production of Quebec films. However, the status of co-production does not make a "majority Quebec" film more likely to be successful in France at the box office; witness, for example, the fate of *Les Portes tournantes* (1988), which included a French star (Miou Miou) but whose subject matter, setting, and source (the novel by Jacques Savoie) were all Québécois and which failed dismally (less than 10,000 spectators in France).

Moreover, co-productions provide an interesting case of discourses circulating round the question of "national" culture. On the one hand, their proclaimed goal has been that of promoting (to the point of helping to create, as with the Canadian example) the "national" cinemas of the signatory countries faced with the power of Hollywood. The Franco-Italian co-production agreement, for example, produced nearly 2,000 films between 1949 and 1976. On the other hand, that very transnationalism of co-productions can be perceived as creating a standardized product that is associated with the pervasiveness of American films because it is cut off from "authentic" cultural sources, ending up with the "denaturalized hybrid of internationally attractive product."[22] However, if any "grounded" or "authentic" national culture is always already in dialogue with the forces that would redefine and even dissipate it, then co-productions can be seen as a specific variation of something that exists in every film text. Co-productions are an interrelation of two national-allegorical tensions on the terrains of "the world" and of the special histories of the two countries' cultural connections. Of course, there are different kinds of co-productions, on a spectrum from little more than a co-financing deal to a film text that disavows its incorporation of the two or more "cultures" or which on the contrary avows it and makes their relationship its central problematic. To an extent, it is a question of spectatorship, in the weaker sense that readings will depend on the spectator's own insertion within the national-transnational relationship and the two "cultures" concerned; but in the stronger sense that, when the knowledge of co-production is brought to bear in the act of viewing, the queerly hybrid notion can emerge of looking and being looked at, of being both subject and object of the camera's gaze, or in-between.[23] Is "my country" being seen through members of my national community, or by members of the other?

The complication by the fact of co-production of the processes of recognition in national cinema is augmented when the film's connections are understood temporally as well as spatially. *Maria Chapdelaine* (Carle, 1983) provides a fascinating example of this process, as it is located within a whole history of rewriting and appropriation on both sides of the Atlantic, even as the status of its novelistic "source" is as an ur-text of French-Canadian (self-) representation. The film versions, and the contrasting uses to which the novel has been put, demonstrate the twin pulls of homogeneity and heterogeneity, of what we might term origin/authenticity and intertextuality/plurality. The latter clearly characterizes all texts, including that of the nation: "If on the one hand, it [intertextuality] has transformed the unity and self-presence of the text into a structure marked by otherness and repetition, on the other hand it has suggested that the exterior of the text is not a monolithic real but a system (or an infinity) of other such textual structures."[24] As we argued in chapter 1, however, such texts are to be characterized not in terms of complete dispersion, but as located in a ceaseless play of identity, provisionality, and dispersal.

Maria Chapdelaine was first published in the French newspaper *Le Temps* in 1914, shortly after its author, Louis Hémon, was killed in a railway accident. Hémon was born into an academic Catholic family in Brest in 1880, but he had abandoned the career pathways planned for him and travelled to Quebec in 1911, working as a farm labourer in the Lac Saint-Jean region where the novel is set. In the novel, Maria Chapdelaine is the unwed daughter of farming parents who are located on the edge of French-Canadian settlement. Maria has to choose between three suitors: the family's neighbour, Eutrope Gagnon, who offers her a life similar to but slightly more settled than that of her mother, Laura; Lorenzo Surprenant, who has emigrated to Boston; and François Paradis, a *coureur de bois* figure with whom Maria falls in love but who dies when journeying in winter from the lumber camp to the Chapdelaine home. In the end Maria opts for marriage to Eutrope.

The novel, and its context, were understood quite differently in France and in Quebec. In France, the imperial projects of the Third Republic, coupled with the political polarizations around the Dreyfus case and the separation of church and state in 1905, had provided a context in which traditionalist and often Catholic and monarchist élites had looked to *le Canada* as offering a model of rural, Catholic life untainted by 1789 and its aftermath. *Maria Chapdelaine* thus appeared on a well-prepared terrain which would constrain its meaning and influence as offering an enticing if ambiguous play of similarity and difference: the exoticism of a branch of France lost or transplanted in the dehistoricized, "natural" setting of *l'Amérique*, but also a connection with an eternal, mythical France unspoilt by modernity, "a France outside France, far from the contingencies disfiguring it, where different social and political utopias can run free without the constraints of the real."[25] Its sales far outstripped any previous book on Canada. In addition, *Maria Chapdelaine* could be slotted into two contemporary cultural currents. The "voices" that Maria hears, and that eventually guide her to the choice of Gagnon, and the construction of the novel as invoking an "eternal France," point almost inevitably to Joan of Arc. Joan's beatification in 1909 and canonization in 1920 were determined by factors such as the relationship between republican legitimacy and compensation for secularization, as well as traditionalist lobbying and the heightened need for national symbolizations owing to the First World War. The second current is more problematic. Maurice Barrès (1862–1923) exemplified that current in right-wing thinking that combined the modernity of individualism, a kind of Nietzschean cogito (*Le Culte du moi*, 1888–91), with a grounding (*racinement*) in place and in nationalism, in his case inspired by Lorraine and the widespread *revanchard* feeling provoked by its loss to the Germans in 1871. For Barrès, Catholicism was significant for its "eternal" presence in, and co-extension with, France. He also articulated these themes via a female protagonist (*Colette Baudoche*, 1909). As we shall see, even as these right-wing discourses developed and were transformed in time from 1914 to the contemporary period, *Maria Chapdelaine* remained for the French the founding representation of French Canada in the twentieth century,[26] spawning, owing to illustrators such as Suzor-Côté, a whole iconography of snow, log cabins, churches, furs, and firs.

In Quebec, *Maria Chapdelaine* was co-opted by the clerical-nationalist élites in the 1920s, particularly for the project of internal colonization, the creation and settlement of new agricultural land in Abitibi and elsewhere which would perpetuate Quebec's rural, traditional, and Catholic vocation and obviate the need for urbanization or emigration to industrial jobs in the United States. The first edition, published in Quebec in 1921, was subsidized by the government. In the contemporary period, the volume of essays *Le Mythe de Maria Chapdelaine* vigorously denounces that operation from the point of view of post-Quiet Revolution modernization, nationalism, and feminism. As the editor, Nicole Deschamps, cogently argues, a colossal mismatch was implied in the official efforts made in the 1920s to equate the new colonizing endeavours of the French Canadians with those of the French and British empires: "The colonizing figure being proposed as model is, unwittingly, colonized."[27] The volume ends with the following condemnation which can be tested against the film texts to be analysed: "In all its manifestations, the myth of *Maria Chapdelaine* thus appears as the expression of a museum-society which lives on its memories and which refuses, probably involuntarily, to create a new history for itself."[28]

It is pointless to propose a "true" reading of *Maria Chapdelaine*, still less of Hémon's intentions, to counteract either the official appropriations or the recent hegemonic debunkings of the novel. Instead, it is possible to suggest several points of tension or contradiction which pull against the totalizations of these readings and threaten, like Deleuzean lines of flight, potentially to take it somewhere else. Hémon himself is a rather baffling figure. Like Barrès (and arguably Kipling, several of whose short stories he translated into French), he is marked by a productive tension between individualism and nationalism, but in his case it produces wanderings or *errance*, the construction of a life narrative (and tragic death) marked by a strong sense of the physical and masculine but also of romance and loss. His Breton identity factors in a more complex set of cultural references than Barrès's Lorraine, for they can be located both temporally and politically on the margins of modern nation-building. Moreover, it is equally unclear to which genre(s) *Maria Chapdelaine* belongs: partly melodrama, in that "the sacred" is transferred to the domestic and sentimental realm; partly epic, in that Maria becomes the protagonist of an age-old collective narrative which binds together the sacred and "the people" in a common set of references and values; partly the popular adventure story because of its American setting, the role of François Paradis, and the role of untamed, mysterious nature; and partly, of course, romance, in that Maria has to negotiate the attractiveness but also shortcomings and even dangers of heterosexual masculinity in three different avatars. This latter description is perhaps a clue to the novel's appeal beyond clerical-nationalist appropriations, and it ties in with the notion of a "national" romance, in which the "nation-family" is legitimated "through love."[29] Unlike, however, nineteenth-century Latin American romances, in which the heterosexual couple hegemonically unifies the nation by reconciling (sometimes racial) contradictions and pursues "the bourgeois project of co-ordinating feeling with reason, passion with productivity,"[30] and unlike Scarlett in *Gone with the Wind*, whose choice between Rhett Butler and Ashley Wilkes reveals the inadequacy of both versions of masculinity, the union of Maria and Eutrope Gagnon is overdetermined by Maria and Quebec's *situation*. It is twicefold a *pis-aller* or second best, and this leaves a yawning gap at the heart of the construction: François Paradis, the real object of her passion, is dead; Lorenzo Surprenant offers the enticements of modernity, but *in English*.

In fact, the two key male figures in the novel are François Paradis and the father, Samuel Chapdelaine, who are both *coureurs de bois manqués*. Samuel had aspired to the freedom of the forests and would never settle his homestead in one place. It is for this reason that the Chapdelaine family lives on the society's spatial edge, in-between the *habitants* and the woods. One of the strange occurrences in the novel is the death of François, for it contradicts the *coureur de bois* figure as potential source of masculine potency. François loses his way, but this is only partly due to his incompetence (an expected train fails to leave). Rather, he has to die for three reasons. First, to draw a line under the *coureur de bois* legacy, inconsistent not just with the clerical order after 1837–38 but with the whole hegemonic entreprise of nation-survival or nation-building. Too many lines of flight take the figure out of the society and into the liminality of the Indians, a set of identity implications denied by the French Canadians precisely because of the resemblance they provide of their own fate under the British. Secondly, François's death is a result of a masculine hubris that is also partly responsible for the death of Maria's mother at the end of the novel, in that Samuel's aspirations and demands had given her a harder life than necessary. Thirdly, Maria thus comes to emerge as the identity pivot of the novel: Lorenzo means the loss of identity, while Eutrope has property but no symbolism to offer. The risky symbolism of François (differentiation in nature and otherness) is replaced by the semiotic power of Maria, who is able to articulate that exciting relationship to nature and space with a sense of place, linguistic place, and time, and therefore "home":

The very names of this her country, those she listened to every day, those heard but once, came crowding to memory: a thousand names piously bestowed by peasants from France on lakes, on rivers, on the settlements of the new country they were discovering and peopling as they went ... How dear and neighbourly was the sound of them, with a heart-warming friendly ring that made one feel as he spoke them: "Throughout all this land we are at home ... at home ..."[31]

On the one hand, Maria is the synthesizing figure in the novel's dialectic, overcoming contradictions and forging a consensus. On the other hand, her choice, that consensus, are simultaneously very contingent and provisional, and very much located in a history of repetition, not change. It is not surprising that those writing from a post-Quiet Revolution position are dismayed by the novel's conservatism. But that conservatism is enacted and performed by Maria in a manner that is interesting in terms of gender. She chooses (within the parameters available, parameters that she recognizes). And, while that choice may coincide with the clerical-nationalist project of the time, it is not totalized by it. Rather, the third "voice" that Maria hears at the end is a supremely synthesizing one, *which she embodies*:

The voice of Quebec – now the song of a woman, now the exhortation of a priest. It came to her with the sound of a church bell, with the majesty of an organ's tones, like a plaintive love song, like the long high call of woodsmen in the forest. For verily there was in it all that makes the soul of the Province: the loved solemnities of the ancestral faith; the lilt of that old speech guarded with jealous care; the grandeur and the barbaric strength of this new land where an ancient race [*racine*] has again found its youth.[32]

The ambiguity here owes much to that dichotomy of looking and being looked at. Hémon is displaying his own preoccupations with nationality, physicality, youth. But Maria's role as subject is one that, although rooted, crosses spatial and gender divisions and that is difficult to corral into either a straightforwardly Catholic or a modernizing narrative. The fate of these tensions in the film versions will now be explored.[33]

The first version of *Maria Chapdelaine* was French, directed by Julien Duvivier in 1934, the 400th anniversary of Jacques Cartier's first voyage and the twentieth anniversary of the first publication of the novel. It was produced for the Société nouvelle de cinématographie française in Paris but in cooperation with France Film, the main distributor of French films in Quebec. The film stars Madeleine Renaud as Maria, Jean Gabin as François Paradis, Jean-Pierre Aumont as Lorenzo Surprenant, and Alexandre Rignault as Eutrope Gagnon. The script remains faithful to the novel, with three significant exceptions: a village festival plays a role in the unfolding action and sexual rivalries; the death of François Paradis is portrayed on the screen, whereas it is narrated by Eutrope in the novel; and the final "voice" which Maria hears is actually a priest's sermon. Stylistically, the film is cinematic rather than literary, its meaning led and constructed by sound and image, especially music (extensive use of folk song) and montage (the passing of seasons, Maria waiting for François as he perishes, shots of a city then of the countryside as Maria weighs the proposals of Lorenzo and Eutrope). This is not surprising for a director as experienced as Duvivier in both silent and sound cinema. A closer examination reveals a very French set of preoccupations.

Although Gabin had yet to become the major star of French cinema (this is widely held to begin with another Duvivier film, *La Bandera*, a year later), and thus the connotations of his screen image had yet to coalesce into a star persona, *Maria Chapdelaine* points to the social and cultural context out of which that persona emerged. Vaudeville performance, a notion, from a bourgeois spectator's position, of the "people" as source of (national) authenticity, and the construction of a community, all interact to produce scenes familiar from other French films of the mid-decade, for example the Gabin-Duvivier collaborations, *Pépé le Moko* and *La Belle Équipe* of 1936. While the *fête du village* (where he does sing – "Vive la canayenne" – and where the style of music that comes to dominate is European) and the screen time given to Gabin enhance the role of François Paradis, his combination of masculine hubris and vulnerability eventually do not yet enable him to carry the contradictions of the community and be at its centre. This is why the interiority of the final section of the novel gives way to the exteriority of the priest pronouncing the words about Quebec continuity, while the camera films the faces of the community. For Duvivier, then, *Maria Chapdelaine* is a vehicle for certain preoccupations of French popular culture of the 1930s. The Indians, for example, form a necessary backdrop not unlike those of North Africans in French colonial films of the time,[34] and François Paradis is explicitly differentiated from them as he sets off on his unwise winter trek. Duvivier had, in a newspaper interview in Montreal in July 1934, emphasized the "Frenchness" of the inhabitants of Péribonka: "these great French peasants transplanted to Canadian soil and taking root there."[35] For this reason, it is arguable that Duvivier stresses in his film the sedentary (= French) aspect of the novel to the detriment of the pioneer and nomad (= American, Other).

The film, however, was a critical and box-office triumph in Quebec (70,000 spectators in a week), aided by the pre-publicity associated with the period spent shooting on location in Lac Saint-Jean and by the simple fact that so few cinematic images of Quebec were available to the Québécois. However, discrepancies were perceived which imply that the film was caught in a complex process of recognition and misrecognition, of Quebec spectators looking at themselves and looking at themselves being looked at: the desire expressed for a French-Canadian cast vetoed by the French producers who knew that distributors in France insisted on French stars;[36] the blueberry picking (quintessence of the Quebec and particularly Lac Saint-Jean landscape) taking place in a daisy field; and the diction of Paris and the *Comédie française* shining through, despite the great efforts of the actors and the dialogue coach. Most notably, the use of the priest for the final sermon was seized upon by those of a clerical-nationalist bent to appropriate the film as part of their hegemonic project (although the rest of the film, notably the first encounter of François and Maria in the street rather than on the church steps, the *fête du village,* and the priest's uncomprehending dialogue with Maria, strikes a rather secularizing note appropriate to the French context).

The Marc Allégret version of *Maria Chapdelaine* is a Franco-British co-production of 1949 entitled *The Naked Heart* and therefore involves a rather different slant on the question of transnational cultural relationships. The reasons for the concoction lie in the context of European film production in the early post-war period, and the role of Allégret within it. The renewed offensive of Hollywood cinema in especially French film distribution, and the attempts in both countries to bolster and renew national film production, dominated the years 1946–48. In France, the economic agreement reached between the American secretary of state James Byrne and the French envoy Léon Blum in 1946, which shored up France's finances and increased the openness of its market to American products, had been followed by protests in the French film industry and the partial reinstatement in 1948 of quotas of dubbed American films. (By 1950, French box-office receipts again represented over 50 per cent of the home market.) In Britain, the 1947 imposition of a tax on US imported films by Board of Trade president Harold Wilson had been followed by an American embargo and an agreement the next year which allowed Hollywood product again to pour into Britain.

The Naked Heart is one of three films in this, Marc Allégret's "British," period, but it is the only one containing French as well as British stars (Michèle Morgan as Maria, Françoise Rosay as Laura) and involving French scriptwriters (Allégret and Roger Vadim) and producers (Régina/Louis Demazure). Allégret's reputation as one of the leading French film-makers of the previous two decades (*Fanny,* 1932; *Gribouille,* 1937), especially noted for technical and financial efficiency and valued for his virtual bilingualism, had led to him being solicited by certain players in the British film industry and to accepting their advances, given the immediate post-war difficulties on the other side of the Channel. Anthony Havelock-Allan of Cineguild, part of the consortium Independent Producers set up by Rank, thus brought him to Pinewood studios to inaugurate its new technicolor system and make *Blanche Fury,* a melodrama starring Stewart Granger released in 1948. Its success led to two other commissions, *The Naked Heart* and *Blackmailed* (1950). In addition, Michèle Morgan had followed her wartime Hollywood career (notably *Passage to Marseilles,* dir. Michael Curtiz, 1944) with an appearance in Carol Reed's 1948 British film, *The Fallen Idol.* Françoise Rosay had mainly been in British pictures during and after the war, notably for Basil Dearden (*Halfway House,* 1943; *Saraband,* 1948).

In terms of production, *The Naked Heart* can be understood in two ways. *Blanche Fury* had been an attempt by Cineguild to outdo, in terms of production values (colour) but also of cultural prestige, the popular melodramas made by Gainsborough Studios. A constant of twentieth-century British culture has been the homology of Frenchness and high-cultural legitimacy, an additional quality afforded by Allégret. On the other hand, the very temporary shortage of American films in distribution provoked by Harold Wilson's tax led to the hurried assemblage of British film productions (often with ad hoc production companies, in this case Nelson Scott's "Everest Pictures") which then enjoyed a diminished profile when Hollywood movies flooded back. *The Naked Heart* was to suffer this fate.

In terms of meaning, however, what is extraordinary in the film is the way in which Canada and Quebec are used, and are able to be used, to produce a landscape and community recognizable both to British and to French audiences. Whereas Duvivier's film had taken some pains to ensure "authenticity" of language and setting, and its agenda had been precisely that of Franco-Québécois relationships, all these signs are evacuated in *The Naked Heart*. The film is in English. Apart from the two female leads and Philippe Lemaire as François, the other male leads are British: Kieron Moore as Lorenzo, and Jack Watling as "Robert" (as opposed to the exotic, for both British and French audiences, "Eutrope") Gagnon. The landscapes were shot in France, in the Haute-Savoie. What is important here is not so much the bracketing out of Québécois cultural specificity, which can occur in other English-speaking films set there, but the way in which Canada and Quebec can usefully be made to condense the signs of anglophone and francophone cultures for the purposes of multi- or transnational film-making. *The Naked Heart* thus anticipates not so much a film like John Greyson's *Lilies* (1996; made in English, based on a Quebec play set in the Quebec past) as *The English Patient* (Minghella, 1997), in which the combined presence of a French and American star, in this case Juliette Binoche and Willem Dafoe, can be justified by making them both come from Montreal, in contradiction to the actors' real nationalities or the Toronto origin of the nurse's character in Michael Ondaatje's novel. This, of course, fits neatly into that film's problematization of fixed identity assignments and foregrounding of cultural hybridity. In *The Naked Heart*, these commonalities are announced in terms of the supranational notion of premodern rural society and of "spirit." In the title sequence, the helpful map of Canada fades to the announcement that "the French peasant" (for French Canadian) was "moved by spiritual values that we have almost lost today."

So, while the film is very broadly faithful to the main canvas of the novel *Maria Chapdelaine* (the deaths of François and Laura, Maria's final choice of Robert/Eutrope), Vadim and Allégret clearly realized that something more than subtle musings on Quebec identity needed to be injected. This extra spice comes from scenes of cinematic spectacle that have no equivalent in the novel, notably, François's early rescue of Lorenzo and his father from a frozen lake. Moreover, largely one suspects because of the weight of melodrama in contemporary British film production, Lorenzo Surprenant, outlandishly, is here a villain fleeing home after a botched bank robbery in Quebec City. Ironically mocking his family's way of life, he is finally shot by the police as he looks back towards Maria silhouetted against the horizon. But while Lorenzo figures the corruption of modernization, the "spiritual values" that the film offers are decidedly on the secular side. They are vehicles for notions of "truth" (as opposed to Lorenzo's falsehood), "feelings," and "happiness." Maria has to sort out her true feelings and clear up misunderstandings with François. Lorenzo's downfall is precipitated by his belated "sincerity." Even the priest, while warning Maria of the likes of François, urges her to accept "love" and not waste the life God has given. It is these elements, juxtaposed with the authenticating natural landscapes, which give the film a certain Gidean ring. Allégret, of course, had been in a relationship with Gide since he was a young man. He had missed the opportunity of directing Michèle Morgan in Jean Delannoy's 1946 adaptation of Gide's novella *La Symphonie pastorale*, in which a Swiss Protestant pastor struggles with his amorous feelings for a blind girl against the authenticating and ambiguously "pure" natural background of snow. *The Naked Heart* provided the opportunity of making a version of that film. Even Laura Chapdelaine, in Françoise Rosay's big death scene, explains to Maria her own marriage in terms not of piety or tradition but of sincerity, choice, and will, a "quiet happiness" which is "made" and not "found."

Radio versions followed of the novel in the 1940s and 1950s in Quebec. The intertextual persistence of Maria's story manifests itself in modern rewrites. Gabrielle Gourdeau's 1992 novel, *Maria Chapdelaine ou le paradis retrouvé*, presents Maria as an old lady in the 1970s, passionately committed to Quebec sovereignty, dying at the time of the 1980 referendum result, and thus avoiding the demoralization that followed. More important for our purposes, Gilles Carle's film *La Mort d'un bûcheron* of 1973 had cast Carole Laure as a contemporary Maria, the innocent young woman arriving in the city from Chibougameau, seeking her lost (murdered) father, and meeting a photographer, François Paradis (Daniel Pilon). When Maria is employed in a bar, her name is first anglicized and she is then herself transformed into Mary

Lasso, the first topless country and western singer. Typically, Carle's movie simultaneously condemns ethnic, class, and sexual exploitation while remaining complicit with the latter in its representation of Carole Laure's body. The whole narrative of the film is in any case a variation on that of *Valérie*, but, significantly, the heterosexual couple is not formed at the end. However, the final shootout in the countryside underlines the history of exploitative labour relations there, partly owing to the co-screenwriting credit for Arthur Lamothe, director of the socially committed documentary *Les Bûcherons de la Manouane* of 1962.

The choice of Carle as director of the *Maria Chapdelaine* of 1983 was mainly due, however, to his recent success on another adaptation of a best-selling Québécois novel, *Les Plouffe* of 1981. Like this film, the new *Maria* would have a theatrical and a television version and be a Quebec-France co-production. The collaboration of the still state-owned Télévision française (TF1) in this enterprise signalled a French strategy of addressing, through television finance, expanding production costs, falling cinema audiences, and increased competition among TV channels, but all these factors were equally relevant for the Canadian film industry and for Radio Canada as it, too, established its deal with the Quebec production company Astral. The film's status as co-production thus permitted a larger budget ($4.6 million) and seemed to build on the Quebec-France subtext of the novel itself and the uses to which it had been put. Crucially, it also impelled the use of certain stars: the French actor Claude Rich as the priest, and especially Carole Laure as Maria.

Moreover, the relationship of this version of *Maria* to the national past that is being represented is completely different. For the gap between the *énonciation* of the moment in time of the narration (the relationship between narrator and implied reader/viewer) and the *énoncé* of the events being narrated is now the gap between a pre- and post-Quiet Revolution Quebec, and thus between two competing strata of national definition. Modern "Quebec" needs to construct that past as both similar and different. Its (and any) national text is always both an authenticating narrative of origins (where "we" have come from) and an elaboration of national truths and values (what "we" are now). As Homi Bhabha argues, post-structuralist notions of the splitting of the subject in/and of language can enlarge this notion of an enunciatory gap in historical narrative to embrace a fundamental split, in "the writing of the nation," between the "pedagogical" and the "performative."

This tension is signalled in various ways in the film, from the early sequence in which Maria crosses the lake on an old and barely functional steamer and a gramophone record plays opera. As ever, the (past) Other's adjacency in this representation of, for "us," "archaic" technology emphasizes difference more sharply than might that of a more profound cultural gulf. But it is particularly the casting and performance of Carole Laure that pulls against a linear construction of the past as unproblematic authentic origin. Her star persona was intimately linked to the cinema of Quebec modernity, and, although her status as sexual and "liberated" was complicated by the highly sexualized use to which her body was put by directors like Carle in particular, these embodiments place her in the film as astride another historical break, that of feminism. Maria is here more active: she writes, and she defies her father's instructions to wed Eutrope. The loss of François Paradis becomes necessary as the loss of the modern (Québécois) heterosexual couple which the "past" could not deliver anyway (similar to James Cameron's *Titanic*, 1997). Her final choice of Eutrope (novel *oblige*) cannot cancel out this excess.

These traces of technology are also important for the way in which the film refuses to settle for a representation of the past as static, as a mere enactment of age-old rhythms and activities associated with agriculture in which, moreover, collective and personal apprehensions of time were as one (what Pierre Nora calls "the close fit between history and memory").[37] It would then fall to a film like *Maria Chapdelaine* to incarnate a *lieu de mémoire* in contemporary society, in which individuals isolated in their private memories are invited to connect with that surviving rallying cry to *histoire-mémoire*, the nation, and in which what "we" are is deciphered through what "we" no longer are. However, the film emphasizes the uncertainty of the past-present relationship, not least because, as Lise Noiseux has pointed out,[38] Péribonka is portrayed as a site of passage in nomadic space, a place of flows, rather than as a settled, unchanging agricultural community. The *postière*, Marie-Ange (played by Marie Tifo, and a character created for the film), plays an important role in the circulation of news, messages, and goods. (Carle would develop such a character further in his 1992 film *La Postière*, set in 1930s small-town Quebec.)

Carle emphasizes these flows and their relation to the natural scene, rather than Maria's choice of Eutrope and the structures of Catholic belief traditionally underlined in the novel. The opening sequence of the film has a voice-over by Samuel Chapdelaine which repeats part of the famous speech by the "third voice" Maria hears at the end of the novel narrating the historical destiny of the French-Canadian people. However, over shots of the lake and, moreover, of an Indian settlement, it deviates from Hémon's text: "But perhaps it would have been better to know the millenary magic of those who preceded us. For here the demons of boredom [*ennui*], cold, anger, bitterness, even the demons of love prowl around in freedom." Although, as Bhabha suggests, "the recurrent metaphor of landscape as the inscape of national identity emphasizes the quality of light, the question of social visibility, the power of the eye to naturalize the rhetoric of national affiliation and its forms of collective expression,"[39] the space of the nation no more escapes contradiction than its time. For the "people" tenuously constructed across the time-frames of costume drama "are neither the beginning or the end of the national narrative; they represent the cutting edge between the totalizing powers of the social and the forces that signify the more specific address to contentious, unequal interests and identities within the population."[40]

It is not surprising, given Carle's early upbringing next to a reservation and the presence in his *oeuvre* of the 1969 film *Red* (to be discussed in chapter 9), that the native peoples, present it is true in the novel, should be given greater visibility in this film version. They are used to represent a line of flight away from Catholicism and sedentarism and to embody a pagan relationship to nature which Carle even connects with Hémon's native Brittany. However, the Indians are, of course, always seen from the outside, and the *sauvagesses* – in clichéd manner – represent the availability of freer sexual pleasure for François. Ultimately, the film manages to steer through the contradictions it sets up, largely through the enhanced role for Samuel Chapdelaine, whose embodiment of the tension between *habitant* and *coureur de bois* grants him the function of reconciler, despite his admission that his choice of peripheral *habitant* life had contributed to the death of his wife. This reconciling role is available to a much lesser extent from the problematic Maria/Carole Laure, still less François, whose death, it could be argued, is the result of male hubris coupled with a relationship of excess with regard to Indian culture ("Where the Indians go, I go") which respects nature more than he does.

However, this attempt at "hegemony" through Samuel is far less important in the film than the way Carle's particular construction of "nature" is used to compensate for the ultimate depthlessness of the project. (The "supernatural" does, however, have the narrative advantage of helping to explain the incongruous death of François.) This *Maria Chapdelaine* looks backward and forward. In the wake of the 1980 referendum, it poses searching questions as to what the national myth represented by this novel can now actually be about. It anticipates the "native peoples dimension" that now blazes so strongly in Quebec politics in the aftermath of Meech and Oka, as well as the massive investment in the past and in historical costume-drama series by Radio Canada in the following decade (*Les Filles de Caleb*, 1990–91; *Shehaweh*, 1992; *Blanche*, 1993–94; *Marguerite Volant*, 1996–97). It also reveals that other tension, when the *lieu de mémoire*, subtly positioned between past and present, collective and private modes of remembering, tips over into the simulacrum of past as undifferentiated text and image, pastiche and allusion. (The *Filles de Caleb* theme park at Saint-Jean-des-Piles, where the series was filmed, here comes to mind.) For the 1983 *Maria Chapdelaine*, this tension is compounded by its status as co-production, both the pan-Canadian element (the dubbed Italian-Ontarian actor Nick Mancuso as François) and the French, rendering problematic the position(s) of spectatorship it constructs (looking at "us"/looking at "us" being looked at, even without the complexities of the past/present relationship) and thus any stable notions of national authenticity. The film invites postmodern readings of identity as provisional, as performance. *Maria Chapdelaine* as a novel was already that paradox of a transnational work serving as founding authenticity for a national discourse. The 1983 film, at the levels of both production and text, suggests new tensions between national and transnational in terms of the flows of the image industries and the nation's external and internal heterogeneities.

5 Sex and the Nation

The chapter in Benedict Anderson's *Imagined Communities* devoted to "Patriotism and Racism" seeks to elucidate the phenomenon of political love, in which affection for the "nation" can go as far as to lay down one's life, and is, as is commonplace, so often couched in terms of kinship and home. However, Anderson is wary of investigating the historical construction of "the family" itself, and is simply content to make links, based on their respective, non-chosen airs of purity, between the "disinterested love and solidarity"[1] it contains and that extended to and demanded by the nation. The inconsistency of his scare quotes reveals, however, some uncertainty: "Both idioms [kinship and home] denote something to which one is naturally tied. As we have seen, in everything 'natural' there is always something unchosen." Similarly, he later argues that "fond imagining" plays a role in both personal and national affections, in terms very relevant to the case of the linguistically constituted national community of Quebec: "What the eye is to the lover – that particular, ordinary eye he or she is born with – language – whatever language history has made his or her mother-tongue – is to the patriot. Through that language, *encountered at mother's knee* and parted with only at the grave, pasts are restored, fellowships are imagined, and futures dreamed."[2]

This chapter seeks to draw out the full implications of these parallels. For Anderson is coy about the historical link between the modern emergence of the nation and the roughly simultaneous assertion of the nuclear family with its rigid sexual division of labour and the disempowerment of children. In fact, the "kinship" affections do not simply parallel the national, the national is actually constituted through them, and they are not of some random kind. Language is learned at mother's knee and not uncle's, for example. When we seek to understand the way in which national affections and identifications are burned into one's subjectivity and even libido, an encounter with psychoanalytic theory seems unavoidable, for at its best it can offer a materialist account of the emergence of individual and human subjectivity as the infant begins the long history of its interactions with society. However, the questions arise: what kind of psychoanalysis for what kind of national identification and what kind of nationalism?

One response, with a high profile in accounts of Quebec cinema, has been the Freudian model of the family romance. In his essay of 1909,[3] Freud draws links between parental and collective identifications by describing the way in which the child develops from an exaltation of his or her parents to discovery of their imperfections, thus impelling the fantasy of in fact having a different, nobler birth. In this way, dreaming of the royal family points to the memory of the days when the child's parents were considered to be god-like, and indeed to some extent all national identifications can be thus explained. However, that fantasy of nobler birth takes first the asexual form of being a foundling, and then the sexual form of being a bastard, in which the "real" father is a usurper. So the family romance partakes of the child's entry into the Oedipal scenario, in which, in the case of the male child, the desire for the mother is eventually renounced, under threat of castration, in favour of an identification with the father. The advantage of the family romance is that it seems, temporarily, to conjure away that castration threat, for the father is not "killed" but simply eliminated from the family circle while an ideal father is imagined and taken as model to aspire to, and a form of intimacy, but not union, with the mother is made possible.

Much can be made of this scenario for general theories of culture, and they are often contradictory. Marthe Robert sees this creation of a fictional world in which its author can reign supreme, this cycle of transgression and guilt organized through dissimulation, intrigue, and conspiracy, as a paradigm for all fiction and especially the novel.[4] One obvious complexity lies in the centrality of sexual difference to the scenario, and the way in which women (in the form of the mother) not only represent the ground on which father-son conflict is played out, but in addition play a silenced role in which the politically specific positions of gender assignment are neglected. In any case, readers of Freud are familiar with the difficulties he had in recounting the Oedipal scenario for little girls.[5] Reaction to this can take the form of a feminist critique of Freud and/or a contextualization and therefore relativization of the almighty Oedipal scenario within the development of Western society. This is the route taken by Raymond Bellour, for example, whose work on the consequences for film narrative and spectatorship of the earlier and simultaneous development of the bourgeoisie, industrial capitalism, and the nuclear family was taken up by feminist film analysts in the 1970s and 1980s.[6] Bellour argues that classic Hollywood cinema orders and organizes its representations from the position of male heterosexual desire occupied by director, protagonist, and implied spectator. Its narratives are usually characterized by an Oedipal trajectory in which the hero comes to accept a positive relationship between his desire and the Law, that is in marriage.

The conjunction of Oedipus, the family romance, and nationhood is played out in striking and specific ways in Quebec cinema and readings of it. Theorists in the 1960s, with its conflict of generations and hegemonic rejection of the old, Catholic, "Canada français," also employed such vocabulary. An article by the editor of *Parti pris*, Pierre Maheu, in 1964 illustrates this point when he argues against the compensatory myths articulated by the "false fathers" or "pères en jupe/ fathers in skirts" of the Catholic Church. In its place he seeks a subjectivity which gets beyond the mere readjustment offered by Trudeau and *Cité libre* (in which Duplessis/the traditionalist father was seen as the cause and not the symptom) and which seriously seeks to tackle the legacy of Quebec's "colonial Oedipus."[7] That subjectivity purports to be a universal-national one, but in fact it is profoundly gendered and heterosexualized. Instead of a failed and castrated "virility" which is afraid to speak its name and to act, Maheu seeks a new paternal position, what Robert Schwartzwald has termed a "phallo-national maturity":[8] "The world of the father is the universe of *hard* objects, of objectal reality, of concrete achievements, of work and efficiency; the Father is praxis, and our myth sentenced us to *sterile* projections" in which there was an "absence of vital energy and sense of adventure" (my emphasis). For Maheu, Quebec man is Oedipus because he marries his mother, who is herself "abandoned to frigidity" because she castrates her sons and husband, refusing them "any *authentic* encounter with masculinity" (my emphasis). Against this phallo-national maturity, this plenitude of virility associated with the nationalist project, is posited the traditional world based on the cult of the mother eternally fixed and rooted in nature. As a result, all wholeness and plenitude are lost: "We live in a disintegrated culture, a life reduced to scattered crumbs. We lack the social structures essential for integrating the individual and show him a role to play, diversified, efficient, paternal institutions ... depersonalization is that social mush that threatens to swallow us up in the shifting sands of the Mother."

Surprisingly, however, this masculinism is qualified by the need to differentiate it from the liberal, modernizing, and federalist discourse of *Cité libre* or the Lesage Liberal government in Quebec, which has simply substituted one myth, agriculture, with another, industry and technology, and which has equated the needs of the bourgeoisie with that of the nation as a whole. Maheu is astute enough to seek to include women in his national project, but it is, he believes, by resurrecting and transforming the idea of "la Terre-Mère/Mother-Earth" that the nation as *totality* can be embraced once again. It is in this way that the article is a very 1960s text, mistaking, in the name of a liberation yet to come, its own highly gendered position for a universal one and suggesting (sexual) emancipations for both men and women which are highly one-sided: "Make woman into lover and wife and free us from the Mother by bursting from her breast once more, armed and ready for a new battle." The vision is no longer one of the colonial Oedipus but it remains very Oedipalized in its proposed "solution" of the Oedipus complex, in the sense of retaining fixed assignments of gendered subjectivity and male power in the family romance or in genital heterosexuality. The whole scenario is in fact a disavowal of that lack, that tension, at the heart of national or any other identity.

It is certainly the case that the father-son relationship is often privileged in Quebec cinema (or conspicuous by its absence, which usually amounts to the same thing) and often within the diagnostic logic described in the Maheu article. One memorable example is a film made just after the 1960s, Francis Mankiewicz' *Le Temps d'une chasse* of 1972. Here three working-class men from east Montreal set off into the countryside on a hunting trip: Lionel (Pierre Dufresne), Willie (Guy L'Écuyer from *La Vie heureuse de Léopold Z.*), and Richard (Marcel Sabourin), accompanied by his ten-year-old son Michel (Olivier L'Écuyer). The hunt is in fact a ritual of masculine prowess that ends in failure, with the rotund, drunken Willie, determined to show he is "capable," finally shooting Richard dead by accident.

Within the logic of *Parti pris*, the men's failure to achieve either hunting or sexual success would be bound up with the colonized history of Quebec and its failure to attain phallo-national maturity. The effectiveness of the hunt as metaphor is certain, since it also metonymically relates to the "real" status of hunting in the cultural practices of that class of men. However, the film also implies a whole set of ambiguities. Hunting in Quebec is also bound up with the hybridity of its culture in relation to the native peoples; indeed, the kind of masculine identity for which it is a vehicle carries with it connotations of the *coureur de bois* comingling with native culture and escaping not only the hold of the French or any other state or nation-state but rationalist forms of modernity itself. (This is a point missed in contemporary analyses of the film, in which the men's failure to attain "authenticity" is seen as matched by their "inauthentic" response to the natural scene so perfectly captured by Michel Brault's camerawork: The question arises as to what that "authenticity" might be.)[9] This is part of its appeal for these working-class men, but it would have been difficult to co-opt even a successful trip into a straightforward narrative of unified national subjectivity. This is especially so because the homosocial relations between the trio of adults (bonds between men predicated on the exclusion of women and the disavowal of anything remotely homosexual)[10] are seen to possess an undercurrent of violence.

Famous films such as Carlos Saura's *La Caza* (1966) or Jean Renoir's *La Règle du jeu* (1939) treat the hunt as a metaphor for the "real" violence lurking underneath society's façade. How does *Le Temps d'une chasse* diagnose that violence? It is a fine line between a critique of failed masculinity (the "Oedipe colonial" position) and a critique of masculinity itself. In fact, *Le Temps d'une chasse* is also marked by the transformations in sexual politics, most especially the renewal of feminist politics, which had taken place since Pierre Maheu's 1964 article. Whereas the logic of the advancement of Quebec's national (masculine) self could be construed by some in the 1960s as "déshabiller [undress] la Québécoise" (*Valérie* and its aftermath), in *Le Temps d'une chasse* the position in the social order and in cinema spectatorship of heterosexual masculinity is dealt a severe blow, most notably in the famous striptease scene in the motel. Lionel and Willie pay a waitress, Monique (Luce Guilbeault, one of Quebec's greatest actresses), $20 to take her clothes off in their motel room. The point-of-view shots of her dancing and stripping, defamiliarized by the lack of music, alternate with reaction shots of the men which in a sense are more voyeuristic, for they are revealing of a "truth," a lack within them. Finally, Willie's giggles provoke defiance from Monique, but unlike Judy/Maureen O'Hara's tirade against the male audience in Dorothy Arzner's *Dance, Girl, Dance* (1940), she also reveals her own fragility and sobs, "Je suis tannée/I'm fed up."

The film is also multilayered in relation to the child, social class, and the differences between the men. Michel's presence is imposed by his mother, who does not want to look after him over the weekend. For the men, he is largely an intrusion, but he and the relationship with his father are subtly altered during the film. On the one hand, there is the possibility that Michel will learn the social roles and turn into a version of these men, as when he successfully fires at the beer bottle. On the other, his games in the forest have him fantasizing about killing them, as shots are filmed from his point of view of taking aim at the adult trio. Of course, the Oedipal story suggests that these attitudes are two sides of the same coin, symbolically killing then identifying with the father. However, Michel's distance from the masculine game of the hunt is represented in the one scene of bonding with his father, who is visibly ill at ease with the whole entreprise. In this scene, Michel is playing with frogs near the lakeside, and Richard teaches him how to hypnotize them by stroking their stomachs. The frog is then set free. Similarly, Michel's horrified reaction to the dead squirrel shot by Willie suggests a radically different mode of being in nature and relating to animals (this point will be explored further in our analysis of *Bach et Bottine*).

The difference between critiquing masculinity or critiquing "failed" masculinity, between "lack" as potentially productive or lack as failure, cannot be separated from questions of class. If these were three middle-class protagonists, it would be a different story. Working-class disempowerment and alienation can be made to stand in for a general national oppression. Or else the film can be seen as in some senses a "world" text, since all Western societies contain class inequality and are going through a process in which traditional gender roles are being questioned. In some ways the trio is reminiscent of the representation of the French working classes in the 1930s. There, a dominant populism produced the spectacle of the working classes as degraded or as authentic. Moreover, the male protagonists were seen similarly to lack a means of surpassing their condition because of their low social status and also because of the impasses of masculine identity associated with it. In this way class division prevented them negotiating the Oedipal scenario and emerging as "full" male citizens or agents. Often the differences between the male characters would describe the various modalities of this defeat: here, Willie is aging and overweight, the most sexually insecure; Lionel barricades himself within the false certainties of his role; Richard, more than the others, sees the vanity of the enterprise, but his sensitivity is no good to him, since it is coded as non-masculine and he lacks the verbal skills to express his feelings, hence the aborted relationship with the equally defeated waitress (Frédérique Collin). The difference from 1930s French films, however, that which makes *Le Temps d'une chasse* very much a product of this national cinema, is the absence of the Jean Gabin figure, the reconciling male hero who, as in, for example, Julien Duvivier's *La Belle Équipe* (1936), is able to absorb the contradictions of the community in a minimalist way, by simply not embodying their excesses, and whose star persona is able to assemble a coalition of French national symbols and connotations.[11]

It is possible, then, to detect two strands in Quebec cinema and in critical positions on that cinema: one that constructs a national position read in unified, masculine, heterosexual, and Oedipal terms; and one that is more heterogeneous, challenging that dominant masculine position, qualifying it by seeking to articulate with it other key terms such as class or jettisoning unity and the national-Oedipal scenario altogether. Narratives of failed masculinity or of alternative gender and sexual identities may point to the historical specificity of Quebec's position as "minor" rather than "major" culture, and to the desirability of exploring the positive implications of that status rather than rejecting it as deficiency.

What happens, for example, when it is not fathers and sons but mothers and daughters? Mankiewicz's second feature, *Les Bons Débarras* of 1980, is one of the most famous Quebec films and provides such an example. Set again in the forest and lake region of the Laurentiens north of Montreal, it recounts the story of Michèle (Marie Tifo), a single mother who runs a ramshackle business delivering wood to wealthy second-homers, her twelve-year-old daughter, Manon (Charlotte Laurier), born of an unknown father when Michèle was eighteen, and her brother Ti-Guy (Germain Houde), mentally handicapped after contracting meningitis in childhood. Michèle is going out with a policeman, Maurice (Roger Le Bel), and discovers she is pregnant by him, which outrages Manon who is professing an intense love for her mother and who wishes to eliminate rivals. She suggests that Maurice has made sexual advances to her and incites a drunken Ti-Guy to kill himself at the wheel of their van.

The film has been subjected to readings determined to allegorize it for Quebec national "identity." Ian Lockerbie argues[12] that each of the three main protagonists represents a different aspect of Quebec across the generations. Ti-Guy is the subordinated self, imprisoned and disempowered. Michèle, "the character with whom the spectators identify," is the conquered self, brave but ultimately defeated, a fact symbolized by the scenes in which she is immobilized by a tire puncture or falls into mud. Manon, however, represents the Quiet Revolution generation which is assertive and self-confident, combining imagination, creativity, and aggressivity, "the aggressivity which will be necessary for Quebec to overcome its historical handicaps and to launch a social dynamic."

Heinz Weinmann, in his stimulating study *Cinéma de l'imaginaire québécois*, places the film within his analysis of Quebec's own "family romance," in which the changing dependencies of "French Canada" (orphaned by the loss of France, alienated by Britain in 1837–38, embracing Canada in 1867 but transferring its devotion to the church and the patron St John the Baptist), mapped onto the Freudian scenario, are surpassed by the foundation of "Quebec" (which he dates from the October crisis of 1970). Although *Les Bons Débarras* was released just two months before the failed sovereignty-association referendum of May 1980, in which the dependency of the Québécois in relation to Ottawa was reaffirmed, it seems to point to a different outcome. For one thing, Weinmann reads it intertextually as the revenge of "la petite Aurore" from the most famous and successful French-Canadian film of the immediate post-war period, *La Petite Aurore l'enfant martyre*. Based on an equally successful play, this film told the story of Aurore, who is raised by her father but also a wicked and sadistic stepmother, Marie-Louise (Lucie Mitchell), who Aurore knew had poisoned her natural mother. Marie-Louise's crimes are discovered and punished too late, for Aurore dies from the abuse meted out. Weinmann argues, rather contortedly, that the film is a reverse family romance, since it is the lost parent (in heaven) who is idealized and the replacement denigrated, a usurper who symbolizes, inevitably, the British conqueror. But the historical compensations fail to function, since the representative of the church is useless, Aurore, by keeping her secret, fails to live up to the reference to the *saints martyrs canadiens* of the seventeenth century, and the film symbolically refers to the repressed scene of the St John the Baptist story, his beheading on the orders of a woman. *La Petite Aurore l'enfant martyre* thus marks the beginning of the disengagement of "French Canada" from its family romance and the process of its increasing autonomy. (The other hit of this period, *Tit-Coq*, directed by René Delacroix and Gratien Gélinas in 1952, is about an illegitimate soldier who loses his love.) *Les Bons Débarras*, in contrast, features a daughter who is addressed as "boss" by her mother and who is a master of language. Manon, by refusing to choose a new, "nobler" father in the form of Maurice or even the more likeable garage mechanic Gaëtan (Gilbert Sicotte), is thus opting out of the family romance. This is why she eliminates – the "good riddance" of the title – the real child in the film, her alter ego, Ti-Guy, who is "in a way the transexual incarnation of Aurore who has survived her stepmother's torture."[13]

Although these two readings of the film are different, they share the tendency to create a master interpretation which in turn is able to totalize "Quebec" in its reading of the narrative and characters. Lockerbie in particular seems to accept as part of a project of national plenitude a kind of eugenics in which the "abnormal" or "subnormal" can be happily sacrificed. Indeed, Weinmann rightly points out that the relationship between Manon's passion for her mother and any national or collective identifications is highly problematic. "Love" is the terrain on which all identities are constructed and therefore in Quebec as elsewhere a shared structure is there to behold ("aimer à mort/love to death" betokening both the high suicide rate among the young and the fear of collective disappearance, the happy birthday song "C'est à ton tour" – featured in the film – as quasi-national anthem). Manon idealizes her real mother and not a fantasy parent, but that love is not extended to anything representing the collective: She despises representatives of the state such as Maurice, the police in general, and, inappropriately for an embodiment of the Quiet Revolution, school.

The family-romance interpretation relies on an excessively literal reading of Freud, for it is the force of Freud's argument that the child's fantasies are precisely a way of retaining affection for the parent, in particular the father. The process of debasement and idealization are forever, and subtly, linked. Moreover, both Lockerbie and Weinmann, by prioritizing national over any other identifications, neglect those aspects of the film that undermine such a totalizing and overriding identity, namely, class and gender. "Le petit peuple" can certainly be made to stand for the national community, and frequently are in Quebec cinema; Mme Viau-Vachon (Louise Marleau), the wealthy *bourgeoise* to whom the family delivers wood, is certainly an unattainable fantasy figure for Ti-Guy, who is unable to occupy an adult male heterosexual position (this is his problem rather than being stuck in the family romance) and symbolically smashes his windscreen before he drives to his death, just prior to which he envisions her welcoming arms. But the dominant *mise en scène* of the film is that of realism, the material day-to-day struggle for survival of this economically marginalized group, the contrast with Mme Viau-Vachon's home, and the sombre light of Brault's cinematography which refuses to prettify the milieu, even less so than in *Le Temps d'une chasse* (*Les Bons Débarras* was shot in autumn).

Given these points, and also that Weinmann argues that Manon opts out of the family romance, then why retain it as the master decoding? Manon's androgyny, a mixture of power and flirtatiousness, and her infatuation with her mother, seem to pitch us into a different sexual economy altogether. Manon's refusal to be interpellated as citizen or as national-governed raises the non-differentiation of mother and daughter as a potential problem. On the other hand, it also sends us out of history and into the realm of myth. Through its literary references in particular, *Les Bons Débarras* offers an alternative and oppositional myth of non-Oedipal, non-patriarchal, minor rather than major identity construction. Réjean Ducharme's 1966 novel, *L'Avalée des avalés*, echoed in the film in the place name Val des vals, also portrayed a demonic and assertive young heroine resisting the codings of Oedipus and nation. Bérénice Einberg's long monologue explores a conflict between flows of desire (for her brother, in relation to the flora and fauna of their island in the St Lawrence) and the codings society would impose even as they are in conflict with each other (the parents raise the two children in two religions, Bérénice samples life in New York). Like Bérénice, Manon is perverse, in that she has turned away from the "normal" organization and trajectory of desire. Indeed, the Nietzschean and Dionysiac aspect of Ducharme's writing seems pretty much to the fore,[14] with the will to power expressing itself mainly through Manon's creative/destructive use of language.

The references to *Wuthering Heights* intensify the other-worldly, anti-patriarchal myth-making of the film text. For the significance of Emily Brontë's novel in *Les Bons Débarras* goes well beyond the mere paralleling of an intense and passionate love. As Georges Bataille argued in *La Littérature et le mal*, *Wuthering Heights* describes a love which not only goes against social convention, a common trope in many a romance, but whose transgressiveness is completely independent of an order to be created and therefore goes on to imply a loss of self in the other and, ultimately, death. Cathy and Heathcliff represent a quasi-incestuous passionate attachment (they were raised as brother and sister) which, played out in the landscape of the moors, comes to be a story of forces rather than people, in which elements of the self are to be found in others ("Nelly, I *am* Heathcliff"). In *Les Bons Débarras*, we find that same non-separation, that same embrace of "savagery" against the "civilized" (we should recall, however, that in *Wuthering Heights* society continues, but in reworked form after the deaths of Heathcliff and the older Cathy). Manon's refusal of adult subjectivity need not therefore be read as a regression, but it is certainly not the paradigm of full nationalist subjectivity suggested by Lockerbie. The attachment of daughter to mother could be read as a refusal of the Law (literally, in the form of the buffoonish Maurice) and thus to be of great significance for sexual politics, because Manon, without being able to return to the Imaginary in which, according to Lacan, the infant does not differentiate itself from the mother's body or the outside world in general, is proposing a new order based not on lack and not therefore on the phallus-governed entry into language. However, as befits an art movie, the ending of *Les Bons Débarras* is ambiguous, as Manon's victory is obtained at the price of a kind of stasis, an attempt to arrest the flows of desire and most notably the flow of time, be it the linear time of the nation or any other configuration (Manon will age, Michèle's baby will be born.) Nevertheless, the film is an interesting example of a strangeness or even queering of familial relationships which has problematic implications for the connection with national identifications.

There are few such ambiguities in Jean-Claude Lauzon's first feature, *Un Zoo la nuit* of 1987, a *policier* owing its sets, decor, and iconography (notably the villainous police) to Jean-Jacques Beineix's *Diva* (1981), but with very national-Québécois features too. Marcel (Gilles Maheu) is released from prison after serving a two-year sentence for involvement in a drug scam. The two policemen who set him up now want the money. With the help of an American former cellmate, the police are killed. Meanwhile, Marcel has renewed contact with his divorced father Albert (Roger Le Bel), whom he takes from his hospital bed on one last hunting trip before he dies, to a zoo where he shoots an elephant.

For Weinmann, the film is further proof of the maturing of Québécois identity, in that Marcel is able to recognize his father (it is even suggested that the person of René Lévesque – as father of the nation – had contributed in the 1970s and 1980s to the rehabilitation of the figure of the father in Quebec culture). For this to happen, of course, the "bad father," George (Lorne Brass), the sadistic, crooked, gay, and *English-Canadian* policeman, has to be physically eliminated. This occurs when he is lured for sex with the ally from the United States.

However, the examples of *Les Bons Débarras* and even *Le Temps d'une chasse* are there to denaturalize and demystify this masculinist national narrative which is in fact full of sexual anxiety. Weinmann misses the point when he writes, "By eliminating George, he eliminates at the same time his own homosexual drives towards his own father which prevent the expression of their father-son relationship."[15] This spectacular disavowal (gay-baiting and murder, "justified" by the spectacle provided of George's sadism and by the prisoner he sent to rape Marcel in his cell at the start of the film) is necessary to legitimate the extraordinary final scene when Marcel washes Albert's naked body and then climbs, naked himself, into bed with him. As in *Parti pris* writing of the 1960s, the "feminization" of the conquered Quebec is reversed so that it is the English Canadian, and the "fédéraste" pro-Canada Québécois such as Trudeau, who are tainted with (passive) homosexuality. The terror of anal penetration is rife throughout, as when Julie (Lynn Adams) suggests to Marcel, "Your club sandwich, you can sit on it."[16] Notably, Julie, the only woman in the film who is not a mother-figure, is a prostitute, and Marcel's dominance over her is asserted when he first has sex with her after his release, a forced coupling filmed with him standing up.

The film clearly presents the source of these anxieties even as it seeks to disavow them. Robert Schwartzwald argues that the 1960s discourse of decolonization in Quebec eventually opted for the assertion of new whole identities rather than the deconstruction of those fixities handed down from the past. What won out was "the primacy of a political moment in which the task was to constitute whole Subjects capable of finding a *way out* of the very fragmentation that constitutes the generative moment of postmodernist thought."[17] *Un Zoo la nuit* thus favours a "major" rather than "minor" response to the changed status of women (Albert's wife has left *him*; Julie's defiance is subdued and she can be inserted into a rescue narrative) and also to immigrants and multiculturalism, globalization, and the relationship in content and form between the traditional, the modern, and the postmodern.

Albert belongs to the urban working class that emerged from modernity and industrialization. That culture is made to lock seamlessly into more traditional, that is, rural, practices of hunting and fishing (the bonding with Marcel when he teaches him fishing lore on the lake) to form a national historical plenitude. (Weinmann, like Lauzon, neglects the fact that the transmission of that culture from the native peoples to the *voyageurs* and *coureurs de bois* is problematic, not a source of plenitude.)[18] We are far from the alienation in nature of the working-class men of *Le Temps d'une chasse*. Albert, however, has lost his job to the process of globalization, as his factory closed and the production process moved to the United States. When Marcel presents him with a 1957 Buick, he remarks, "The Japanese wouldn't have made that," locating him within the certainties of post-war Fordism (and, by implication, 1950s sexual roles). The Italian community within which he lives, and which Marcel initially seems to embrace as a substitute family, is also viewed competitively. The restaurant owner Toni has accompanied him on the hunt, and so the elephant shoot represents one up on him. Marcel is the urban artist (musician), living in a loft and defining himself through consumerism and its fractured identities, most notably the consumption of drugs. The dialogue with Albert takes place at first in the interface of those worlds, a disembodied message from Albert on Marcel's answering machine that stresses the contrast of generations and epochs ("I'm your father and you're my boy. That still means something to me"); Albert hides the drug money in that metonym of working-class life, his old lunch box.

Albert thus represents an "authenticity" under threat, and while the film does not suggest a return to the 1950s, far from it, it works, primarily through its Oedipal, homosocial, and homophobic narrative, to renew contact with that identity while reworking it for the present. Marcel's proclaimed love for his father reaches its apotheosis after he has gone on his own hunt, the *chasse à pédé* which kills the policemen. That action is itself a reassertion of his prowess after the momentary defeat when Julie is threatened with death behind the peep-show glass partition. Marcel's active virility is able symbolically to penetrate that screen, to cross it so that he is able to impose his own reality on it (the whole film presents a gradual breaking down of barriers, symbolic or otherwise, from the opening in which Marcel's rape is filmed through prison bars to the partitions demolished at Albert's home and finally the passage through the enclosures of the zoo). He is thus able to prove he can actively get beyond mere questions of style, hedonism, and consumption and correct Albert's assertion that "you young people think you've changed the world just because you wear dark glasses at night." In turn, Albert's last venture is aided by a sniff of cocaine provided by Marcel. Significantly, however, the Oedipal narrative's impetus does not carry Marcel as far as the formation of the heterosexual couple, the classic formulation of the reconciliation of desire and the Law of the father.

Moreover, the form or forms of the film belie any linear and totalizing reading. Clearly, what is unusual about *Un Zoo la nuit* is its combination of *policier* violence and family drama. However, that contrast represents two distinct kinds of film-making for two distinct worldviews which explain the federating market success of the film but undermine its professed coherence. Marcel's eventual "crossing" of the peep-show barrier into his own action is in fact a passage from one film quotation (Wenders' *Paris Texas*, later to be followed by a reference to *The American Friend*) to another (the designer violence of contemporary American mob movies as well as French films such as *Diva* and *Subway* [Besson, 1985]: The violence is explicit but filmed in a highly stylized *mise en scène* of orange light, shadows and corridors at a seedy hotel). In contrast, the scenes with Albert in the milieu of the Italian restaurant, for example, are shot by cinematographer Guy Dufaux according to the dominant Quebec realist style with painterly, rich, Brault-like flourishes for the fishing sequence. The very gendered national "authenticity" at the heart of the film is thus demonstrably a construction, its neurotic masculinity finally unable fully to fill the lack, to stitch together the unravellings provoked by historical, economic, and cultural globalization and the detraditionalization of identity. Albert's home is literally rebuilt around him, and it is unclear what shape it will metaphorically take following his death.

The tension between centipetal and centrifugal notions of identity also informs Lauzon's extraordinary second feature, *Léolo* (1992). Again, Ducharme's *L'Avalée des avalés* functions as intertext. It is the only book in the working-class east Montreal home of Léo Lozeau (twelve years old for most of the film) and becomes his obsession. Like Bérénice but also Manon, Léo has an artistic and Nietzschean disposition which collides with the restrictions of his milieu, so much that he fantasizes, in his own outlandish version of the family romance, that his real progenitor is an Italian peasant who masturbated over a shipment of tomatoes into which his mother (the singer Ginette Reno) fell at her local market. Léo finally succumbs, however, to the family mental illness (which Lauzon claims is a release).[19] Lauzon breaks with the documentary realism of much Quebec cinema to present an exaggerated, grotesque realism, much influenced by Fellini (the scenes with the "word-tamer" are filmed in Fellini's statue warehouse at Cinecittà) and tinged with fantasy. This style and humour, as well as the stances of the film's narrative, intensify *Léolo* as very much a working-class fantasy, in which the substitute father is not sought from the nation's élite and in which national hegemonies such as clerical nationalism or modernizing technocracy are happily ignored or labelled as failures (Léo's school is useless, but it is unclear how we are to judge this because of the vagueness of the film's temporal setting: the presence of Ducharme's novel would place it in the late 1960s, but otherwise the feel is 1950s.) This marginalized popular culture, far from the notion of "pure laine" or indeed any purity, also expresses itself through Rabelaisian grotesque bodies that seem to break out of their bounds, through scatology, and also through the provocations of brutality (the rape of a cat by a group of boys). The soundtrack is international and daring (Tibetan chants, Rolling Stones, Tom Waits). However, the film restrains itself from a complete reversal and inversion of norms. Léo still clings to the Oedipal family romance. Anality is a source of order, not pleasure (the family's obsession with regular shitting is echoed in its attitude to money). There are bad "fathers" or authority figures, and good ones, notably the "word-tamer," played by former nationalist politician and teacher to Lauzon, Pierre Bourgault. Léo's brother Fernand falls victim to an anglo bully (played by the tormentor from *Un Zoo la nuit*, Lorne Brass): The joke is that for a long time "I thought the English [*Anglais*] didn't have any." Any hint at polymorphous perversity is undermined by the developmental treatment of Léo's evolution into heterosexual masculinity, through masturbation, voyeurism on his young Italian neighbour, Bianca (Giuditta del Vecchio) (who nonetheless gives his grandfather hand-jobs for money), and encounter with a prostitute (because "I didn't have the courage of my love for Bianca"). Similarly, the unfurling of set-piece sequences begins to resolve itself into a narrative – of failure: Fernand is bullied again despite his body-building, Léo fails to kill his grandfather who earlier had tried to drown him.

On one level, "perverse" Quebec children in the form of Manon or Léolo can be read as antidotes to the characters of one of the key specialisms of Quebec cinema over the past thirty years, the "children's film" and especially the *contes pour tous* or "tales for all" produced by Rock Demers (b. 1933). The origins of Demers's interest lie in the distribution company, Faroun Films, that he founded in the 1960s and that specialized in the import and export of children's films, including those from Eastern Europe. This led to investment in the first "children's feature" made in Quebec, *Le Martien de Noël* (Bernard Gosselin,

1970). In 1980 he set up a production company, les Productions La
Fête,[20] and set about creating a series of (initially twelve) films, in English and in French and dubbed in each, specifically for children. The
first was *La Guerre des tuques* (André Melançon, 1984).[21] Other films in
the series have taken advantage of Demers's Eastern European connections and included co-productions with Czechoslovakia (*The Great
Land of Small*, dir. Vojtech Jasny, 1987), Hungary (*Bye Bye Red Riding
Hood*, dir. Marta Mészàros, 1989), and Romania (*The Champion*, dir.
Elisabeta Bostan, 1990).

Of course, the notion of "children's film," and the relationship between these terms, is a problematic one. Demers has explained that
his films "usually have an affirmative and reconciliatory tone designed
to bring children and adults together," and positions them against
Hollywood fare, which give children "entertainment" rather than
"peace and warmth."[22] As Philippe Ariès has pointed out, "childhood"
as a concept has not always existed: in the European Middle Ages children were not separated from, but were considered a part of, adult
society after they ceased being physically dependent, and "modern"
concepts of childhood are closely bound up first with the Counter-
Reformation and then with the ascendancy of the bourgeois family
within the class societies of industrial capitalism, along with the Enlightenment emphasis on discipline and schooling.[23] Heavily influenced by the work of Foucault and Deleuze, Guy Hocquenghem and
René Schérer have taken this historicization of "childhood" to one
conclusion, arguing that the "child" as "little person" is a product of
Enlightenment discipline, and favouring a breakdown of the adult/
child distinction through an emphasis on the latter's polymorphous
perversity, psychic mobility, and the blurring of the reality/fantasy distinction.[24] In her work on *Peter Pan*, Jacqueline Rose has written of the
impossibility of children's fiction, in that it rests on an evasion, the notion that the "child" is something simple and straightforward to know,
rather than a construction and investment of the adult: "If children's
fiction builds an image of the child inside the book, it does so in order
to secure the child who is outside the book, the one who does not
come so easily within its grasp."[25] The image of the child is used by
adults to deny the difficulties of, and therefore to naturalize, the way
in which adult subjects are constituted, "a process which the adult
then *repeats* through the book which he or she gives to the child."[26]

This is why it is appropriate to look at the *contes pour tous* in the context of sexuality and the nation. The liberal (non-sexist, non-racist,
multicultural, and individualist) world of the films and the reconcilia-
tions of their narratives hinge on processes of identification, recognition, and belonging which make links between the family and
friendship formations depicted and the wider society, although only

those films shot in French and in Quebec are really relevant to a discussion of national-sexual identity formation. The protagonists of the films are aged between ten and twelve and so on the cusp of the formation of sexual identities and adult personhood and responsibilities. The tension of forces in these films is between the pull towards the polymorphous perversity of early childhood and the "finished" (Oedipalized) persons ready to take their place as adults in society. Just as *E.T.* (Spielberg, 1982) spun an Oedipal tale in which the extraterrestrial functioned in a relay of phalluses between loss (the absent father) and the child's ability to take his place in the world,[27] so Marcel Sabourin's Martian in the 1970 Gosselin film indulges the children's oral fixations and hints at the possibility of replacing the father as more playful, generous, and powerful (in the Father Christmas sequence), while at the same time making sure that both he and the kids return to their respective homes ("c'est bien chez vous") and families. It is not a huge leap here to Weinmann's argument about the family romance, to read the Martian as a substitute for older belief systems (Catholicism) and the ending of the film as a reconciliation in Quebec society between social order, technology, pleasure, and consumerism.

This is not to argue, therefore, that the *contes pour tous* are simply a form of social dressage of children by adults who create the stories and films, but rather that they unwittingly represent a contested space by dint of their presentation of events from the child's point of view, between different forms of subjectivity and, by extension, different ways of being in society and the world. This is perhaps best illustrated by the role and portrayal of animals in the films. Instead of the "becoming-adult" (in which the "adult" is the fixed and end result) that the narrative impels, other becomings are imaginable, notably "becoming-animal." There is no animal that is "become" at the end of this process. Deleuze and Guattari are referring to the non-hierarchical symbioses, states of in-betweenness or "transversal communications between heterogeneous populations" that occur between "humans" and animals.[28] In *La Guerre des tuques*, however, Cléo the St Bernard dies when the snow fort collapses on her. She thus acts as a relay between the "warring" groups of human children and represents a means by which they pass through an apprenticeship of adulthood, with a "couple" tentatively forming between the lead boy and girl protagonists. In *Bach et Bottine* (Melançon, 1986), the biggest box-office success in Quebec of its year, Fanny (Mahée Paiement) adopts a skunk (Bottine) and a whole menagerie of pets which disrupt the adult world, notably the closed-off "personhood" of her "bachelor" uncle Jean-Claude (Raymond Legault), who spends his time practising the organ and listening to Bach on headphones. Temporarily, there is also a flight, when Fanny and the boy next door spend an idyllic day wandering around a wintry Quebec City before returning home. However, this last sequence in fact represents the "home" – security and freedom – to which Fanny aspires, a lack represented in the first sequence of the film, when she dreams she is with her dead parents. This lack must be filled, and the film's narrative organically builds to a filling of that lack, when a new family is formed with Jean-Claude and his schoolteacher colleague Bérénice (Andrée Pelletier). Fanny teaches him to "love": the animals are transitional objects, the mediators of something all too human, and enable Fanny to find her place within an adjusted but unquestioned order. (Whereas she, too, represents a kind of revenge of la petite Aurore, it is this that distinguishes Fanny from the perverse, protesting, but ultimately trapped Manon of *Les Bons Débarras*). Fanny's Rubik's cube consisting of photos of her parents and Jean-Claude is "solved," and a "truth" is revealed in the film when we learn that Jean-Claude had been in love with Fanny's mother (and so *could have been* her father).

Examples so far suggest that the distinction or boundary between heterosexuality and homosexuality is central to constructions of Quebec nationhood, although it may not be the only sexual-identity configuration which upsets the most unified and centripetal versions of it. A typical Claude Fournier comedy of the early 1970s, *La Pomme, la queue et les pépins* (1974), crudely expresses that combination of nationalism, heterosexism, and profound sexual anxiety. A Liberal, Martial (Donald Lautrec), becomes sexually impotent after his wedding but is cured when he discovers this is caused by the carnation he wears like his hero Trudeau (!), and the film ends in a sea of semen. A camp gay bookshop owner played by Jean Lapointe becomes the butt of the anxieties provoked by this (hetero)sexual dysfunction: he has to be absolute Other to the straight man's problems, or else the regime of heterosexual and with it gender normativity would be under threat. Such films share characteristics with certain British 1970s sitcoms, for example, as being located in a historical transition between 1960s "liberation" and the full flowering of the women's and lesbian and gay men's movements' correctives to that decade's sexism and heterosexism.[29] However, within Quebec there are certain specificities. Despite the rich popular and televisual culture from which film comedy emerged, there was little indigenous camp culture lurking at the centre of the official culture and ready to be decoded, no Frankie Howard or Kenneth Williams, for example. In addition, as we have seen, the whole relationship with Canada had for long been expressed in highly gendered and sexualized terms which precluded the juxtaposition of "Quebec authenticity" and "homosexuality." But because "high culture" was differently and distinctly configured in a Quebec peripheralized in relation to France and "colonized" in relation to Britain and Canada, the emergence of homosexuality as a fruitful problematic addressing this nation's peculiar situation came from the stage, in that dialogue between class, nation, and sexuality achieved in the works of Michel Tremblay. For long, however, as Tom Waugh points out,[30] the representation of gay men in Quebec cinema was as predators and freaks, which rendered all the more astonishing Jutra's "coming out" in *À tout prendre.*

The representation of homosexuality in Quebec cinema can thus be analysed in several ways. As with representations of immigrants or native peoples, it provides a test of a film's capacity to articulate an idea of the nation that is inclusive and plural rather than exclusive and unified. Moreover, its representation crucially affects what Eve Sedgwick calls the "habitation/nation system" and its relation to "the sex/gender system," as we have seen in our previous examples in its relation with "phallo-nationalism." These can in fact take many forms: "It may be that there exists for nations, as for genders, simply no normal way to partake of the categorical definitiveness of the national, no single kind of 'other' of what a nation is to which all can by the same structuration be definitionally opposed."[31] These first two points I make also relate to Sedgwick's evocation in *Epistemology of the Closet* of the twin poles of universalizing and minoritizing discourses on homosexuality. The former sees homo/heterosexual definition as "an issue of active importance primarily for a small, distinct, relatively fixed minority"; the latter "as an issue of continuing, determinative importance in the lives of people across the spectrum of sexualities."[32] My third preliminary point would be to read these issues diachronically in relation to the emerging lesbian and gay movement and the subsequent expressions of gay film-makers, as well as to differing articulations of what we might call the modern-national and postmodern-transnational.

However, before we can examine how examples of more "gay-friendly" films articulate the relationship with nationhood, we must also bear in mind the specificities of the Quebec historical case. Indeed, just as gay identities qualify the national, specific national cultural traditions and histories qualify "gay," which must be equally problematized. Here we must take into account the way in which Montreal developed, during American prohibition and especially during the Second World War when it was a main transit point for Canadian and American troops, an industry of sex and sexual spectacle which obviously collided with the agenda of clerical nationalism but which in turn produced identities, most notably around a francophone working-class drag culture. Since the Quiet Revolution, there have been many important law reforms, including the decriminalization by Trudeau's federal government in 1968 of the sodomy laws, the incorporation in 1977 into the provincial Charter of Rights and Freedoms by the Parti Québécois government of a provision, the first of its kind in North America, outlawing discrimination on the grounds of sexual orientation, and the federal government's legal recognition of same-sex couples in 1999. Significantly, the passing of the 1977 provision followed increasing police harassment of gay spaces in Montreal, especially during and after the 1976 summer Olympics. Interestingly, the "homosexual" becomes above all a factor of modernity, part of a Quiet Revolution legitimizing national narrative within the discourse of the then minister of justice, Marc-André Bédard: "There is no comparable case in the West or in the World of a society that has gone as quickly as Quebec society, and in such an *adult* way, with so few negative aspects, from a closed, authoritarian, obscurantist society, to a society that is open, daring and well-articulated."[33] This demonstrates the fact that there are different kinds of nationalisms and that some can be pluralist and inclusive, but also the way in which the letter of the law, and of this law, can be at odds with the forms in which other versions of nationalism constitute themselves.

Undoubtedly, it is the 1973 film adaptation of six of Michel Tremblay's plays,[34] *Il était une fois dans l'est*, which marks, after *À tout prendre*, the most significant manifestation of homosexuality within Quebec national cinema. The film is structured around three disappointments or defeats. In the middle of the film, the old transvestite la duchesse de Langeais (Claude Gai) engages in a monologue with a young married couple on the plane back from Mexico, but her fantasy of a fanfare welcome back to Montreal ("ce sera tout un retour/what a return it's going to be") is punctured when only his semi-estranged sister Robertine (Béatrice Picard) is there to greet him at the airport. When Germaine Lauzon (Manda Parent) invites her friends round to stick the discount stamps she has won into the relevant books, the evening degenerates into mutual back-stabbing and theft. Hosanna (Jean Archambault) is humiliated when he turns up to a special night at the club chez Sandra dressed as Cleopatra, only to discover that his friends/enemies have outdone him and done the same. Finally, the waitress Lise Paquette (Frédérique Collin) dies from an illegal abortion.

The film portrays alienation and defeat but also some solidarity and defiance: the duchesse tries to warn Hosanna, the lesbian waitress Hélène lambasts the assembled conspirators. The traditional nuclear family is demolished and the possibility of an alternative, extended non-biological family is hinted at. As Tom Waugh points out, the real setting of the film is 1965, therefore pre-Stonewall, devoid of any sense of a lesbian and gay political identity and not without an attitude of self-loathing. Instead, the lot of Tremblay's waitresses, housewives, drag queens, and lesbians is daringly attributed to economic, sexual, and also national alienations. The marginals of east Montreal are therefore not only to be included in the national community, they actually symbolize it in its unfulfilled truths and masquerades, its internalized oppressions, its hierarchies, and also its defiances. The impact of the first performance of *Les Belles-soeurs* in 1968 was no less bound up with Tremblay's use of *joual*, the Montreal working-class dialect, full of anglicisms and slightly feminized, which was both an indicator of colonization and alienation and a vehicle for their overcoming, as a new "authenticity" was claimed in contrast to the performance in Quebec theatre of international or metropolitan French. The episode *chez* Germaine Lauzon in fact demolishes the linear notions of progress and the promises held out by the Quiet Revolution. The drag queen himself/herself is perhaps too fragile an edifice, however, on which to hang a notion of sexual and national "truth" beneath the masquerade, for what in these circumstances can that "truth" be? The whole drag performance can in any case be seen to be built around a lack, in Lacanian terms that phase in the child's development when it tries to identify itself with the mother's object of desire in order to be that object of desire, while in addition harbouring desires for her. That object is the phallus, with which the transvestite "identifies" as hidden under the mother's clothes and becomes the displacement of the phallus for her. However, that phallus represents the paternal law of symbolic castration which prevents mother-child unity, and so the whole of human subjectivity is based on a lack, a lost maternal object it is impossible to symbolize. *Il était une fois dans l'est* is perhaps the ultimate example of the minor as opposed to major configuration of Quebec nationhood, and of the universalizing as opposed to minoritizing representation of homosexuals, but it hints even that the authentic truths of sexual and national identity it postulates are in fact very provisional performances, and that this artifice is not simply a tragic function of the disempowerment of the protagonists but a fundamental aspect of contemporary culture and cultural identities. Judith Butler in *Gender Trouble* defends drag against those feminists who criticize it as degrading to women or complicit with sex-role stereotyping. Her grounds are that gender is performative (originally a linguistic term to denote a speech act that enacts a reality, such as "I pronounce you man and wife"). The implication is that identity is not a question of interiority but of an organization and coding of surfaces:

Such acts, gestures, enactments, generally construed, are *performative* in the sense that the essence or identity that they otherwise purport to express are *fabrications* manufactured and sustained through corporeal signs and other discursive means. That the gendered body is performative suggests that it has no ontological status apart from the various acts which constitute its reality. This also suggests that if that reality is fabricated as an interior essence, that very interiority is an effect and function of a decidedly public and social discourse, the public regulation of fantasy through the surface politics of the body, the gender border control that differentiates inner from outer, and so institutes the "integrity" of the subject.[35]

Drag therefore points at the mask, revealing the contingent, imitative basis of gender itself and the way in which biological sex and gender as cultural product are distinct and only falsely unified. The duchesse de Langeais, Hosanna, and the others are such tragic figures because their class and historical situations prevent them from seeing that the truth lies in the imitation and not in an essence supposedly hidden away. Thus the stunning Hélène (Denise Filiatrault), so validated when she makes her entrance chez Sandra in *Il était une fois dans l'est*, is as much an imitative play of surfaces as any of the drag queens.

Having directed *Il était une fois dans l'est* and the previous year a short, *Françoise Durocher, waitress*, based on a Tremblay script, André Brassard did the same with *Le Soleil se lève en retard* (1976), Tremblay's first full-length original screenplay. This tale of a wedding and two funerals can at first sight be located within the romance genre. Gisèle (Rita Létourneau), a thirty-year-old secretary who lives with her parents and unmarried younger sister and older brother, is frightened of becoming an old maid, especially after the wedding of her brother Louis that opens the film. She goes to a dating agency which eventually produces the timid Jacques (Yvon Deschamps) as her ideal partner. The success of this relationship coincides, however, with the deaths in a car accident of the husband and children of her elder sister Marguerite (Denise Filiatrault). As befits the negotiations of the genre,[36] the film presents the attractions and dangers of male heterosexuality from the point of view of the women (various fantasies of sexual murder and white slavery are expressed, Gisèle fends off a predator in the street), rings the changes on the ways different women cope via the gaggle of secretaries that range from the sexually assertive to the aphasic, and inscribes this within the changes in Quebec society that result in love and marriage being articulated, owing to the agency's computer, within a discourse of "science" and consumerism. As an example of (late) 1970s Quebec popular comedy, the film can be read as a corrective to the male comedies of sexual potency from the beginning of the decade.

However, the film is relevant for the representation of homosexuality because Gisèle's quest is overlaid with a certain denaturalization of heterosexuality and the family through the comic portrayal of institutions and rituals (marriage, funerals, courtship: Jacques first meets her at the chapel of rest) and a play with identification and spectatorship which surprisingly works both to centre and decentre Gisèle's quest. The film makes clear that it is social pressure which is her prime motivation. A young gay actor chats her up on the Metro, and she encounters him again as he argues with his boyfriend. On several occasions Gisèle and Jacques walk past a rowing couple on whom the camera lingers. Just as *Il était une fois dans l'est* represented gender (and therefore transgender) performance in all its excessive masquerade, *Le Soleil se lève en retard* transplants that rhetoric and *mise en scène* to "normality" and defamiliarizes it. Claude Gai is no longer the duchesse de Langeais but dresses soberly and sticks stamps in his album at home with mother. Denise Filiatrault as Marguerite adopts a masculine voice to probe the dating agency over the phone. Above all, at the funeral of her nephews and brother-in-law, an enigmatic smile comes over Gisèle's face. (The third film for which Tremblay wrote the screenplay, Jean-Claude Lord's *Parlez-nous d'amour*, also from 1976, will be discussed in chapter 7.)

In the 1980s and 1990s, and thus following the legal changes outlined above, the representation of gay men in Quebec cinema partly followed North American and Western European evolutions in culture but also industry practice, with the construction of an international gay audience through film festivals and other forms of marketing. A certain cinema emerged which articulated a gay identity in an exportable way, that is, in which the specificities of the Quebec context could be downplayed either by audiences or film-makers. This gay identity could take the form of, for example, Tremblay's adaptation of his novel for a television film, *Le Coeur découvert* (Yves Laforce, 1987), or *L'Escorte* (Denis Langlois, 1996), in which are explored the sentimental tangles of middle-class gay citizens living in the plateau district of Montreal. The weight of the Catholic past and of Quebec history still plays a role, however, as in Anne Claire Poirier's television film about elderly gay men in a nursing home, *Salut Victor* (1991), and especially *Lilies* (John Greyson, 1996), the English-Canadian adaptation of Michel-Marc Bouchard's 1987 play *Les Feluettes*. In the latter film, however, the specificity of the Quebec context – a boys' love triangle in 1912 and its tragic *dénouement* re-enacted by prisoners in 1952 for a bishop implicated in the affair – is evacuated because of the use of English. Despite the casting of Québécois actors, such as Marcel Sabourin in the role of Bishop Bilodeau, *Lilies* becomes an (aesthetically subtle and effective) intervention in North American and world sexual politics rather than an example of Quebec national cinema.

The "New Queer Cinema" that emerged briefly in the early 1990s in the United States was, along with academic and subcultural appropriations of the word "queer," bound up with attempts to reinvigorate "gay" as cultural and political identity. A discourse of civil rights and strategy of minoritized acceptance was eschewed in favour of the "in your face" provocations of generalized perversity which, influenced by the postmodern, sought to embrace all "deviant" sexual practices and get beyond binaries such as that between homo and hetero. Films such as Greg Araki's *The Living End* and Tom Kalin's *Swoon* revealed a fascination with the relationships among homosexuality, criminality, and outlawdom, and they did so by appropriating or pastiching cultural forms such as the road or lovers-on-the-run movie or the Leopold-Loeb murder case of the 1920s. However, "queer" remains uncertain as to whether it represents simply a "funkier" form of identity politics or whether it is really a fundamental deconstructive move, decoupling identity, gender, biological sex, and desire. Gay/queer politics does not escape the distinction between major and minor constructions.

In Quebec, the historical situation was clearly distinct from that of the United States, where the AIDS crisis had combined with a conservative moral and political climate to create a public sphere highly polarized on the issue of homosexuality. As we have seen, Quebec cinema's articulation of national and sexual identities had been sporadic but, in the cases of Jutra and Brassard/Tremblay, revealing. However, their texts really addressed 1960s preoccupations rather than fully confronting the challenges of AIDS, the internationalization of consumer gay identities, and the fall and rise of Quebec nationalism 1980–95; or else, as with *Le Coeur découvert* and *L'Escorte*, they were preoccupied with psychological realism and the making and unmaking of couples. Nevertheless, Quebec theatre in the 1980s continued to foreground and explore homosexuality in relation to other identities,[37] and this is the origin of Quebec's apparent contribution to the *annus mirabilis* of New Queer Cinema, *Being at Home with Claude* (Jean Beaudin, 1992), which was able, or made, to fit nicely into that transnational cinema. René-Daniel Dubois's play, written in New York in 1984, had already had some international success, and it was this that ensured that the play's arbitrary English title was retained. Paul Burston's review in *Time Out* was typical but also telling. The film, he said, "has all the elements that made the New Queer Wave something people sat up and took notice of (sex, violence, a horny piece of stuff in the lead role), but none of the indulgences that finally put audiences off (bad acting, an overreliance on visual noise). It's a film of great contrasts, one that combines outlaw queerness with good old-fashioned romanticism, pure cinema with the compressed power of the stage."[38]

Being at Home with Claude is basically a two-hander between a police inspector (Jacques Godin) and Yves (Roy Dupuis), a male prostitute accused of murdering Claude (Jean-François Pichette). The last ninety minutes of an interrogation that has lasted all night reveal that Yves cut Claude's throat during lovemaking in order to preserve the purity of their love. André Loiselle has argued that the film, successfully and on various levels, constructs oppositions between inside and outside to render convincing and understandable Yves's act. The dazzling prologue consists of a black-and-white montage of Montreal on a hot summer's night, an urban frenzy peopled with brutal or indifferent individuals. The camera literally evades these public spaces and finds refuge at home with Claude, entering the window of his apartment and discovering the men *in flagrante*. Both Claude and Yves are seeking to separate and compartmentalize their love affair from the rest of their lives, Yves from prostitution, Claude from his political activities. The film's structure emphasizes the distinction between cinema's centrifugal tendency to throw the spectator into the world and that of theatre to bring the spectator centripetally into its own light.

However, the provocative nature of both film and play relies on these oppositions in order to transcend them. Dubois, on the one hand, is drawing on French literary antecedents to ground his drama, notably, of course, Genet, but also beyond that the treatments, post-Nietzsche, of similar acts beyond good and evil, most famously the killings in Gide's *Les Caves du Vatican* and Camus's *L'Étranger.* In the latter case, for example, Meursault's murder trial, with its positivistic quest for facts and truth, is seeking retrospectively to impose an order on events that is ultimately untenable. Going even farther back, one can talk of a tradition interested in reversing traditional categories of beauty and sainthood, for example, Baudelaire's *Les Fleurs du mal.*

This French tradition, which often associated criminality and sexual deviance, depends upon a fundamentally Catholic or Christian hegemony in order to retain its force. *Being at Home with Claude* is yet another example of a Québécois cultural artefact seeking to break with Catholicism and yet retaining its logic. As the epigraph indicates, Yves represents "a reverse sainthood." But, although the notion of sainthood has thus dramatically shifted from the seventeenth-century martyrs or John the Baptist, its terms remain the same. The interrogation of Yves produces a confession, and there is a passage from inarticulacy to articulacy. And that confession, articulated in the closing twenty-minute monologue, is the "truth" of the film. Of course, this is very ambiguous, for it is possible to argue that the process of interrogation has itself *produced* this discourse, and its verification lies only in the words Yves uses. As Michel Foucault has argued, the Catholic confession is the precursor of modern discursive practices in which the "truth" of the self is produced.[39] However, *Being at Home with*

Claude disavows the notion that Yves's "truth" is anything other than an essential verity unveiled.

That "truth" is obviously located within a social and historical context, but the film's romanticism depends on constructing this as an alterity to its subject's *amour fou* and not what constitutes it. However, the tour de force of the prologue fails to demonize the city "out there," precisely because the rapidity and heterogeneity of the montage generate "pleasure" and quote the style of rock video. One suspects that for this reason the camera is made to linger a little less momentarily on a child molester stalking his potential victim/trick. The effect of this is to tip Yves into the camp of "normality," a mode reproduced in the only other moments when the film represents the world that is other to the interrogation: the domestic scene (the inspector calls his wife), or the garden (the inspector takes a break). The inspector at the end *recognizes* Yves's discourse as one that, as "moving" as it is, can be integrated into general notions of romantic love, if not the written law. As the speaker of "truth," Yves also invites *identification*. Through the most extreme and potentially othering act imaginable, the homosexual lover is in fact socially acknowledged.

The exportability and title of *Being at Home with Claude* can be explained by its construction of this universal. Homosexuality is not here universalizing in the sense of being an issue of determinative importance for everyone (see Sedgwick above). It is universal because its radical difference is merely apparent, its excesses of behaviour merely attributable to an excess of alienation which is nonetheless universal. This is why both the play and the film place "politics" within the contingent and possibly threatening Other. The play, set in 1967 at the time of Expo, has Claude a member of the Rassemblement pour l'indépendance nationale (RIN), a precursor of the PQ. The film, set during the Montreal jazz festival in 1991 for budgetary reasons, has Claude a member of the PQ. This is not to say that the work takes an anti-nationalist line, merely to suggest that it proposes that the nationalist master narrative is unable to soak up all these issues, notably homosexuality and human intimacy. The question of homosexuality, unbound to that of the nation, must therefore be given a "home" in the widest possible sense.

However, this "home" is also extremely narrow. Unlike in *À tout prendre* where the radical difference of homosexuality was linked to a general questioning of fixed as opposed to provisional identities, *Being at Home with Claude* proposes an identity – the universal – that is both fixed and meaningless. Its solution is one of transcendence rather than the messy working through of what an engagement of sexuality, nationhood, and modernity could possibly mean. This is confirmed in

Yves's construction of the sexual act, when difference is abolished.[40] Its international distribution fits perfectly into this evasion, but it is less clear how the film might fit into "New Queer Cinema." In films by Araki, Jarman, or Kalin, queer criminality or difference is unassimilable. They do not attempt to sway mixed or straight audiences or the representatives of the law. *Being at Home with Claude* comes out of a very Québécois context, in the sense not of specific interactions of gay and national cultural and political traditions but of a specifically francophone and post-Catholic way of exploring the relationship between good and evil. However, there is one element, the "horny piece of stuff" (see Burston above), which, beyond the logic of the film, represents the inseparability of national and sexual cultural elements. Roy Dupuis in a gay role raises numerous questions of spectatorship and nationhood. For the international gay audience, of course, he fulfils the straightforward requirement of object of desire. In Quebec, his star persona is already replete with connotations of national masculinity. Jean Beaudin, having worked with him the previous year on *Les Filles de Caleb*, insisted that Dupuis have the role.[41] The connotations of his persona extend beyond the combination of soft emotion and muscular animality to embrace national iconicity, especially in relation to the image of the *coureur de bois* and his relationship to nature and the law. The combination of masculinity and body to be looked at and invested in homoerotically produces an instability for a Québécois audience which will be developed in the chapter on popular cinema.

If there is little in Quebec cinema that can approximate to the British and American New Queer Cinema of the early 1990s, a truly penetrating meditation on gender, sexuality, and nation can be found in Yves Simoneau's second feature, *Pouvoir intime* of 1986. With a script written by Simoneau (b. 1956) and one of the film's stars, Pierre Curzi, *Pouvoir intime* is basically a heist movie with intimations of the postmodern. Two corrupt officials, chief of police Meurseault (Jean-Louis Millette) and the Ministry of Justice security chief, H.B. (Yvan Ponton), recruit a thief, Théo (Jacques Godin) to steal from a security van containing money but also an incriminating document. Théo in turn recruits his teenage son, Robin (Éric Brisebois), and another professional criminal, Gildor (Pierre Curzi), who then recruits an ex-lover, Roxanne (Marie Tifo). Their action goes wrong from the start: the guard accomplice absents himself, Robin panics and shoots three guards dead, and the team have to drive the still locked van to their hideout and attempt to get the surviving guard Martial (Robert Gravel) to leave it, a struggle that takes up a third of the film. By the end, the conspirators and thieves are all dead except for Roxanne and Janvier (Jacques Lussier), Martial's gay lover whom Roxane had brought to the hideout in order to put pressure on Martial. They go on their separate ways with some of the loot.

Discussion of the film has made much of the gay element in what seems after all to be a genre movie. Gilles Thérien, in a survey of 1980s films that for him bear the mark of the failed sovereignty-association referendum, argues that it is another example of the way in which homosexuality represents an identity dead end for Quebec. Partly drawing on Jacques Lavigne's work *L'Objectivité* of 1971, Thérien argues that homosexuality involves a failure to engage with the Other. The tragedy of *Pouvoir intime* lies in the collapse of all its relations of alterity: law/not law, male/female, father/son. We are left with the Same, the gay man and the androgynous woman who then separate: "real homosexuality, false feminine, victory of the homoethical, horizontal level against the vertical hierarchy of power."[42] Homosexuality thus summarizes Quebec's intermediary situation, "in between" the self-isolation of the Duplessis era and the uncertainties of struggle and liberation "out there" in the world. Once again, Quebec is seen as peculiarly lacking a national father-figure, and this prevents it launching into an Oedipal revolt. It is "incapable of reaching the Other as Other, alterity as heterogeneous social given, and of going back to take up the question of origins, the question of identity."

Robert Schwartzwald's efficient demolition of Thérien's arguments forms part of his ongoing work on the persistence of phallocentric and homophobic discourse in Quebec nationalism,[43] Suffice it to say here that Thérien presents "Quebec" and "homosexuality" as mutually exclusive, his developmental model is highly dubious, and his notions of Same/Other seem to be as lacking in engagement with alterity as the texts he criticizes. There is no logical reason why a homosexual relationship should automatically imply a relationship to the Same rather than between two highly heterogeneous entities marked by a multiplicity of discourses of social position. Thérien's quest for identity through alterity in fact proposes a highly homogenizing mapping of binary oppositions and a master discourse of heterosexuality. As for the film, it provides no evidence that its arrangements are to be considered as anxiety-ridden impasses.

In contrast, Henry Garrity argues that *Pouvoir intime* articulates an effective subversive discourse and valorizes the critique of "vertical hierarchies of power."[44] He uses Deleuze and Guattari's *Anti-Oedipus* to analyse the thieves as the agents of a molecular defiance and dispersal of the molar structures of state power. The police are entirely absent apart from a second-long glimpse of vehicles going in the wrong direction and the sound of sirens. Those most locked in the structures of group or territorialized identity fail, those who "deterritorialize by refusing predetermined roles" succeed (including Martial who dies but prevents the principal robbery). The final, heavily symbolic scene as Roxanne and Janvier share the cash in an abandoned and burned out church – a reverse marriage ceremony in the landscape of Quebec's post-Catholicism – represents the final triumph of the individual over the macrostructures.

While this analysis is certainly on the right lines, the equation of subversion and individualism needs to be questioned. The radical decodings that occur in the film go against any Oedipal, masculinist, and individualist outlook. They involve sexual and gender roles, as well as attitudes to the state, but also the way in which desire is organized in the genre movie. *Pouvoir intime* is in this sense the most radical Quebec film since *À tout prendre*, not simply because of its sympathetic gay characters but because it questions and renders provisional all social identities while at the same time offering an enticing glimpse of possible utopian futures.

The first reason for this is the place of the film within genre cinema. As we shall see in the following two chapters, the dominant auteurist strain in Quebec cinema from the establishment of regular production in the early 1970s was accompanied by the attempt to create a "popular" cinema, but mainly through comedy and a symbiosis with television performers and performances. Unlike, obviously, in Hollywood or even in France, where comedies and *policiers* play an important role in the film industry, genre remains a marginal activity within Quebec production. It is therefore interesting to see the reworkings to which a Quebec genre film is submitted. *Pouvoir intime* refuses the pleasures and identifications of the Hollywood thriller or even heist movie, in which the emphasis is on the spectacle of male bodies tested, on the relationship to the Law (even an alternative law among the thieves), and on the preponderance of a single, privileged point of view. For Jean Larose, the film's distinctiveness is attributable to this refusal of "cinema" (whereas *Un Zoo la nuit* suffers from an excess of this and a denial of reality).[45] None of the protagonists offers a hero figure to the "spectator": they are "endowed with too many faults and human qualities to take their cinematographic task to conclusion," and they are ultimately "defeated because they were not able to defeat themselves, suppress their intimate desires and play their roles of heavies [*durs*]." He thus sees *Pouvoir intime* as "an allegory of Quebec cinema and the difficulties it has in becoming great [*grand*]," because it symbolizes the tendency in Quebec culture to privilege a debilitating interiority which prevents self-assertion.

On the contrary, *Pouvoir intime* glories in the "minor" appropriation of cinematic genre. It not only avoids the Oedipal closures described by Raymond Bellour, it actively discredits them, as father and son self-destruct and a heterosexual couple is decisively not formed and desire not reintegrated into the Law. The phallic knife and gun are rejected by Roxanne and Janvier, who are at the end deterritorialized, single people without a centre but nonetheless, as Deleuze and Guattari say of the "bachelor machines" in Kafka's work, "plugged all the more into a social field with multiple connections,"[46] one of which has been their own. While the film has relatively few point-of-view shots, they are highly multiple, a fact emphasized by the rapid cutting in the three crisis scenes when a gun is fired. If anything, it is Roxane who is privileged, in the low-angle shot that introduces her and in her role as voyeur as she learns of Martial and Janvier's relationship in the *men's* toilets. Of course, other heist movies portray the gap between the planned operation and a failed reality caused by factors such as luck or human failings, and it tends to be in comedic variations that this is attributable to the construction of gender and sexual difference (Michael Caine and Shirley Maclaine in *Gambit*, dir. R.Neame, 1966: he gets the girl in the end). Larose's use of "role" (see above) in fact suggests another fundamental way in which the film renders inoperative any "major" use of the genre, namely, the foregrounding of performance. The hideout is a theatre warehouse full of props, dummies, and masks which also recall the early panoramic shot of Roxanne and Gildor at the station, meeting beneath the cenotaph juxtaposed with the marginal, drunken down and out. Roxanne has to change her hairstyle because, for Théo, she does not look the part, she is not "feminine" enough. The crooked guard has the equivalent of stagefright. Roxanne and Janvier make their escape from the building via the stage, the empty theatre shot from their point of view. Rather than fixed and naturalized connections being made between action and masculinity, *Pouvoir intime* proclaims the provisionality in performance and repetition of all social identities, including memory if we recall the cenotaph and Martial's contemplation of the photographs of his couple (at the robbery, there is a cut from one holiday snap to the hoarding advertising the tropics behind Roxanne). In turn, it creates a distinct kind of spectatorship. On the one hand, it provides the suspense associated with the genre, in which the viewing subject is caught in the play of process and position, incoherence and fixity, and organized so by the narrative. On the other hand, it takes away any confirmation or mastery implied by that trajectory through the surprising and innovative ending, the reflexive *mise en scène*, and the ambiguous relationship between a universalizing discourse of human frailty (and by extension, Quebec's national diffidence) and the heterogeneous positions being represented. It can usefully be compared to *Reservoir Dogs*, in which Tarantino subverts or rather renews the genre by self-consciously portraying the heist and its protagonists as a play of permanent and ongoing quotations from mass culture, an approach that allows him to emphasize the ironic twists of narrative as variations on that culture. In *Pouvoir intime*, the generic raiding takes place across frontiers and languages and thus further denaturalizes the structure, pushing the reflexivity as far as emphasizing the constructed and performative provisionality of all social positions. It is because of the "major" position of Hollywood that questions of identity, which abound in Tarantino's two features, fail to gct beyond the quotation (from popular prejudice and the experience of mass culture) and thus are flattened out with all the other signifiers.

Significantly, *Pouvoir intime* does not attempt to render the surviving identities in major mode. Its representation of homosexuality is distinct, needless to say, from the abjections of *Un Zoo la nuit*, but also from the identities suggested in *Il était une fois dans l'est*, *Being at Home with Claude*, and *L'Escorte*, in that there is no suggestion that "gay" or "queer" is being asserted as a new hegemony. The film renders gay identity in minor mode as well, and this is highly relevant to its portrayal of state power and the line of flight at the end. Roxanne and Janvier are not parading completed identities from which they can oppose the system brought metaphorically to collapse in the previous scenes of the film. On the contrary, they embody deterritorialized but also non-limitative and horizontal relations, not molar entities but molecular potentialities, which break with the verticality of power which has demonstrably depended in the film on father-figures and hierarchical succession.[47] *Pouvoir intime* works with genre to produce an economy of desire and identity which is arguably more radical than that permitted by the ambiguities of "queer," with its tendency to fall back on to binary oppositions and to constitute a group. Rather, such stable cultural images of unity are rejected in favour of a process of becoming something else, a heist movie becoming a psychological and humanistic art movie (the "all too human" *pouvoir intime*) becoming a nomadic road movie, a traversing of national cinematic frontiers, groups, and couples becoming individuals becoming sets of potentialities. This is not to argue that *Pouvoir intime* completely rejects stability, but rather, in the manner of the national-allegorical tension, that that stability is always provisional and in process, consisting of forces of homogenization (the cause-and-effect linear narrative, the forms of recognition of and address to "Quebec") and heterogenization. Moreover, while it refuses to focus on a gay identity that must be included in the molar structure of the nation, it is no accident that the gay man and androgynous woman occupy the final scene, for it is their economy which offers an alternative to the Oedipalized impasses of much of Quebec cinema.

6 Auteurism after 1970

This periodization marks, like all periodizations, a transition. It is bound on one side not only by the emergence in the 1960s of a Quebec national cinema, but by the putting into place of political, cultural, and institutional arrangements which would structure in the following decades the paradigms in which that cinema and that society imagined itself and its contradictions. On the other side lies a new turn, the contemporary period, in which the ever-present exigencies of the "national" (as illustrated by the renewal of Quebec nationalism following the collapse of the Meech Lake Accord in 1990) have to contend with the inescapability of a globalized economy of cultures, identities, and cinematic practices. The work of "auteurs" in and after, roughly speaking, the time of Denys Arcand's *Le Déclin de l'empire américain* (1986) – which represented the triumphant culmination of Quebec cinematic efforts on both the national and the international level – was porously interconnected with the agendas set by new global realities, and so it is more appropriate to discuss this subject in the final chapter.

The transformations in this period can be plotted by looking at the fates of the public and private sector, most notably the relationship between the National Film Board and the changing cinematic economy. As was its purpose, the SDICC/CFDC had impelled in the early 1970s an industrialization of film production in Canada, which meant a particular fillip to Quebec production, with its head start over anglophone Canadian cinema at that time. This industrialization was accelerated by the creation in 1974 of a tax shelter for film investment, the capital-cost allowance, which was to shift support away from directors and scriptwriters to producers and thus to bigger budgets and pre-distribution and pre-sales deals with television and interests abroad. One perverse effect of this was to be the proliferation of such quintessentially "Canadian" productions as *Porky's* (Clark, 1982), a teenage sex comedy set in Florida and which is still the most successful "Canadian" film ever at the US box office. While the use of a hidden tax-shelter subsidy to produce such works led to an attempted tightening of the definitions of a "Canadian" film via a points system of participants, such developments were part of a north-south North American economic logic whereby Canada was becoming, as in the car industry, a branch-plant cinematic economy, assembling American products for the American market. (Jacques Godbout, for example, would rail against the consolidation of this policy in government proposals in 1984 but in terms that illustrate the problematic nature of the debate, arguing that the definition of "Canadianness" should lie not in the nationality of the film-makers but in the cultural "authenticity" of the product. Opposing in the familiar way "industry" and "culture," he nonetheless claimed that culture has a function, namely, the legitimizing of the state.)[1] While the injection of money into the Canadian film industry (175 features financially assisted by the CFDC from 1968 to 1979, tax-shelter money rising to $150 million by 1979) led to an increase in production and employment in the 1970s, another effect was to inflate production costs enormously and to place power in the hands of middlemen such as accountants rather than creative personnel. To an extent, Quebec cinema had the worst of both worlds by the end of the 1970s: high employment but inflated costs of production in Montreal for what were principally English-language films, and little money going to francophone production because of its smaller potential market. The effects of the 1979 oil shock and the downturn in Western economies in the early 1980s led to near catastrophe for Quebec cinematic production in the private sector. The economy of the city of Montreal had by the mid-1990s still not totally recovered from that period, unlike Quebec cinema, owing to the evolving state sector, television (Radio-Québec, founded in 1969; increasing involvement of CBC/Radio Canada in film financing; new cable subscription channels such as Super Écran specializing in first-run movies), and the proliferation of video (by 1987, income from video rentals had already equalled that from cinema tickets). After 1983, television was in the driving seat as far as decisions over film production, especially in the private sector, were concerned. That year, the CFDC became Telefilm Canada, with annual budgets of $30 million to aid film production (specifically feature films) and $50 million for television.

It is in this shifting context that state institutions, both federal and provincial, had to intervene and adapt. In Quebec, laws to promote the Quebec film industry were passed in 1975 under the Liberals and in 1983 under the PQ. The 1975 law, of which the 1983 one is a continuation, came into effect in 1977 after Lévesque's victory in November 1976 and seeks the promotion of "a cinema which reflects and develops the cultural specificity of the Québécois."[2] The most significant development was the creation of a provincial equivalent of the CFDC/Telefilm Canada, but with little money for television, first as the Institut Québécois du Cinéma (IQC), then, with the IQC retaining a research and advisory role to the minister of culture, the Société Générale du Cinéma du Québec (1983–88), fusing with other cultural activities to form the Société Générale des Industries Culturelles (SOGIC) from 1988 onwards and then SODEC. By 1994, for example, SODEC's aid program to cinema amounted to over $13 million, which included $3.4 million in production aid for feature films but also money for development, promotion, and distribution and even an $11,600 subsidy for the film magazine 24 Images.

But it was the National Film Board which remained a, if not the, cornerstone of Quebec cinema, perhaps miraculously given the political climate of the 1980s and the private sector's jealousy of its funding. The report of the Applebaum-Hébert Commission in 1982, largely written, according to Godbout, by the private film producer Denis Héroux,[3] had recommended the cessation by the board of the production and distribution of films. It was not taken up by governments but hung like a sword of Damocles over the institution. Essentially, the story of the NFB in this period, through its various budgetary crises (3.75 per cent of the total culture budget in the early 1970s, a 17 per cent cut between 1978–79 and 1979–80) is one of adaptation to the new realities. The advent of video meant a new and growing source of income, surpassing that from film sales by 1984. Its culture was dominated by that of permanent staff with the protected status of civil servants, but also included that of freelance independent film-makers employed on contract before returning to the private sector, the "revolving doors" effect. This was an option more available to francophone than anglophone film-makers, with the much larger francophone private sector in Montreal. Forced, in addition to budget restrictions, to compete for sponsorship contracts (films made for government agencies) at the end of the 1970s, the NFB in the 1980s increasingly cooperated with the private sector in co-producing and co-financing, and from 1984, under the new Conservative communications minister Marcel Masse, it developed a more market-driven approach to film-making. Its sustained production of features, roughly two francophone and two anglophone per year after the mid-1970s, was encouraged by certain critical and box-office successes in the 1970s, as we shall see.

The relevance of these developments for "auteurism" is complex. Clearly, the work of *auteurs* such as Arcand and Jutra is going to be not only influenced but to a certain extent structured by the material processes and production context in which they are working. However, those processes also structure the meaning of auteurism itself in this society and the relationship between "art" cinema and popular cinema. In turn, this debate is crucial for the notion of a national cinema, for it involves processes that are centripetal and centrifugal, simultaneously unifying and destabilizing meaning.

For example, the auteurist approach to film criticism and production, which favours the notion of a unified body of work by a director, is useful for the creation of a national artistic élite. In turn, a canon of directors can take its place in the international pantheon and, more important, can be marketed, sold, and consumed in the international networks of film festivals, film-studies courses, and arthouse cinemas. At least at the beginning of Quebec cinema in the 1960s, a semi-artisanal cinema could emerge which was not required to seek out an audience of any size, and with it a list was founded of names who were later to be recognized as constituting an *oeuvre* (Arcand, Jutra, Lefebvre) even beyond the time when they still had something to say (Carle).

However, the specificities of the Quebec situation force an interrogation of auteurism in relation to national cinema. The unit system at the NFB, along with the circumstances of the late 1950s and early 1960s when there were relatively few film-makers in Quebec, encouraged team effort as well as personal vision in what was seen by many as a collective endeavour. Because of the interchangeability of the *équipe*, it is not always easy to identify authorship, a problematic notion in any case because of the industrial nature of cinema. The case of Michel Brault demonstrates this. Director of relatively few features, his "authorship" or at least input is crucial as chief cinematographer on Perrault's *Pour la suite du monde*, Jutra's *Mon oncle Antoine*, Mankiewicz's *Le Temps d'une chasse*, and *Les Bons Débarras*, to name but a few. Moreover, the auteurist discourse in Quebec is articulated, as in other countries, against the star and studio system of Hollywood but is also *problematically* linked to France. The French New Wave is the origin of these discourses, especially but not only in francophone countries, and coincided historically with the origins of Quebec cinema itself. We saw in chapter 3, however, how the New Wave's relationship with American culture was highly ambiguous, and also how the importation of French cultural models into Quebec is a highly contested and contestable move. If "French" (and even Gaullist) modernity was a discourse available to Quebec nationalists in the 1960s and even 1970s, it nonetheless continued to contain cultural baggage to which sectors of Quebec society remained resistant. In the same way, as we shall see in the next chapter, that it is misleading to seek to map Pierre Bourdieu's descriptions of cultural stratification in 1960s France on to Quebec society then and now, it is also necessary to call into question the auteurist discourse in Quebec cinema even as it practises it itself, for the simple reason that it is a small nation which lost most of its élite in 1760, was colonized, and later used the notion of "the people" to create a new legitimacy in the modernity of the Quiet Revolution.

And so, auteurism, rather like "national cinema," is a term that must be simultaneously deployed and resisted, because its practices and procedures do precisely the same. Auteur cinema in Quebec can be "popular," even if we limit the word's definition for now as attracting a wide audience. As a leading film intellectual in the 1960s, Denys Arcand offered an agenda that prophetically announced the *film à fesses*, beginning with *Valérie* in 1968, which effectively launched popular Quebec cinema: "From the time filmmakers forget their mom in order to undress serenely their neighbour called Yvette Tremblay or Yolande Beauchemin, in the full light of day and with a well-focused wide-angle on the camera, from that time, we could envisage like Jean Renoir a cinema which is free and at the same time fiercely national. A cinema of joy and conquest."[4] When Jutra's *Mon oncle Antoine* was shown on Radio Canada in October 1973, it obtained half the francophone audience. In these circumstances, it is perhaps appropriate to talk of a *cinéma de qualité*, on (again) the French model, where *Jean de Florette* and *Manon des sources* (Berri, 1986), with their high production values, were able to articulate the national in distinct ways for home or international audiences, and to be read more as "popular" or more as "art" cinema depending on that audience and the presence or absence of subtitles. The holy grail within the multiplicity of Quebec cinema is an auteur cinema which seeks a wide audience in the nonetheless exiguous home market but which, as a vehicle for cultural prestige, is able to attract investors. For Marcel Jean, that holy grail is represented by *Le Déclin de l'empire américain*, the triumphant Quebec production which in a sense closes our period. On the other hand, that term, *cinéma de qualité*, is a highly contested one, not only because it was the "*tradition de qualité*," the studio-bound, script-led literary adaptation that was lambasted by Truffaut in 1954, but because that differentiation and articulation of international arthouse standards and national cultural discourses can fail, fall between the stools, and blandly conform to "the international aesthetic."[5]

As we shall see, Quebec has one trump card: a much more developed and, to an extent at least, culturally esteemed television culture, and much higher television audiences for indigenous fictional product than English Canada. Television has played an important role especially in Quebec popular cinema in terms of performers, but as it has become involved more centrally in the Quebec film industry, it has articulated centripetal, "national" concerns against those other centrifugal forces which form the tensions of globalization.

In the relationship between auteurism and the national, it is possible to plot the fate of a director's *oeuvre* in the vicissitudes of production described above, and also the particular take or takes a director may have or develop on the national-allegorical tension. How, for example, does the debate on identity initiated in *À tout prendre* develop in Jutra's later works?

Materially, Jutra's output is marked by the difficulty of production, to the point that he was forced to work in Toronto in the lean late 1970s and early 1980s. But a coherence can be grasped in the explorations of adolescence, and also of the national past, which characterize his most important films. Just as *À tout prendre* articulated the tension between forces of heterogeneity and homogeneity in the construction of identity, in terms of a prolonged adolescence which was in fact a source of creativity, so do Jutra's documentaries later in the decade address the world of young people: the documentaries *Comment savoir ...* (1966) (on the then innovative use of computers in teaching) and *Rouli-roulant* (1966) on skateboarding, and especially *Wow* (1969). Of his four francophone feature films of the 1970s and 1980s, two place childhood and adolescence at the centre (*Mon oncle Antoine*, with a quasi-autobiographical script by Clément Perron, 1971; and *La Dame en couleurs*, with a script by Jutra and Louise Rinfret, 1984), while the adaptation of Anne Hébert's novel *Kamouraska* (1973), co-scripted with Hébert herself, emphasizes the profoundly gendered nature of the relation between the fixed and unfixed in identity construction. Moreover, all three films situate their debates across the "before" and "after" of the Quiet Revolution, a narration of national past from the national present which leads to further ambiguities. Only *Pour le meilleur et le pire* (1975) and the anglophone productions *Surfacing* (1980) and *By Design* (1981) are set in the contemporary period, and they set out radically to question normative sexual arrangements.

Mon oncle Antoine is set at Christmastime in the 1940s in the small town of Black Lake, in the asbestos mining region of Estrie, between Montreal and the American border. Life there centres on the shop, which doubles as a funeral parlour, run by Cécile (Olivette Thibault) and Antoine (Jean Duceppe), assisted by Fernand (Jutra), their adopted "nephew" Benoît (Jacques Gagnon), and another adolescent in their employ, Carmen (Lyne Champagne). On Christmas Eve, Antoine and Benoît set out on a horsedrawn sledge through the snow to collect the body of the Poulin family's fifteen-year-old son, but on their return journey the coffin slips off and the drunken Antoine is unable to help Benoît to recover it. Back home, Benoît discovers Fernand in bed with his aunt, but he nonetheless returns with Fernand to the Poulin farm only to discover the family gathered round their son's open coffin, discovered by his father as he got back from a lumber camp for the holiday.

It is likely that the film's success as a reliable workhorse on the art-cinema circuit is due to its combination of universal and particular concerns, or to put it another way, its dovetailing of anthropological and social-historical discourses. In other words, the moment of adolescence is poised between, on the one hand, that childhood tension between polymorphousness and oedipal identification, and, on the other, that adult tension between fixity and contradiction. The order of the adult world is thus relativized, its constructions and illusions laid bare. The specificities of *Mon oncle Antoine* lie in the social and historical context of 1940s Quebec, but also in the juxtaposition with death that qualifies and indeed drives this identity quest (as in *À tout prendre*).

The consequences for the semiotics of the film lie in the use of point of view and the foregrounding of performance and an almost slapstick deployment of what we might term structuring discontinuities. It is Benoît who is the principle focalizer in the film, and this role is supplemented by voyeurism (he and the other employee, Maurice, watch the lawyer's wife Alexandrine [Monique Mercure] undress) and a more studied observation in which he watches the world of adults (beginning with the early botched funeral ceremony) with a reaction shot inviting a decoding of his expression. This structure, of observation, reaction, and (putative) action on the part of Benoît (what Deleuze would call affection-pulsion-action), forms the core of the film, ending, of course, with the freeze-frame on his face looking through the window at the Poulin house. The close-ups of Benoît's face are, however, ambiguously embedded in the film's action, because he participates for better or for worse in a network of looks (his own outward, but also on him from the community and from the spectator) that structure the present and what his own future might be. The only other bearers of the look are Fernand (in the early sequences towards Cécile and Carmen) and the community (towards Alexandrine as she makes her dramatic entrance; and towards Benoît himself: once he is invalidated by the denial of the look, following the snowball attack on the anglophone boss, and once he is validated by it, as he proudly accompanies Antoine out of town).

This play of looks invites several interpretations: an existentialist one, as Benoît momentarily and comfortingly coincides with a preordained role; a Foucauldian, as his subjectivity and that of the whole community is brought into being by a collective, internalized, panopticism. But the point is that, as an adolescent, Benoît has only a provisional future: the film is the drama of what becoming like the others would entail, as it analyses the processes which render adult life possible but also so unattractive. Thus the close-ups of Benoît link him rhetorically with both Fernand (as bearers of the look, and in the second sleigh ride) and Antoine (the cut between them in the first sleigh ride) in a problematic relationship of similarity and difference. He has the potential to become either, or neither.

That adult world observed by Benoît is predicated on performance and seduction played out in the troubling and disrupting context of death. Throughout the film a play is made of veiling and unveiling, and this has both sexual and theatrical connotations. Carmen tries on the bride's veil. The shop's nativity scene is revealed to the waiting public as a curtain is opened (and collapses in mishap). Cécile and Fernand's lovemaking behind a closed door is discovered. The ultimate unveiling, of course, is the lidless coffin of the Poulin teenager. The performativity central to identity and community is unavoidable and can mean different things. Cécile's song reinforces the community through performance but also hints at non-consummation and the unhappiness of her own marriage. The rituals of Christmas and church are similarly exposed, the former scene re-enacted as the Poulin family gather round not a manger but their son's coffin. Antoine's performance of masculine bravado is revealed under the influence of drink to be a mere show covering up his own fear of death and corpses. The inevitability of performance implies ambivalent, provisional identities that in everyday life are covered up. It is thus difficult to see Benoît's destiny as a linear one leading through revolt to new certainties. Any "certainties" are bound to be similarly provisional and prone to disruption. The figure for this in the early part of the film is the barrel of nails (used by Antoine for the coffins), delivered to the shop but constantly in the way: finally it is Carmen who stumbles over it, cutting short the boys' observation of Alexandrine. Not only does the barrel neatly structure the film, announcing the lost coffin (Madame Poulin also stumbles on her way back home where her son's illness is announced), it also serves to disrupt the continuous and coherent space constructed by the film's classical *mise en scène.*

However, attempts have been made to appropriate *Mon oncle Antoine* for a grand narrative of the emergence of a more mature and finished Quebec identity than that portrayed in the film. For Weinmann in *Cinéma de l'imaginaire québécois*, the film's overthrowing of certainties connected to the church, and Antoine's final rejection of his adoptive parents and, by implication, wider authority, make it fit into his notion of the Quebec family romance. (The other "absent" father is Jos Poulin, who abandons his work for the *Anglais*'s mine to spend winter in the lumber camps and is thus a twentieth-century equivalent of the *coureur de bois*.) Again, however, Weinmann's one-to-one allegories, with Benoît gazing on the possibility of the death of Quebec itself in the shape of a corpse his own age, recreate the authority and authoritativeness which Benoît and the film are supposedly calling into question. For Ian Lockerbie, the final scene also warns of the death of the nation, but, for him, Benoît is now in a position to act, and this "founding work of Quebec cinema" establishes him as a precursor of the Quiet Revolution and of modern Quebec nationalism.[6]

It is beyond question that *Mon oncle Antoine* mobilizes collective, national discourses as well as individual and "universal" ones. The very opening scene is quite unusual in Quebec cinema: it portrays a confrontation across the linguistic dividing-line, with Jos Poulin walking out on his anglophone boss. Moreover, the setting inevitably recalls the key strike at Asbestos in 1949, which became a cause célèbre for modernizing intellectuals against the Duplessis regime and has been inserted into a whole linear and teleological history of Quebec culminating in the Quiet Revolution. However, it is difficult to ascribe to Benoît any of that linearity (despite the snowball incident), since the technocratic discourse is absent from the film, and in any case it could lead to Trudeau's federalism as much as Lévesque's nationalism (Trudeau supported the strike and published a book about it in 1956, *La Grève de l'amiante. Une étape de la révolution industrielle au Québec.*) As Jocelyn Létourneau has pointed out,[7] this appropriation of the Asbestos Strike is a highly discursive (and thus *performative*) act, as provisional as any of the social half-solutions in the film. In a sense, Lockerbie is employing the same discursive procedure for *Mon oncle Antoine* as the 1960s technocracy did for the strike, with a little bit of Oedipus added. For he deploys totalizing assumptions about age and gender roles. Fathers have again failed; Jos Poulin is a "révolté impuissant/impotent rebel." This neglects the fact that the *coureur de bois* figure offers a potentially different sexual and racial economy from Quebec familial discourse. Similarly, the coupling of Cécile and Fernand could be read as liberating – the older woman gets herself a younger lover – but, for Lockerbie, it represents "the regressive character of a relationship in which the age difference is shocking." (This reading is influenced by Benoît's point of view, but is this to do with age gap or the disruption of expected "family" behaviour?) More severely still, Weinmann sees Cécile as a "guidoune/whore," in Benoît's eyes. Similarly, whereas Lockerbie sees Antoine's fear as "neurotic" but "natural" for an adolescent, it is possible to see here a vindication of the film's extension of adolescence's denaturalizing gaze to the whole of this society of appearances.

It is clear that any reading of the film must take place across the caesura of the Quiet Revolution and its aftermath. However, instead of a linear, totalizing reading, that relationship between past and present must partake of the national-allegorical tension. The past is both similar (the origins or previous incarnation of "us," "our" ancestors) and different (its ignorance and poverty, infant mortality), often undecidably so (the status of the Québécois). The result is a transtemporality, a relatedness, a to-ing and fro-ing between temporal periods and cultural/political epochs. We shall discuss this further in relation to Jutra's next film, *Kamouraska*. Suffice it to say here that *Mon oncle Antoine* challenges both the authority structures of the Duplessis era and a comfortably installed identity of self and nation. It does this not by debunking identity and community but by emphasizing their provisionality and lack of groundedness, their "lies" but also the "truths" they can offer in snatches. There is the pleasure of community in the film, notably when the announcement of the wedding is celebrated in the shop, but that, too, is balanced by the bleakness of the marriages represented, its commercial and commodified dimension, and, of course, the proximity of death. Similar comments might be made of Benoît's burgeoning sexuality (the emphasis in the film on close-ups of his face ambiguously eroticizes him as much as the women he looks at). The film thus recalls Renoir in its historical construction of a community, the "illusions," "grand" or not so grand, by which it lives, and the way in which "theatre" is extended to the whole of social relations. Like Renoir, Jutra masterfully conveys a sense of place, whether of the town or the family shop, and choreographs his characters within it. However, more bleakly than in Renoir, the relation between inside and outside is marked not by depth of field emphasizing the interconnectedness of social and spatial relations (as in the shots through the windows in *Le Crime de Monsieur Lange*, or the beckoning landscapes in the final part of *La Grande Illusion*), but by the all-pervasiveness of performance in identity construction, the corollary of which is death.

The success of *Mon oncle Antoine* led to the biggest film budget of that time ($750,000): a literary adaptation, co-produced with France, *Kamouraska* (1973). Anne Hébert's novel, originally published in 1970, recounts the story of Elisabeth d'Aulnières and her marriage in the 1840s to Antoine de Tassy, *seigneur* of Kamouraska, who turns out to be drunken, violent, and abusive. She takes a lover, Dr George Nelson, an

Empire loyalist, and together they conspire to kill Antoine. But after the murder Nelson flees to the United States and Elisabeth is put on trial. She is freed, but in effect a new "sentence" begins, with her marriage to the respectable Quebec City bourgeois, Jérôme Rolland. However, this *fabula* (chronological story) of the novel gives way to the complexities of its narrational arrangements, the *syuzhet*. Indeed, telling and remembering are the fundamental problems of the novel, as the *fabula* is recounted from Elisabeth's position as she sits up awaiting Jérôme's death twenty years after the events, which she recalls in a confused, guilt-ridden, and half-drugged state. (The film exists in two versions: a 124-minute theatrically released version from the 1970s; and a 173-minute video re-edited by Jutra for television in 1983.)

Clearly, there is much potential for reading the film *Kamouraska* as Quebec's great national romance. But, instead of a foundational fiction that legitimates the nation-family, *Kamouraska* portrays the impossibility of romance in the colonized space of French Canada. In the aftermath of the defeat of the Patriotes' Rebellion in 1837–38, it depicts a Catholic society that stifles women, a Law that is literally in English (the trial), decadent aristocratic remnants, and an ultimately unreliable lover who possesses the freedom that Elisabeth ("that damned woman") lacks. Such a reading would require a linear, progressive relationship between that past and this present, that of the mature Quebec of the Quiet Revolution and its aftermath.

Kamouraska resembles *Maria Chapdelaine* in these and other respects such as landscape and the "national," but Hébert and Jutra's project can partly be read as an attempt to problematize some of the linear spatial and temporal readings to which that work has been put. Unlike in *Maria Chapdelaine*, the myths of heterosexual romance and of national survival are to be found wanting, and as in *Les Bons Débarras* the diabolical comes to be the preferred figuring of feminine (dis)empowerment. The fact it is a co-production with France means that none of the characters (in the theatrical version) speaks with a marked Québécois accent, with the possible exception of the one lower-class character, the maid and childhood friend Aurélie (Suzie Baillargeon), so that the audible "inscape" fails to participate in the production of nationhood. The casting of Philippe Léotard as Antoine, while he is arguably too "attractive" for the role, does enable his decadence to be tarred with the feudal remnants of "Frenchness" (although a reading is also possible which sees him as very "Canadien" in his powerlessness: Elisabeth does comment early in the relationship that he is very "unhappy," and it is clear that his stern mother is the one who fulfils the patriarchal role both before and after his death). Geneviève Bujold as Elisabeth is cast not only for her undoubted talent but also as, at that time, the only Québécois "star" on the international and therefore co-production circuit. Above all, the problematizing of narration places the novel in traditions of European modernism themselves influenced by cinema (Anne Hébert had been living in Paris since the 1950s, before which she had written scripts for NFB documentaries). In the film, the fragmentation of Elisabeth's narration and the fragments of her story are translated into an extensive use of flashback, especially temporal cutting in the same scene, shorn of a voice-over narration but partaking of what Deleuze via Bergson calls "the memory-image." However, the tension in the film is between what we might call a will to chronology, in which the memory-image actualizes a former past in a way that can be reinserted into a cause-and-effect narrative, and a time-image in which actual and virtual ("pure memory," where the past is preserved in itself) are indiscernible. The novel more radically disrupts and even renders impossible the process of re-membering. As Bergson and Deleuze argue, "not being able to remember" is often more significant than remembering, because then the present image "rather enters into relation with genuinely virtual elements, feelings of *déjà vu* or past 'in general' ... dream-images ... fantasies or theatre scenes."[8]

The film uses the techniques of basically 1950s and 1960s art cinema to dislocate the relationship between landscape and inscape, between the workings of individual and collective memory and the physicalities which purport to be continuous and given. For nothing is given in *Kamouraska,* and this is basically because of the relationship between gender and history. As we shall see in chapter 8, Quebec women's cinema set out to challenge many of the totalizing linearities of Quiet Revolution hegemony, and *Kamouraska* to an extent participates in that early 1970s moment. The fate of a woman is for the first time at the centre of a Jutra film, but this seems strikingly appropriate for the *cinéaste* of provisionality and performance. Elisabeth's negative view of motherhood, despite her numerous children, means that she rejects the filiation on which the national family, particularly one called into being by the *revanche des berceaux,* depends. Benoît in *Mon oncle Antoine* and Elisabeth here are made to share the motif of gazing through windows, one to contemplate a problematic future, one a problematic past. That image connotes not past or future plenitudes but the dichotomous relationship between the spatial and the temporal/subjective which maps the arbitrary gender roles Elisabeth at some points in the film (the hunt scene) challenges. When Elisabeth looks out of the window, in fact she looks in. This means that the spatiality in the film becomes part of an undecidability of identity which is basically temporal, in that it both sets up boundaries and narratives and then problematizes them: Sorel and Kamouraska (Elisabeth in the first, the murder in the second, linked by Elisabeth's litany of the place names linking them), Canada and the United States, Canada and Europe (the bourgeoisie's desperate imitation of European culture in this colonized and "primitive" space), and, because of the film's co-production, a (this time) highly appropriate hovering between Quebec and France. Above all, it is that undecidable relation between the *énonciation* of the moment in time of the narration (the relationship between the film's "omniscient" narrating camera and the implied spectator) and the *énoncé* of the events being narrated. What marks out *Kamouraska* as an art movie rather than a "popular" representation of the past is the fact that ambiguity is already self-consciously constructed into the narration. Bhabha, of course, wishes to deconstruct the totalities of "nationness" via an engagement with its literal minorities and the renegotiation of historical and contemporary narratives. Arguably, this procedure is particularly appropriate for Quebec's specific history as simultaneously colonizing, colonized, and post-colonial, "major" and "minor," for Hébert's investigation of women's historical experience and problems of representation, and for Jutra's sensitivity both to the non-linear provisionality of identity and to the persistence of ideas of "home":

Minority discourse acknowledges the status of national culture – and the people – as a contentious, performative space of the perplexity of the living in the midst of the pedagogical representations of the fullness of life. Now there is no reason to believe that such marks of difference ... cannot inscribe a "history" of the people or become the gathering points of political solidarity. They will not, however, celebrate the monumentality of historicist memory, the sociological solidity or totality of society, or the homogeneity of cultural experience.[9]

Jutra's articulation of these problems in relation to gender, sexuality, and childhood can be seen in his later films. *Pour le meilleur et pour le pire* (1975), whose mixed critical reception at the time did nothing to help Jutra's career, is daring in both its form and its content. It condenses over a twenty-four-hour period four seasons and seventeen years of married life of an advertising executive, Bernard (Jutra) and his wife Hélène (Monique Miller). Her time is divided between domestic work and visits to a divorced, "liberated" neighbour (Monique Mercure). Bernard leaves for work, is fired for being late, and, obsessed with the notion of his wife's infidelity, invites to dinner a man he supposes to be her lover. After that fiasco, the couple confront each other with recriminations and at one point a gun. Their now late-teenage daughter leaves with her boyfriend, never to return. Bernard and Hélène retire to bed, resigned to endure each other.

Jutra's break with the realist tradition of Quebec and Canadian cinema is as decisive here as in *À tout prendre*. In addition, the devastating satire of the institution of marriage, present in his previous two films, was still relatively rare in Quebec cultural production. Marriage is seen as particularly damaging to the woman's mental health, irrelevant to the child, who develops autonomously from the adults as in other Jutra films, and in general productive of misery all around. Moreover, this social comment is hitched to an innovative temporal structure. Whereas *Kamouraska* was preoccupied with the (doomed) attempt to unify sheets of past time in a coherent, teleological memory-image, the time of *Pour le meilleur et pour le pire* is contracted in a way that renders indiscernible the division between past, present, and future. Welles's *Citizen Kane* had portrayed a decaying marriage through a montage of newsreel-like clips which represented a succession of "former presents" akin to the imperfect tense in French or the habitual past in English. If anything, it is the future, not the past, that gives a perspective to the events in Jutra's film, but that future is one of repetition in the most negative sense, as the outcome will be death ("till death us do part"). It is as if each moment of their relationship contained the past, present, and future of Bernard and Hélène. This is another element in the film, along with the mutual torment, which evokes Sartre's play *Huis Clos*, set, of course, in a hell, in an afterlife (Bernard: "I see Hell but the Hell you see is better than seeing nothing").[10]

The one point in the film in which communication, dialogue, and solidarity seem possible is found in those pre-climactic scenes which evoke the shared memory of a film musical. But, whereas in musicals the transition from "normal" action to song and dance signals entry into another world or worlds, and thus a liberating movement in which characters are depersonalized and swept into a generalized *mouvement de monde*, in *Pour le meilleur et pour le pire* the couple's performance is one that re-enacts in a different form the movements, choreography, and sentiments of their stifling existence.[11] (Hélène: "We can't change what we think but we can change the way of saying it.") Prompted first by the "happy" memory from early in their marriage of going to see in New York *Rio Rita* (Simon, 1942), a musical starring Kathryn Grayson but also that dysfunctional "couple" Abbott and Costello and with a wartime plot, Bernard and Hélène proceed to recite names of stars, reminisce briefly in English, but then waltz around singing lyrics about mutual detestation and sexual repulsion. This "dancing" ends with

Bernard's "orgasm" as they clutch each other. Jutra was to continue his interest in sexual politics in the films he made in Toronto: an adaptation of Margaret Atwood's novel *Surfacing* (1980), and a film about a lesbian couple seeking to have children, *By Design* (1981), which happily denaturalizes received perceptions of masculinity, femininity, heterosexuality, and homosexuality.

La Dame en couleurs (1984) is set in the 1950s in a children's home, doubling as a mental asylum, run by the church. Opening with a new batch of arrivals that reproduces the spectator's point of view, it evokes the strict regime ("licence to circulate" is needed) and generalized sexual repression. The fourteen-year-old Agnès (Charlotte Laurier, Manon in *Les Bons Débarras*) represents temptation for her tutor, sister Gertrude (Paule Baillargeon), who ends up walking out of the institution and the church. This world is then bypassed by the children as they discover a secret access to the institution's cellar, where they seek to create an alternative domain with the help of an adult epileptic painter, Barbouilleux (Gilles Renaud, Cuirette in *Il était une fois dans l'est*: the role was to be played by Jutra himself). The enterprise fails, brought on by conflicts with Barbouilleux and an escape attempt, abortive for most of the kids. A coda in the "present" has the "adult" Agnès, having refused to join another child in escape, now one of the mental patients. Again, the film could be read in linear fashion to "justify" the Quiet Revolution and demonize the Duplessis era, with consumption (the kids raid the cellar's provisions, including its narcotics), art and sexuality breaking loose in the alternate subterranean domain. However, just as in *Kamouraska* the feminine position is used to disrupt that linearity and the costume drama to inhabit the split in national subjectivity, so do the kids in *La Dame en couleurs* contradict "national" ideas of maturity and plenitude, and the representation of the past impels a problematic relationship to the present. Childhood and adolescence are confronted with the grids of authority imposed by the state: in a recollection of the *coureur de bois* tradition, the kids in the subterranean passageways ask, "Who'll be the Indian chief?" As we saw in the analysis of some of the *contes pour tous* films, Western civilization depends on the suppression of the child within. Jutra's "home" portrays that hierarchy of child and adult in the blurring of the distinction between the two (the kids are "enterprising," the patients are like children). The subterranean cultural resistance, however, ends in failure, and the contemporary coda, seen by some critics as unnecessarily pessimistic,[12] in fact hurls the critique beyond that of a mere period in Quebec's history or even a problematization of the similarity/difference of past/present. The onset of Jutra's degenerative mental illness, which eventually drove him to suicide, adds an extra dimension to the film. "We don't think the same way when we're small as when we're big," asserts Barbouilleux in the final confrontation with the children, but "for a grown-up it's much more difficult." Partly perhaps because of the film's uneven plotting, a fruitful alliance is not and cannot be built between the alienated artist and childhood. Is it Jutra himself talking as he tells the kids in the cellar, "There's no one on my side, neither here or up there"?

While Denys Arcand is best known outside Quebec for the highly exportable films he made from the late 1980s onwards, he had already made before then four feature-length fictions and three feature-length documentaries. In contrast to Jutra, his films are informed less by autobiographical self-consciousness than by a profound sense of Quebec history. Quite apart from certain differences in class (Arcand's father was a *marin-pilote* in the village of Deschambault near Quebec City, although his family were imbued with middle-class culture)[13] and sexuality, the ten-year age difference is telling. Whereas Jutra was already a sceptical thirty-two-year-old when he made À *tout prendre*, Arcand is very much a child of the Quiet Revolution, a member of that generation which was in its twenties in 1968. All his films are informed by the need to take account of the socio-political possibilities and limitations of that decade and its protagonists, and this includes an engagement with those elements in Quebec society which are of long duration, notably Catholicism. But although Arcand is more "social" than Jutra, he and his films are similarly reluctant to embrace explicitly political points of view founded on positivity rather than critique. As he insisted in a 1989 interview, any militant activity in his life has been restricted to membership of the Parti Québécois during the two years preceding its 1976 election victory.[14] In the interviews with Michel Coulombe, he even goes as far as to say that today he has no interest in politics, including the issue of Quebec independence.[15] Indeed, Arcand's "pessimism" can be understood more clearly in the comparison with Jutra, for whom the provisionalities of identity and choice could, as well as affording a critical standpoint, themselves be made into sources of pleasure and art.

After the student film *Seul ou avec d'autres* in 1962, Arcand had joined the NFB, where in the mid-1960s he made three short historical documentaries: *Champlain* (1964), *Les Montréalistes* (1965), and *La Route de l'Ouest* (1965). These are already notable for his use of parallel editing to accentuate contrast and conflict, and for his interest in history, which he had studied at university. For example, the second film plays on the contrast between the religious origin of the foundation of Montreal and its later commercial and military role, emphasized by a sequence featuring a modern-day fashion shoot in the Jeanne Mance

Museum (Mance being one of the city's founders along with de Maisonneuve).[16] Despite his closeness to the *Parti pris* group, Arcand took an approach that was therefore less influenced by *le direct* than by a historicizing *longue durée* which in its use of often ironic counterpoint challenged the orthodoxies of the NFB's official discourse, the techno-cratizing confidence of the Quiet Revolution, and even the optimistic teleologies of Marxism and socialism.

His 1970 feature-length documentary (running-time 159 minutes), *On est au coton*, is one of the great *causes célebres* of Quebec cinema. Its title refers to its subject matter, the textile industry in Quebec, the province's biggest employer at the time, but is also a Quebec idiom meaning "we're fed up." The original idea had been a documentary on the Quiet Revolution technocrats who would be confronted with the impossibility of resolving the crisis of this industry in terminal decline. The film parallels the working day of a textile worker and an employer, features the harsh working conditions and illnesses the work provokes, and adds the historical perspective of past strikes. Its scathing judg-ments led it to being banned from distribution (on the grounds of bias and factual inaccuracies)[17] by Sydney Newman, then NFB com-missioner (it was not to be shown officially until 1977), but it met hos-tility, too, from many on the Left who disliked its refusal to question the workers' resignation. Arcand's next feature-length documentary, *Québec: Duplessis et après* ... (1972), and his last for the NFB, engages more closely with politics and political discourse in Quebec, portraying the 1970 provincial campaign in several constituencies fought over by various minor players within Quebec's political class. The discourses portrayed are compared to those of previous epochs, most notably to Maurice Duplessis's *Catéchisme des électeurs* of 1936, which, in a manner similar to that of contemporary candidates including those of the new PQ, argued for Quebec's economic liberation. But, if Duplessis's *grande noirceur* hangs over the film and Arcand's reading of the electoral campaign, so do Lord Durham's dismissal of the "credulous" French Canadians in 1838 and, ultimately, the conquest of 1759.

Arcand's critical-historical realism depends on a subtle relationship between scepticism and belief that ties in interestingly with this book's exploration of Quebec national identity as in-between assertion and dispersal, or major and minor discourses. His intellectual mentor here was the historian Maurice Séguin, whose view, cited by Arcand in 1987, was that

the Québécois were both too numerous and too well organized inside a fron-tier to fear disappearing in the short term, but were at the same time not pow-erful enough, not rich enough and not organized enough to hope to attain independence and form a country. So for the foreseeable future we were condemned to a sort of eternal mediocrity, oscillating between disappearance and assertion, falling between two stools. I can't see anything at present which would allow me to contradict this statement and I find that very unsettling.[18]

The question remains, however, what kind of specifically cinematic practice for such a view? While Arcand's distance from some of the nationalist and progressive orthodoxies of the 1960s partly announces the general problematics of modernity and post-modernity to be found in *Le Déclin de l'empire américain* and *Jésus de Montréal* (1989), it is nonetheless informative to examine the three very different cinematic explorations to be found in his fictional films of the 1970s.

La Maudite Galette (1972) is a piece of genre cinema in determinedly minor mode. Made in the private sector (Jean Pierre Lefebvre's Cinak) from a script by the novelist Jacques Benoît, the film recounts a tale of alienation, criminality, and family betrayal among the marginalized working class of modern, North American, transforming Montreal. Berthe (Luce Guilbeault) and her scrapdealer husband Roland (René Caron) go to murder their rich uncle Arthur (J. Léo Gagnon) in his house for money ("la galette"), but Roland and an accomplice are shot dead by hired man and lodger Ernest (Marcel Sabourin), who had overheard and followed them, and one accomplice is killed by Berthe by mistake. Ernest escapes with the loot and Berthe, having set fire to the house and disposed of the tortured uncle's body. Having made love to Berthe but then left her for dead in a hotel room, Ernest avoids local gangsters and presents the money (and a gift of jelly beans) to his elderly impoverished parents. However, Berthe reappears and they shoot each other dead. The last shot of the film has the parents setting off for Florida in a convertible.

Unlike *Pouvoir intime*, *La Maudite Galette* disrupts the "B" movie generic expectations through an unrelenting moral abjection which is depicted as part of a wider social and cultural context that is very Québécois, and not only in the language. The familiar trademark of Arcand's parallel montage yields, in this his first fictional feature, to the pro-filmic, in a deep-focus *mise en scène* which figures crucifixes in the domestic interiors of the older characters, kitsch popular taste (a pastel of ballerinas) in the home of Berthe and Roland, and advertising hoardings in the urban landscape that is traversed. The malaise produced by the lost moral centre and rampant materialism is not far removed from *Le Déclin*. The role of Berthe as dominating wife cannot produce in reverse reaction a coherent Oedipal or phallic position for a male protagonist. In any case, Marcel Sabourin's screen persona, whether as Abel in *Il ne faut pas mourir pour ça*, the cuckolded husband in *Deux femmes en or* (Fournier, 1970), or the childlike extraterrestrial in *Le Martien de Noël*, is as far removed from the male action hero as one can imagine; hence the deliberate incongruity of his metamorphoses in this film from simpleton to gun-toter to devoted son (linked, however, by his impassivity). Actions embarked upon lead to misunderstandings, mistakes, death; hence the black humour in the scene at Arthur's house. Even the cry of revolt that Arcand refers to in connection with the film (he links it to the dead ends of Quebec politics in the early 1970s, and to the violent despair of the FLQ)[19] is too affirmative a position from which to read it, for spectatorial distance is created and sustained throughout by the eschewal of identification (shifting central protagonists) and above all by the use of long takes, especially in the scene at Berthe and Roland's house. Arcand's approach is in this sense Godardian, taking genre conventions and then assaulting the points of view and rational chains of cause and effect that characterize bourgeois narrative.

Réjeanne Padovani, made at Cinak the following year but with a bigger budget thanks to CFDC money, draws on other cinematic and cultural references but continues the dark portrayal of contemporary Quebec society. Indeed, this critique is heightened by the long perspectives gained from Buñuel, Renoir, Rosi, opera, and Tacitus. Vincent Padovani (Jean Lajeunesse), contractor for an urban motorway and a gang boss, is entertaining at home those members of the city elite close to the project, the mayor (René Caron), the minister of public works (J.-Léo Gagnon), his two assistants (Jean Pierre Lefebvre and Roger Le Bel), and their wives. Their attendants, servants, and barmaids entertain themselves in the basement. This bourgeois social affair eventually reveals its violent underside: two journalists arrive and are roughed up; Padovani's men beat up the organizers of a demonstration against the project and ransack their headquarters; and Réjeanne Padovani (Luce Guilbeault), Vincent's ex-wife who had been banished to the United States after leaving him for the son of a rival Jewish gang, returns to claim her children, only to be murdered and her body buried in concrete as part of the motorway which is opened with ceremony at the end of the film.

This devastating critique of contemporary Quebec society captures some of the atmosphere of Montreal in between the October crisis and the first Parti Québécois government, between Expo and the Olympics, when the long-serving mayor Jean Drapeau was embarking on grandiose urban development in cahoots with land speculators and developers. Arcand's project was also to represent in fiction some of the shenanigans observed during the 1970 electoral campaign for *Québec: Duplessis et après ...*, when Union Nationale candidates were visibly enmeshed with the underworld.[20] However, he also wished to avoid making a film *à clef* in which political problems could be reduced to mere questions of personnel.[21]

As Gene Walz has pointed out,[22] comparisons with Renoir's *La Règle du jeu* (1939) are compelling. In both films, the setting of an isolated grand house outside which violence is wrought, the multiple sexual infidelity, the portrayal of masters and servants, the presence of an outsider, all work to produce a drama of modern ethical crisis. Certain details in *Réjeanne Padovani* self-consciously invoke the earlier film, for example, the greenhouse in which Réjeanne pleads for her life recalls that in which Jurieu died. However, whereas Renoir in *La Règle du jeu* was to a certain extent leaving behind the more particular and concrete *engagements* within French politics that had characterized the period from *Le Crime de Monsieur Lange* (1935) to *La Marseillaise* (1937) and *La Bête humaine* (1938) in favour of the critique of a whole civilization, Arcand in *Réjeanne Padovani* makes coexist long-term and short-term historical contexts and is much more explicit about political and economic power and their imbrications. As we have seen, he was approaching the sole period of his life in which he was a card-carrying member of a political organization. The film not only portrays recognizable characters from contemporary Montreal, it also represents a dissident, if defeated, element in society. Moreover, the film works gradually to centre on intermediate characters who are both dependent upon and share in the power and wealth of those at the top. These are Padovani's secretary Caron (Lefebvre) and his wife Hélène (Frédérique Collin), the lawyer Desaulniers (Le Bel), and Di Muro (Pierre Thériault). They all lucidly prosecute their own agendas of personal advancement (Hélène ends the film as Padovani's new mistress) but in that lucidity display a knowledge of the system which the other characters are unwilling, or do not need, to make explicit. To this intermediate group may be added Réjeanne herself. The build-up to her death is based on a two-shot with the henchman Ferrara (Gabriel Arcand) in which victim and killer are framed in the point of view of the other, but where hers dominates because of the slow reverse-tracking shot as she backs away. These centerings of certain characters place the spectator in positions that are uncomfortable because of their incapacity to alter the power structures represented.

The other obvious intertext is Buñuel's *Le Charme discret de la bourgeoisie* released the previous year, with its demolition of bourgeois manners around the ritual of the dinner party. In that film, the upstairs-downstairs configuration is momentarily broken when a chauffeur is invited in to have a drink with the guests and then sent back out, only to have his drinking gestures analysed and invalidated by the bourgeois. Buñuel's grotesque and excessive humour with its anarchic potential have no place in the universe of Arcand's film. The main scene in which the hierarchical space is undermined has been analysed in some detail by Pascal Bonitzer of *Cahiers du cinéma*.[23] When Mme Stella Desaulniers (Margot MacKinnon) gets up to sing an aria from Gluck's *Orpheus and Eurydice* (a piece repeated over the film's concluding shots of urban demolition and construction), a series of shots shows the reactions of other guests and then, in a close-up equivalent to the preceding shot of Desaulniers, of the barmaid Micheline (Guylène Lefort). Arcand's analogy of social and material (scenographic) space has here produced a momentary crisis or scar, exacerbated by the fact that the shared or even transcendent appeal of opera might now smuggle *value* into this universe as opposed to merely restating legitimate taste and bourgeois hypocrisy. However, the scar is healed when it becomes apparent that Micheline was serving the minister champagne. The same shot of her is transformed, without an editing cut, when the camera pans down to the minister eating like a pig, oblivious to the music. The final images contrast the long shots of the guests comfortably seated and the others crammed onto the landing leading to the basement. As with the elimination of Réjeanne herself, order is restored, political and spatial power structures maintained.

Gina (1975) was Arcand's last fictional feature for eight years, and in very hybrid manner it engages with documentary and fictional-spectacular ways of making political cinema (Its bigger budget – at $360,000 more than twice that of his previous two features – was enabled by the Carle-Lamy production company.) This hybridity is mapped on to a continuing use of diagrammatic parallelism between three groups. A team from the "Office national du cinéma" headed by the director (Gabriel Arcand) sets off for Louiseville to make a documentary about the textile factory. Gina (Céline Lomez), a striptease artist, is also sent there to perform by the violent male gang who employ her. In obvious references to the still banned *On est au coton*, the director attempts to manipulate the employers (dressing in a suit, speaking English, shaking off the public-relations man) in order to portray the "truth" of the factory. In particular they interview a worker, Dolorès (Frédérique Collin). Gina is staying at the same hotel and comes into conflict with the local snowmobile gang by beating them at pool (she is on the side of the film-makers) and by besting them at banter when she performs her act. That night she is gang-raped by them in her hotel room, while the sound recordist reads obliviously in the next room. The rest of the film is the story of her revenge. With the help of her employers, the gang is wiped out in a spectacular pursuit and bloodbath. In the end, Gina leaves for Mexico, Dolorès is married, and the director, his documentary cancelled, is last seen shooting a rather tawdry-looking melodrama in Montreal.

Parallelisms of form map those of content: black and white 16 mm. documentary interviews of Dolorès speaking the same words as a worker in *On est au coton* are edited into the spectacle of Gina's strip-tease. But Arcand's procedure innovates in this film: social contradiction is articulated across women's bodies, raising a whole sexual political agenda largely absent from his previous films. Gina's strip-tease is filmed both glamorously (unlike that of Luce Guilbeault in *Le Temps d'une chasse*) but also from multiple, differently motivated points of view. There are shots of Gina and the audience, creating a voyeurism on the voyeurs, as well as of the snowmobile gang, their woman member, Carole, teased about Gina's slim figure, the film-makers (one of whom retires to bed in the middle of the act), and most notably Dolorès. In her intervention, she ambiguously sets out the exploitative nature of her work but also the snatches of autonomy it allows her. The two women had been framed in a shot preceding the show, making themselves up in the mirror of the ladies' toilets and discussing their relative incomes (Gina earns five times more). This shot sets up a complex set of similarities and differences between their conditions, but it is not just about the "knowledge" the spectator can extract from their encounter. The shot is the problematic suture of the film, in that it sets up a precarious cinematic relationship between what Denis Bellemare calls "the fantasm of the imaginary body of the dancer and ... a real documented body of the worker."[24] Problematically, the rape of Gina comes also to stand for other, collective structures of domination. It is immediately followed by Dolorès's account of the strikes of 1952 when police fired on the workers; and, in a gesture which announces the generic excess which will come to overwhelm all other discourses in the film, the rape takes place while "Oh Canada" is played in the closing-down sequences on television. It is this kind of procedure that Bart Testa calls the "cartooning of significance" in the film,[25] in which obviously over-signified scenes (he cites the interview in English with the factory manager) make up for the deliberate non-centring of the diegetic director or anyone else as beacons of the "truth" of the film.

This latter point hints at some of the specificities and indeed peculiarities of Arcand's approach in the 1970s to "political" cinema. His brand of realism generates generic surprises, but it is difficult to make a convincing case for some great Godardian imprint on his cinema. Even Gene Walz admits, in a telling comparison with *Tout va bien* (1972), which similarly features a film team visiting a factory and mixes fiction and documentary, that by the time of *Gina* the relationship is extremely tenuous. Despite the presence of a film crew in the diegesis of that film, Arcand's cinema lacks that reflection on form which *Screen* theory in the late 1970s and early 1980s deemed essential if the contradictoriness of the real is to be fully articulated and the hierarchical discourses of truth to be found in the "classic realist text" are to be replaced with a more radical and open text that prevents the construction of comfortable, stable subject positions for the spectator.[26] In addition, the parallelisms of Arcand's narrative practice are not, despite his protestations,[27] part of a dialectic in the future-directed Eisensteinian sense; still less, however, do they tend towards the creation of an organic whole in the sense of Griffith or classic Hollywood realism (or, adds Testa, of "the Quebec narrative 'art film'").[28] In a sense, Arcand's practice is in-between Griffith and Eisenstein, parallel montage with a sense of history (as in *Intolerance*), with the notion that oppositions are not given but produced by social and historical contradictions. For Arcand, perhaps, there is nothing new under the sun. (Notably, none of his films provides an Oedipal resolution, in which a male protagonist assumes a "mature" and socially integrated heterosexual position, or even shows the slightest interest in sketching an Oedipal trajectory.) Nevertheless, Arcand's films do succeed in placing the spectator "at some critical remove from the diegesis."[29] For, while Arcand's procedure is not Brechtian in the sense that he chooses not to disrupt realist space and time or to invoke a future, it nonetheless relentlessly historicizes and renders provisional its characters and discourses. Fundamentally, history in its *longue durée* judges the present;[30] in turn, the different discourses in the present, as in *Gina*, as products of history and of histories, interrogate each other. Hence the emphasis on groups and contrasting pairs rather than "individuals," and hence also the surprising movements characters and situations make from background to foreground in his texts, a spectrum from visibility to invisibility, so that the status of characters as major or minor is always undecidable. Arcand's cinema is fundamentally suspicious of institutions, of power and those who wield it. This would seem to be an appropriate form for a Quebec national cinematic text in determinedly minor mode, as it explores that oscillation between assertion and disappearance that is, for Arcand, its most telling characteristic.

In the lean years that followed *Gina*, Arcand wrote the screenplay for the Radio Canada television series *Duplessis* (1977), directed three episodes of the CBC English-language series *Empire Inc.* (1983), and also completed the direction, begun by Gilles Carle, of the series/feature film that was *Le Crime d'Ovide Plouffe* (1984). However, his most significant achievement of this period was a film that announced many of the preoccupations of the late 1980s, a documentary for the NFB on the failed 1980 sovereignty referendum, *Le Confort et l'indifférence* (1981).

Here Arcand uses Machiavelli, quoting extracts from *The Prince* in period costume in an office overlooking Montreal, to comment on the way in which Lévesque and the nationalists were outmanoeuvred by Trudeau and the federalists. The latter's victory was due to their relentless insistence, against the "dream" of their opponents, on the material risks the Québécois would run by voting yes. Ultimately, it was consumerism which put paid to Quebec's national collective project. Arcand's classic procedure of accentuating conflict through montage of the two sides and then assessing their perspectives via historical distancing was also, however, criticized for missing an opportunity of examining more profoundly the ambivalent heritages within Quebec culture. Whereas *Le Devoir* criticized Arcand for insulting the "people" for their stupidity,[31] Fulvio Caccia, an important figure, as we shall see, in the pluricultural turn later taken by much intellectual debate in Quebec, saw Arcand hiding behind the "objectivity" of Machiavelli and thus perpetuating in inverted form the image of the "self-seduction," the narcissistic inward-looking, of the Québécois.[32] Nevertheless, it is clear that, for Arcand, 1980 was a turning point, for it marked the death knell of collective struggle and the possibility of social change in his lifetime: "The night of the referendum, there was no longer to my mind a collective struggle."[33] His later films explore the consequences of this belief.

In the 1970s and 1980s Jean Pierre Lefebvre was able to continue, via his production company Cinak, an *oeuvre* which wove links between personal, interior worlds and the collective reality, and specificity, of Quebec. Indeed, those links form part of a cinematic strategy which consciously seeks to defy, in true "national cinema" fashion, the global image-making industry centred on Hollywood: "We must fight for the continuity of a cinema which must ensure and believe in the continuity of the country, this geographic and human space in which we can be free to become what we are and to think what we think." The implied unanimity of the nation is partly qualified by what follows: "provided we share these privileged freedoms with those, of all races, cultures and religions, who wish to inhabit it with us."[34] Quoting approvingly Buñuel on the political and military power crucial to the fame of American writers, Lefebvre is also acutely aware of Quebec's "minor" status: "Since elsewhere major galaxies gobble up minor ones, why persist in expressing points of view that are singular, mine, ours? ... There can only be a collection of small answers to such 'big' questions."

Two of Lefebvre's most critically acclaimed films of this period illustrate the advantages and limitations of this procedure. *Les Dernières Fiançailles* (1973) recounts the last days of an elderly married couple, Armand and Rose Tremblay (J.-Léo Gagnon and Marthe Nadeau), who own a small farm in rural Quebec. They are the only characters in the film, apart from the doctor (Marcel Sabourin), who tries unsuccessfully to persuade Armand to go to hospital. The couple's only son died in the Second World War. The spartanness of the décor, typical for Lefebvre, is extended to the film-making itself: This is a film about time and light. It opens with dawn rising over the house. A shot of a cuckoo clock (connoting both time and the "home" itself) is followed by a clock face (Armand's hobby is to repair clocks) with, on the soundtrack, the loud ticking which will accompany most of the interior scenes. After a shot of the crucifix above the bed, the camera pans down first to Armand, then left to Rose, and it then follows her as she goes about her daily routine (an editing cut separates the shots in the bedroom and living area). This five-minute sequence is repeated in simplified form the next day, fifty minutes into the film. Armand dies on the third. Lefebvre has described the way in which the film is structured by rhythm, that of a cardiogram, a regular beat that then stops, as in the camera's slow half-circles which come to rest in a long take, as in the depiction of death.[35]

Lefebvre claimed that the slow pace of his films was partly to do with the specificity of the Quebec "milieu ambiant"[36] (such as the long winter and bare immensity of the landscape), partly to an epicurean predilection for *durée* or duration.[37] (Indeed, the question of time goes to the heart of all the financial considerations, such as relations with Hollywood, which bedevil independent and non-English language film making).[38] Rather like *Pour la suite du monde, Les Dernières fiançailles* is ambivalent about its representation of time. The old couple embody continuity, cyclical rather than linear progressive time, but also, conceivably, immobilism. The sense of living in time is palpable, but it is rendered indirectly, by, for example, the ticking clock, rather than by any disruption or indiscernibility of past, present, and future. The film's investment in repetition, as in the daily rituals, is the reverse of Jutra's *Pour le meilleur et pour le pire*, clearly, and is harnessed to a more conservative aesthetic. The one exception is the final scene in which, after Rose has decided to die next to her husband, two angels appear and escort them away through the orchard, placing two seeds in their hands. This is a projection of the belief system of this generation of Québécois, but it also raises questions of spectatorship and a possible split: in a manner analogous to viewing a costume drama, how does a younger, contemporary cinema audience relate to the *difference* represented by the culture that preceded the Quiet Revolution? Moreover, does the sentimentalization of the couple, and the emphasis, typical for the pre-1960s generation, on private life as opposed to a collective happiness or project, undermine the real if subtle links between the personal and the social that have always characterized Lefebvre's work?

These questions are confronted directly by Lefebvre in his 1981 film *Les Fleurs sauvages,* which precisely plays on the problematic relation between continuity and difference. It also stars Marthe Nadeau, as Simone, a seventy-year-old mother of eight who for a week in July goes to visit her daughter Michèle (Michèle Magny), who lives in rural Quebec with her second husband, Pierre (Pierre Curzi), and her two children, Éric and Claudia (Éric Beauséjour and Claudia Aubin). The differences in generation are palpable: mother and daughter enact the classic struggle over differentiation. Simone is a practising Catholic who inwardly disapproves of Michèle's smoking and sexual openness and who insists on performing lots of domestic tasks during her stay. In a memorable scene in which Michèle, Pierre, and their friends gather for an open-air meal and each recount how they met (these are all heterosexual couples), Simone is obliged to tell the story of her marriage, which, although it lasted for fifty years until the death of her husband, was arranged by the respective parents.

Lefebvre suggests these potential, subterranean conflicts through a series of techniques. In the opening sequences, what seems at first sight to be a parallel editing structure (with Simone travelling on the bus and Michèle driving to meet her) is complicated by the relation between sound and image. For example, as Simone knits, gazing out of the bus window with the camera reproducing her point of view, her voice-over alternates with that of her daughter. This blurring of the editing dialectic, coupled with the abortive interpenetration of discourses, underlines at one and the same time the attempt at dialogue and the improbability of a unity being formed. The insertion of still images such as family photographs, and, moreover, of black-and-white sequences which express the virtuality of a moment, complete this tendency. That virtuality can be one of conflict (Simone commenting negatively on her grandson's appearance and behaviour), of memory (Simone comparing the parent/child relationships of previous generations with this one), or of the closeness to which Michèle in particular aspires (as when mother and daughter walk down a country lane and Simone tells of her friend who had died in the nursing home, the black-and-white shots expressing the emotions and physical closeness absent from the preceding colour sequence). These "crystalline" techniques, in which a virtual (memory or dream) image corresponds to an actual description and is to an extent indiscernible from it,[39] supply a cinematographic equivalent of the film's theme of generation, in that they are linked to the overriding question of time. As the camera tracks the movement of the bus, the two women's voice-overs speak of change (Simone: "Tout change trop vite ..."). The virtual black-and-white sequences and the to-ing and fro-ing between sound and image are consistent with Deleuze's analysis of time-images which provide a direct representation of time that is not subordinated to movement. *Les Fleurs sauvages* is therefore interested in strata, in terms of the Quebec nation and in particular the status of women: "History is inseparable from the earth [*terre*] ... and if we want to grasp an event, we must not show it, we must not pass along the event, but plunge into it, go through all the geological layers that are its internal history ... To grasp an event is to connect it to the silent layers of earth which make up its true continuity."[40]

The "peasant" aspect of *Les Fleurs sauvages*, in a society that has precisely left behind its traditions, is conserved in the film's attitude to commodities and exchange. Refusing commodity status itself, it problematizes this status for all the characters. Michèle and Pierre have opted out of urban living. He makes money from photography (such as the wedding early in the film) but seems to live for the "pleasure" of his creative and family projects. Michèle is a potter and is seen discussing their precarious financial situation with her friends and colleagues. Arguments occur with the children about their access (or lack of it) to money. Time is money. A stance against its empire, in terms of the fabrication and distribution of this film and in terms of the relation to a non-capitalist past, forms one of the threads of the film. Indeed, the title denotes not only the gift of wildflowers from childhood that Michèle tries to reproduce for Simone (producing the "narrative" "resolution" of Simone, who repeats the gesture and includes the daisies which she had originally disdained), but also a memory, an image, an object of beauty with no exchange value. Flowers, however, fade. The centrality of time to the film also addresses, therefore, that ultimate disjunction of its positing of continuity and conflict, and that is death. (Simone: "It's funny to think of the past, when we've just got the present to live, when the future can stop any time.") It structures the relation to the past (memory, photographic or otherwise, as the only access to lost loved ones), and its proximity renders more poignant and urgent the relation to the present that passes and the future that is continually becoming. In 1982 Marguerite Duparc, Lefebvre's wife, film editor, and partner in Cinak, died at the age of forty-eight.

Lefebvre's unquestioning investment in the heterosexual couple as locus of meaning and fulfilment has a more interesting flipside, however. As Pierre puts it in *Les Fleurs sauvages*, "It isn't always easy to be a man and to be Québécois." Whether in the figure of Abel or in the central roles played by women protagonists, Lefebvre's films since the late 1960s can be read as rather "feminizing." He himself recalls that, during his adolescence, "poète rimait avec tapette ['queer']."[41] This "becoming-woman," befitting a cinema determinedly both national and minor, means that, while *Les Dernières Fiançailles* and *Les Fleurs sauvages* are very distant from *Pour le meilleur et pour le pire*, they are equally so from *Un Zoo la nuit*. His two feature films of the 1990s are in the mode of gentle fantasy and the links between generations. *Le Fabuleux Voyage de l'ange* (1991), on a bigger budget than usual for a Lefebvre film, is a quest narrative combining the worlds of *bande dessinée* and live action. More successfully, *Aujourd'hui ou jamais* (1998) attempts to bring the Abel trilogy to a conciliatory close, following *Il ne faut pas mourir pour ça* and *Le Vieux Pays où Rimbaud est mort*. Abel's father, Napoléon (Claude Blanchard, only a few years older than Marcel Sabourin), after fifty years in Brazil returns to Quebec. Abel is running leisure flights from an aerodrome in Estrie, but he is traumatized by an accident that killed his partner fifteen years earlier and is only just working up the courage to fly again (before a particularly precious light plane is repossessed). The film can to an extent be seen as an allegory of Lefebvre's life and career in cinema, with commerce, ageing, and death setting obstacles to the business of poetry, dream, and fantasy, here rendered through the metaphor of flying (frontal point-of-view shots of clouds from an aeroplane, memories of flying rendered through sepia 8 mm., references to Saint-Exupéry) and the unity of time as the sun sets and the light gradually changes. However, since the relationship with the father, absent from the first two films, remains sketchy, the film's purchase on the collective meaning of "Quebec" and what has happened since the 1950s is less integrated to the personal than in Lefebvre's earlier films.

It seems more appropriate to place discussion of Gilles Carle's output since his 1960s films in the context of his role in constructing a Quebec popular cinema and a cinematic "people." Defending the large budgets for *Maria Chapdelaine* and *Les Plouffe* (1981) – small in comparison with Hollywood and other cinemas – Carle criticized Lefebvre's notion "according to which if a director makes films in a small country, he must make small films."[42] Discussion of Carle's films is spread across several chapters in this volume, a testimony to the eclecticism and reach of his preoccupations. However, the Carle-Lamy production company in the key period of the early 1970s was crucial to the careers of not only Carle but also Arcand and Jutra (*La Maudite Galette*, *Kamouraska*, and *Pour le meilleur et pour le pire*), and, as we saw in chapter 4, the role of Carle was central to the mini-vogue for Quebec auteur cinema in France in the early 1970s. Certainly, the persistence of what we might term "institutional auteurism" well into the 1990s has permitted Carle to continue feature film-making (*Pudding chômeur,* 1996). His fifteen features over thirty years do contain recurring characteristics, preoccupations, and style, and these consistencies are paradoxically attained, given the tendency of his films, particularly those he has scripted himself, to narrative digression and polyphony, which he defends by invoking Kundera, Buñuel, and Lake Superior Indian chants.[43]

The cultural location of Carle himself is to be found in a shifting and pluralizing play of centre and periphery. He was born in 1929 in Maniwaki near an Algonquin reservation and partly of native descent, and his upbringing also included Catholicism, American popular culture such as country and western,[44] and the multiculturalism of the Abitibi region, recently opened up for internal "colonization" and immigration from abroad: "This created a modernity in Quebec which people are only just beginning to live through elsewhere."[45] He has turned his hands to other media, such as poetry, but also advertising. His reputation still probably depends on his 1970s output, and particularly on *La Vraie Nature de Bernadette* (1972). Here Bernadette Brown, maiden name Bonheur (Micheline Lanctôt), leaves her husband and flat in the city, taking her young son to rural Quebec where she has acquired a run-down farmhouse and intends to live "close to nature," a notion that includes both vegetarianism and "free love." These dreams collide with the economic difficulties facing the farmers (literally so when, driving to her new home, she encounters her neighbour Thomas [Donald Pilon] protesting against conditions by blocking the road), sexual exploitation (her masturbation of old men, including Thomas's father, is milked for comic effect), Catholic superstition intensified by the media (she is taken for a saint when she apparently "cures" a mute child), and straightforward greed (theft and the murder of Rock [Reynald Bouchard], the young handicapped man in love with Bernadette, the giving away of her urban possessions). The film ends in conflict, with the peasants emptying their fruit and vegetables on the motorway and Bernadette firing on the motorists.

Rather than the psychological intimism of a director like Lefebvre, or the painstakingly constructed and contextualized dialectics of Arcand, Carle typically opts to take ideas and run with them, skimming a multitude of surfaces. Bernadette is a composite of irreconcilable discourses: already her name connotes Saint Bernadette Soubirous and Bernadette Devlin (the conflict in Northern Ireland was then at its most intense), but she is also mother, whore, revolutionary, ordinary. Like Buñuel's *Viridiana* (1961), *La Vraie Nature de Bernadette* critiques charity and religion, but it is more of a post-Catholic film, in that Bernadette refuses to assume sainthood and her initial idealism is a secular one, syncretically spiritualizing "nature" and the material world. The film's procedure is based on the reversibility of categories such as saint and prostitute, or "the return to nature" as progressive or reactionary. This produces a mosaic-like narrative which eschews closure or a clear couple formation by the end. There is no "true nature" of Bernadette or anything else, no fixity, just "movement towards."[46]

However, this pluralism of surfaces has its limitations, for Carle's cinematic practice also includes the slippery reversibility of critique and spectacle. The mosaic of cultural stereotypes of "woman" is both criticized and enjoyed *as spectacle*, even as the notion of spectacle (the media circus) is also critiqued. This can reach the point where it is the "naughtiness" or "joyous immorality"[47] of the film which is remembered by audiences, not its satire. In addition, the centred viewing and also social position is that of heterosexual masculinity, both in its "down-to-earth practicality" (Thomas as the "raisonneur" – as in Molière – to Bernadette's excesses, although she wins battles of emotional insight with him) and in its anxiety and failure (Rock). In this way, Carle's films are in their sexual attitudes very much of the 1970s. Just as they purport to reveal the incongruities of differently layered social and historical discourses (such as Catholicism and consumerism), they have blind spots as to their own location within or between those strata. In *Les Mâles* of the previous year, Carle had cast René Blouin and Donald Pilon as two sex-starved marginals living outside society in the woods. Their escapades, particularly their abduction and adoption of pliant young women, form the basis of a challenge, via 1960s counter-culture, to the small-town rural attitudes of the Duplessis era. In turn, the pretensions of the counter-culture are undermined by a centred and unchallenged populist masculinity dressed up in the quintessential if exaggerated Quebec garb of the *coureur de bois*. Nevertheless, Carle's film-making style is rather distinctive within Quebec cinema and in particular its auteur mode. The only other director to resemble him is really the only film-maker who began producing a consistent *oeuvre* in the 1970s and continued into the 1990s. Like those of Carle, the films of André Forcier (b. 1947) can most fruitfully be looked at via the notions of the baroque, magic realism, and affinities with Fellini.

Beginning with *Le Retour de l'Immaculée Conception* of 1971, Forcier has directed eight feature films from his own screenplays (five co-written with Jacques Marcotte). He has been among the staunchest defenders of an independent auteur cinema in Quebec, helping to found the distribution company Cinéma libre in 1973. During his time in the late 1960s at Pierre Lamy's Onyx Films, Gilles Carle was instrumental in the genesis of Forcier's career.[48] Forcier's films combine a social "realism," in the portrayal of a recognizable working class or even *lumpen* Montreal milieu, with excess, caricature, and even fantasy. The naturalistic aspects of *Bar Salon* (1973) and *L'Eau chaude l'eau frette* (1976) evolve into the dream worlds of *Au clair de la lune* (1982), in which an albino, from the land of "Albinie," inhabits a parked car with an arthritic sandwich-board man who advertises the joys of the local "Moonshine" bowling alley in which he used to star, their lives set against a neon-lit nocturnal winter cityscape traversed by tireless cars; and *Kalamazoo* (1988), in which a lovelorn fifty-three-year-old virgin summons into being a mermaid corresponding to an image seen on a bookcover.

L'Eau chaude l'eau frette is probably the most accomplished film of this period of Forcier's output and reveals many of his preoccupations, actual and potential. Within a twenty-four-hour period, it traces the lives of the inhabitants of a rooming-house and other denizens of their *quartier*, culminating in the birthday party held for Polo (Jean Lapointe), racketeer and money lender. He is sexually involved with the *concierge* Clémence (Élise Varo) and also Carmen (Sophie Clément), who runs the local laundromat and who pays the rent through the favours she offers him. Her adolescent daughter Francine (Louise Gagnon), along with her boyfriend Ti-Guy (Réjean Audet), hates Polo. Francine's life depends on a pacemaker, the batteries of which she is constantly recharging but which she also uses to jumpstart the motorbike and sidecar driven by Julien (Jean-Pierre Bergeron), secretly besotted with Carmen, and the delivery boy for the bulimic Françoise (Françoise Berd) who runs the local snack bar. Other characters include the pretentious (and homosexual) Croteau (Albert Payette), "member of the French-Canadian Academy"; Mlle Vanasse (Anne-Marie Ducharme), the "old maid" besotted with him; and Panama (Guy L'Écuyer), the gay chef recruited by Croteau for the party, who is violently beaten by Polo's cronies. The plan hatched by Francine, Ti-Guy, and Julien to shoot Polo fails when one of the latter's debtors, trussed up for the party, is hit. Francine and Ti-Guy ride off on the bike and sidecar, leaving Julien behind to shoot himself after being rejected by Carmen.

In the amoral, despairing world Forcier frequently depicts in these films, the figure of Guy L'Écuyer acts as an exemplum of the director's procedure. Rotund and with a limping gait, combining a humorous *bonhomie* with a certain tragic affect, he was the classic Québécois "little man" of Gilles Carle's *La Vie heureuse de Léopold Z.* and Francis Mankiewicz's *Le Temps d'une chasse*. In Forcier's *Bar Salon*, he plays Charles, the bankrupt bar-owner betrayed by his friend: his bodily movements are given a surreal and oniric twist amidst the hyper-naturalism of the film in an unforgettable dance sequence. In *Au clair de la lune*, he is the sandwich-board man, Albert. His more minor role in *L'Eau chaude l'eau frette* forms part of a system of meaning and suggestion in the film which, leaving behind the metonymy of realism, both caricatures the protagonists and hints at a world beyond of dream and despair. Urgently material concerns – money, debt, death, food and drink, un-reciprocated desire (including here a cameo of Forcier and Carole Laure as a couple in crisis) – are magnified to the point (but not here beyond that point) of floating free of referents and the sensory-motor patterns of mainstream cinema. In this way, Julien, young, slender, and vertical, is a counterpoint to Panama. Both are physically uncoordi-nated and "miss" their targets (there are scenes in which Panama is made a fool of with a baseball, and Ti-Guy trips him when, limbering up like a bull, he attempts to break down a door). The tracking shot that follows Julien from the snack bar to Carmen's laundromat is echoed when, in Françoise's storeroom – full of potato sacks – he moves away from Francine and Ti-Guy, who want to have sex, and masturbates.

In a suggestive article, Jocelyn Deschênes has used the term "baroque" to describe the films of Carle and Forcier.[49] There is much mileage in this term and the way in which it describes certain films' dependence on spectacle and artifice, digressions, proliferation, and becoming:

Classical compositions are simple and clear, each constituent part retaining its independence; they have a static quality and are enclosed within boundaries. The Baroque artist, in contrast, longs to enter into the multiplicity of phenom-ena, into the flux of things in their perpetual becoming – his [sic] composi-tions are dynamic and open and tend to expand outside their boundaries; the forms that go to make them are associated in a single organic action and can-not be isolated from each other. The Baroque artist's instinct for escape drives him to prefer "forms that take flight" to those that are static and dense; his liking for pathos leads him to depict sufferings and feelings, life and death at their extremes of violence, while the Classical artist aspires to show the human figure in the full possession of his powers.[50]

The baroque not only suggests a certain textual reflexivity in its articu-lation of spectacle and "the real," it also raises questions concerning modernity and postmodernity. The baroque is an alternative cultural-historical resource to Enlightenment categories of self and other, iden-tity and non-identity. At the same time, it potentially offers an alterna-tive to contemporary postmodern accounts of society as a proliferation of surfaces that we shall explore in the final chapter of this book. The relevance of Carle's and Forcier's films to questions of Quebec modernity should not be underestimated. Even the terms "poetic realism," with the prestige it carries from an anxious but very integrated French national cinematic culture of the 1930s, or "surrealism" (Forcier is frequently compared with the anarchist Jean Vigo) seem inappropriate to the Quebec context.[51] As Fredric Jameson has argued in connection with magic realism in Latin American and Eastern European cinemas, the incongruities we find in such films are connected with the disjunctures of what we might term the historical embedding of the societies being depicted. In the case of working-class francophone Montreal (as opposed to the countryside of *La Vraie Nature de Bernadette*), this means not so much "the overlap or the coexistence of precapitalist and nascent capitalist or technological features," but a cultural and economic peripheralization which in turn produces a reality that is already magical or fantastic (including for example the films' evocation of kitsch) because of "the articulated superposition of whole layers of the past within the present."[52] Elementary forms of bodily experience form building blocks of meaning which neutralize the process of narrativization in these films and emphasize instead "a seeing or looking in the filmic present." For Jameson, such films create a way of dealing with past and present which is radically distinct both from the straightforward chronologies of the historical novel or film and from the surface gloss of the nostalgia film. Such analyses help to distinguish the different ways in which Quebec *auteurs* all address the same historical and cultural issue, that of the relationship between the national present and past. Unlike the trans-generational intimism of Lefebvre, carefully drawing links between the private and collective, or the broad historical sweeps of Arcand, or the radical moral questioning of Jutra, Carle and Forcier, faced with the decline of the historical and temporal roadmaps of modernity and its Quebec avatar, a collective national project,[53] opt for a proliferating "present of uncodified intensities."[54]

The comparison with Fellini represents another way into these messy and uneven *oeuvres*. Fellini's scriptwriter, Ennio Flaiano, was a friend of Carle and worked on the script of his *Red* (1969). Both Carle and Forcier tend to emphasize some kind of spectacle in their films (the country-and-western dance club of *La Mort d'un bûcheron*, the party in *L'Eau chaude l'eau frette*) and to blur the distinction between spectacle and "reality." Deleuze's analysis of Fellini in *The Time-Image*, following the work of Barthélémy Amengual, stresses the different ways in which Fellini's use of spectacle contributes to the construction of an "intermental" world, a world for everyone, in which psychology and psychologism, as well as the distinction between spectator and participant, are left behind and an artificial, depersonalizing movement sweeps the characters along. Fairgrounds play this role in Fellini's films, and affinities can be drawn with aspects of two later films by Forcier, the fairground and hypnotist's show of *Le Vent du Wyoming* (1994) and the circus of *La Comtesse de Baton Rouge* (1997). In Deleuze's theory of the time-image, these procedures are crystalline (indiscernible facets of the "real" and the virtual) and testify to a Nietzschean "power of the false" which injects a new belief in the world into the world by sidestepping the "truth" of self-identity. Forcier's cinema in particular is very Nietzschean, but a certain amount of existential despair underlies the intensity of the worlds he creates.

Analysis of auteurism in this period reveals a number of challenges which overflow the term itself and the parameters within which it obliges the film student to work. The transformations in the Canadian and global film industry, and the undermining of the industrial and aesthetic assumptions associated with an earlier film "modernism" and art cinema, form part of that challenge. The example of one of the main film auteurs to emerge in the 1990s, Robert Lepage, complicates the issues because of his multimedia practice, the collective emergence of his scripts and projects, and his "globalized" place in Canadian cultural production, as we shall see in the final chapter. That of the other, Robert Morin (b. 1949), stems from the importance of video and its presence in visual art, news-gathering, and the home.

Morin was one of the founders in 1977 of Coop Vidéo, devoted to independent production and to exploring the interface between documentary and fiction impelled by video technology. (In that decade, many Quebec film-makers, including Charles Binamé and Pierre Falardeau, had cut their teeth on the emerging technology, thanks in part to the NFB's creation of a production centre, Vidéographe.) With Lorraine Dufour collaborating on production and editing, Morin's output in the 1990s, beginning with his first 35 mm. feature, *Requiem pour un beau sans-coeur* of 1992, helped to reinvigorate Quebec cinema with a formally innovative approach which challenged the boundaries of experimental and popular film.

Requiem is partly a genre film about a gangster's three days of liberty following a prison break-out. There is a suspenseful narrative about the outcome of a police raid and the identity of the gang member who gave away the location. However, "objective" omniscient narration is eschewed in favour of a series of eight vignettes which tell the story of Régis Savoie (played by the popular singer Gildor Roy) from eight often contradictory points of view, the camera reproducing their "subjective" positions: the young son visiting at the moment of the breakout, the assistant to the violent policeman on Régis's tail, the journalist chronicling his career, the lawyer, the mother, his fellow bandit Tonio (Jean-Guy Bouchard), the two girlfriends.

This approach has a long cultural history. Modernist fragmentation narrating same scenes from different perspectives is to be found, for example, in William Faulkner's *As I Lay Dying* (1930). In mainstream cinema, the experiment with a subjective camera has been short-lived, an example being *The Lady in the Lake* (Robert Montgomery, 1947), really a one-off in Hollywood and popular film. More recently, however, rock and other video expression since the 1980s has loosened up the grammar of film and television narrative, so that the relentless demand for narrative has become compatible with the foregrounding of its operations, as in the films of Quentin Tarantino. But, for Morin, the liberating potential of video is linked to a critique of the media. In *Requiem*, there is no objective, totalizing or totalized "truth" of Régis; he is a reflection of the look of others. In two of the sequences he is seen to protest against the circulation of images, when he complains about the journalist's stories (a headline says he took his son hostage in the escape; this is absent from the son's narrative: who can tell?) and when he shoots a gun at a television showing a crime story. When in the film's coda he films himself, it is to resolve a narrative enigma (as at the end, unrecognized by the journalists, of *Citizen Kane*) but in fact to self-destruct *in representation*: proclaiming, "OK, attention, ça continue," he puts the camera down at an angle and is heard to be phoning the police to come and get him.

As Morin was himself aware, the 35 mm. format militates against "the illusion of the real."[55] Often in *Requiem*, the camera functions as in mainstream film, for example, in the use of point-of-view shots, despite the fact that they "originate" in the look of the subjective position at the second protagonist who is looking at something else (as when a shot of Régis is followed by that of a roadblock). These procedures help to rein in the film's narration and flatten out the different reading positions. Morin went much farther in *Quiconque meurt, meurt à douleur* (1998), a video feature about a police raid on a drug den which goes wrong, with a news cameraman held hostage along with two cops and forced to film the duration of the siege. The film is partly about social marginals attempting to take over the power of the image, with jokes about the NFB and "Oh Canada" marking the end of transmissions on CBC/SRC (when the cameraman is tied up at night) and with the tables turned when he is himself filmed on the toilet. The film ends with a TV news report summarizing the siege and its outcome in a few minutes, before passing on to trivia.

Quiconque meurt is certainly troubling, as the hand-held camera refuses the spectator a comfortable viewing position. However, Morin perhaps establishes too great a polarity between the "reality" of this procedure and the "constructed" and commodified news story. While video provides a way of intensifying the direct cinema legacy and providing it with a dose of – avowed – "subjectivity," the images in the film also refer to other images, most notably of reality shows and even of spoofs of reality shows (the proliferation of parodies of *The Blair Witch Project* on the web testifies to its potential here). Morin was more effective in his 1994 video feature, *Yes Sir! Madame ...*, which refused to take itself seriously and whose humour was based on a subversion of "official" images and messages coming from above. Purporting to be the video and film diary of one Earl Tremblay (played by Morin himself), this "real fucking Canadian movie" traces the story of the bilingual and rather marginal Earl from his childhood to his unlikely election as a Conservative Member of Parliament in 1988, after which he has a breakdown and disappears in the woods. The "silent" home-movie footage (supposedly a number of reels provided by his mother), which includes his "childhood," Brian Mulroney in the election campaign, and a montage of shots of him in the House of Commons in Ottawa, is narrated bilingually (Earl translates himself immediately). This, plus sound-effect voice-overs, blank screens, and clanking beer bottles, serve to undermine the "truth" of every image, as well as to explore the underside of Canadian society. Gradually, the bilingual commentary collapses, with one language correcting the other's perceptions, until Earl is at war with himself. Morin's exploration of the image is thus accompanied by, and perhaps predicated upon, an unambiguous Quebec nationalist stance (blood had already spattered the Queen's portrait in the prison sequence of *Requiem pour un beau sans-coeur*). The alienation has its ultimate source in a "lack" which official bilingualism cannot fill. The most famous shot from *Yes Sir! Madame ...* has Earl filming his multiple reflections in a bathroom mirror, a row of them on either side of the screen ("pea soupers" and "têtes carrées") as he proclaims, "On a décidé de se séparer pour toujours. Yes sir, oui madame."

Other challenges to an auteurist approach are thematic: for example, the preoccupations with nature and the native peoples to be found in Carle, Lefebvre (*Les Maudits Sauvages*, 1970), and Morin (*Windigo*, 1994) need to be located within broad frames of cultural, political, and epistemological analysis. Significantly, all six film-makers discussed so far in this chapter tend to decouple the "people" they represent from political agency. This runs the risk of precisely that postmodern "flattening out" of experience and relativization of meaning which they would all nonetheless refute. The one exception to this is the work of Gilles Groulx, which continued a strong political agenda from the 1960s but was cut short by a serious accident in 1980. *24 Heures ou plus* (1976), banned by the NFB for five years, is a montage film which combines shots of the present, archive material from the early 1970s, and

Groulx and fellow-scriptwriter Jean-Marc Piotte addressing the camera to denounce the state of Quebec society. *Au pays de Zom* (1982) is an audacious musical piece, its dialogue sung in entirety, about the epony-mous Montreal financier. Brechtian distantiation via the opera form thus seeks to defamiliarize the workings of capitalism. The marginality of characters in Carle and especially Forcier, however, testify less to the existence of a *lumpenproletariat* than to marginality, and the absence of community, as a symptom of a wider malaise.

As we shall see, auteurism also persists into the 1990s as the domi-nant mode in women's cinema in Quebec. The masculinism and het-erosexism of those baroque Benny Hills, Carle and Forcier, need to be challenged from that perspective. There is also the question of audi-ence and gender, which comes to intersect with the evolving commer-cial considerations of the period. From this point of view, perhaps the most significant film of this period is Jean Beaudin's *J.A. Martin photo-graphe* of 1976, which provides a chronological and conceptual link be-tween the high-art movie status of *Kamouraska* and the more televisual *Maria Chapdelaine*, which, as we have seen, in turn inspired some of the 1990s costume dramas on Radio Canada.

In the film, set in turn-of-the-century Quebec, Rose-Aimée (Monique Mercure, who won the best actress award at Cannes) is married to the taciturn J.A. (Marcel Sabourin), a professional photographer. Against convention and the wishes of her live-in mother-in-law, she decides to accompany her husband on his annual summer itinerary. Their jour-ney through rural Quebec, stopping off to take photographs of J.A.'s regular customers, permits an investigation of both the state of society (exploited workers including children, wealthy anglophones) and the state of their marriage, notably in a scene in which Rose-Aimée has a miscarriage but also a visit to the hotel in which they spent their honey-moon, an encounter with a former lover of Rose-Aimée, and a wedding party in which desiring extroversion is expressed. The return marks a certain, if subtle, re-equilibrium in their relationship.

The success of the film lies, first, in the cinematography, with an even light emphasizing the "naturalness" of the stunning Quebec land-scapes. Pierre Mignot would later work with Beaudin on *Cordélia* (1979) and *Mario* (1984) (and with Robert Altman in the 1980s): his cinematography combines documentary (consistent with NFB tradi-tions and experience and with one dimension of this film) with paint-erly style; indeed, it is reminiscent of some of the landscapes and still lives of Ozias Leduc (1864–1955), whose output coincides with the pe-riod in which *J.A. Martin* is set. The second strength is the performance of Monique Mercure, for her judgment in dosing elements of moder-nity (associated also with elements of her cinematic persona, if we think of her roles in *À tout prendre, Mon oncle Antoine,* and *Deux femmes en or*) with tradition, assertion, and acceptance, is crucial to the meaning of the film. Like *Kamouraska, Maria Chapdelaine, Cordélia* (in which a nineteenth-century woman is hanged), and the *téléromans* of the 1990s, *J.A. Martin* places a woman at the centre of a period costume drama in which the similarity or difference of the national "we" is played out across the caesura of the Quiet Revolution. In a suggestive article, Joan Nicks argues that this film's articulation of landscape, cinematography, and photography in fact produces disjunctions, between the static male, professional, enclosing gaze and the discontinuous, non-linear, and open horizons, both literal and metaphorical, inhabited but also aspired to by Rose-Aimée. As in the miscarriage scene, insuperable gender differences played out "at the edges of cultivated society" mean that both pastoral and national myths unravel and prove illusory.[56] The (beautiful) landscape is not just a photographer's backdrop but, for Rose-Aimée, a multilayered space of work, life, and death.

What I would argue, however, is that the film is able to function as an example of national cinema in its very ability to hold in tension opposites, to knit together spatial, temporal, and ideological opposites. This is partly achieved by the ambiguity so central to the art-movie tradition: the last scene in which Rose-Aimée and J.A. lie in bed, their relationship changed, adjusted, improved perhaps but not transformed, is redolent of that. But it is mostly to do with the relationship with the national and personal past, the play of similarity and difference, the past people as origin but the present audience as the performative reality, and here photography plays the crucial role. The diegetic photography of J.A. and the cinematography of Mignot in their different ways refer to and enact the workings of personal and collective memory. In a process that reaches its apogee with *Les Filles de Caleb,* an adaptation of a family memoir, the combination of costume and intimist drama creates a *lieu de mémoire* that is a bridge between private and collective (particularly national) memory. The *lieux de mémoire* are the sites of the labour of memory around the nation, the last incarnation of a past, traditional epoch when collective history and private memory were as one. Just as the family-photograph album produces a sense of individual identity through private memory, so does a *lieu de mémoire* such as a monument or an audio-visual text contribute to processes of collective recognition and belonging in the context of contemporary individualization and atomization.[57] But in the undecidability of the meaning of the relation between past and present, *J.A. Martin photographe,* rather than perpetuating the bourgeois myth of technology defeating death or at least time and decay, reminds its audience that the survival of the photographed forms part of the "history of how a person *lives on*, and precisely how this afterlife, with its own history, is embedded in life."[58]

In 1954 François Truffaut wrote his famous article lambasting the script-led *tradition de qualité* in French cinema.[59] While undoubtedly cinematic, *J.A. Martin photographe* was a federating text which, with its slow pace, fades, and long takes rendered itself distinct from popular cinema but, with its emphasis on identification, linear narrative, psychological "realism," ideological consensus, and aesthetic practice (beautiful images of beautiful things), was also different from much Quebec art cinema of the 1960s and early 1970s. One has only to juxtapose the film with Jutra's *Pour le meilleur et pour le pire*, for example. In France, the *tradition de qualité* fled to television with the onset of the *nouvelle vague*, but it re-emerged in the 1980s and 1990s with costume dramas and heritage films, some linked, appropriately in a new audio-visual era, to television distribution (*Jean de Florette*, dir. Claude Berri, 1986). Beaudin's film announced similar processes in Quebec, with the added urgency of creating and nurturing an economically viable auteur cinema. However, a Quebec popular cinema had begun to exist, with an emphasis on stars and genre in an admittedly exiguous industrial context, and its significance must not be underestimated.

7 Popular Cinema

If, as Eric Hobsbawm has pointed out, nationalism precedes the nation,[1] then the "people" are not a given but have to be created and produced. The journalism of the nineteenth century, radio from the 1930s and television from the 1950s, and manifestations of direct cinema such as *Les Raquetteurs* and *Pour la suite du monde*, all contributed to the construction of French-Canadian and then Québécois identity through narratives and representations of its ordinary people. When we speak of popular cinema, however, we come up against the conundrums posed by terminology. The confrontation of the "popular" with a "mass" cultural medium raises the question of the meaning of both terms and the specificity of Quebec society and history in relation to them.

In Perrault, as we have seen, despite the elements of invention and becoming, the "people" are linked to notions of authenticity which in turn depend on putting reworkings of traditional practices into discourse. However, this is not a viable approach for a wider Quebec cinema in a modernizing society, still less for a cinema wishing to reach mass audiences. In this chapter I shall take "popular cinema" to mean those attempts in Quebec cinema at reaching a mass rather than merely *cinéphile* audience. "Popular" thus slides into "mass" here, but the reality of contemporary capitalist culture is to do just that, to link together, transform, and rearticulate elements of traditional society for the purposes of commodification. "The people" must become "audiences" for those commodities; they are the (active) consumers and not producers of this culture. Obviously, much is at stake symbolically as well as economically in the enterprise that is Quebec commercial cinema. Popular cinema provides some of the clearest sources of visual and aural recognition of "Quebec"; indeed, one of the distinctions of the popular as opposed to art or auteurist work is its intertextual connections with other *spoken* entertainment forms. Stuart Hall thus argues against seeing popular culture as merely manipulative or, like the Frankfurt School, instrumentalized: "If the forms of provided commercial popular culture are not purely manipulative, then it is because, alongside the false appeals, the foreshortenings, the trivialization and shortcircuits, there are also elements of recognition and identification, something approaching a recreation of recognizable experiences and attitudes to which people are responding."[2] At the same time however, Quebec popular cinema represents a faultline, indeed several faultlines, within those processes of recognition.

The first is that between change and continuity, and, within these terms, between the nation and capitalism. Quebec popular cinema constructs a "people," represented in the diegesis and/or assembled in its audience(s); that "people" is both origin and always, as we shall see, in a process of historical change which, more visibly than for many other national "peoples," affects its very being and self-definition. In Quebec, the "people" is always becoming something else, and the "nation" represents change as well as continuity or origin. In addition, that process of becoming is one that is currently being integrated into a North American and world economic system of trade and commodity exchange, a becoming-capitalist or becoming-global which is mirrored in the film industry itself. Simon Frith prefers the term "capitalist culture": "culture defined, that is, not in terms of the production of commodities (though this is involved) but as the way in which people deal with/symbolize/articulate/share/resist the *experience* of capitalism (including, but not exclusively, the ideological experience of capitalism)."[3]

The second faultline arises from the complexities of the first. The way Quebec popular cinema tends to deal with the problem of the nation-becoming-global and its own complicity with that process is to place American culture at the centre of its preoccupations. There is even more at stake here than in Western European societies, because of the minority status of a francophone society in anglophone North America, and also because of that temptation of Québécois or French-Canadian identity represented by the vast spaces and possibilities of *américanité* rather than nationhood modelled on the *habitants'* home or a defensive territorialization such as that which characterizes modern France. The United States can also be seen as the touchstone of success and upward mobility.

The third faultline emerges from the play of identity and difference implied in the second. If, as Hall points out, one definition of the "popular" is "all those things that 'the people' do or have done,"[4] then the question arises, who or what is included and excluded here? If popular culture often raises to a higher power society's wider preoccupations (through schematization, caricature, its colossal investment in recognition), then in Quebec this can take the form of a heightened sense of self and other, of the frontier between those that belong and do not belong, that are "us" or "not us" (witness, for example, as we saw in chapter 5, the homophobia of early 1970s comedies). However, it is not enough to speak of a mere intensification of anxieties. "Popular culture" always points also to its own society, implying differentials and distinctions to which we must now turn.

In *La Vengeance de la femme en noir*, directed by Roger Cantin in 1996 as a sequel to his successful comedy thriller *L'Assassin jouait du trombone* of 1991, a whole comic sequence is built on the eating practices of two policemen staking out a suspect. The pleasures of bread and caviar are decisively rejected in favour of doughnuts, a simple gag that is, however, a metonym for more complex social phenomena. The joke is partly to do with the recognition of a cultural and generic cliché ("cops eat doughnuts," endlessly recycled in the television comedy show *Rock et belles oreilles*) but also of the cultural capital, as well as, if not more than, financial capital which is involved in having a taste for and knowing how to eat caviar. Audiences are caught between a relationship of difference with the police (as unsophisticated) and one of identification (as embodiments of popular taste) which mirrors their dual role in the film as antagonists and allies of the little Québécois hero. Pierre Bourdieu's monumental work on the sociology of taste locates practices such as eating caviar (or doughnuts) and liking modern art (or ice hockey), and their meaning or indeed "value," within a structure of distinction that assigns cultural capital to individuals and groups in society as unequally as financial capital. The education system differentiates not only in the award of diplomas but in the unequal distribution of cultural capital and ability/willingness to participate in the most prestigious cultural tastes and practices. For Bourdieu, legitimate taste's "aesthetic disposition," in which material urgencies are bracketed out in favour of a preoccupation with form, is in a mutually dependent binary opposition with popular taste, which favours identification and participation rather than distance, and which refuses legitimate taste's refusal of itself.[5]

Suggestive as they are, Bourdieu's schemas can be imported only problematically into other societies beyond that of 1960s France, where his original research took place. (We shall delay until the final chapter discussion of the implications of postmodernism for the high/low cultural distinction.) Quebec here provides a dual profile. On the one hand, its size and history imply different understandings of social hierarchy. Its first élite, the ruling personnel of New France, disappeared along with its culture after the conquest of 1759. Even in the years of clerical nationalism, there was, and continues to be, a massive investment in "the people," in those bereft of economic and political power, as source of the nation's symbolic legitimacy. Its small population of 7 million people makes it analogous to Western countries with, supposedly, milder social differentiations such as Scandinavia or the Netherlands. The embodiments of wealth and legitimate taste in Quebec have historically been the anglophones and an indigenous bourgeoisie which looked to France for its high culture.

On the other hand, while class distinction is partly subsumed in the construction of the Quebec nation, it cannot be completely, particularly since 1960 and the expansion of the francophone bourgeoisie. That bourgeoisie, from whose numbers are drawn much of Quebec's *cinéphile* audience and many *cinéastes*, is both dependent on the "popular" bias of Quebec national definition and often concerned to displace cultural distinction onto the "outside," high for France, low for the United States. This contradiction may be one of the sources of the shortcomings of Quebec cinema analysed by Ginette Major in an influential study published in 1982, which argued that the "Québécois audience" (itself a homogenizing abstraction, unfortunately), preconditioned as it was by Hollywood cinema with its emphasis on entertainment and utopia, was failing to recognize itself in the resigned and fatalistic portraits to be found in the slow, intimist dramas of much Quebec film production: "Quebec cinema will rediscover its lost audience when it stops being the complacent mirror of an enfeebled society."[6]

We traced in chapter 4 the problematic relations between French and Quebec cinema. It could be argued that that space in between France and Hollywood is a potentially fascinating one to be in, particularly as the latter pair both possess their own quotient of cultural hybridity. Two polarities, however, have tended to be sketched out for Quebec cinema: a refusal of the world economic system (and film industry), or a complicity with it, with all the risks and opportunities that entails. In a sentence already rather dated, Fredric Jameson had listed, in an influential article in 1979, the *roman québécois* (along with black, gay, women's, and Third World literature, blues, and British working-class rock) as an example of "authentic cultural production" drawing on "the collective experience of marginal pockets of the social life of the world system."[7] While he is probably thinking of the novels of

Hubert Aquin,[8] we could suggest cinematic equivalents here, say Gilles Groulx and Jean Pierre Lefebvre. Over the last three decades, Quebec cinema has experienced modes of film-making which have continued that avant-garde tradition, created spaces for a more mass-audience-friendly auteur cinema (Arcand, Beaudin), or gone all out to maximize audiences at home and/or abroad (the ultimate logic of which, of course, is to shoot in English). It is these latter texts that have, by and large, been anathematized, ignored, or at best neglected by the Quebec critical apparatus,[9] and on which francophone avatars this chapter concentrates.

The approach to them has partly to be a diachronic one, since definitions of "the popular," and of the high/low cultural distinction, can change historically and are themselves the products of history. We saw in chapter 3 the beginnings of a commercial film industry in Quebec in the late 1960s: the creation of the CFDC, and the success of *Valérie*. Denis Héroux was to continue that strain, with *L'Initiation* (1969: also starring Danielle Ouimet), *L'Amour humain* (1970), and *Sept fois par jour* (1971). The two other major names in this period of construction are Claude Fournier and Jean-Claude Lord. Fournier (b. 1931) had been a scriptwriter and director at the NFB and then for his own company in the private sector, where he made his first fiction film, *Deux femmes en or* (1970), the first Canadian feature in colour, seen by two million spectators in Quebec and making $4 million from an original investment of $218,000. The film inaugurated the sex comedies with a dose of nationalism that would characterize his output in the early 1970s. Violette Lamoureux (Louise Turcot) and Fernande Turcot (Monique Mercure) are two bored suburban housewives living in Brossard on the south shore of Montreal. Yvon Turcot (Marcel Sabourin) works for an anglophone insurance company based in Toronto: after a comic conversation in English with his superiors, his work is rewarded with a portrait of the queen which he takes home. Bob Lamoureux (Donald Pilon) is a salesman who philanders on his travels. When the two wives discover Bob's infidelities, they decide to get their own back by doing the same, seducing the various handymen and delivery boys who come their way. A pet shop salesman expires in the act with Violette, and the women are arrested for his murder, since their activities had become known because of Fernande's confession to the magazine *Midinette*. However, they are acquitted because of a sympathetic judge (played by the union leader Michel Chartrand), become celebrities, and have their lives turned into a musical on Broadway.

The film can to an extent be seen as a parody of *Valérie*, as Gilles Blain has argued.[10] The "erotic" scenes are in fact de-eroticized because of the comic element, and because of, for the Quebec spectator, the parade of well-known comedians and monologuists such as Yvon Deschamps who are seduced.[11] However, breasts are bared at an early stage, and it is not at all clear that the American climax is meant to satirize Héroux's film-industry ambitions – quite the contrary, it imitates them. But at this stage in Quebec history, before the 1976–85 *péquiste* governments and their language reforms, and in the context of this irreverential film, the preoccupation is not with the low status of American culture but with English Canada and federalism as Other to the community of the Quebec comic audience and as the butt of its jokes: the scenes in Toronto, a montage of Trudeau blowing his nose, Bob's "Les Anglaises dans le lit c'est pas un cadeau/English girls are appalling in bed." The film therefore embodies the three faultlines outlined above: the role of America, but, more important, the structures of inclusion/exclusion and also change and continuity; the film constructs its content and audience as in process and incomplete in terms of national identity but also gender and sexual roles. Having emerged from Catholicism and having extensively modernized (suburbanized) itself, the society is negotiating change through a play of autonomy and dependency (to a heterosexual-male look) for women and a debunking of traditional machismo. Fournier's films of the 1970s become progressively cruder, partly because they are centred on male protagonists. *Les Chats bottés* (1971) includes a striptease to the tune of "God Save the Queen" by an Elizabeth II lookalike.

Jean-Claude Lord emerged from the Coopératio venture in the 1960s. The family melodrama *Les Colombes* was a major box-office success in 1972. Lord's wife, Lise Thouin, plays Josiane Boucher, a budding pop singer from a working-class family in the east end of Montreal who marries Julien Ferland, the schoolteacher son (Jean Besré) of a wealthy lawyer (Jean Coutu). Formally, the film combines the diverse narrative strands of television soap opera with the short takes, narrative pace, and parallel editing of mainstream Hollywood cinema, particularly to illustrate class difference: the bus/Jaguar used by the two families to return from the wedding, the contrast between the communal working-class *cuisine* and the large spaces of the bourgeois *salon*, between emotional expression and reticence. It proposes, however, a rather backward-looking articulation of these well-implanted myths of Quebec culture. The "authenticity" of the "people" (among whom Josiane's mother, played by the remarkable vaudeville performer Manda Parent, is the most spectacular embodiment), counterposed to the bourgeoisie, commerce, and corruption (Josiane's pop career), opens not onto political action but to the trope of childhood. Young Nadine Ferland joins the list of dead children in Quebec cinema when her uncle Albert (Jean Duceppe), whose own children had been killed in a car accident by his drunken brother and who has since been reduced to a broken, childlike, and disruptive state, accidentally/deliberately lets her suffocate during a hide-and-seek game. The "doves" of the title refer not only to the birds sacrificed at a leftist theatre performance to *épater le bourgeois* and comment on an "oppressive" society, but also to children and childhood as sites of cultural value (the lyrics of the title song). *Les Colombes* is significant for its reworking of 1950s Catholic melodrama for the 1970s, in which the sacred has been left behind but stays in the family through this rather overdetermined and politically arresting emphasis on childhood (the leftists are portrayed in caricatural fashion), and in which, in a manner typical of Lord's output, the denunciation of consumer society takes place by putting it into spectacle.

Lord's other successes in the 1970s were thrillers with a political theme, which got him dubbed "the local Costa-Gavras."[12] *Bingo* (1974), a transposition of the October crisis, was discussed in chapter 2. *Panique* (1977) was a thriller about industrial pollution, again with animals and children as the main victims. Most of Lord's films after 1980 were made in English, although he did direct the television hockey saga *Lance et compte* (SRC, 1987–89) and the sixth *conte pour tous*, *La Grenouille et la baleine* (1988).

None of the texts so far mentioned in this chapter really articulates "the people" as founding myth or legitimacy for their enterprise. *Deux femmes en or* is too much about change and suburbia, which are not articulated with origin or a notion of the "authentic." Fournier's other comedies are too crudely sexist to be truly federating. Genre requirements prevent Lord portraying a social fresco, if that was ever his intention, so that "the people" cannot found anything and are in any case defeated. However, at the NFB in the early 1970s, attempts were made to participate in the development of this popular cinema. The most notable example is probably Marcel Carrière's *O.K. ... Laliberté* (1973). This tale of forty-somethings, neither bourgeois nor workers, relies for its pleasures on a combination of realism, a product of Carrière's documentary experience, and performance, especially that of Luce Guilbeault. She plays Yvonne, a tenant in a boarding-house in the Carré St-Louis, transfixed by consumerism but sensual and nostalgic, who embarks on an affair with the newly installed Paul Laliberté (Jacques Godin), whose marriage collapses at the start of the film. The debts that the couple run up are eliminated by an amateurish but successful robbery. The tale thus manages the effects of change and individualism, negotiating a modest path for its protagonists between winning and losing, freedom and constraint. Significantly, Carrière and his NFB team took the trouble of testing both the synopsis and a two-and-a-half-hour-long cut of the film on audiences before the film's release.[13]

To an extent, of course, the job of founding "the people" had already been done: the oral "people-in-becoming" of Perrault's Île-aux-coudres trilogy for art cinema, the radio and then television serials for popular culture. Of these, the most important had been SRC's first, *La Famille Plouffe*, which ran from 1953 to 1957. Roger Lemelin's 1948 novel about a working-class family in Quebec City was turned into a blockbuster cinema and television version in 1981, directed by Gilles Carle.

Les Plouffe is set in 1939–40 with a brief coda located at the end of the war. The family live in the lower town of Quebec City and consist of the matriarch, Joséphine (Juliette Huot), and the father, Théophile (Émile Genest, who had been in the TV series), a typograph for the newspaper *L'Action chrétienne*. Three of their children work in the local shoe factory: Cécile (Denise Filiatrault), unmarried, in her forties, carrying on a chaste friendship with her married childhood sweetheart Onésime (Paul Berval); Napoléon (Pierre Curzi), who helps his tubercular lover to recovery; and Ovide (Gabriel Arcand), who has pretentions of performing opera. He is in love with the flighty Rita Toulouse (Anne Létourneau), whose flirtations drive him to the monastery but whom he eventually marries. The youngest son, Guillaume (Serge Dupire), is a champion *anneaux* player and is recruited by a visiting pastor, Tom Brown (Paul Dumont), to play professional baseball with a team in Cincinnati. This falls through because of the war, which Guillaume decides to spend in the Canadian army.

The film had at that time the biggest budget in Canadian history, at $4.8 million, and this is testified to by not only its length but its lavish use of costumed extras in crowd scenes. The money was assembled by the International Cinema Corporation, the predecessor of Alliance Films, which had been founded by Denis and Justine Héroux (b. 1942) along with former NFB producer-director John Kemeny (b. 1925) in 1979. As well as public investment from the CFDC, the SRC, and the Institut québécois du cinéma, the film benefited from private sponsorship, notably from the Banque Royale and Alcan, which got access to TV advertising time and space on the publicity posters. *Les Plouffe* was part of a series of high-profile films International Cinema produced in this period that were directed by established French names and/or made into a parallel TV version: *Atlantic City USA*; *Quest for Fire* (Annaud, 1981); *Hold-Up* (Arcady, 1985), set in Montreal and starring Jean-Paul Belmondo, made in French from an American novel, and remade in Hollywood as *Quick Change* (Franklin, 1990); *Louisiana* (de Broca, 1983), made in English with a CBS television version; and *Le*

Sang des autres (Chabrol, 1984), made in both English and French versions. Apart from *Maria Chapdelaine*, the only two other "Québécois" films of this period were a sequel to *Les Plouffe*; *Le Crime d'Ovide Plouffe* (Arcand, 1984), the script for which Lemelin was persuaded to write for $250,000 and which features Ovide transmogrified into a *Cité libre-*type intellectual (this was also made into a TV series, with the first episodes directed by Carle; only Arcand's episodes were translated into a theatrical version); and *Le Matou* (Beaudin, 1985), of which more later.

Intriguingly, then, *Les Plouffe*'s production parallels the play of centripetal and centrifugal, homogenizing and heterogenizing forces which characterize the protagonists' fates and those of the people of Quebec. Because of the need for French distribution, care was taken to render the dialogue comprehensible across the Atlantic, extra effort even being made at the post-synchronization stage by actors redubbing their dialogue.[14] A French actor, Rémi Laurent, was cast in the role of Denis Bouchard, the nationalist journalist and friend of the Plouffe family who, in a major change from the novel, has lived in Paris and has a French mother (Stéphane Audran) who is consoled by the neighbours when France falls. *Les Plouffe* meticulously traces the forces that are disrupting and will disrupt the settled nature of this society, from the early shot of "zapping" across different (foreign and American) radio stations through the references to baseball and the consumption of American mass culture (Rita) to, of course, the outbreak of war and the controversy surrounding conscription. (The 1950s television series had replaced baseball with the more territorialized ice hockey.) Against these centrifugal forces are pitted the centripetal forces of church, tradition, and traditional nationalism: Théo is so ardently anti-English that he named his youngest son after the kaiser; Joséphine will not let the Anglican priest re-enter her house; Guillaume is nearly arrested when he uses his pitcher's skills to disrupt the visit of the king and queen to their street, an event for which the Plouffe are the only family to refuse to hang flags in recognition. Théo is sacked from his job for this, which provokes an ultimately successful strike at the newspaper but also a stroke which leaves him half-paralysed. These events are punctuated by set-pieces in which crowd scenes (at the sports events, the parades, and demonstration) emphasize both collective identities and the popular cultural mode of identification and participation which characterizes the film itself and its classic montage and *mise en scène*.

Quite apart, then, from the tensions we have previously observed in the relation between present *énonciation* and past *énoncé* where the costume drama is concerned, *Les Plouffe*, paradoxically and triumphantly, simultaneously represents an origin and change, an origin-in-becoming. (This is acknowledged in one of the publicity slogans for the film: "a people on the brink [*frontière*] of a profound evolution but whose identity remains essential to its survival.") The construction of self/other (with regard to the "English") is strong, but problematized, not the least example of the past/present enunciatory gap: "we" know what the meaning of the Second World War and Nazism was. The older generation are trapped, but the young men escape and fulfil their goals to an extent. Significantly, it is the daughter, Cécile, whose destiny, caught in parallel editing with that of Ovide and Napoléon, ends in catastrophe and defeat, with the bus crash that kills Onésime. This in-betweenness is conveyed spatially as well as temporally (the passing years that convey change): the staircases leading up to the upper town are not only emblems of hierarchical space but spaces of transition, out of the house, where Guillaume and Ovide's first sexual encounters take place. The gallery and staircase leading to the Plouffe home are also emblematic of the continuity of private and social/collective space,[15] as well as being the space in which melodramatic confrontations are staged (Guillaume returning after going off with Rita).

There are two more points to be made, one to do with content, the other with form. Few other Quebec fictional features represent the Second World War: *Je suis loin de toi mignonne* (Fournier, 1976) and *Bonheur d'occasion* (Fournier, 1983) are the exceptions.[16] This is because, unlike for Britain (which probably, with the former Soviet Union, holds the record for mass-cultural representations of the period) and most of the other Allies, the war cannot serve as a founding moment of national unanimity for the Québécois. Conscription in the First World War had met with considerable resistance, with riots in Quebec City in 1917. The federal Liberal government had promised no conscription in the second world conflict of the century, and when it asked the public for the right to change its policy in a pan-Canadian referendum in 1942, there was a pro-yes vote nationally but a 72 per cent "No" in Quebec. (The provincial Liberal government subsequently lost the 1944 election.) Catholic and conservative opinion played a strong role in this, and in the film most of the characters are portrayed leaving the procession when the cardinal of Quebec comes out in favour of conscription, contradicting Father Folbèche (Gérard Poirier). (Significantly, *Je suis loin de toi mignonne* portrays the Québécois as spectators to history, its male characters being Rosencrantz and Guildenstern figures at the 1943 Quebec conference, one of them losing Winston Churchill's bag: a truly minor treatment of the war-movie genre.)

Les Plouffe adheres to melodramatic and soap-opera formats, but with important variants which underline Quebec's specificity. Whereas nineteenth-century melodrama in Europe marked an acknowledgement of the desacralization of society and the massive reinvestment in the home and sexual relationships as sites of new meanings and moral polarities,[17] in Quebec melodrama (in the novel *Les Plouffe* or the contemporaneous film output) emerged as Catholic melodrama, a site of competing discourses and genres, between the "private" or "individual" as sites of struggle and goal construction, and a collective sacred and ethnic destiny. This is precisely the contradiction embedded in *Les Plouffe*. In addition, this is a melodrama or soap opera which is centred on men, not women. Joséphine and then Cécile, in their different ways, have their options closed off. Rita develops and "matures," but only to be gazed at and exchanged between men. The men's "melodramatic" domestic relations come to bear such symbolic weight because they themselves are feminized by their circumstances. Geoffrey Nowell-Smith has written of a fundamental characteristic of Hollywood melodrama:

In addition to the problems of adults, particularly women, in relation to their sexuality, the Hollywood melodrama is also fundamentally concerned with the child's problems of growing into a sexual identity within the family, under the aegis of a symbolic law which the father incarnates. What is at stake (also for socio-ideological reasons) is the survival of the family unit and the possibility for individuals of acquiring an identity which is also a place within the system, a place in which they can both be "themselves" and "at home," in which they can simultaneously enter, without contradiction, the symbolic order and bourgeois society.[18]

The negotiation of social and domestic roles is as problematic for men as it is and has been for women in "normal" societies in which melodrama has emerged and flourished.

To that extent, the film can be seen to represent an Oedipal trajectory in which men find their social and (hetero)sexual place in the world (despite, in this case, the weak father). However, the final shot, which at first sight seems rather lame after three hours' projection time, is a freeze-frame of Joséphine on the gallery having just discovered that Guillaume after all has actively participated in the war and "killed men." As well as a loss of innocence for her, this is a double-edged gender victory for him if ever there was one, Oedipus legitimating killing. It is therefore difficult to concur with Jean Larose's condemnation of the film's symbolic system, with Joséphine as castrating mother, a "sub-priest without a penis"[19] who with Folbèche forms the "real couple" of the film. Réal La Rochelle, in an article in *En lutte!* of May 1981, condemns the film for its lack of working-class militancy and, more pointedly, for its project of selling Québécois picturesque on the international market.[20] It is precisely the film's production of a space-time *between* the plenitudes of identity which makes it all the more remarkable as embodiment of a founding myth of a "people."

Adapted from Yves Beauchemin's best-selling novel which sold 200,000 copies in Quebec and a million in France, *Le Matou* followed the same production basis as *Les Plouffe*, a co-production with France with two versions, one theatrical, one a television series. Set in contemporary Montreal but in the anonymously picturesque old quarter rather than the vibrant and cosmopolitan plateau of Mont-Royal, it tells the rather picaresque story of a married couple, Florent and Élise Boissonnault (Serge Dupire and Monique Spaziani), whose lives become entangled with a mysterious and sinister stranger, Ratablavasky (Jean Carmet), when he offers them the possibility of fulfilling their ambition of owning a restaurant. The "cat" of the title is the pet of a neglected street-child, Monsieur Emile (Guillaume Lemay-Thivierge), who is looked after by Florent and Elise but who is killed in an accident when searching for the cat in a disused building. The creature also comes to connote destiny and fate, and introduces, with Ratablavasky, an element of the fantastic into this realist text. In the film, any "strange" or "uncanny" elements as such are limited to the last shot, of the cat framed in the window while the silhouette of Ratablavasky passes in the street. However, both book and film work hard to establish the married couple as "centred" and "normal" and to create a caricatural confrontation with the machinations of the Slavic, immigrant Other and the anglophone Other, Florent's former colleague and double-crossing business partner, Slipskin (Miguel Fernandes), with whom Ratablavasky is in cahoots. (Florent to his anglophone boss: "Trouve-toi un autre nègre/Find yourself another nigger"; to the hotel manager who announces Ratablavasky's – false – death and asks if he is a relative: "I'm Québécois through and through [*pure laine*], don't I look it"). Beauchemin was a PQ member and passionately committed to the sovereignty project. What is striking in these texts, however, is, first, that the goals and resolution of the antagonism are read not only in individual but in individualist terms, with Florent as the 1980s self-advancing entrepreneur, the "homme performant" which Jocelyn Létourneau sees as the new avatar of Quebec identity.[21] Florent and Elise thus come to embody a kind of hegemonic transmission belt, in which old and new and different time-frames are balanced: traditional Québécois cuisine with a metropolitan French cook (played by Julien Guiomar, owing to the co-production), a new business founded on selling antique furniture, and, moreover, the familiar dead child of Quebec masochism and defeatism (shades of *La Petite Aurore l'enfant martyre*, but also *Mon oncle Antoine, Les Colombes*) replaced by the end of the film with their own offspring. Secondly, the mysterious, fantastic, "magic" element in the film functions (as in Forcier's films but with less sense of community) as a textual element signalling the coexistence and embeddedness of different phases of capitalist development and culture. However, in *Le Matou* this depends on that uncanniness associated with the Other, as the texts show no awareness of the fact that boundaries are about internal limits (Žižek), and that the notion of the uncanny is closely related to what *is* "homely"/ *heimlich*, in that it is about the return of the repressed (Freud).

A reliance on these *valeurs sûres* ("dead certs"), represented by adapting for the cinema and/or television series best-selling books, is one possible approach when seeking to create a regular output of, and audiences for, a popular cinema. Another is, of course, the resort to genre. Famously, American film companies during and since the studio era developed genres as a way of organizing audience expectation, of promising and signalling something different but also something familiar (a "western," a "musical"). It was a system appropriate for regular film production and film-going and for the phenomenon of repetition which characterizes the practices of commodity culture. The structures of Quebec cinema obviously lend themselves with more difficulty to this kind of repetition, given the ad hoc nature of assembling film projects and submitting them to Telefilm Canada and other agencies (with the exceptions of highly specialized activities such as animation – associated especially with the NFB and its legacies – and the children's film). Genre cinema is thus a rarity in an industry still centred on a *cinéma d'auteur rentable* (viable or lucrative auteur cinema). When it emerges, however, it inevitably raises important cross-cultural questions, because it must always position itself in relation to American codes and conventions.

Although there is a Québécois western of sorts (*Mustang*, dir. Marcel Lefebvre, 1975), in Quebec the space occupied by this genre in American culture is that nexus of relations with the native peoples and with the natural wilderness, the truly indigenous *pays d'en haut* genre that developed out of literature, radio, and television earlier in the century, as we shall see in chapter 10. There are only three examples of musicals in Quebec cinema (which is, after all, dominated by realism): *Pas de vacances pour les idoles* (Héroux, 1965), Jacques Godbout's *IXE-13* (1971: a parody of the – federalist – pulp serial tales of "the ace Canadian spy" which began in 1947),[22] and Gilles Carle's *Fantastica* (1981). These are exceptional, for it is a genre that relies on large budgets and especially a more regular indigenous theatrical and recording output of that kind of musical product than one-offs like Luc Plamondon's *Starmania* (first performed in Paris in 1979) and *Notre-Dame-de-Paris* (1998; both works co-written with the French composer Michel Berger).

Given the budgetary constraints and the cultural context, the two most likely candidates are comedy and the crime or police thriller, which form the basis of genre cinema in France. The *policier* there is embedded in several cultural histories: the experience of nineteenth-century modernity and the city as first represented in the crime narratives of Eugène Sue but also Hugo and to an extent Balzac; its continuation in the twentieth century from the point of view of the bourgeoisie (Simenon's Maigret series) but also the lower classes (Léo Malet's Nestor Burma series), and its representation in cinema from an early stage;[23] its complex reworking via American culture and the transnational encounter of the *série noire* and the *nouvelle vague* auteurs (as we saw in chapter 4), as well as existentialist thought eager to see some of its agendas played out in late 1940s Hollywood *film noir*; and the different political uses to which it has been put in the post-1968 era, asserting authentic "French" values or denouncing entrenched corruption or social inequality.[24]

Quebec cinema and culture have only the American connection to work with, and its presence is more massive, the relationship more unequal. In addition, the Law/not Law distinction and the assertions of masculine identity the genre traditionally requires are problematic within the "minor" status of Quebec culture. The approach of Quebec film-makers has been various. In their radically different ways, Lauzon in *Un Zoo la nuit* and Simoneau in *Pouvoir intime* had dealt with that minor status, the first by revisiting the sources of masculine identity (father fixation and homophobia), the second by dispersing them. Roger Cantin in *L'Assassin jouait du trombone* and *La Vengeance de la femme en noir* had opted for a postmodern comedy pastiche of the genre, setting the first in a film studio in which his little Quebec hero is employed as a watchman, and peppering both films liberally with cinematic quotations. In addition, the American thriller has in the past three decades been able to globalize its purview of crime and corruption, so that the Law/not Law distinction plays itself out in relation to organizations (for which read big business) and is generically articulated for audiences living and negotiating the realities of the capitalist culture represented. American crime films, in their explorations of American power, often have global implications.[25] For Quebec, this is not possible because of its minority status and because of the unavoidability of the national question. Arcand's solution in his 1970s films was to open out through references to history the punctual denunciations of Quebec society permitted by his depiction of crime milieus.

In recent years, however, the *policier* has manifested itself more in Quebec cinema, partly as it is able to articulate both auteur and commercial preoccupations in a way appropriate to the current climate. *Rafales* (André Melançon, 1990) is a hostage drama which uses the snowbound Montreal winter as an indigenous cityscape and mindscape in a manner analogous to the urban iconographies of Hollywood. *La Conciergerie* (Michel Poulette, 1997) casts Serge Dupire as a police officer whose partner is killed in a drive-by shooting. Via a whodunnit structure that unmasks one of the eccentric denizens of the eponymous halfway house as the murderer of its property-speculating owner, Dupire is also able to reveal two of his superiors as guilty of his partner's death. This Oedipal narrative ends with him reconciled with his estranged wife and family. The most successful film of this current crop at the box office is *Liste noire* (Jean-Marc Vallée, 1995), which made $1 million in Quebec and did better than *Le Confessionnal* (Lepage, 1995) and *Léolo* in the United States, grossing just over $800,000 there.[26]

Liste noire is set in Quebec City and stars Michel Côté as Jacques Savard, a new member of the provincial Supreme Court. After a judge is found *in flagrante* with a prostitute, Gabrielle Angers (Geneviève Brouillette), the latter, in order to avoid prison, threatens to reveal to the press the list of names of other judges and lawyers whom she services. Her own lawyer, who had threatened to blackmail them, is murdered. The murderer is eventually revealed to be Savard himself, who had been one of her regulars, a false name representing him on the list. He is shot dead by the off-duty policeman Michel Gauthier (André Champagne) – who defies orders not to protect Gabrielle – a split second before Savard's wife Francine (Sylvie Bourque), who has worked out the truth and trailed him, would have had to decide between shooting Savard to save Gabrielle or shooting Gabrielle to save the family's reputation. The conniving chief police investigator Claude Laberge (Raymond Cloutier) destroys the evidence against the others, and the system continues as before. The film deals with the paradoxical situation of "Quebec noir" by in fact turning into an abstraction. The dark cinematic potential of Quebec's capital, so intelligently explored in *Le Confessionnal*, is here avoided in favour of generalized night scenes in bourgeois houses and their adjacent driveways and gardens. The denunciation of "corruption" and conspiracy has none of the purchase on contemporary Quebec society that characterized Arcand's *Réjeanne Padovani* and *Gina*.

One prominent Quebec critic's condemnation of *Liste noire* emphasized its imitation not only of American film style ("an excrescence of what American cinema serves up to us every week")[27] but also its rather un-Québécois puritanism (the exaggerated condemnation of infidelity). This would seem to miss the point of a film which, like a half-hearted *Pouvoir intime*, explodes and dissipates the notion of a single male hero, setting up actual and potential alliances between women (Francine and Gabrielle, but also Savard's secretary who puts Francine on the right track) even as it exposes the homosociality lurking behind the principles of the Law. The film is thus "Québécois" in minor mode in terms of narrative structure (no Oedipal resolutions, father and son figures are equally complicit in the charade and exploitation of women) but completely abstract in terms of its referents.

The question of imitation is central to the workings of the main Quebec cinematic genre of the 1990s, namely comedy. There is some discussion of why comedy should attain this status, on stage as well as in the cinema: in 1996, 70 per cent of all theatrical presentations in Quebec were by comedians. Indeed, comedy has become a veritable industry, embodied by the Montreal comedy festival (Just for Laughs/ Juste pour rire) held in August each year. In an article in *Le Devoir* at the time of the 1997 festival, Pierre Cayouette speculated on the reasons for this boom.[28] As well as "global" explanations such as Gilles Lipovetsky's analysis of the relaxed informality of postmodern society,[29] Cayouette cites the specificity, that is to say, morosity of Quebec society after the 1980 referendum and during the economic recession of the early 1980s from which Montreal was by late 1998 only just beginning to recover (stand-up comic shows are cheap to put on and take on tour). However, his view is critical: contemporary Quebec humour is apolitical and fails to challenge the status quo, unlike the humour of the 1960s, and concentrates on the absurd and on self-mockery. I would like to argue, however, for the significance of this *autodérision* for Quebec cultural identity and even a cultural politics.

Comedy is the popular genre par excellence in that it constructs a shared experience, a community of laughter, and is highly participatory: "Like language and 'texts' in general, the comic is plural, unfinalized, disseminative, dependent on *context* and the intertextuality of creator, text, and contemplator. It is not, in other words, just the *content* of comedy that is significant but also its 'conspiratorial' relationship with the viewer."[30] But what are we to make of the spectators' relation with the targets and butts of humour, and with the comic personage him/herself? Within the multifarious theories of the comic, it is striking how often recur figures of duality, which can be understood either as contradictory or incongruous opposites, or as ambivalence. Comedy is about "a combination of control and freedom, an awareness of stated or implied rules/codes, and the imagination/fantasy to manipulate them."[31] Arthur Koestler[32] and Jerry Palmer[33] argue respectively from logic and semiotics that humour results from the mental encounter of two self-contained logical chains, or two syllogisms, marking the intersection of the plausible and implausible. However, there are also involved processes of inclusion and exclusion, identification and disavowal, in which the integrity and protection of the ego (that is, narcissism) are at stake. Freudian theory makes a distinction between humour and the comic. Whereas humour involves a narcissistic disavowal of "the provocations of reality" and a repression of the true butt of humour, namely death and castration,[34] the comic sets up someone observing a butt or a comic person from a superior position and thus a different structure of disavowal: "Laughter marks a disavowal of what one once was, a refusal of identification, a differentiation of ego and other. The aggression involved, though, stems not from any impossibility of identification, from any absolute distinction between other and ego. It stems from an identification that the laughter disavows, thus from an ambivalence inherent in identification itself."[35] "What one once was" is the child. Steve Neale and Frank Krutnik add Lacan's mirror phase to this scenario, so that the comic presents the opposite of that unified, coordinated (and misrecognized) ego.

All this is very suggestive for the Quebec context, first of all because of the comic's dependency on the clash of two syllogisms (it is difficult not to think here of Canada's "two solitudes," but the relationships with France and the United States also correspond), and secondly because the comic, in its momentary, heavily cued, and usually instantly restored suspension of decorum, verisimilitude, and convention, needs a set of shared (social, adult) norms in order to function. That is why some comedy, but not all as we shall see, draws on stock deviations from the "norm," such as the drunk, the homosexual, and the foreigner.

The eponymous hero of *Elvis Gratton* (Falardeau, 1981–85) is one such example of the mercilessly mocked butt of comedy. (This feature film, in fact a collection of three shorts, is the Quebec film most rented at video stores.) Bob "Elvis" Gratton (Julien Poulin) is an obese and physically uncoordinated garage owner obsessed with Elvis Presley who wins an Elvis impersonation competition and with it a holiday on the god-forsaken Caribbean island nation of Santa Banana. Back in Montreal he suffocates to death during a performance in an excessively tight Elvis suit. Falardeau's nationalist credentials (we recall that he was the director of *Octobre*) has him overlay the visual gags with a strong political message. Gratton is a federalist (a "Non" referendum poster hangs prominently in his home) and a reactionary, his Elvis-obsession to be read as an example of cultural alienation and colonization. He is also blind to the American-inspired injustices and inequalities on Santa Banana, whose President "Ricochet," a midget (shades of Vigo's headmaster in *Zéro de conduite* [1932], but consistent with the film's corporeal "norms" that Gratton also transgresses), turns up at Montreal airport in a Mountie uniform.

The relentless lack of subtlety here contributes to a very successful comic effect. A postmodern argument could be developed against Falardeau's notion of "authenticity," for Gratton might be read as creating a *bricolage* of images and identities, foregounding the latter as performative rather than essential.[36] However, I wish to remain with the specificity of *Elvis Gratton* as comedy, and in particular to tease out the implications for Quebec identity of the ambivalences outlined above. Gratton as butt of humour, as the inferior observed by the superior observer, is also a mocking of oneself, of "what one once was." This can be the child (Gratton's infantile relationship with objects in the world) but also that Lacanian mirror phase in which the ego is like the Other while simultaneously the Other is distinct. In other words, the self/other relationship is a fiction. "What one once was" is also, for Falardeau, the colonized past of Quebec, which is prolonged into the present and future through cultural colonization by the United States. The first part of the film ends with a repeat of the opening shots in the supermarket, but this time the customers all wear Elvis masks. (The amalgamated feature ends with the very 1980s admonition, "Peuple à genoux attends ta délivrance/people on your knees, await your liberation.") The notion, however, of self and other held together in an unseparable dance, the simultaneous reading of Gratton as "us" and "not us," point to an ambivalence and impurity within popular Québécois identity which is condensed in *le quétaine*.

Le quétaine is the visual and iconographic equivalent of *joual*, an impure, culturally delegitimized Anglo-French hybrid of borrowings and copies. Significantly, the word's etymology has migrated from an English to a Québécois context and ultimately embraces the two. According to Gilles Colpron's *Les Anglicismes au Québec*, the word originated in the provincial town of Sainte-Hyacinthe earlier in the century and is a corruption of "Keating," a Scottish family famed for their impoverishment (or in alternate versions, for the unrelieved junk sold in their shop).[37] By the time it reached Montreal, its designation of cultural rather than material poverty become dominant, so that it basically means "backward" or "kitsch." It was popularized in a SRC sitcom starring Denise Filiatrault and Dominique Michel entitled *Moi et l'autre*, which first ran from 1966 to 1971. *Le quétaine* is thus a spatial but also a temporal concept, with its connotations of "old-fashionedness," of a cultural habitus that has been (should have been, Falardeau would say) left behind.[38] Whereas costume drama opened up an enunciative gap between past and present based on the discrepancy between origin and performance, *quétaine* comedy's play of similarity to and difference from the spectator's position partakes of the genre's ambivalences of recognition. Elvis Gratton's life, taste, and decor are relentlessly and ineluctably *quétaine*, and the comic aspect of the film is based on a profoundly ambivalent recognition of self and other, self as other, and self as process. Is this what "we" have left behind since the Quiet Revolution, or is it still what "we" are, a part of "us"? Is it alienation or in fact does "our" identity consist of this constant conversation with that which is not "us"?

Quebec comic films of the 1990s tend to base their humour on one of two sets of incongruities, two ambivalent recognitions. On the one hand, there is the comedy of gender identity and (hetero)sexual relations: *Cruising Bar* (Robert Ménard, 1989), which helped to reinaugurate the genre, casts Michel Côté in four different sketches relating to heterosexual male seduction; *L'Homme idéal* (Georges Mihalka, 1996) casts stand-up comic Marie-Lise Pilote as a single woman in her mid-thirties looking for love and someone to father her child. Both these films include temporal and spatial variations within the structures of recognition, playing on class and subcultural differences, social hierarchies of taste, and the distancing effect of behaviours coded as "old," "new," or "emerging."

Cruising Bar employs the classic scopic regime of men looking at women. However, although this can be used to generate humour (a particularly distasteful scene in which an attractive-looking woman is revealed to be deformed from the waist down), the film is overwhelmingly about masculinity, the forms it takes, its ultimate failure: yuppie, narcissistic Jacques *dit* le Paon turns out to be impotent; suburban middle-aged garage-owner Gérard *dit* le Taureau has his multiple infidelities discovered by his wife in disguise; head-banging film set assistant Patrice *dit* le Lion loses his woman when he succumbs again to drug-taking; and nerdy Serge *dit* le Ver de terre wanders mistakenly into a gay disco and and is trapped into sex with a leatherman. The film is about men being caught looking, at women and themselves, with the boundaries and mastery associated with traditional masculine identity undermined to comic effect. (To take two examples: le Paon collapses in a coughing fit after sipping tabasco-spiked beer, a good example of Bergson's association of laughter with *le vivant* bursting through *le mécanique*, but also of the body erupting through the sedateness of bourgeois formalism; le Taureau's encounter with female sexuality has the woman's orgasm echoing through the dance hall and the entire city.) While this comic premise is shared with other Western cultures, it has particular resonances for Quebec national cinema, so much of which is, as we have seen, preoccupied with masculinity and, moreover, the mapping of its inadequacy onto the national context. The extent to which these complexes are being set aside depends on whether a "centred" position can be discerned in the film from which relations of alterity, no matter how ambiguous, can be established. The nucleus of the film is the Paon/Taureau pairing, because they represent exaggerated versions of residual and emergent identities and tastes, popular/ *quétaine* and upwardly mobile/modern(ist), what "we" once were, what "we" might become. The parallel editing, at one point contrasting false teeth and electric toothbrush, reinforces this. Around them circle le Lion and le Ver de terre, whose misadventures are due to the childlike behaviour and knowledge of their adult masculine personae, who are unable to cope physically with the world or socially with its codes. (Le Lion is the one who is nearest to a "mature" relationship, and so the film has to work hard on his physical "otherness" – wild hair, prominent teeth – to compensate.) Here we have a clue to the centred position which the comic effect of the film requires: audiences are placed both in possession of that knowledge and in a median situation compelled by the categories of residual and emergent. On the other hand, the film's investment in recognition (of social types, of Michel Côté in disguise, of different performances of the masculine within Quebec culture: the slogan on the video cover is "You'll recognize them all!") means that that position of superiority is but part of a more complex play of similarity and difference ("us" and "not us") associated with the comic. *Cruising Bar* also succeeds in federating male and female audiences, partly owing to its team of male (Côté, Menard) and female (Claire Wojas, Véronique Le Flaguais, who plays le Taureau's wife) scriptwriters. The duality of laughing at oneself/not oneself is thus mapped on to male/female positions of spectatorship.

L'Homme idéal, while centring on a woman protagonist and a coterie of female friends, also takes masculinity as its prime comic butt. Just as *Cruising Bar* adapted the sexual preoccupations of *Le Déclin de l'empire américain* for popular comic effect, so does this film take on board the changed status of women and fertility in post-traditional Quebec society. The unmarried Lucy Saulnier (Pilote) is a yuppie, an editor of a fashion magazine, but wants a baby. Not only does the film's narrative have to negotiate this familiar dichotomy in a not totally detraditionalized society, its very comic effect depends upon the relationship between old and new. Lucy's mother (Rita Lafontaine), from the Saguenay region and pressurizing her about grandchildren, inadvertently pours a sperm bank sample over her Chinese take-out food. Among the men Lucy encounters (with astounding ease, it should be noted), there are Bob (Rémy Girard), an ex-alcoholic who has embraced feminism to the point of going through birthing rituals and demonstrating a fake orgasm in a restaurant like Meg Ryan in *When*

Harry Met Sally (Reiner, 1989); and Pierre (Cédric Noël), a mummy's boy gynaecologist who romantically saves her life but who is too bourgeois, too old money (significantly, he is French). Otherwise the men are just too young or too "male" and philandering. Clearly, there is no problem in this film as to the centred position from which the comic effect is enounced. The hegemony constructed around Lucy extends to the politics of language. Because he is in an ethnic restaurant, Bob insists on speaking English to the staff. Lucy is differentiated from her dyed-blonde bombshell assistant (Macha Grenon), whose "inauthenticity" includes a discourse peppered with an excess of anglicisms. However, hegemony is not without its contradictions. The "solution" to Lucy's dilemma lies in the Hungarian chef Laszlo (Grégor Hlady), with whom a romance and courtship is barely represented if at all, and a character who is overwhelmingly associated with a feminine space, the restaurant regularly frequented by Lucy's band of *copines*. His profession of chef is re-feminized by the knowledge that it is a come-down from his post as university professor in Budapest. His boss, Martin Drainville in a blonde wig, is feminized to the point of being desexualized. The old/new dichotomies that are the comic butt of the other men are neatly sidestepped by Laszlo, who is conveniently "foreign," representing an older, barely known culture and a new (neo-) Québécois. This *deus ex machina* for Lucy miraculously rescues the family unit. Without it, the film might have slipped into a denaturalization of heterosexuality itself, because, not only would it have figured it as impossible, it would have cast it into a play of similarity and difference, like *le quétaine*, rather than as an unsurpassable horizon.

On the other hand, in 1990s comedies there is the encounter with the Other. *La Florida* (Mihalka, 1993) stars Rémy Girard as Léo Lespérance, the appropriately monickered Montreal bus driver who takes early retirement and invests in a hotel in Hollywood Beach, Florida, taking his wife, Ginette (Pauline Lapointe), and two teenage children with him. On the one hand, the film is about the formation and reassertion of Québécois distinction vis-à-vis American society. Conflicts with the other Québécois hoteliers, notably Daddy Bolduc (Raymond Bouchard), are eventually forgotten in a dispute with American land speculators, and even then the rival and cuckoo in the nest, Jay Lamori (Jason Blicker), is assimilated into their community, in a novel reversal of Quebec's traditional nightmare scenario, when the grandfather, repository of memory and genealogy, establishes that his name is a corruption of "Lamoureux" and that his ancestors emigrated from Quebec to Massachusetts. There is even a priest in attendance. This modern-day *famille Plouffe* by the ocean shows the process by which Léo is sucked into American values (individualism, indifference to a death in the hotel, phoney market-driven smiles) only to resist them in the end. However, the binary oppositions are not always clear-cut. The differentiation made with the violence of American society (from the outset the television news reports one violent crime after another, and Léo and Ginette are robbed at gunpoint) is one which all Canadians would make, and in any case violence (against property) is also imported into Hollywood Beach via the pair of biker brothers (Martin Drainville and Gildor Roy) who are in love with Léo's daughter. Moreover, the comic mode helps to relativize the "superior" position of the Québécois audience vis-à-vis the "butt" that is American society. In an overturning of the habitual syllogisms, Léo has to deal with monolingual hispanic construction workers and cries, "Doesn't anyone speak English around here, tabarnak!" Iconographies and visual gags are set up for audiences to laugh at the Québécois abroad, an oscillation of spectatorship reminiscent of those to be found in co-productions (the syndrome of looking at "ourselves" being looked at which we observed in *Maria Chapdelaine*). Thus the film plays on the reports in Florida tabloids that year ("They're back!") of middle-aged male Québécois beer bellies damaging the aesthetics of the state's beaches by including not only a montage of said protuberances but comments by Léo and Jay on the different operation scars to be observed on them.

These oscillations continue in *Ding et Dong le film* (Alain Chartrand, 1990), produced by Roger Frappier at Max Films (stable of *Le Déclin de l'empire américain*). The film was based on an established stage act starring Claude Meunier and Serge Thériault (who would go on to feature as husband and wife – "Popa" and "Moman" – in the hit SRC sitcom *La Petite Vie* from 1993). The producers' deliberate strategy was to target the Christmas and pre-Christmas audience: "It's a cultural choice, so that the Québécois have the chance to see a comedy made here, in French, at this time of year."[39] Although the film is really a series of sketches, there is some kind of narrative progression, from desperately unsuccessful performances (they are nearly chain-sawed at a quintessentially "French-Canadian" lumber camp) through failed auditions as newsreaders, farcical "pitches" at a film company, a disastrous job as car stunt men, and finally the acquisition of a prosperous inheritance when they entertain a wealthy denizen of Westmount on his deathbed. Until that point, the aural and verbal humour of the film had largely relied on the ambivalent relationship with American language and culture, the incongruity between its connotations of success and the dismal antics of the protagonists: the ironic John Williams-type score over the opening sequence as they drive into the countryside, and the masquerade in English as Hollywood producers which merely doubles the pretensions of the employees of the production company (ending in the chaos of shouting into the boss's speakerphone, "Shut up you Spock"). When Ding and Dong ascend socially, the comic confrontation is with high, and therefore French, culture. They buy a theatre and bring in a director from Paris (Yves Jacques) to put on Corneille's *Le Cid*, in which they star with predictably chaotic results which nevertheless establish a community of mirth as the diegetic Montreal audience reacts favourably and the carnivalesque return of the body (splashings of theatrical blood) overwhelms the solemnities of the legitimate stage. The debunking of high language and culture that takes place throughout the film never, however, posits a stable position of Québécois authenticity from which to judge it. Québécois audiences are placed in between performances of Americanness and Frenchness and at a distance from the childish grotesqueries of Ding and Dong's bodies and (impeded) language and diction, so that identifications are always highly ambivalent. This prevents the mocking of their vaguely foreign landlord from tipping into racism, because their admonitions for him to "articulate" better French collide with their own strangulated syllables.

If, as critics of films like *Liste noire* have argued, Quebec cinema loses its way when adopting televisual practices of film direction and audience address, then it is not surprising that the two Quebec films which take television as their subject are both relentlessly hostile. The first, *Parlez-nous d'amour* (Lord, 1976) has a script by Michel Tremblay and assimilates television with *quétainerie* as cheap, compensatory substitute for real life and empowerment. "Jeannot"/Jean-Claude Michot (Jacques Boulanger) is a pop singer and host of a prime-time television light-entertainment show whose audience primarily consists of middle-aged women. Like a Québécois version of *Network* (dir. S. Lumet), released the same year, the film satirizes the power, manipulation, and commercial premise of television but concentrates on its culture more than its demagoguery. The attitude of Jeannot and the television company to their audience is contemptuous. The film maps the distinctions of "taste" and their attendant inequalities of power. While the television studio is a carnivalesque and participatory space of shared enthusiasm, Jeannot's home, which he shares with his "sophisticated" and socially empowered wife (Monique Mercure), a children's writer, is "modern," rectilinear, and full of abstract art, precisely marking their possession of the bourgeois aesthetic disposition. (This contrast is emphasized by numerous edits between the decor and the tawdry objects exhibited on the show.)

However, *le quétaine* as alienation emerges more ambivalently than in *Elvis Gratton*, and this is because of gender. The contradiction in Tremblay's work since *Les Belles-Soeurs* had been to set up working-class women, those possessing the lowest social status, as symbols of a whole alienated and colonized nation, while at the same time endowing them with a language and even charisma which made them interesting *as women* and which foregrounded gender rather than class or nation as the prime issue. In other words, to see the women as embodying sheer negativity would be to re-enact the disempowerment that the work was supposed to denounce. Rather, this contradiction opened up the possibility of women's space and culture representing a resource for Quebec rather than the expression of its past defeats.

In *Parlez-nous d'amour*, popular culture is provided for the women, but they in turn make something out of it. The television studio is a kind of battleground between the agenda of the program-makers and the communal enthusiasm of the female audience which succeeds in creating connectedness even as contemporary society sweeps away the old forms. Some are easily humbled or see that their fantasies fail to measure up to reality (Rita Lafontaine as the fan from Rimouski whose sexual encounter with Jeannot ends in fiasco), while others are disruptive. The formidable Ruby (Françoise Berd), leader of the bus-load from Drummondville (epitome of the *quétaine* provincial town), having mocked a sales assistant's pretentious French ("J'ignore."/–"Ignorant!"), brashly goes for Jeannot's flies. His eventual physical violence towards her lays bare the power relations involved. The last straw for him is the obscene puppet he is presented with on the show. The audience as active rather than passive extends even to the film diegesis, as, when some of the main protagonists begin to argue at the final party, a member of the public (echoing perhaps a film spectator) proclaims her delight that "Ça tourne au vinaigre/It's turning sour." The film underestimates the power of the women, even as it emphasizes the way the power relations it represents are overwhelmingly to do with gender. In a long scene, a group of men pretending to run an audition humiliate a woman by insisting, from their unseen position in a control box, that she strip naked (the scene recalls that in *Le Temps d'une chasse* for its negative exposure of the male voyeurs, a fact emphasized here by the glimmers of a conscience revealed in the close-ups on Jeannot). Mirroring this are the expressions of sexual longing of the audience, and the status of Jeannot as sex object whose "cul" is bought and sold by the advertising industry. The practices of the television studio attempt to control and manipulate this lust, but can only partly do so: Mignonne, played by Manda Parent, spots a mile off the crotch padding used by singer Pierre Vignon (Benoît Girard). To re-universalize and re-centre the film's message as one about capitalist consumer culture and its attendant alienations, Jeannot must become a more mobile signifier, suffering pangs of conscience (especially after the death of Mignonne from a heart attack provoked by his momentary rejection of her), differentiating himself from the other repellent male figures, and deciding to leave the show. The centre of the film returns to the middle-class husband and wife and especially the "empowered" women such as the latter and one of the show's producers, who had been horrified by the telethon's representation of handicapped children.

The other Quebec comedy about television also coincides with (two) Hollywood movies. Both *The Truman Show* (Peter Weir, 1998) and *Louis 19 le roi des ondes* (Michel Poulette, 1994) portray "little men" whose lives are broadcast live on television twenty-four hours a day. But, whereas the American film feeds on increasing global preoccupations with virtual reality and surveillance, tipping into science fiction, and never shows "the real world" outside the practice of television viewing, *Louis 19*, the biggest-grossing Quebec film of the first half of the decade, attempts to counterpose Quebec specificity to the global society of the spectacle. (It was remade as *EDtv*, directed by Ron Howard and starring Matthew McConaughey, in 1999.) Louis Jobin (Martin Drainville), a timid assistant in an electronics shop, is selected in a "Big Star" competition to have his life broadcast. He gains in self-confidence as his fame spreads, conjuring up for the television producer (Patricia Tulasne) a massive audience and coalescing diverse sections of the Quebec national community (including Marcel Leboeuf and Gildor Roy as a gay couple). However, he quits the show when it becomes clear that his love affair with Julie (Agathe de la Fontaine), and even a mugging he experiences, have been manipulations. Hunted through the city via the tools of private surveillance (cameras, camcorders) now available to the population, he agrees to continue the show to which he is contractually bound, but, with the help of the now reconciled Julie, he puts on such an outrageous sexual and scatological performance that the plug is pulled. He and Julie ride off on a motorbike.

The film is very self-conscious about the Quebec context, interspersing Louis's adventures with critical comments from pretentious members of the Montreal intelligentsia which pre-empt that of the film audience: comparisons with NFB direct cinema, and the appropriateness of a "petit peuple" wanting a "petit héros." The American networks catch on to Louis's story, and they mangle the representation of him, and his French. The Foucauldian aspect of the film, in which the technologies of surveillance produce new subjectivities and an inward self-surveillance, has Louis performing "good deeds" for the camera (giving up his seat on the bus to a pregnant woman – although when he acquires fame she does the same for him) but also performing "good cultural behaviour" and "good French": his domineering mother (Dominique Michel) wants him not to make her ashamed, and to express himself well. (The film is a co-production with France.) However, the film loses sight of that self-consciousness and basically produces an unquestioned Oedipal narrative in which the mother is left behind (as well as the harridan producer), and a heterosexual male identity is assumed and fulfilled (with a French nymphette).

In an article on Quebec cinema and *américanité*, Louise Carrière argues that *Louis 19* represents a conflict between the French culture of the mother and girlfriend, and the American culture of the mass media.[40] This is to underestimate the globalized culture of spectacle, surveillance (and of virtual or indirect belonging) represented in the film and the difficulties of disentangling the mass media and its images from some "true" identity, of standing outside that mediated reality. Louis and Julie, after all, escape the media and in the end enact a cinematic cliché. The role of stars is in fact central to the construction of personal and national identities, and this activity plays itself out across different international but also national star systems.

The exiguity of the Quebec film industry means that no star system can exist within it, in the strict economic sense of the term, in which a star is considered to be a commodified individual whose "persona" exists and proliferates beyond a film or films across several media texts. A star, like genre, is part of the promise of a film, a promise of familiarity and difference ("going to see a Tom Cruise film"). Star studies have explored the clusters of connotations surrounding star personae as they articulate questions of gender and cultural identity.[41] In Quebec, of course, there exist two star systems, a French and American. Significantly, the only two Quebec performers to have achieved an international film career did so mainly in one of the two systems, Geneviève Bujold in Hollywood (especially after the failure of *Kamouraska*),[42] Carole Laure in France. Their star personae in Quebec have become closely bound up with that internationalization, while in general their "French-Canadianness" is not an important part of their international image. This is not to say that either Bujold (b. 1942) or Laure (b. 1948) are ignored by the secondary texts that circulate in Quebec (*Echo-Vedettes* has a circulation of 115,000) or that their status as *Québécoises* is in any way elided. Bujold in the 1970s in particular made a declaration in favour of René Lévesque and the Parti Québécois, and it is a straightforward process to insert her in a Quiet Revolution narrative (she was educated at convent school) of upward mobility (her father was a Montreal bus driver) which takes her from being host of a TV pop show in the 1960s to world fame, and to draw on the rebellious, mischievous ("espiègle") and individualist aspects of her persona. It is necessary to seek elsewhere those personae around whose images and connotations important aspects and contradictions of Quebec identity construction have coalesced.

If stars are thin on the ground in Quebec, celebrities are not. While there have been attempts to construct films as vehicles for a star from the music industry – the pop singer Mitsou's disastrous *Coyote* (Richard Ciupka, 1992) and *Prince Lazure* (Danièle J. Suissa, 1991) – it is the role of television which is crucial. John Ellis in *Visible Fictions* attributes the distinction between star and celebrity to that between cinema and television. Whereas cinema-going commands rapt attention in the dark, television mobilizes casual looking, the glance rather than the gaze. Whereas film stars are located in a play between ordinariness and extraordinariness, "the television performer exists very much more in the same space as the television audience, as a known and familiar person rather than as a paradoxical figure."[43] (This is underlined by the lack of heroes and winners in Quebec cinema.)[44] Whereas the play of ordinariness and extraordinariness places Bujold simultaneously inside and outside Quebec culture, television celebrities are very much on the "inside," inevitably given the almost total inexportability of Quebec television but fittingly given the domestic setting of the medium's consumption. The actor Gabriel Arcand has emphasized this ordinariness, indeed neighbourliness, of Quebec performers: "The general public knows and loves its actors, but when you see Gilbert Sicotte or Guy L'Écuyer in a film, it's a bit like seeing your neighbour, your brother-in-law or the garage-owner down the road. Gabriel García Marquez called it 'the theory of the village.' "[45] This takes us back to Benedict Anderson and his idea of the nation as imagined rather than physical community. Quebec television's massive success among the population makes it, moreover, a fertile and indeed essential seedbed for film productions that have the ambition of seeking an audience. Thus Martin Drainville, for example, star of *Louis 19*, was already well known to Quebec audiences from television, in particular for his role as Tintin in the SRC series *Scoop* (1992–95).

This osmosis between cinema and television, in which performers invariably move back and forth between the two media, is central to the two perhaps most culturally significant stars/celebrities of the past three decades. "Notre Dominique Michel nationale"[46] (Aimée Sylvestre, b. 1932) had four "star vehicle" films made around her in the 1970s, and this was based on her television success. (So central is she within Quebec popular culture that SRC broadcast a three-part documentary on her life and times in prime time in March 1992.) By far the most successful of these films (and of all the "nationalist comedies" of the period, Michel's vehicles can be seen as audience-federating, "family viewing" antidotes to the *films à fesses* of the period) was *Tiens-toi bien après les oreilles à papa,* made by the same television and light entertainment man, Jean Bissonnette, who had directed her in the TV sitcom *Moi et l'autre* as well as the SRC New Year's Eve show *Bye Bye.* The scriptwriter, Gilles Richer, was also from the same stable.[47] Michel plays the role of Suzanne David, who works as a secretary in an anglophone-run insurance company, where work is conducted in English – as in *Deux femmes en or* – and there is an unusually high death rate among the policy holders. After being fobbed off with vague and unfulfilled promises of a pay rise (the francophone employees are paid less than the anglophones), she begins a counter-attack which has her move out of the family home and into her own apartment, attempt to organize a union, and hoist the Quebec flag over the building. She eventually forms an alliance – and marriage – with salesman Jacques Martin (Yvon Deschamps), who has in secret been sabotaging the company by altering medical reports. The film's coda has them both welcomed as employees in a new insurance company, their old one having gone bankrupt.

While its proposed political praxis seems somewhat limited, the film nonetheless effectively articulates many of the Québécois's aspirations at the time: whereas Suzanne's parents (and, ostensibly, Jacques) are resigned to their allotted place in society, and in Canada, Suzanne is a *batailleuse* (the title means "hold on tight," or "fasten your safety belts"), with the narrative organized around her setbacks and repeated defiance and anger. It begins with her waking and dressing for work, the *mise en scène* and costume emphasizing the constrained role she is being forced to play in the anglo world. But the film is in comic mode, its politics expressed through parallel editing (Suzanne's journey to work and that of her boss), the linguistic and cultural gag of both Suzanne and Jacques completely mangling the prayer required as they attend a customer's funeral, and the ironic voice-over of the opening montage, a spoof travelogue on Canada (example: "What surprises the uninitiated visitor to Montreal is the preponderance of French" – cut to signs and billboards in English).

The other Michel vehicles of the 1970s are less effective but not without interest. *J'ai mon voyage!* (Héroux, 1973; again with a Richer script) casts her as Danielle Sylvestre, the wife of Frenchman Jean-Louis Cartier (Jean Lefebvre), who sets off with his family in a trailer from Quebec City to Vancouver in order to gain a lucrative position there in his insurance company (*encore*). The fact that the film is a co-production with France accounts not only for the presence of Lefebvre but also for the informative as well as satirical opening sequence tracing the history of Canada through cartoons and once again an ironic voice-over; the preponderance of visual humour (physical disasters reminiscent of the Lucille Ball/Desi Arnaz film *The Long Long Trailer*, dir. V. Minnelli, 1954); verbal comedy which is as relevant to a French as to a monolingual Québécois experience (this is why they are not a Montreal family), in that the misunderstandings are based on *total* incomprehension; and a range of constructions of the Other which are either very French (the long fantasy cowboys and Indians sequences) or totally ungrounded (Ontarians as sex maniacs, exactly the opposite of the Quebec clichés about them, and the Vancouver business community dancing reels). The Quebec/Canada relationship is thus not really explored, and, apart from the sequence when "military camp" is understood as *camping* and the family are caught up in military manoeuvres reminiscent of the October crisis, it is only at the end that a political message is asserted, when, on the way home, they are unable to converse in French in Montreal and have "Speak White" hurled at them. "J'ai mon voyage!" ("I'm fed up," I've had enough") thus comes to refer to the subordinate status of French and even to Quebec's continued membership in the federation.

Les Aventures d'une jeune veuve (Roger Fournier, 1974) casts her as another woman of the people from east Montreal. Widowed shortly after marrying the head of a textile company, she proves that she is not a *tête d'oiseau* and foils a plot hatched by sinister Japanese businessmen (the film's racism also extends to its representation of Cree Indians negotiating about their land, although the film also mocks the Quebec government's high-handed attitude towards them). *Je suis loin de toi mignonne* (Claude Fournier, 1976) was marketed as a reunion of Michel with Denise Filiatrault, who had played her flatmate in *Moi et l'autre*, and is set at the time just before conscription in the Second World War when there was a rush of weddings before it came into effect, married men being exempt. It also portrays an abortive attempt to rescue the anti-war Mayor of Montreal, Camilien Houde, from internment. Here Michel has a relatively straight role and is just one of many characters (notably, Juliette Huot, later to play Madame Plouffe, receives, alone and confused, the news of her son's death from a telegram in English), and one of the main interests for Quebec audiences is that play of similarity and difference between past and present, between Michel and Filiatrault's marriage-centred domestication and sexual naivety, and the liberated girls they had played in the 1960s television series.

In these films and other texts, Michel's persona is that of the ordinary or little person (she is diminutive of stature) proving themselves and winning against the odds. Her gender, of course, renders non-pertinent the analogy with a male action hero in a goal-centred narrative (in *Les Aventures d'une jeune veuve* her non-eroticized body

undergoes numerous physical ordeals in a slaughterhouse): The fact
that a woman is cast in these roles both mirrors Quebec's subordinate
position and qualifies the masculinism of much nationalist discourse.
(Of course, her victories are meant to signify cultural as well as physical survival.) In other words, she is able both to represent the nation
and to express her gender: the unconvinced male colleagues in *Tiens-
toi bien après les oreilles à papa* are only interested in the "sexual revolution" which would make her available to them. In two of her films, she
is sexually assertive and her marriage either comes at the end and fails
convincingly to erase her autonomy (rather like the marriage at the
end of Douglas Sirk's *Written on the Wind* of 1956 which cannot rescue
the film's earlier demolition of the institution) or is swiftly terminated
through death. The uneasy professional marriage of Michel and
Lefebvre in *J'ai mon voyage!* is paralleled by the incomprehensibility of
her character's position in the diegetic one. Importantly, while she is
always seen as a member of a family (the great vaudeville comedienne
Rose Ouellette – "la Poune" – passes the generational baton to her as
her mother in *Les Aventures d'une jeune veuve*; in the 1990s she became
co-presenter of a TV magazine entitled *Ma Maison*), it is only in the
unconvincing *J'ai mon voyage!* that she is cast as a mother. Crucially for
the post-Quiet Revolution Quebec femininity she represents, the maternal is absent as a referent from all but one of her films (even and
especially *Le Déclin de l'empire américain*) and also from the secondary
texts. Michel's "authenticity" is marked by her accent, the energetic
"naturalness" of her physical comedy, the feisty anger that builds and
propels the narrative forward,[48] and her very lack of glamour (which
also provides a rare space in popular culture for the image of the
older or aging woman): "Dominique Michel, is like Ms Everybody, the
neighbour, the workmate, the anonymous women who wander into
our lives, but with a generous dose of guts and artistic flair. A woman
like everyone else, not more beautiful and not less, who has accumulated over the years experience, wisdom and knowledge."[49] How
significant, then, that her comedy act is also based on imitation and
mimicry (in *Les Aventures d'une jeune veuve* she impersonates a geisha),
producing in her persona a dialectic of authenticity and performance,
actual and virtual, highly appropriate to the national-allegorical tension of Quebec culture. (Interestingly, the Marie-Lise Pilote persona
in a film like *L'Homme idéal* marks a kind of update of that of Michel:
ordinary and centred, but upwardly mobile through her own – career
– efforts; childless but aspiring to renegotiate the maternal role for
the contemporary situation.)

   We saw in chapter 5 how the Fournier comedy *J'en suis* battled with
the homoerotic implications of the star persona of Roy Dupuis, as well
as his marketing appeal in the pseudo-Queer Cinema enterprise that

was *Being at Home with Claude.* Whereas Dominique Michel's "ordinariness" and age allowed her to become a typical heroine for the Quiet Revolution generation, Dupuis's appeal is that of youth, a naturalness and authenticity based on the body rather than the social, and a federating but problematic mixture of virility and sexual ambivalence, a capacity to look and be looked at, power and vulnerability. This is manifest in the plethora of publicity photographs of him, which have to deal with the pitfalls, in what remains a male-dominated society, of the male pin-up.[50] In many, there is the standard expressionless male gaze seeking to compensate for being the object; but in others his mouth is open in an expression of inviting lack (he is rarely smiling, unlike Roch Voisine), and there the carapace of the male body is prized apart and its usually policed boundaries transgressed. On the one hand, he is the *coureur des bois*, the extra-social man of nature from the forests of Abitibi. On the other, he is also feminized (and redomesticated) as object of the look, as "Québécois" and thus part of a minor culture, as an actor taking his art seriously (because it allows him to be "vulnerable"), and as a person bearing internal scars.[51] The result is a classic Quebec masculinity which is resolutely non-communicative, at opposite poles from the voluble and gestural Dominique Michel, hence his famed mumbling delivery, his body reduced to animal pacing in *Being at Home with Claude.*[52] Like Michel, however, he is able to federate audiences, as object of desire and identification, as bridging outer and inner, high and low culture (and also an older "authenticity" and more contemporary modernity; witness the simultaneous modern architect and seeker of objects with an aura – to the point of pleistocene figures – in *J'en suis*).

All this, however, is largely constructed out of television, his fame dating from *Les Filles de Caleb.* His only other starring roles for the cinema are in two films obscure even by arthouse standards but which emphasize, through theatricality, the links in his persona between inner and outer experiences of masculinity. In *C'était le 12 du 12 et Chili avait les blues* (Charles Binamé, 1994), he plays a pious and blinkered vacuum salesman in 1963, marooned in a railway station by a snowstorm, and living a love affair. In 1993 Michel Langlois, with Denis Langlois the only openly male gay film director making features in Quebec and scriptwriter or co-scriptwriter on three of Léa Pool's films, directed Dupuis as a fisherman in *Cap Tourmente*, a bizarre melodrama set in the lower St Lawrence in which all the members of an extended family are intensely but not always avowedly in love with one another. (Langlois had directed Dupuis in a bisexual triangle in a short film made in 1988, *Sortie 234*). With hair streaked blonde (supposedly by the sun), Dupuis in this feature bears a physical resemblance to James

Dean in *Giant* (Stevens, 1956). While the comparison is moot because of his sexual ambivalence and method-acting intensity which links brooding interiority and explosive action, the Quebec and generational specificity of his persona means that instead of embodying youth identities grappling with the crisis of older authority provoked by post-war modernization, this persona encapsulates an unresolvedness in the general construction of masculine identity and its relationship with narratives of nation and nature. That Québécois incompleteness has also manifested itself in Dupuis's career, which has taken him out of Quebec and the French language and into a CBC/CBS miniseries on the Dionne quintuplets (*Million Dollar Babies*) and the syndicated series *Nikita*, playing the Tcheky Karyo/mentor role from Luc Besson's film.

Les Boys (Louis Saia, 1997) had by spring 1998 grossed nearly $5.7 million in Quebec, making it in box-office terms the most popular Quebec film ever. *Les Boys II* was released in December 1998. A sequel or even series forms a kind of micro-genre, organizing expectations, promising familiarity and difference. In this case, the hockey film, as well as fitting into the Hollywood subgenre of the sports movie, works as a Quebec equivalent to other genres that emphasize the conflicts and struggles of the homosocial group, notably the war film and particularly its "guys on a mission" variant (a configuration completely unavailable in Quebec cultural history). In *Les Boys*, Stan (Rémy Girard), owner of a bar and manager of an amateur hockey team, contracts a gambling debt with the sleazy Méo (Pierre Lebeau). In order to avoid physical retribution, a deal is made whereby it all hangs on a hockey game which Stan's team has to win if Méo is not to take over his business. After a brutal battle with the team Méo has assembled (which includes ex-professionals), Les Boys win the match, which takes up the last third of the film, by one goal.

If we recall Ginette Major's diagnosis of the failure of Quebec cinema to find an audience in the 1970s, then the success of *Les Boys* is obviously based on the feel-good factor, that euphoria so lovingly milked at the end of the film. Its euphoria is based on homosociality, the eradication of (some) social differences through unanimity but the perpetuation of other boundaries, and on performance in the sense of effort tending towards victory. We are now worlds away, it would seem, from the defeated working-class Québécois men of *Le Temps d'une chasse*. This later film of low cultural status provides what popular taste demands: participation and the abolition of distance, factors reinforced both by the shots of the diegetic audience (cinema audiences often applauded the equalizer) and the filming in the thick of the action, with intense sound effects of clashing bodies and sticks. Significantly, that victory is achieved not through an individual hero but through a team or community, and from the position of under-dog, a staple of American films of this type but one appropriate to Quebec identifications. (The TV series *Lance et compte*, which also starred Marc Messier, filmed its matches from above like real televised games and dealt with the milieu of professional stars.) Although the team adopt a will to win drawn from American culture ("the mental," in English in the film), their victory is not followed by the resolution of any of their own personal problems (except Stan's).

The team is assembled out of a variety of social positions: fitness video producer Bob (Marc Messier), real estate agent Ti-Guy[53] (Patrick Huard), surgeon François (Serge Thériault), garage mechanic Mario (Patrick Labbé), and, from both sides of the law, a policeman, Boisvert (Dominic Philie), and a coke-snorting guitarist, Julien (Roc Lafor-tune).[54] The parallel editing at the start of the film establishes the differences between the men even as it has them converging towards the same destination. This is echoed in the narrative when the conflicts between them, and the different secrets that are exposed (Bob's bankruptcy, François's wig, the policeman's domineering wife), are overcome. The film's inclusion runs to that of a gay character, lawyer Jean-Charles (Yvan Ponton), who scores the equalizer. This is a com-ment on the evolution of Quebec society since the early 1970s, but even here boundaries are constructed: Yvan's partner is extremely effeminate and given to fits of jealousy, although his public outing of Jean-Charles and declaration of love do inspire the goal. Jean-Charles's acceptability as a "real man" is reinforced when he assaults Méo in the toilets by soaking his trousers, forcing him to change, humiliatingly, into feminizing new red ones. His sexuality is not made to render am-biguous any of the male bonding; indeed it is used by the film and by the characters to reinforce the crucial homosocial/homosexual dis-tinction. The whole sexual economy of the film is profoundly Oedipal, with Stan as the good father figure and Méo as the bad, and Stan's obese, inexperienced son scoring the winning goal.

The hockey game, one of the prime sites of the construction of both masculinity and communal identities and allegiances in Canada (450,000 people in Quebec play the amateur game), has also gener-ated here a fiction of exclusion. While it would have been inappropri-ate to demand an equal-opportunities approach to the team to make it more ethnically diverse, this only begs the question. If it is an amus-ing joke to claim that winter sports were created so that there would be some physical activity black people were not good at,[55] the choice of hockey rather than baseball (the opposite procedure from the film version of *Les Plouffe*) does permit a wholly white narrative to unfold. The absence of anglophones becomes all the more glaring.

It is, of course, women who are the main group excluded from this film, this, along with the disavowal of homosexuality, marking one of the poles of homosociality itself. While in roles that provide service for the men they are made to show defiance in the first part of the film (unflattering comments about the policeman's penis size), this is used to set up the reassertion of masculinity that will occur by the end. In similar vein, the barmaid says she loves Stan "like a father." By the end of the film, they are reduced to the roles of manipulated sexual partners who are less important than the hockey game, or, literally, as spectators. François and Boisvert resolve their differences when the former keeps quiet about the latter's domineering wife; Ti-Guy covers up Mario's marital infidelity. The film's success suggests a highly federating text. However, it is difficult to see what there is in the film for a female spectator who is not already a hockey fan. From the point of view of the heterosexual female gaze, the camera hardly dwells on the eroticism of the men's bodies: the brief shower scene is overwhelmingly homosocial in its emphasis.

It is striking, then, how francophone Quebec identity is still bound up with masculinism. It is useful to compare *Les Boys* with its contemporary British phenomenon, *The Full Monty* (Peter Cattaneo, 1997). Whereas the Quebec film traces an upward trajectory of masculinity around national identifications, *The Full Monty* traces a downward trajectory, partly in connection with the declining nation, partly with the diminished traditional working class. Men's bodies can and are to be sold as objects of desire. (This is not to forget the ambiguity of the final scene, in which the "object" can be seen to reassert itself by proclaiming once again that it possesses the male genitals.) Both films, however, trace the consequences for older national and regional cultures of the "new," that configuration of individualism, post-industrialization, post-Fordism, and gender instability which might be explored under the heading of the "postmodern." In this way, *Les Boys* can be seen to address the contradictions and shortcomings of this transition, but principally through avoidance, as the world outside (Huard's yuppie, his work observed – and satirized – in most detail, would here become central) is left behind in favour of a utopian scene of success and performance read in communal terms, with a masculinity under siege reasserted via the most minor of adjustments.

Les Boys II takes most of the same characters to a club tournament held in Chamonix, France. Despite the predictable jokes about French plumbing we have noted, the film follows roughly the same pattern, with this time Julien's place in the homosocial thrown into crisis and then redeemed. Even Méo is integrated into the team and helps the men deal with the hostile (criminal) environment. Romances with

French women take place and form important plot elements, but on the gay side Jean-Charles's dalliance with a man he meets on the plane is marked only by his repeated absences. Contemporaneous with the two *Boys* films were two popular comedies that emphasized all-female groups and that obtained significant box-office success, if at a lower level than for *Les Boys*.

Denise Filiatrault directed both *C't à ton tour Laura Cadieux* (1998) and *Laura Cadieux ... la suite* (1999). The first, adapted from Michel Tremblay's novel, was marked by all the ambiguities of Tremblay's portrayal of women, some of whose subtleties were lost in the cinematic form. Thus the ambiguities of Laura's narrative voice in the novel (for example, her popular appeal but also her racism) were lost in the film, particularly as she was played by the charismatic Ginette Reno. The second film, however, based on the same characters but leaving Tremblay's authorship behind, is paradoxically rather freer to explore this all-female popular genre, reminiscent of TV sitcoms and also *The First Wives' Club* (Hugh Wilson, 1996). The group of women friends meet regularly at a doctor's office, and one day they head off on a cruise down the St Lawrence without their menfolk. Whereas the *Boys* films were concerned with managing the tension between performance/ success and community via a "game" that allowed them to be both responsible and irresponsible, the preoccupations of the women here are with the no less real and urgent problems of power in the domestic space (one woman is fleeing a violent husband, Laura herself is tempted by shipboard romance) and the possibilities held out by consumption. (The other male passengers are either gay, and accepted as such, nothing more [Donald Pilon], or bumbling but in the end sexually successful Québécois little men [Martin Drainville].) These domestic dramas are, however, played out via national narratives, both spatially and temporally. The cruise (no doubt for budgetary reasons) is not in the Caribbean but traverses Quebec's heartland. One companion, Mme Therrien (a splendid comic turn by Pierrette Robitaille) misses the boat and ends up on a Russian cargo ship in which she engages with the Other, and prepares and explains the history of various Quebec dishes, before insisting on being let off because she "misses home." Laura exchanges family history with the captain and notes that, although her daughter is a successful businesswoman, she, as a child of *la grande noirceur*, had no such opportunity. The conflicts the film's narrative contains, and the way they are resolved, display a certain management of change and nostalgia, around spectacle and identification (the final diegetic shipboard entertainment the women put on) and via the balance provided by the exclusion of the violent husband and the return to the "ordinary," loving one (both outcomes engineered by Laura's active child).

The construction of the "popular" in Quebec cinema is therefore traversed by anxieties around change and around therefore the *differences* which the "national people" visibly contain. The fact that the *Laura Cadieux* pair plays second fiddle to the *Boys* in terms of audience and budget (and the leaving of Quebec) is less important than the surprising fact that their preoccupations are imagined in such gender-polarized terms. The next chapters must deal further with these differences within "the people." Why, for example, is the only black character in *Laura Cadieux ... la suite* the piano player? This chapter ends, fittingly, on two films directed by a woman: the delayed presentation of women's cinema in Quebec must now play its full role in our analysis.

8 Women's Cinema

"Women's cinema" does not here necessarily mean feminist cinema, but simply films made by women. It holds out at least the possibility of alternative film-making practices to a bogus cultural universalism that is in fact very situated, that takes the particularity/ies of masculinity as a norm which establishes difference and alterity. Establishing even "women" or "women's cinema" as categories, however, involves some of the pitfalls and issues – those of homogeneity and heterogeneity – that pertain to "the national." On the one hand, it is a category refused by certain women film-makers in Quebec.[1] (The dominance of auteurism in film discourse in Quebec is an important factor here, as we shall see.) On the other, we have seen that much Quebec cinema, particularly as it constructs the national, has been profoundly gendered and has had great difficulty in coming to terms with "the feminine." The project of the first collection of essays on this issue, *Femmes et cinéma québécois*, edited by Louise Carrière in 1983, was precisely to link critiques of the representation of women in Quebec cinema (their absence, or presence as foils to the men, as young and sexually available, as restricted to a limited number of archetypes such as the waitress or mother) with the new possibilities offered by the increasing presence of women in the film industry. If "women's cinema" is a viable working term, essential if the analysis of gender constructions in Quebec cinema is to be complete, then certain questions arise. What histories of women and women's movements are specific to Quebec within the overall context of Western societies and their "modernization"? In this way, how can the idea of "the national" be articulated with "the feminine," both in general and in particular? And what particular cinematic practices, for the institutions, creative personnel, and audiences, are implied by such an articulation?

For women in Quebec, the Quiet Revolution, that particularity of Quebec history which at the same time meant a "catching up" with the rest of the Western world, marked a profound shift from the Catholic discourses of motherhood and tradition which had preceded it. While Quebec women had obtained the right to vote in federal elections in 1918, they had to wait until 1940 for the equivalent right at provincial level. (Indeed, some of the founding fathers of French-Canadian nationalism, such as Louis-Joseph Papineau in the 1830s, had opposed suffrage – mainly because it benefited anglophones – for the very few women entitled through property qualifications to vote at that time, and this right was withdrawn in 1849.) For the Catholic Church and the clerical-nationalist élites who dominated Quebec life from 1837 to 1960, *la survie* had meant their own classic articulation of femininity and the national, namely, the demographic urgency of a high birth rate (but which had already begun to decline in the late nineteenth century with industrialization and urbanization). Since 1960, women in Quebec have indeed "caught up" with their sisters elsewhere in the West: secular and mixed education, with men and women in equal numbers in higher education; in 1964 the juridical equality of husband and wife (a hundred years after the rest of Canada); divorce-law reform in 1968; the legalization of contraception in 1969; the long battle to decriminalize abortion and make it easily available, ending in a Canadian Supreme Court ruling in 1988. All these changes were accompanied, as elsewhere, by the lively agitation and organization of groups and movements in Quebec civil society such as the Regroupement des femmes québécoises, founded in 1977 by Parti Québécois militants, or, more recently, FRAPPE, Femmes regroupées pour l'accessibilité au pouvoir politique et économique.

The picture is complicated, however, by several factors. First, the technocratic-teleological narrative of the Quiet Revolution must always be qualified. As Micheline Dumont has pointed out, since female members of religious orders dominated the structures before 1960, the Quiet Revolution in fact marked a profound masculinization of authority in health and education.[2] The modern (female) citizens of the new order are still interpellated by the nation's need to produce babies (the Quebec government's *prime* for the third child, Lucien Bouchard's unfortunately natalist remark to this effect in the September 1993 federal election). It is in this sense that women in Quebec can be understood to have moved from a private patriarchy (exclusion from public life) to a public patriarchy (no longer excluded from the public arena but subordinated within it).[3] Secondly, although feminism in Quebec was overwhelmingly influenced by Anglo-Saxon models (Firestone, Greer, Millett after 1970, despite the longer-term reach of Simone de Beauvoir's *Le Deuxième Sexe* of 1949), it is often greeted with some incomprehension in English-Canadian feminist circles because of its relationship with nationalism, considered by many as antithetical to what feminism stands for and to the necessary prioritizing of gender as site of struggle. For, despite the attempts by the anglophone media, for example, in the 1980 referendum campaign, to portray Quebec women as hostile to the sovereignty project, in fact women and feminists were more or less equally divided on the issue. In general, the Parti Québécois in government has a positive record on women's issues (it was the first to develop specific policies on women, and created a *secrétariat d'État à la condition féminine*). Feminist positions in Quebec cannot be easily mapped onto either pro- or antisovereignty stances. However, this is not to say that nationalism has an accidental or contingent relationship with it. The best analogy may be with May 1968 in France, a profoundly male-chauvinist occasion which nonetheless impelled second-wave feminism in France for reactive reasons and also for the anti-traditional ideological turmoil it articulated in a climate of late and therefore accelerated modernization, as well as for the direct political action it inspired outside older legitimate élite power structures. The Quiet Revolution was in a sense the May 1968 for Quebec feminism, in that the interrogations of collective identity and of modernity which accompanied it inevitably interpellated women, their role and status, particularly as it was a revolution marked for many by incompleteness and lack of closure. As Dumont puts it: "Feminism in Quebec was stimulated and nurtured by the powerful nationalist movement which swept Quebec between 1963 and 1990,"[4] an example of which would be the Manifeste des femmes québécoises of 1971, which adopted the colonizer/colonized vocabulary of nationalist analysis in talking about women's bodies and subjugation.

However, the incompleteness of this process was manifested in the most dramatic and tragic form possible by the massacre of fourteen female engineering students at the École Polytechnique in Montreal in December 1989 by an armed man labelling them as "feminists."[5] It is impossible to answer, but equally unavoidable to interrogate, the "Quebec specificity" of this event. Nonetheless, it underlines not only the persistence and indeed rearguard violence of older attitudes, but also the urgency of the questions of gender construction and of representation which this work and, moreover, which women image-makers are seeking to explore, despite the disavowals quoted earlier. Patricia

Smart's deft analysis of representations of the feminine in Quebec women's writing in fact relies on metaphors of physical damage or even disappearance. In a literary context in which symbolic violence is done to women (in the flip side to the clerical nationalists' idealization of the mother, the *roman de la terre* writes them out of the story/history in the person of the mother-figure: Laura Chapdelaine is but one example), the project of women writers to grant a subject position to women has dramatic consequences: "As soon as 'the object' begins to perceive itself as a subject, the very foundations of the house are shaken," that "house," that space or territory, being that of the patriarchal order itself.[6]

The question remains, however, what were and are the specifically cinematic articulations of these urgencies and dilemmas? In the domain of film theory, Anglo-Saxon debates over the past twenty-five years have tended to emphasize, since, for example, seminal articles by Claire Johnstone and Laura Mulvey in the 1970s, women's cinema as a potential counter-cinema to, respectively, an investment in realism that affirms common-sense notions of the given, comfortingly reconfirming the non-contradictory nature of the self and the real; and a mainstream (Hollywood) cinematic apparatus tainted by a centred heterosexual male gaze constructing women and women's images as other (non-male to *him*) in an Oedipal paradigm which sees her as castration threat.[7] Lacanian versions of psychoanalysis have been influential in arguing that a symbolic system – language – that is founded on lack and the phallus is not one that permits a position from which women can speak, and so it is on the terrain of signification itself, on new ways of speaking and representing, that women writers, artists, and film-makers should work.

These propositions have been much debated and reworked. We shall see that the agendas they raise – the investigation of representation, the refusal to take for granted, and the desire to get beyond, structures of looking that are in fact profoundly gendered as straight male – are present in nearly all Quebec women's films to some degree. However, as Maria Lauret has convincingly argued,[8] it is important to avoid ethnocentrism when discussing the contexts and strategies for politically conscious women's film-making. First, the theoretical agenda of what we might term *Screen* theory was posited in an Anglo-Saxon context which eagerly embraced French Marxist and psychoanalytic theory in order partly to counter and get beyond some of the perceived impasses (auteurism, empiricism, humanism) of their colleagues, and partly as an act of *distinction* within the hierarchies of their society and profession. In Quebec, while French theory certainly makes its presence felt in the academy and intellectual circles, it tends to be neither harnessed to identity politics on the Anglo-Saxon model nor embraced as a conscious cross-cultural strategy for circumventing the shortcomings of indigenous agendas and traditions (we have seen the highly ambivalent relationship with French culture that has characterized Quebec before and since the Quiet Revolution). This tends to mean that experimental film in Quebec is not "theory film" in the sense of the avant-garde movies made by Sally Potter or Mulvey/Wollen in Britain in the 1970s.

Secondly, the tradition of documentary realism in Quebec and Canada collides somewhat with Claire Johnstone's criticism of what she understood as *cinéma vérité* in the 1970s: "The sign is always a product. What the camera in fact grasps is the 'natural' world of the dominant ideology. Women's cinema cannot afford such idealism; the 'truth' of our oppression cannot be captured on celluloid with the 'innocence' of the camera: it has to be constructed/manifested."9

While such reservations are by no means rejected by Quebec women film-makers, they tend to be held in tension with other urgencies, particularly, but not only, the national project. As Terry Lovell pointed out in her 1983 work *Pictures of Reality*, realism is rescuable for feminist and socialist practice, which, for her, must engage with real audiences rather than just the textually implied spectator and concern itself with the constitution of collective as well as individual subjects.10 E. Ann Kaplan forcefully argues this point in relation to women as a collective subject as well: "Women have been forced to develop a semiotics of the cinema that would include a theory of reference, since our oppression in the social formation impinges on us daily. But as our oppression emerges from our (mis)representation in signification, how can we avoid dealing with representation? Since our voices have never been heard, how can we avoid attempting to locate a voice, a discourse?"11

Thirdly, while, as we have seen, many dominant images in Quebec cinema lend themselves all too easily to feminist analysis and criticism, it is a cinema that in many ways cannot be read as "dominant," although it may sometimes seek to imitate dominant modes. We have seen how, for example, a self-consciously "minor" treatment – in *Pouvoir intime*, in certain films by Arcand – can produce narratives, even "genre" narratives, that avoid the totalizations and teleologies of Oedipal narratives and gazes. Anglo-Saxon gaze theory thus has its uses in this analysis, but it is only part of the picture.

Two ways to grasp Quebec women's cinema in its specificity are to investigate how it addresses a community of women as well as a national community (how it constructs them as spectators), and how it is situated in relation to the major/minor tendencies of Quebec culture. The first task is to marshal those key elements in the construction of the nation and of national cinema and see how they function in relation to "feminine" positions, thus opening up faultlines in now non-totalizable domains. The first concept, recognition, is obviously important for the capacity of film images to create a commonality of women's experience. We examined in chapter 1 the different ways in which culture and cinema construct national identity. However, whereas, as Eve Sedgwick points out, one result of nation-building is to have us believe we have a nationality in the same way we have a gender, the result of women's cinema is not to construct gender identities or "women" – the wider culture and cinema by and large get on with that quite blithely – but to probe them, investigate them, problematize them through their very representation, through their being put into some kind of reflexive discourse. We saw via Kristeva how time as gendered, how the cyclical and monumental aspects to "women's time," might problematize the time of the nation. The same can be said of space, which is obviously profoundly gendered as well. Women's relation to urban space, its ownership, its dangers, plays a major role in Quebec women's cinema. And the traditionally feminine domestic space is equally explored, introducing difference in the space of the nation between constructions of "public" and "private," articulating its vastness with the confines of kitchen and home.

Most feminist debates on ontology/identity have tended to call into question the Cartesian and Enlightenment heritage of the fixed and finished consciousness and the instrumentalism that goes with it, or the Freudian construction of "normal" Oedipal trajectories that can be seen to accompany it.[12] In section ten, "1730 – Becoming-intense, becoming-animal, becoming-imperceptible," *of Mille plateaux*, Deleuze and Guattari's emphasis on becoming rather than being, and radical investment in heterogeneity, give women and sexual politics a crucial role in possible future liberations. In this post- or anti-Oedipal, indeed post-human universe, sexual difference is infinitely pluralized: "There are as many sexes as there are terms in symbiosis, as many differences as elements contributing to a process of contagion. We know that many beings pass between a man and a woman; they come from different worlds, are borne on the wind, form rhizomes around roots; they cannot be understood in terms of production, only in terms of becoming."[13] The molecular as site of human endeavour is the domain of becoming, where the category "man" (in its most gendered sense) can finally be undermined in its fixed and finished sense, as the categories "animal," "child," and "woman" ("the key to all other becomings")[14] already are. Crucially for the relation to Quebec cultural identity, Deleuze and Guattari agree that not only can "molar" woman exist (with an assigned social and ontological place), but she must do so in order to exist as subject rather than object of enunciation. However,

that entity must coexist with that other molecular vocation of innovation, proliferation, undermining of boundaries, becoming the other:
"The woman as a molar entity *has to become-woman* in order that the
man also becomes – or can become – woman. It is, of course, indispensable for women to conduct a molar politics, with a view to winning
back their own organism, their own history, their own subjectivity: 'we
as women ...' makes its appearance as a subject of enunciation. But it is
difficult to confine oneself to such a subject, which does not function
without drying up a spring or stopping a flow."[15] Quebec women's
cinema, in the tensions between, in turn, gender and national self-
affirmation, and a broader provisionality and self-questioning, opens
up a potential space for Quebec culture to develop its "minor" vocation, to reject and undermine both linguistic and sexual positions of
mastery, and to develop new cinematic communities and spaces.

In reality, by the end of 1998 fifteen women film-makers in Quebec
had directed or co-directed a theatrically released fictional feature,
and of these only five had directed more than two films. (The numbers
are more extensive as far as shorts, television films, and documentaries
are concerned. Immigrant women such as Marilú Mallet and Tahani
Rached provide particularly interesting examples of the latter, and
they will be discussed in chapter 10.) With the exception of the *Laura
Cadieux* films, all the women's feature films can be classified as art or
auteur cinema; no other woman in Quebec has yet directed a film that
could be described as genre, commercial, or "popular," and this confinement is producing problems for women as the auteur tradition
wanes, as we shall see. A sociological study, *Septième art et discrimination*,
traces the institutional and attitudinal obstacles facing women in the
Quebec film industry, and confirms that they are mostly located in subordinate roles, with a high concentration, in particular, of film editors.[16] *Cinéma femmes* was founded in 1984 to promote women's work
in the film industry through production, distribution, and exhibition,
in particular organizing *Silence elles tournent*, the Montreal international
festival of women's film and video. *Moitié-Moitié* is a current organization that lobbies for parity funding for women's films (only 10 per cent
of Telefilm Canada and SODEC funds go to women).

As with the general history of Quebec cinema, so with the women:
the National Film Board, and with it the figure of Anne Claire Poirier
(b. 1932), are of central importance for the emergence of women's
cinema. Although the first film made at the NFB by a francophone
woman on women's issues was Monique Fortier's 1964 ten-minute
documentary *La Beauté même* (Fortier's career after that was as one of
Quebec's foremost film editors, working, for example, on *Le Déclin de
l'empire américain*), Poirier's career there as a director was the most

sustained and the most engaged, with three documentary and four fictional features as well as six shorter films. Although the 1967 documentary *De mère en fille*, on childcare, is described by her as "an unconsciously feminist film,"[17] she was able in the 1970s to use her position at the organization to connect the NFB with the changing status of gender relations and identities, if not with actual feminist militancy. With other women she was instrumental in launching, within the *Société nouvelle* program, the series "En tant que femmes" (1972–75), although she refused the model of the English side's women-only unit, Studio D.[18] To an extent, the aims of "En tant que femmes" can be situated in that positivist NFB tradition of "showing Canada to Canadians," but the "showing of women to women," while privileging documentary, automatically implies a complex unveiling of that which has been rendered invisible, and an exploration of the images and codes imposed on women, if that already supposed "reality" is to be "seen": "We want this study to be lively and to make woman become aware of the social realities in which she participates – advertising, the media (literature, television, cinema), social and religious morality, the law, family structures, the world of work, etc ... so that she can find out whether they respect her inner reality [*réalité profonde*] and allow her the social behaviour that fits this reality."[19] Thus "women" are to be interpellated and to recognize themselves as a "group," to be provoked into a *prise de conscience*, and to be aroused into some kind of social as well as personal awareness. In order to achieve this, the general strategy was one consistent with auteurism, with "personal" films being made in a collegial context. In addition, the approach was to be direct and emotive without being didactic: "We'd learned that only language that was direct and emotional would let us join with and raise collective awareness."[20]

Content to help launch the series and produce the work of others, Poirier then directed two of the six. The period also marks the beginning of one of the most consistent and fruitful relationships between director and screenwriter in Quebec cinema, that with Marthe Blackburn (1916–91). Both *Les Filles du roy* (1974) and *Le Temps de l'avant* (1975) explore and evoke the relationship between women's emancipation and Quebec history, and the tensions and uncertainties aroused: adjustment within or challenge to the national project and the progressivism of the Quiet Revolution? The first is an hour-long documentary exploring the status of women in Quebec society from the seventeenth-century to *Valérie*. The fictional feature *Le Temps de l'avant* effectively establishes a discourse of (national) sexual reconciliation via an examination of change. Hélène (Luce Guilbeault) is forty and married to Gabriel (Pierre Gobeil), who works in merchant shipping and is often absent from home. With three children already, unable to continue taking the pill and now pregnant, she debates whether to have an abortion first with her younger and more "liberated" sister Monique (Paule Baillargeon: this two-hander takes up a long central section of the film). The film threatens to fall into didacticism here as it constructs its "nous autres/we" of women, but it is able to rescue itself through the performances and the care taken to delineate both gendered spaces (kitchen/bar) and gestures, particularly those associated with work (Hélène's loom, kneading dough) and national-symbolic itineraries and spaces: the family home, between Montreal and Quebec City, is on the riverside, and the crucial discussion between husband and wife takes place there. The river also connotes time, of course, as we have seen in Perrault (Michel Brault is the cameraman on this film, too): the sepia memories of courtship, collective history, the absences of the father analogous to a certain Quebec past of lumber-camp employment. The film's emphasis on choice, then, is quite radical, in that, as Deniz Kandiyoti has pointed out, nationalist discourses that emphasize the "naturalness" of belonging rely on the mother figure: "Nationness is thus equated with gender, parentage, skin-colour – all those things that are not chosen and by which, by virtue of their inevitability, elicit selfish attachment and sacrifice. The association of women with the private domain reinforces the merging of the nation/community with the selfless mother/devout wife."[21] The ending of the film is uncertain, and it is not clear that Hélène's insistence that "it's no longer as before," in its positing of choice and self-empowerment for women, has been translated by Gabriel into that general lesson of the new realities of modern Quebec society which might counter the memory he has of the humiliation of his father at the hands of local *notables*.

The year 1975, International Women's Year, added some outside pressure to the NFB's development of women's film-making, although a 1978 study on equality in work concluded negatively on the position of women there. Studio D created high-profile efforts such as Bonnie Sherr Klein's denunciation of pornography, *Not a Love Story*, in 1981. Francophone women participated in this with the *Regards de femmes* program after 1987. Poirier continued to be the only woman making fictional features at the NFB until the co-productions with the private sector of the later 1980s. *Mourir à tue-tête* (1979) remains her most discussed film and the one that, through television (over one million viewers when broadcast on Radio Canada in January 1981), has attained the highest audiences. For this study of rape, Poirier sought to bring together two strands to her approach, strands with both risks and advantages for a women's film-making seeking to break with dominant representations. While never losing sight of what the Quebec feminist writer Louky Bersianik has called "the female anthropology that is urgently needed,"[22] that is, that documentary unveiling of the hitherto "invisible" in women's lives consistent with NFB realism, Poirier is also interested in opening up cinema to poetry and theatre (she had studied at drama school, and one of her first shorts – *30 minutes, Mr Plummer* of 1963 – is about an actor preparing for his performance): "I'd even dream of being able to make films like those of Marcel Carné or Jean Cocteau in which transposition was obvious and the cinema had nothing to do with an emphasis on the real [*le vérisme*]. I don't like that emphasis much. I think that what you encounter everyday must be communicated as you feel it and not as you see it."[23] This statement, while surprising (although we have noted the polysemy around the St Lawrence, as well as the emphasis on feeling and emotion in *Le Temps de l'avant*), points the way to a complex interaction between the two modes in her second feature. (In fact Poirier and Blackburn's original project was to make two films on the subject, one fictional, one documentary.)[24]

Molly Haskell's argument is well known: the violence against women and the dearth of strong female parts to be found in Hollywood films of the 1970s is to be explained as a backlash against the emerging women's movement.[25] Her work has been rightly criticized for conflating real women and their representations. However, the emergence of Quebec national cinema in the 1960s and early 1970s, particularly in its more populist modes, had produced a plethora of rapes, which, while not always inviting "titillating" readings, were always adjacent to notions of the modern and of liberation which involved undressing *la Québécoise*. There was thus some urgency, in national-cinematic terms, in Poirier's project. While today some of its rhetoric seems rather heavy-handed, this in fact can be read as a tribute to the activity of those feminists who were determined to end the trivialization of rape and to place male power and violence not only in the analytical spotlight but firmly on the political agenda.

In *Mourir à tue-tête*, a nurse (Julie Vincent), on leaving the hospital, is dragged off at knifepoint by a man (Germain Houde), tied up in the back of a van, and subjected to an ordeal of insults and violence, culminating in rape. Unable to pick up the pieces of her life or renew her relationship with her boyfriend, Philippe (Paul Savoie), she commits suicide. This narrative, however, is just part of the film's strategy. The rape scene places the viewer in the same position as the victim, since it is filmed entirely from her point of view, with the drunken, distorted face of the rapist, in close-up or medium shot, hurling abuse, spitting, pouring beer, urinating on her, her terrified whimpers on the soundtrack. This identification is interrupted with a freeze-frame on the rapist at the point of orgasm: cut to the "film-maker" (Monique Miller) and the "editor" (Micheline Lanctôt) discussing the nature of this *representation* they are creating. The film also includes footage of other assaults on women (the Vietnam War, clitoridectomy in Africa, shaving women's heads in France at the Liberation), and its final sequence of length is that of a theatricalized court scene in an ecclesiastical setting, in which initially masked women of various ages accuse the judicial system, against the protests of an unseen male judge, of neglecting rape as a crime. These extra-diegetic scenes take up a third of the film.

The film thus plays on various rhetorics of hyperrealism (the urinating penis, for example), identification and point of view (camera angle and position are repeated for the victim's medical examination and police questioning), breaks in rhythm, distance, and self-reflexivity. It is an effective example of women's cinema as counter-cinema, in that it calls into question the transparency of the real as given and natural, setting it up only to undermine it, employing neutral establishing shots but, needless to say, abandoning the conventional "neutrality" afforded by the shot/reverse shot. Its inspiration is Godardian and Brechtian, but with a gendered emphasis. Radically different spaces are constructed for men and women through the point-of-view device. Victim and rapist/doctor/policeman are never figured in the same shot after she is confined in the van; Julie is figured with her boyfriend, but this in time proves to be an impossible coexistence, cinematically or in the narrated life. The rapist is body, semi-articulate, filmed as pure physicality; the judge as Law is unseen, is voice. The three other men, whatever intentions they may have (for example, the policeman, played by Pierre Gobeil, is officious but not obnoxious, the boyfriend is well-meaning), are positioned in relation to these two configurations of masculine power.

Poirier's approach, however, has not been without its critics. Although a montage of shots at the beginning of the film shows Germain Houde playing different social types, a freeze-frame immobilizing him while a female voice-over accuses him of rape, the scene in the van emphatically gives us a working-class rapist. The emphasis on his body exacerbates not only the "classism," it also has connotations of naturalism, of man as determined by animal urges, a reverse sexism and an evacuation of social determinants. Although director and editor discuss this point, with the director insisting on its maximum shock value, Poirier has been criticized for not trusting her audience, which might have been titillated by the sight of a handsome rapist.[26]

However, while it is true that much NFB output, including by women directors, deals mainly with, and addresses, the (new) middle classes, there is a Quebec specificity to the rapist's masculine persona and Houde's performance, not just the *joual* but the failed masculinity articulated around beer and male bar culture (biting off the bottle top). In a culture that has gained much of its authentication from notions of "the people" as opposed to those of a conquering bourgeoisie, and in a national cinema replete with homosocial spaces and discourses (Carle, Forcier, *Les Boys*), the rapist is significantly both very situated and very universalizable.

It could be argued, however, that Philippe is unfairly treated. An analysis of masculinity and patriarchy as constructions, while necessary and interesting, is not one of the film's priorities, since it considers with some justification that the effects of these constructions on women need first, urgently, to be exposed. More important, the film can be seen to perpetuate victimology.[27] Carole Zucker has also argued that the rape scene does not successfully avoid "pleasures," because identification is not necessarily limited to the almighty point-of-view shot (exposed as artifice anyway when the urine splashes on to the camera lens' smooth surface), but can wander into depth of field and close-up too, that is, to the rapist. The ingredient of suspense adds to this effect.[28]

Different critical positions are articulated around the final sequence, when the camera scans deserted city spaces, spaces of danger for women, and then the soundtrack echoes to a cacophony of women's whistles. The starting point for this is the judge's suggestion that women carry whistles for their defence. Is this scene a feeble gesture of defence, consistent with the film's victimology (Zucker), or in fact a satirization of the judge's idea? It would seem rather that the sequence represents a "collective political call,"[29] a culmination of the voice-off soundtrack that has progressed from the victim's whimpers through the court scene to this decisive, dissident, and disruptive protest by a constituted community of women, of political subjects.

Poirier's later feature films, all at the NFB, include *La Quarantaine* (1982), in which a group of eleven forty-somethings, all members of a gang of childhood friends, who loved each other "by choice" in "our own family," gather for a weekend together after thirty years. Typically for a Poirier film, the narrative is interrupted, by Monique Mercure as the articulate journalist Louise, to comment on the action and performance. Male space does not come to rival that of women; couples are not formed. The film, rather morosely in the post-1980 referendum context, is about "Quebec." This is the generation marked by the

Quiet Revolution, with its various empowerments, transformations, and failures. Louise, for example, is of the first generation of women really to gain personal autonomy. One character, Jacques (Benoît Girard), has since come out as gay. The disillusioned Tarzan (Jacques Godin), estranged from his children, commits suicide. While the film takes an interesting idea and effectively develops the theme of choice and modernity which had dominated *Le Temps de l'avant,* it deploys too many characters and relies too much on character "type" and personality really to have an effective purchase on the relationship between collective and individual development.

Poirier's next features were the telefilm *Salut Victor* (1988), and a fifty-year anniversary archival anthology of the NFB's representation of women in *Il y a longtemps que je t'aime* (1989). *Tu as crié "let me go,"* released in 1997, recounts her daughter's drug addiction and murder. Clearly by far her most personal work, it nevertheless continues her preoccupation with maternity, which can be seen as central to her conception of femininity. In an interview in 1985, she even places it at the centre of masculine definition, in which masculinity is figured as itself a "lack," a compensation for the inability to bear children: "They try to make up for a less total and conscious participation in life itself through social, intellectual and material things,"[30] which some might argue confirms some of the essentialism they discern in her work. The film, made in black and white, combines a documentary analysis of the drug trade, calling for its legalization, with lyrical interludes in which Poirier herself reads a text written for the film by Marie-Claire Blais, and ice falling off glaciers figures death and loss.

Mireille Dansereau was the first woman to direct a feature film in the private sector. Born in 1943 in Montreal, she had studied dance and law and spent the year 1968–69 in London studying for a Master's at the Royal College of Art. *La Vie rêvée* (1972) was one of the first films produced by the Association coopérative des productions audiovisuelles (ACPAV), a production cooperative set up by and for young film-makers to encourage first features and to bypass the burgeoning commercial cinema represented by private companies such as Carle-Lamy. The film also benefited from CFDC money.

La Vie rêvée recounts the friendship of two young women, Isabelle (Liliane Le Maître-Auger) and Virginie (Véronique Le Flaguais), who both work for a private film studio which seems mostly to make ads. There is a narrative, basically revolving around Isabelle's crush on Jean-Jacques (Jean-François Guité), her finally arranging to see him in Virginie's flat, and their final dismissal of him after Isabelle and he have sex. What is important in the film, however, is the element of *rêve* or fantasy and its relationship with the women's situation. Through editing, *mise en scène*, and mobile camerawork, the film at every moment locates the women both in the concrete spaces of the city, parental home, work, and landscape and in a world of images and sounds that are external and interiorized, that come from elsewhere but inhabit the self in such a way that the development of identity is dependent upon their exploration, acceptance, or rejection. The very first scene with Isabelle and Virginie together has them framed in the mirror of the toilets of their workplace, the impelling of the identity exploration underlined by their conversation about make-up. The linear narrative is frequently interrupted by fantasy sequences, of holidaying by the sea with Jean-Jacques, and of frolicking naked in the countryside with him. Virginie, who works in animation, has a flat festooned with collages of consumer images of mostly men and women. These are triumphantly torn down after the sexual debacle with the dream man, Jean-Jacques.

The Quebec film that *La Vie rêvée* most resembles is *À tout prendre*, for its ludic exploration of the self and its construction, its refusal to take plenitudes of identity seriously, its attention to fantasy and sexuality, its playful attitude to cinema and images. *La Vie rêvée* was greeted with similar incomprehension and disapproval: ACPAV pronounced that it did not provide "a dynamic and stimulating reflection of Quebec's female collectivity,"[31] its attention to emotion and the "private" a diversion from the agenda and approach of a more concretely militant film.[32] (This is echoed in the film when Virginie's working class brother condemns women's preoccupation with "affaires de coeur et de cul/affairs of the heart and the ass.") This, of course, is Dansereau's point. Her version of "women's cinema" is to question the boundaries of private and public space (physical, politico-psychological, cinematic) that a patriarchal society has established. In addition, it succeeds in gendering the preoccupations of *À tout prendre*, where Johanne, trapped in the fantasies and expectations of heterosexual romance, did not enjoy the same access as Claude to the putting into images of a ludic and fragmented self. Isabelle and Virginie – and it is surely significant that there are two protagonists, a connection between women rather than a beleaguered narcissism – are clearly located in a nexus of economic and political power which is in a continuum, however complex, with the fantasies they inhabit. The ads are grotesquely (and amusingly) sexist: an aerosol sprayed into a female armpit is, typically, milked for bathetic humour. The boss of the studio gives Isabelle her notice, in English, and assures her that she will soon find a husband. The point of view of his gaze momentarily and fetishistically focuses on her legs, but the result is irony because of the undermining both of his position and of image-making that has previously taken place. A similar distancing is achieved when an Anglo-Canadian porn director inspects a series of naked women, framed from waist to mid-thigh.

The date of the film, 1972, is also important, and not only for its intervention in a Quebec cinema then dominated by sex comedies. It comes at the tail end of a process of modernization and consumerization in Quebec society that has rejected tradition but is still searching for modes of living with the new. Within this, women have ceased to be the national mothers but are continuing to be exploited in body and conditioned in mind, a situation to which the new wave of feminism is beginning to respond. (1972 is also the year of Jean Eustache's *La Maman et la putain*, which in ultimately more sombre vein examines the fallout of the 1960s and particularly May 1968, with its highly ambiguous consequences for women, and looks uncertainly at the future, all within a strong sense of public time and place: *La Vie rêvée* similarly alludes to historical events such as Northern Ireland and the October crisis.) Although a reading of the film is possible which emphasizes a teleology, a trajectory of truth and liberation that finally tears off the masks of obfuscation and mystification (witness the final tearing down of posters), the subtle strength of the film is that at no point are the women or their fantasies to be understood as "silly." Their situation vis-à-vis their "dreams" is always already ambiguous. The sequence of the little girl lifting her dress in the garden to the father figure can be read both as an Oedipal trap, rhyming with the encounter with *le boss* and the infatuation with the idealized Jean-Jacques, and as a gesture of defiance. The momentary euphoria of the final, literally iconoclastic sequences cannot disguise the fact that identity formation is an on-going negotiation of social discourses that will include prefabricated pleasures where the relation between autonomy and appropriation to the system is at best uncertain and may even lose its meaning. The images on Virginie's wall are already a collage, a juxtaposition of fragments from which she is attempting to make sense of her existence. At the end, the wall is blank, to be covered by what? Perhaps the same images, but in quotation marks, to be read ironically? This anticipatory postmodern lesson is made clear in the sequence in the countryside, when the myth of nature (marked by means of a zoom on the group tormented by insects whose noise increases in volume on the soundtrack) is exposed as just another discourse bound up with consumer and male pleasure: the supposedly "alternative" Reichian analysis made by their male companion as he tries to get them into bed. North American counter-culture, it could be argued, provided one way for advanced capitalism to renew itself from the late 1960s onwards.

Louise Carrière, writing in 1983, criticized the childlike nature of the women (how else can a film be ludic?) and, moreover, the fact that the film is unclear about representing and denouncing the fantasies: "You can't tell if she is distancing herself from the dream images or if she misses them."[33] However, this is the point. "Femininity" is that ambiguity, as Patricia Smart argues: "The only trait that is truly characteristic of the feminine ... is the *absence* of a territory and the impossibility of distinguishing between what we 'are' and what culture has made of us."[34] Interviewed in 1972, Mireille Dansereau made an analogy with the situation of Quebec, but at the same time she made a breach within it: "The search of women to create and to exist is the same process as what is happening in Quebec. It is the same pattern for any sort of colonized/colonizer relationship. The same problems exist for women as exist for Quebec in relation to the rest of Canada. It is very difficult for a woman in Quebec."[35] In this way, "Quebec" is simultaneously affirmed (in relation to Canada) and, as a patriarchy, undermined as a totality. As with *La Vie rêvée*, the only response can be an exploration of the provisionality, the ambiguity, the molecular status of identities and their location in the flow of social discourses.

Since *La Vie rêvée*, Mireille Dansereau has made mainly documentaries, such as those at the NFB in the 1970s exploring the evolution of marriage and the family in Quebec: *J'me marie, j'me marie pas* (1973), and *Familles et variations* (1977). Her second feature, *L'Arrache-coeur* (1979), concentrates on the mother daughter relationship as a decisive site of the construction of female subjectivity. Céline (Louise Marleau, who won best-actress award at the Montreal Film Festival for her performance) is a struggling writer who lives with her husband, an equally struggling independent avant-garde film-maker, and her four-year-old son, Samuel. However, the crucial relationship in her life is with her mother (Françoise Faucher), and the film proceeds to analyse the daughter's classic struggle to achieve a satisfactory balance between intimacy or complicity with, and differentiation from, the mother. One image of this is the breast cancer from which the mother had suffered and which Céline is constantly monitoring in herself. There is a Quebec specificity to this: the mother is the strong figure in her marriage, the father has "décroché," is unemployed, has opted out of career and public empowerment in the public sphere. The parents' ultimately happy marriage was a shotgun affair in a conservative milieu. Céline's husband is an immigrant, and he is experiencing alienation in domestic and public "homes," and in work (the anglophone film executives are dismissive of his art; it has to be said that the brief extract from his rather pretentious and derivative work is one of the few moments of humour in this film). In the end, mother and daughter reach a new understanding based on the relationship between generations, past and present, the *legacy* of anxieties and fear that is passed on to one's children, and Céline's concern about repeating this with Samuel.

While the film leaves many questions unanswered, such as the nature of Céline's own work and the country of origin of the husband, the film does succeed in exploring cinematically the issues and spaces associated with this domestic drama which could have been very televisual. Most notably, depth of field is used to map the hierarchies and territories of the home, as when Céline prepares breakfast in the foreground while the husband, berating the child at the table in background right, eventually strikes him. It also enables the camera to convey metaphors of depth, reflection, repetition, and identity in frequent scenes when Céline's image is caught in mirrors, even in several mirrors at once, juxtaposed with that of her mother, in the sequence at her parents' home. A shot of Céline on the telephone to her mother is followed by that of Samuel playing with yarn like an umbilical cord. Céline is often photographed through glass, and the transitions these scenes denote (the car windshield, the door leading to her psychiatrist's bureau, the windows of her mother's real estate agency) all suggest crisis, until the final shot of the film pans up and out from the reconciled husband and wife to the life outside the apartment. To a much lesser extent than in *La Vie rêvée*, fantasy and memory sequences follow close-ups of Céline.

This is the technique that dominates Dansereau's third feature, *Le Sourd dans la ville* (1987), an adaptation of Marie-Claire Blais's 1979 novel. This was a challenging work to adapt for the cinema, since it is basically a novel in polyphonic free direct discourse in which the voices of several characters can inhabit the same lengthy sentence. In her adaptation, however, Dansereau has both achieved a cinematic equivalent of this interiorization and provided a centred, guiding thread. This is Florence (Béatrice Picard), a middle-aged *bourgeoise* whose husband has left her and who leaves her luxurious apartment overlooking the city, through which she wanders, ending up in a sordid hotel run by Gloria (Angèle Coutu) and inhabited by her young, terminally ill son Mike (Guillaume Lemay-Thivierge), two other children, teenage Lucia and baby Jojo, and assorted marginals. In what amounts to a spiritual rather than political journey, Florence receives an education in "human" suffering and endurance (the schoolteacher Judith who knows both Florence and Mike is obsessed with the Nazi concentration camps) and shoots herself in her hotel room.

But, while concrete political references are largely missing from this text, what we might call civilizational ones are not. In its representation of alienation in a city that is recognizably Montreal in the spring, *Le Sourd dans la ville* is one of the high points of a rather elusive Quebec modernism. Florence's peregrination through the streets, and in particular a long scene at Viger Square in which she observes one of the hotel guests, old Tim (Pierre Thériault, an actor himself terminally ill) reminiscing about Ireland to his dog, and also the children playing in the fountains, maps out the city as a fragmented space of loss, sexual and other exploitation, non-communication, and non-reciprocity. However, this assessment, this view in cinematic terms, is possible because there is something else, there is a position from which this can be critiqued, if only in the natural metaphors for and images of escape, for places elsewhere – desert (land), water and mountains (air) – that pepper the film. Thus Gloria and Mike fantasize about the journey west to San Francisco they will make in the summer; Florence ascends the staircase to her decisive rendezvous with death amid a repeated image of snow-capped mountains. Moreover, the film puts Munch's *The Scream* at the centre of its extended meditation on art and painting. The last shot is that of Mike reacting to the sight of Florence's death with the same gesture and facial expression as in Munch. The importance of art is just one of the ways in which the look is examined in the film. In her previous existence, Florence's look had been characterized by either bourgeois detachment and indifference, a visual "deafness," as it were, which is bound up with modernity, or the aesthetic gaze, that bracketing off of art from material urgencies, that primacy of form over content or function, which Bourdieu, for example, sees as playing a crucial role within the social hierarchy of taste. These looks are discredited in the film, and for Florence, by the way in which they are confronted with other forms of looking within a plethora of close-ups of the two main characters.

There is the look that is voyeuristic, and that is bound up with exploitation, for example, that of Lucia's "boyfriend" as he pimps her out to an older man, or the sexual transactions in the hotel. There is the look that objectifies and distances Florence herself, as, object of a suspicious and fascinated gaze, she arrives at the hotel. There is the look that establishes connections with people in the city (the smile of a passing cyclist, Florence observing the children) and in the hotel. Depth of field here shows that there is something to be looked at, something, some truth, to be discovered beyond appearances, for example, in the long perspectives afforded by the dingy hotel corridors. There is the look of escape, which is external (Mike gazing out through the net curtains), and the memory-look, a look of introspection when Florence gazes but sees memories. In the film's long central scene, when Florence sits on the stairs and observes the hotel denizens, art and life begin to interact, the gazes of her culture start to adjust themselves. The high-angle distance shot recalls cinematic perspective itself. At one point, Mike, with whom she comes to share a real complicity, partly as they both face imminent death, is seen by her in terms of Oslo Kommunes' *Sick Child*. The look of compassion and "truth" that Florence achieves ("I repressed life through painting") is the telos or goal of the film, and is announced when one memory-look, interrupted by Mike bringing her coffee, has her recalling the comforts of home: slippers, bed, and a landscape painting which then fades to white. This prefigures the end of her life (amid the whiteness of snow) and the blank screen at the end of the film itself, but perhaps it underestimates the way in which the aesthetic has not been abandoned or located in a binary opposition to "life" – we are watching a film after all – but has become integrated into something wider, a spiritual temptation possibly, but certainly a wider ethical means of establishing a purchase on the catastrophes of modernity following the collapse of religious belief. In short, Florence learns to "see," like the bourgeoise played by Ingrid Bergman in *Europa '51* (Rossellini, 1951), but with the consolation of the sublime.

The film can accomplish these procedures only through the repeated and prolonged silent close-ups on Florence. There are only two scenes in which she speaks at any length, in flashback when she opens up to Judith, and in the hotel with Mike. The film depends on Béatrice Picard's strong performance even more than *L'Arrache-coeur* does on Louise Marleau. These looks and close-ups are a perfect example of what Deleuze calls the affection-image, that intermediary state between an entity perceiving stimuli and acting upon them. The close-up, which invariably means the face, is the site, or "ensemble," of a "reflecting, mobile unity" and of "intensive expressive movements."[36] Florence's face is mainly photographed in terms of the former, namely as an outline, as thinking about something. Only once, when she breaks down with Judith, does her face correspond to the latter definition, when the features themselves enter an intensive series of movement and change. Significantly, the two portraits by Kommunes and Munch respectively correspond to this distinction, which Deleuze makes between the close-up or portrait as *qualité* or as *puissance*. It gives a clue to the kind of cinema presented in *Le Sourd dans la ville*. The playful questioning to be found in *La Vie rêvée* has become a much more serious affair, and not only in the contrast of their two endings. In *Le Sourd*, action itself is held in suspense, and personal identity (Florence has abandoned hers) and concrete spatio-temporal references have become less important than the abstract universalism of the face in close-up. It is the cinema of Bergman rather than Godard. We shall see in Léa Pool how this temptation within Quebec women's cinema continues.

Micheline Lanctôt (b. 1947) was in the 1970s best known as an actress, the star of *La Vraie Nature de Bernadette* and opposite Richard Dreyfuss in the internationally distributed anglophone Quebec film, *The Apprenticeship of Duddy Kravitz* (Kotcheff, 1974). This vocation, and various other autobiographical elements, provide structuring themes and patterns to her four fictional feature films. Her first, *L'Homme à tout faire* of 1980, portrays in some detail and sympathy the gestures and routines of the life of a Quebec suburban housewife, Thérèse (Andrée Pelletier), who finally stays with her husband Bernard (Gilles Renaud), the final shot being of her isolated in the desert-like whiteness of the unfilled swimming pool. It concentrates, however, on Armand (Jocelyn Bérubé), the handyman of the title. He is the archetypal Quebec little man, unhappy and ineffectual in love, wandering across the province according to the demands of work, iconically sporting T-shirts from peripheral regions of the province. This is the source of much bathetic humour, including an effective sight gag which has him rising and descending in the vertical plane as he pursues an abortive love on the Metro escalators. He is the valued embodiment in the film of simple, nostalgic values, carving wood, writing to mother, almost childlike. However, this figure is now marginal within contemporary Quebec: his rival is the *homme performant* Bernard; the old homosociality, in several key scenes with his male friends, is seen not to be functioning. The economy of this ultimately reactionary film therefore needs to emphasize that Armand is not homosexual (as, it could be argued, Armand needs to do himself). There is thus a scene in which, to cries of "maudite tapette/fucking queer," he violently throws out his gay flatmate (Marcel Sabourin) in a series of shots that parallel in reverse, and thus compensate for, an earlier scene when he was pressured by his dishonest friend.

Lanctôt's attitude in this first film is also explained by her visceral anti-Americanism. She lived with Ted Kotcheff in Los Angeles in the late 1970s and denounced American individualism and materialism in a NFB documentary, *La Poursuite du bonheur*, in 1987. In a series of interviews with Denise Pérusse in 1995, she links this with her Quebec nationalism ("I became a separatist in the United States") and her homophobia: in scientific experiments, she points out, "after a certain density rats would show a certain number of aberrant behaviour patterns, such as attacking each other, homosexuality, cannibalism, which we see in American cities." After this extraordinary amalgam, she then emphasizes that "the American model is killing off plurality, diversity, difference."[37]

As critics of Balzac and others have pointed out over the years, even (and sometimes especially) the reactionary position with regard to modernity can throw up interesting insights into its workings. Lanctôt's second feature, *Sonatine* (1983), which won the Silver Lion at Venice, is organized around three movements of roughly equal length: in the first, an adolescent, Chantal (Pascale Bussières), pursues an infatuation with a bus driver, taking the same ride every week until he loses his job; in the second, Louisette (Marcia Pilote) has run away from home but finds temporary affection from a monolingual Bulgarian sailor on a ship in the port; in the third, the two girls make a suicide pact and ride around the Metro with a placard proclaiming their intention. They take the pills, to the indifference and inaction of their fellow-passengers, and die undiscovered because of a Metro strike.

The Metro, far from being the playground of modernity and space of new stimuli that we found in *Valérie*, is now the space of modern alienation, and death, in which the national "people" assembled there neither react nor act.[38] However, the film is not without its contradictions. The film's interesting use of the soundtrack, with its disjunctive noises, the girls' extensive use of the Walkman (filmed in extreme close-up over the opening credits), distorting external sound (Louisette eating cornflakes while her parents argue), could have been developed into a more complex examination of its cultural effects and uses other than its atomization of the young people. (The computers and other technological paraphernalia at school are similarly no help to emotional communication and understanding.) For Chantal, the Walkman constitutes an instant source of memory, as the bus driver calls her beautiful. It has been argued that this is a problem rather than an opportunity: "Chantal and Louisette are able, by the selective recording of their environment, to reinforce the fragmented grasp of things implicit in their passionately incomplete vision, and thereby to strangle at its inception any impulse to life-promoting dialogue with the outside."[39] However, the Walkman does provide this disempowered pair with the opportunity for *bricolage*, for a creative use of these fragments. It has been argued from a postmodern perspective that the Walkman also involves extensions of the self, in the creation of a soundscape, the continuous decontextualization and recontextualization of music on the move.[40] The girls can thus be seen as nomads *sans le savoir*, caught between an autonomy that can creatively weave its way through the fragments, and an autism that leaves them more isolated than ever. While some critics have seen the film as, typically for Quebec, a quest for the father (Louisette's father works there and is glimpsed speeding away on the back of a train), there is some evidence that in fact it is the absence of the mother, as the more distant figure, which is most felt. The Metro is where the girls die: in a reverse of the Orpheus myth, it is because the male figure does not look. Heterosexual romance had already been problematized in the futile hopes the girls had placed in the two men in the first two sequences. The internalized sound of the Walkman could imply some kind of return to the womb, or at least to some pre-Oedipal time before language and the male symbolic order. And yet these more radical challenges are lacking in the film. If one charge against modern North American society is its "narcissism," then the girls are as guilty of this as anyone: Chantal adjusts her appearance in the reflection of the bus window just like passengers in the Metro. The problem that is presented is that of society failing to reflect back to the girls the image they want. An autobiographical reading seems again to be relevant: Lanctôt was anorexic and bulimic as an adolescent, the relationship with her "rational" mother very difficult. The latter had had little sympathy with the two girls on viewing *Sonatine*.[41]

Lanctôt's most recent two features explore personal themes in inchoate fashion but in formally interesting ways. *Deux actrices* (1993), a more artisanal affair (blown up from 16 mm.) made with Canada Council money for $237,000, casts Pascale Paroissien as Fabienne, who unexpectedly turns up to announce that she is the older sister of Solange (Pascale Bussières). Emotionally demanding and unstable, with a lesbian past and a seven-year-old daughter who had been taken into care, she damages Solange's relationship with Charles (François Delisle), and when the two young women visit their mother (Louise Latraverse) the estrangement between Fabienne and the latter is only confirmed. Solange, however, continues to support Fabienne and her baggage of problems. This narrative is interrupted by video segments in which the actors discuss their roles with the director and make links with their own personal experiences: relations with parents and partners, feelings of emotional and cultural estrangement when moving to another country. Jerry White has argued that the film invites reflection on the relationship between performance and identity.[42] The family illusion breaks down, is made strange, and so meanings are constructed "in the *difference* between acting and sincerity." If this were so, this would have radical effects on the film's construction of gender and even the nation (at one point Solange sits on a park bench next to a transvestite and confirms to him that he looks like "a real girl"). However, rather than creating distantiation, the film's device tends to increase the intimacy of the piece and the identification of the viewer. As White himself points out, the actresses in the process come to terms with their identity, that is, delve further into who they "really" are. The "realism" of the video footage is not called into question.

In contrast, Lanctôt's next film was a relatively high-budget affair for Rock Demers's Productions La Fête in co-production with the NFB. *La Vie d'un héros* (1994) deals with a neglected episode in Quebec history, the period during and just after the Second World War when a large number of German prisoners were held in the Eastern Townships region of Quebec and many were employed as agricultural labourers on local farms. For the Québécois family involved and particularly the mother (Véronique Le Flaguais), the handsome German officer Hanibal (Christopher B. MacCabe), from Prussian aristocratic stock, is an exotic and attractive figure. The story of his brief stay is passed down through the generations of women in the family, through Evelyne (Marie Cantin) to her young daughter Amélic (Marie Eve Champagne) in the present day. Evelyne's voice-over narrative periodically transforms itself into the *style indirect libre*/free indirect speech[43] of different family dinner-table conversations from the past thirty-five years. In the present day, Evelyne and Amélie arrive at the family home to help welcome Hanibal on his return visit. He turns out to be an old and unattractive West German businessman, played by Erwin Potitt (Amélie: "He's not like I thought he'd be"). However, the visit ends with reconciliation all round.

The film invites comparison with *Another Time, Another Place* (Radford, 1983), in which Italians are held captive in northern Scotland and the encounter with cultural difference, and "the enemy," is negotiated via the sexual longings of a married woman (although these are never here consummated). *La Vie d'un héros* also contains a direct quotation from *The German Sisters* (*Die Bleierne Zeit*, 1982), when the adolescent Evelyne, until then a dedicated germanophile because of the stories about Hanibal (she was just a baby when he left), attends a screening of *Nuit et brouillard* and walks out, vomiting outside the cinema. For Margarete von Trotta, of course, and her generation of filmmakers, the distinction between "German" and "Nazi" is a problematic one to make. Lanctôt's film is able to unpack the two because of the Quebec context and the remoteness of the hosts from the realities of the war. (It was this that upset some of the Montreal critics, but the film is at pains to debate the issue.)

In various scenes, France for these Québécois comes out unfavourably in comparison; Evelyne's father (Gilbert Sicotte) is anti-British and a Bloc populaire candidate. As it slips between different timeframes, the film shows how we bathe in memory and narrative. The encounter with the German allows a series of reflections on the arguably inevitable role of misapprehension, idealization, and caricature ("A German is clean") in memory's construction of narrative, the self and the Other. The film invites a collective dimension to these reflections. For example, Evelyne's Hispanic husband, who refuses to go to the reunion because he "doesn't fit" into the family, is played by Manuel Aranguiz from *Les Noces de papier* (to be discussed in chapter 10). Evelyne, in classic fashion if we recall Weinmann on the family romance, fantasizes that Hanibal was her real father. However, the film's ambition is really one of *intimisme* around the mother-daughter relationship, with an autobiographical dimension for Lanctôt herself (her parents also owned an apple orchard in Estrie and had put up a German prisoner). The final shots of war footage ("our" historical memory) fail to articulate a relationship between the public and private domains. Interesting and distinctive (within distinctiveness) as Lanctôt's cinema is, it is difficult to disentangle her authorial vision at best from autobiographical concerns, at worst from personal affronts and prejudices.

Léa Pool was born in Switzerland in 1950 and moved to Quebec in 1978. She has achieved one of the most stable positions in contemporary Quebec cinema, equivalent in the private sector to that of Anne Claire Poirier, precisely for her ability to address international art-movie audiences. However, whereas Poirier negotiates the relationship between the "real" and its construction, Pool's is a cinema in between spaces and places, fantasy and reality, with the aesthetic linking the two. Her first feature, *Strass café* (1980), is the most abstract and experimental, with much tracking through deserted city streets, past walls and railway lines, and a female voice-over articulating themes of memory and loss, the possible story of a relationship between a nameless man and woman. *La Femme de l'hôtel* of 1984 represented Pool's breakthrough in terms of festival prizes (Montreal and Créteil), audiences, and her own art, in the articulation of the concrete and the abstract. A Jewish film-maker, Andréa Richler (Paule Baillargeon), has returned to Montreal ("I'm not at home, either here or anywhere else") to make a film. She becomes fascinated by Estelle (Louise Marleau), who, at some unexplained point of crisis in her life, has abandoned a train journey westward and moved into Andréa's hotel. Estelle's story becomes integrated into Andréa's project of recounting the life crisis of a singer, played by an unnamed actress (Marthe Turgeon). Estelle eventually departs on the train, but the possibility remains of the three characters in fact creatively representing different aspects of the film-maker: as in Bergman's *Persona* (1966), for instance, they lose their individuation in the course of the film (although here more by editing and the transgression of a coherent cinematic space-time than through close-ups).

Co-produced on a bigger budget with the NFB, *Anne Trister* (1986) opens with the funeral of Anne's father in the Israeli desert. Anne (Albane Guilhe), a Swiss Jew, seeks to recover from this loss by moving to Montreal to develop her artwork. There she develops an unreciprocated sexual attraction to a child psychotherapist, Alix (Louise Marleau), whose treatment of a young girl, Sarah (Lucie Laurier), is paralleled with Anne's experiences. Anne is injured in a fall at her workspace, which is demolished by developers. Anne and Alix seem eventually to have sex, but Anne returns to Israel. *À corps perdu* (1988) is a loose adaptation of *Kurwenal*, a novel by the French gay writer Yves Navarre. Pool's first international co-production (with Switzerland), it is the first to place a man at the centre. The eponymous photojournalist (Matthias Habich) is dumped by David (Michel Voita) and Sarah (Johanne-Marie Tremblay), with whom he lived in a *ménage à trois*, and is questioning his work and career after a traumatic experience in Nicaragua, when he is blamed by a villager for the death of her child. Like a depoliticized *Under Fire* (Spottiswoode, 1983), the film then has him embarking on an unconventional photo project on Montreal and on a relationship with a young deaf-mute, Quentin (Jean-François Pichette). *Hotel Chronicles* (1990) is a documentary journey across the United States accompanied by a voice-over combining analysis of both its subject and its author. *La Demoiselle sauvage* (1991) is another co-production with Switzerland, where it is set. Marianne (Patricia Tulasne), the young Québécoise of the title, lives a brief love affair with Elysée (Matthias Habich), in hiding between her murder of her lover and her suicide. The film is dominated by the blank, abstract spaces (but which also function as walls) of Swiss mountains, dam and lake dwarfing the human protagonists. In *Mouvements du désir* (1993), a co-production with France and Switzerland, straight-laced computer expert Vincent (Jean-François Pichette) begins a love affair on a westbound train with single mother Catherine (Valérie Kaprisky). The film ends surrealistically: the train does not stop in Vancouver, the love story does not end.

Other studies have commented in detail on these films, particularly *La Femme de l'hôtel.*[44] Pool's work does now constitute an *oeuvre* in the auteurist sense, with recurring formal and thematic preoccupations which are not marked by any specific breaks or departures. It would seem most fruitful to examine these and relate them to questions of gender and national identity. Of course, her persistent and successful break with the dominant social realist strand in Quebec cinema is both praised and derided by critics. The question remains: what kind of politics, particularly gender politics, inhabits these films? Chantal Nadeau has argued coherently that none does at all. By placing women in these in-between, dream-like spaces, Pool's films "deny the positivity of the position of woman-as-other for a feminist practice."[45] This marginalization of women in the name of a dubious universalism would deny them the status of social subjects, and be complicit, not only with the tendency in Quebec political culture to view sexual relations as outside the public domain, but with a whole straight male cinema which places woman as the Other in an existential (or Oedipal, or national) quest for authenticity (the films of Forcier, for example).[46]

There are some cultural specificities here. Francophone and/or Catholic cultural traditions have until recently not yielded spaces in which an identity politics on the Anglo-Saxon model might flourish. That Pool is not more of a militant lesbian film-maker presupposes one particular, indeed ethnocentric, model of how these issues might best be articulated. Arguably, the matter-of-fact portrayal of male homosexual desire (Andréa's brother Simon, played by Serge Dupire, in *La Femme de l'hôtel*; Pierre and David in *À Corps perdu*; even Catherine's ex-lover in *Mouvements du désir*) represents an advance in Quebec cinema, somewhat reminiscent of André Téchiné. The fact that lesbian relations, in *Anne Trister*, for example, are made more of an issue is precisely to do with Pool's interest in sexuality as continuum and in identity as unfixed. Andréa's fascination with Estelle in *La Femme de l'hôtel* is part of that process. Not only, as Janis L. Pallister argues, is the fetishizing of Garbo/Dietrich figures within mainstream cinema refashioned by a woman,[47] the film is also one of those rare occasions in cinema when a woman becomes an object of fascination for another, in fact a radical departure from the woman-as-other-to the subject "man." Like Seidelman's *Desperately Seeking Susan* (1985), the film sidesteps the traps that gaze theory claims mainstream cinema creates for female spectatorship, namely, masculinization, masochism, or marginality, and suggests a new visual economy that posits female-female desires and identifications within a wider context of, for example, mother-daughter relations and their memory.[48]

An assessment of Pool ultimately means an assessment also of those theoretical positions whose arguments have emphasized the formal consequences of sexual difference to be developed in cinema. While the Pool spectator may not be addressed as a concretely situated woman in social conflict, nor is he/she addressed as an Oedipalized assumed male. Pool's "universalism" is about the blurring and dissolution of boundaries, and it is the import of this procedure that needs to be addressed. It is certainly consistent with feminist analyses of women's permeable ego boundaries (Chodorow). So-called "new French feminist" theory has included an interest in the feminine investment of liminal spaces, a cult of marginality, as, for example, when Claudine Herrmann argues that, to avoid the double-bind of silence and/or speaking the language of men, "the only thing left for women to do is to find, and speak from, the empty space, the no-man's land, which she can at least call her own ... ." The void thus becomes a respectable value[49] and can even be productive of the new. Nadeau's critique of Pool is reminiscent of those Marxist criticisms of Italian neo-realism and its passive, confused protagonists, arguments that Gilles Deleuze sought to repudiate by asserting the mutations and disintegration they announced: "It is not the cinema that turns away from politics, it becomes completely political, but in another way."[50] (Similar issues arise when Deleuze and Guattari's anti-Oedipal theories, or the idea of "becoming-woman," are criticized for eliding sexual difference.)

La Femme de l'hôtel practises its own kind of resistance, in Estelle's breakdown, in the actress's foregrounding of performance. The persistence of this theme of the masquerade in the film, of woman as performer rent between an identity constructed by others, and a being that is lost and unnameable, inscribes a notion of feminine specificity as alienation, expropriation, and schizophrenia. Here exile is lived above all as a resistance to social constructions of identity and as the embodiment of a desire that demands but cannot be represented. And in this impossibility, it is a space of madness, of the dissolution of identity induced by the inability to sustain the masquerade.[51]

This dissolution invites connections to be made beyond the signifier "woman." *Strass café* represents one extreme of a procedure that produces "deconnected or emptied spaces" which are not only devoid of characters in "sensory-motor 'motivating' situations" and in "a state of strolling, of sauntering or of rambling"[52] but lack coherent characters at all. Pool's cinema is that of the relation between the *clapotement* (a film's "gaseous state defined by the free movement of each molecule")[53] and the provisional solidities and coherences that form and unform. This formulation of it permits connections between femininity and the nation, the modern city, childhood, and art.

Estelle's first words to Andréa in the hotel lobby had been "Are you Jewish?" The Jewish connection permeates all of Pool's films, since it is able to formulate that undecidable relationship between exile and homeland, instability and stability, the Jew as cosmopolitan or as citizen of a nation-state. Pool's characters are all not only in movement but in flight, but that flight permits joinings and connections to be made in between a lost or traumatic past and a destination which is either nameless or may never be reached. The figure of the child – in *Anne Trister,* in *Mouvements du désir,* and in Pierre's memories and the angelic Quentin in *À corps perdu* – also embodies that propertyless play of past and future, loss and creativity. This is a radical, deterritorializing departure for Quebec national cinema, so preoccupied with constructing notions of the "home." Lanctôt's cinema is full of references to homes, even as it criticizes and problematizes them. The wanderings in *Sonatine* are very different from those in Pool, for they depend on a notion of the home – national or familial – that might grant recognition and plenitude. They do not constitute an *errance.* The hotel in Dansereau's *Le Sourd dans la ville* is a destination as well as a transitory space and is the source of a modernist and even spiritual protest against the world. In Pool, while the notion of loss tends to structure much of the narrative, it is a loss in the sense in which Lacan argues for the persistence of the *objet a*, that memory, which is not even that, of the plenitudinous relation with the mother's body. It is the fundamental lack around which human subjectivity has to be built.

Pool does, however, manage to articulate a relationship between exile and situation. Her protagonists are both in the business of becoming-other and of yearning for lost solidities. One relationship is abstract and metaphorical, through art, notably Anne's mural in *Anne Trister*. Itself a wall (recalling *Strass café* and the mountains and attic that enclose Marianne in *La Demoiselle sauvage*), it becomes the canvas on which she plays out an articulation of movement and stasis (the tumbling chairs), surface, and depth. Anne's painting combines, on the one hand, *pointillisme*, representing the molecular, the fragmentary, and by association the grains of sand of the desert connoting time and death; and, on the other, perspective and line, suggesting connections and the establishment of some kind of subject position from which to make sense of the world. The other site of this process is the city, whereby Montreal is both Montreal "made strange" (the striking greyness of the opening shot of *La Femme de l'hôtel*, Pierre's photographic odyssey in *À corps perdu*) and a universalized urban space (or "any-space-whatever") for our contemporary era.

Clearly, there is in Pool no analysis of power relations, no praxis. Her films articulate perhaps too perfectly the relationship between a text and a practice (international co-productions based in Quebec, international art-movie exhibition). Because her films do not suggest any place from which we might stand outside the fragmentary and the disconnected world she depicts in order to evaluate and surpass it, they can be described as postmodern; because it is loss and alienation that characterize the contemporary condition, they can be seen as modernist. There is no humour, no playfulness, solutions lie primarily in a rather conventional modernist aesthetic. It could be argued that she provides a feminization of modern or postmodern analyses, rather than the reverse, and a cinema of sexual difference that refuses to be bound by Freudian binaries. However, for an evaluation of her purchase on contemporary cultural dilemmas, we have to turn to the category of melancholy, which permeates all her films.

"Melancholy" is a concept often cited by commentators on Quebec cinema. Heinz Weinmann attributes the ambiance and *mise en scène* of *La Femme de l'hôtel* to a post-1980 sense of loss, a mourning of the ideal of sovereignty managed by a self-diminution.[54] This approach succeeds in evacuating both Pool's origins and gender. However, it is true that one of the specificities of Quebec is not fully to share, in the

1980s and 1990s, that euphoria of a victorious world capitalism and triumphant capital-owning bourgeoisie, despite the expanding franco-phone business class and the support for free trade. This was for both economic (the decline of Montreal, the large amount of "older" industries hit by restructuring) and political reasons (the continuing uncertainty of the as yet unattained and perhaps unattainable sovereignty project). Guy Hocquenghem and René Schérer have argued[55] that what can be termed the tradition of melancholy or the melancholic gaze can be deployed to challenge the euphoria of contemporary consumer capitalism. Among those circulating commodities, the updated art-movie ambiguity of Léa Pool provides a way of refreshing our look upon that world while confirming our helplessness within it.

The output of Quebec's other women film-makers is overwhelmingly realist in its orientation. Louise Carré (b. 1936) had a career as producer and scriptwriter at the NFB (she co-wrote Poirier's *Le Temps de l'avant*) before forming her own production company, La Maison des Quatre (producer of *Le Sourd dans la ville*). Carré's first feature, *Ça ne peut pas être l'hiver on n'a même pas eu d'été* (1980), portrays the recently widowed Adèle (Charlotte Boisjoli) and mother of eight grown-up children who in her late fifties rebuilds her life and achieves her autonomy. It is slightly reminiscent of Poirier's *Le Temps de l'avant* for its "centred" and representative setting near the St Lawrence and for its black-and-white montage in flashback (of a lifetime of domestic labour as well as the duty and pleasure of the marriage bed). Carré's second film, the quasi-autobiographical *Qui a tiré sur nos histoires d'amour?* (1986), casts Monique Mercure as Madeleine, a fifty-year-old radio phone-in host in the Sorel/Tracy area outside Montreal, who deals with her own romantic problems and her relationship with her twenty-year-old daughter spending her last summer at home. Both are among the rare Quebec films to portray older women. (This is true of most national cinemas: the other example, of course, is the NFB's most successful film directed by a woman, Cynthia Scott's *The Company of Strangers*, made in 1991).

Marquise Lepage (b. 1959) made her first feature, *Marie s'en va-t-en ville*, in 1987. In a sentimental but effective variation on the "tart with a heart" story, it portrays the relationship between hardbitten prostitute Sarah (Frédérique Collin) and adolescent Marie (Geneviève Lenoir), who has run away from home after being sexually assaulted by her brother. The film emphasizes the commonalities between the two women, including their relation to the dangers of male sexuality and urban space, in a way that sidesteps that between mother and daughter, but the identifications cut both ways when Marie's "innocence" teaches Sarah how to live "authentically" and accept her maturing and aging, symbolized by her ceasing to wear the garish wigs she had donned throughout the film. Lepage's second feature, *La Fête des rois*, made at the NFB in 1994, observes an extended family holiday dinner from a young boy's point of view, when via his voice-over narration he alternately sees and fails to see the truth of the relationships on display. The event becomes simply a stage in his social integration, with a burgeoning "romance" with the girl next door (she is poised and articulate, however, regarding feminist issues), and the nearest there is to revolt is a cousin adopting a Mohawk hairstyle. Two other directors have made a mixture of "issue" films and intimist dramas. Johanne Prégent (b. 1950) has directed *La Peau et les os* (1988), a documentary fiction on anorexia, and *Les Amoureuses* (1992), a "relationship film." Brigitte Sauriol (b. 1945) directed in 1975 *L'Absence*, an intimist film on the lack of a father figure; *Rien qu'un jeu* (1983) on father-daughter incest; and *Laura Laur* (1989), based on the novel by Suzanne Jacob, which falls into the trap of othering a flighty, unstable, and unconventional woman. Apart from *Anne Trister* and Manon Briand's *Deux Secondes* (1998), the only film by a woman director to portray a lesbian relationship is Jeanne Crépeau's *Revoir Julie* (1998), in which an anglophone/francophone friendship is consummated sexually, the realism interspersed with devices that comment on the women's feelings (animation of the Venus de Milo and Mona Lisa, clips of documentaries on geology).

In 1979 the actresses Paule Baillargeon (b. 1945) and Frédérique Collin (b. 1944) directed *La Cuisine rouge*, which schematically but effectively maps out distinct male and female cinematic spaces. Its approach owes much to the Brechtian style of the Grand cirque ordinaire theatre troupe of which Baillargeon was a founding member. As a wedding party arrives at the reception hall, they discover that nothing has been prepared. The men stay in the hall and talk about politics and sport: the argument between the Marxist and the technocratic nationalist is to be read as cliché-ridden and repetitive, its discourse unable to integrate the women's agenda. The women are sent to the kitchen to prepare the meal but instead transform it and the courtyard into a utopian and pagan space of pleasure, conversation, and inactivity. Most of the film consists of a parallel montage of two sequences each for the two sexes. When a man comes into the kitchen to check on the women he cannot see them. One little girl, symbolically for the new generation, escapes through the courtyard to the world outside, while the women return to their "normal" lives and roles. Baillargeon's next feature, *Le Sexe des étoiles* (1993), based on the novel by Monique Proulx about the return of a transexual father, (Marie-)Pierre (Denis Mercier), to Montreal and his relationship with his thirteen-year-old

amateur-astronomer daughter Camille, is ultimately rather conservative in its gender essentialism (despite the physical similarities between
the daughter and the boy at school she befriends), its juxtaposition of
sexual ambiguity and paedophilia, Camille's education in looking
down to earth, and Pierre's ultimate decision to shed his "disguise."

Nonetheless, it is clear that the term "women's cinema" is not without its value when looking at a certain category of film production
there. Despite the wide diversity of film practices it covers, the spaces,
recognitions, and definitions of "the national" are invariably reworked
and redefined in ways that reject the false universality of gender neutrality, refuse totalizing positions of mastery, and yet interact with the
very particular histories and potentialities of Quebec. The cinema of
native peoples and immigrants would seem to offer opportunities of
exploring further the "minor" vocation of Quebec cinema for which
women's films have been so crucial.

9 The Indigenous Other

The native peoples represent one of the key political challenges to the Quebec sovereignist project. Although they represent 1 per cent of Quebec's total population and are scattered among several "nations," territories, and reserves, their general mistrust of Quebec nationalism, and the fact that since Confederation in 1867 and the Indian Act of 1876 most have come under federal jurisdiction, mean that a successful sovereignty referendum would be followed by great uncertainty. The Oka conflict in the summer of 1990, when Mohawk communities in Kanesatake and Kahnawake outside Montreal confronted Canadian and Quebec security forces over the extension of a municipal golf course on to sacred burial sites,[1] was part of a progressively higher profile gained by native issues in the 1980s and 1990s, which included a native member of the Manitoba Legislature, Elijah Harper, helping to scupper the ratification of the Meech Lake Accord, and the incorporation of plans for native autonomy in the (ultimately rejected) 1992 Charlottetown constitutional agreement. The native issue is frequently invoked by English Canadians to discredit the sovereignist project, which exacerbates some of the polarizations.[2] However, a 1992 report found that Quebec contained "the lowest social distance" of any province between the aboriginal and non-aboriginal populations, that the amount of land recognized as belonging exclusively to aboriginal people in Quebec was much higher than in any other province, and that no other provincial government had made the "limited yet relatively concerted efforts" to support the survival of native languages.[3] (The report of the federal Royal Commission on Aboriginal People, published in 1996, reached similar conclusions.) Indeed, the preamble to the Charter of the French Language declaring French to be the dominant language of Quebec (the PQ government's famous Bill 101 of 1977) expressly recognized the right of native peoples to preserve and develop their own languages and cultures, and in 1985 a resolution of the Quebec National Assembly reiterated and extended those rights to questions of self-government, land ownership, and management. Unlike other Canadian provinces, Quebec never promoted the adoption of aboriginal children by white families. Historians also point out the distinctness of the French encounter with the aboriginal peoples of North America when compared to that of the Anglo-Saxons, particularly the greater degree in some periods of suppleness and cooperation as opposed to expansion and extermination.[4]

Native issues complicate narratives of origins, as we saw in *Pour la suite du monde*. Perrault, whose "Amerindian cycle" of documentaries includes *Le Goût de la farine* of 1977 and *Le Pays de la terre sans arbre* of 1980, is prepared to concede the agonizing contradiction of his ethnographic films: "I show them tons of transcultural sympathy and curiosity with no remorse. And in the same movement, I film them like any passing American whose imperialism I nonetheless question."[5] However, at the same time it is clear that old cultural models of rendering the noble savage are operating, when in his horror of American consumerism and youth culture he homogenizes the Amerindians, hypostasizes their supposedly unmediated relationship with nature, and assimilates their alienation (from a formerly full and fixed identity, it is supposed) to that of the Québécois's consumption of baseball and Anglo-Saxon pop.[6]

The complexity of the political issues, then, is matched by these much wider symbolic resonances that native issues have in the construction of Quebec national identity and by extension in the national-allegorical tension of Quebec cinema. Native questions challenge accounts of "pure" identity in favour of *métissage* and hybridity. They suggest a line of flight away from national territorializations and into the vast expanses of "America." The liminal figure in Quebec's historical identity of the *coureur de bois* is a crucial point of tension here: hybrid but very masculinized (French and *canadien* men intermarried with native women and not the reverse), he negotiates Oedipal and non-Oedipal identity constructions. The native peoples as cultural symbols also challenge the grand narratives of modernity and technological progress. This was classically evident in the James Bay controversy when Hydro Québec, in a continuing Quiet Revolution strategy of expansion, collided with the interests of the Cree and Inuit communities, a confrontation resulting in the agreement of 1975 when native title was recognized, compensation paid, and a body of rights granted.[7]

The role of aboriginal peoples throughout the world in the discourses of popular environmentalism and cultural ecology is a significant one and clusters around the seme "nature" and its various implied "others": technology, capitalism, the social itself. "Nature" is, of course, a discourse: "Nature, like everything else we talk about, is first and foremost an artifact of language ... It can be anything but direct and literal."[8] This is never more true than when "nature" is invoked to "naturalize" a state of things or status quo: significantly, both Canada and Quebec, but especially the former because of the weakness of its "cultural" symbols, often deploy "nature" – the landscape, the weather – iconically as signifiers of "the nation." Nature is a part of culture, and the crisis at Oka was in part a clash over the "meaning" of the land. In modernity, the gamut of meanings is run over the earth as "home or habitat, as resource, as refuge and inspiration, as playground, laboratory, profit centre," and also as servant, pet, and victim.[9] These meanings are lived particularly intensely in cultures of permanent crisis and change which are situated at some distance from the "natural" world and police a rigid distinction between the "human" and "non-human." Thus Quebec films representing the native peoples always threaten to take off somewhere else, into the domain of deterritorialized "world-texts," and a certain symbolic labour has to be performed if territorializing discourses around the nation are not to be completely dissipated. The problem is intensified because of the internationalization of film-making and the increasing interest in indigenous peoples by white, ecologically-minded film-makers in the 1980s and 1990s.[10]

Wim Wenders's *Until the End of the World* (1992), to take one instance, exemplifies perhaps some of the major cultural and political paradigm shifts of the contemporary period. A narrative quest that encompasses the globe and thus traces the new universality of reification and commodification of the image ends in an enterprise to capture, in Walter Benjamin's terms, the lost aura. This final setting is among the Australian aborigines, as if, with the collapse of Soviet-style socialism and of the "grand narratives" of historical emancipation, alternative myths, practices, and narratives to the crisis-ridden forward march of capitalism were now to find their inspiration in those remnants of pre-capitalist cultures located at the periphery and, surprisingly, even at the peripheries of "central" economies. The fact that Australia can stand for the latter, while simultaneously being "at the end of the world" and in a peripheral relation to the imperial homelands, in fact reveals the ethnically and racially codified nature of the stakes. It is a question of white and non-white, of the encounter between European (in the cultural and ethnic sense) and non-European cultures, and, in the case of Wenders's film, the not untypical use to which the figure of the non-European is put in order to mediate, define, and transpose preoccupations that are paradigmatically white and/or European.

In addition and in contradistinction to the waves of immigration and general geographic mobility that are characteristic of the post-colonial world, and that, as we shall see in the next chapter, are redefining cultural identities in the new Europe and its individual nation-states, the figure (literary, cinematic, televisual) of the indigenous Other, of the one who was here before, is a vehicle for not only heterogeneity but also more specific interrogations. These are concerned with: pre- and non-capitalist cultures and structures of belief *that are simultaneously marked by racial and ethnic difference*; the meaning of the conquests of European modernity and capitalist expansion, of those grand narratives themselves; and the constitution of the modern nation itself in those places, the way in which a national "people" can be constituted in a culture whose predecessor(s) are visible, adjacent, embedded, entwined, separate, or whatever.

The quincentenary of Columbus's first voyage, for example, thus acquired yet greater significance in the post-"Communist" world and the crisis of the socialist paradigms. Writing in 1981, Tzvetan Todorov drew partly on his experience as displaced if privileged exile in France, as well as of the Bulgarian Communist experiment, in his study of the post-1492 encounter with the American Other, *The Conquest of America*. In the first place, Todorov underscores the event's centrality in the development of modern culture and identity: "It is in fact the conquest of America that heralds and establishes our present identity ... Since that date, the world has shrunk ... men have discovered the totality of which they are a part, whereas hitherto they formed a part without a whole."[11] If the globalization of humanity is announced at this moment, the characteristics of that difference between conqueror and conquered, for example, between Cortés and the Aztec Moctezuma, are revealing for the content of what we consider modern and European culture. While Columbus is both medieval and modern for the way he combines pragmatic and "finalistic" (signs confirm beliefs) interpretations, Cortés, not unlike the figure of Ulysses in Adorno and Horkheimer's denunciation of instrumental reason in *The Dialectic of Enlightenment*, is the arch-pragmatist and improviser, seeking to understand and obtain information about the Mexicans in order to conquer them, his ruses and manipulations exemplifying a discourse governed by its goals rather than by its object or referents. The difference between the cyclical time and epistemic culture ("how to know?") of Mexican society and linear time and praxeological culture ("what to do?") of the Spanish conquerors encapsulates that difference for Todorov between the European and the pre-capitalist, pre-modern, un-modern Other. European civilization of the sixteenth century and after has been based on prioritizing interhuman communicative skills, while the pre-Columbian cultures were primarily based on a notion of communication with nature, of the interaction between the natural and social and religious worlds. The conquest of America is achieved by those with interhuman communicative skills, for whom signs do not flow automatically and necessarily from the external world but are weapons for manipulating others. Oral communication and culture, predicated on notions of presence and immediacy, notably with regard to nature, yield to the written culture of absence and mediation. This also represents a grave loss:

But this victory from which we all derive, Europeans and Americans both, delivers as well a terrible blow to our capacity to feel in harmony with the world, to belong to a preestablished order; its effect is to repress man's communication with the world, to produce the illusion that all communication is intercommunication; the silence of the gods weighs upon the camp of the Europeans as much as on that of the Indians. By winning on one side, the Europeans lost on the other; by imposing their superiority on the entire country, they destroyed their own capacity to integrate themselves into the world.[12]

Todorov's other major point is the relation to alterity, and the way in which he further develops this idea is determined by a culture's symbolic and semiotic system. Already in Columbus could be perceived the "two elementary figures of the experience of alterity"[13]: a consideration of the Indians as equal *and therefore* as the same or identical, *égalité-identité* ("equality-identity"), the logic of assimilation; or a view that sees them as different *and therefore* as unequal or inferior, *différence-inégalité* ("difference-inequality"), the logic of slavery and massacre. The Spanish thus fail to recognize fully the Other as subject; they as *sujets énonçants* projected themselves on the universe, and so their knowledge and communication were subordinated to power and exploitation. Returning to the subject of alterity and difference in 1989,[14] Todorov also noted that, as regards the self/other distinction, alterity is always relative because always defined in terms of the observer rather than bearing intrinsic meaning. This mode of discourse thus applies equally to nationalism and exoticism, including when the latter's laudatory misrecognitions are figured in the noble savage. In eighteenth-century texts, the savage is noble in terms of Otherness ("not France") and homogenization (aboriginal peoples are "all the same"): The resulting tropes fail to get beyond the narcissism of *égalité-identité* and *différence-inégalité*, as the highly selected attributes of the noble savage – egalitarianism, minimalism, naturalism – are used to comment on European anxieties.

Todorov's semiotico-historical investigations of the first European-Amerindian encounter are therefore useful in the domain of race and cinema notably for their delineation of the *égalité-identité* and *différence-inégalité* couples; for their analysis of the social and historical, and specifically Eurocentric structuring of the encounter and its consequences; and also for their suggestions of the inevitable doubleness, mirroring, and narcissism in relations with the Other. Todorov's project is to overcome the old binarisms of alterity so that in the contemporary world we can live "difference in equality,"[15] for which the Bakhtinian notion of exotopy, combining the recognition of the Other's otherness but also status as subject,[16] is put to use.

The way forward thus lies in analysis based on the subversion of the Self/Other, Same/Different binaries, either through undermining via Bakhtinian dialogue the boundaries of the self, or through taking the deconstructive path of regarding the Self as crucially depending on the Other, the Other as inhabiting the Self as its very condition of possibility[17] in the absence of full, intrinsic identity, or of dispensing with the Self/Other binary in the name of Deleuzean becoming. The dominant and the dominated are both located in, and their position constructed by, colonial and postcolonial discourse.[18] Nicolas van Schendel of the magazine *Vice versa* expresses the hybrid and mobile potential of Quebec identity as *identité-mouvance* (movement-identity, the cultural model for which is the *coureur de bois*) as opposed to *identité-appartenance* (belonging-identity).[19] As we saw in chapter 1, Jean Morisset in *L'Identité usurpée* stresses (as opposed to the, for him, totalizations of nationalism à la Lionel Groulx, the alienating liberalism of Trudeau's federalism, or the Parti Québécois modernism that seeks to imitate France) the specifically *American* and therefore profoundly *métissé* identity of the Québécois: "A profoundly hybrid [*métis*], so resistant to purity, which has constantly invented an illusory purity."[20] In the wake of the Morse report on native issue, varying estimates suggested that 60 per cent of the Quebec population have "Indian blood."[21] However, this hybrid potential has not always been realized in Quebec cinematic representations.

The dominance of Hollywood cinema in English-Canadian mass culture meant that for a long time the figure of the Amerindian was filtered through a nationally autonomous American culture, its mythic power bound up with the west and with the English language. Until about 1960, the assertion of a *French*-Canadian and then Québécois nationalism passed not through national narratives of the encounter with the Amerindians but through the survival of the French language and (re)discovery of a history of the French in North America. Quebec cinema arguably lagged behind developments in Quebec literature in which the presence of the Amerindian became relatively common, for example, in the novels of Yves Thériault.[22] There is but a small corpus of narrative feature films in Quebec that deal centrally with the native peoples and the intense problematic that issue generates.

Le Festin des morts, produced in 1965 by the NFB, directed by Fernand Dansereau with a script by Alec Pelletier (wife of Gérard Pelletier, close to Pierre Trudeau on *Cité libre* and in the federal governments he headed), is set in 1639–49 at the time of the Jesuit mission among the Hurons. Significantly, it was the first full-length feature in French to emerge from the NFB's autonomous francophone unit set up in 1959. In a series of episodic flashbacks, the experience of the Jesuits and their leader Brébeuf (Alain Cuny) is seen through the eyes of a young and eventually doubting priest (Jean-Guy Sabourin). The exploration of cultural difference is seen in terms of relativism as opposed to the Jesuits' universalism. The Huron articulate rational arguments (against monogamy because of the low ratio of men to women; for suicide or murder if a delicious life exists after death; and against the absence of Huron in heaven and therefore the isolation of dead Christian Huron). The young priest's voice-over narration meanwhile expresses his growing spiritual and intellectual dismay in the face of both the radical difference of the Huron culture (for example, eating the flesh of prisoners) and its presence within his own subjectivity, in the form of role ambiguity (the spectator/prisoner relation in the torture of the captured Iroquois) and, moreover, sexual temptation. Gazing at a woman's body, he recalls how, as a novice, "I invented penitences while I didn't even know the form of my desire. Eve, who provokes this thirst, and hides your face my Lord, Eve who, however, is your creation ...". There follows a "subjective" sequence, anticipating the final scene, when the priest's staggering through the snow-filled landscape suggests his spiritual disarray. Then, in a two-shot that positions the spectator in the film's metadiscourse rather than the point of view of the priest, a renewed gazing at the woman produces in fact a rather anachronistic voiceover: "So you sent us among them for our flame to die even before it has shone its light? I'm losing my footing. I know that you will never answer. And what if I bore this silence for nothing, and that you didn't exist?" Finally, as their community is crippled by drought, European disease, and Iroquois raids, the Huron turn on the Jesuits, who decide to organize a traditional *festin d'adieu* before they are killed. A brief montage shows the torture and execution of Brébeuf, while the young priest, silhouetted against the unattainable unity and light of the sun, is fated to die in the forest.

With the exception of the French national Alain Cuny, all the actors are white Franco-Québécois, while all the dialogue is in French. The organization of the look in the film reproduces the ethnographic gaze of the white observer. The totality or structure of the Huron's beliefs and practices is not addressed. And since the episode of the "saints martyrs/holy martyrs" became one of the foundational cornerstones of "French-Canadian" identity during the nineteenth century and the hegemony of clerical nationalism, it is obvious to conclude that in *Le Festin des morts* the story and the Huron are being put to use in a problematic of Québécois identity. "The Indian of discourse" prevails over "the Indian of reference," to borrow Gilles Thérien's terms, with the result that "the Indian fails to acquire a dynamic discursiveness through his transformation into an autonomously constituted character with the right of speech." The reality effect evidenced in the sets reconstructing Huronia incoherently encounters the genre effect, reminiscent of the Hollywood western, of having the Indians speak a European language. A catalogue of descriptions for the missionary and colonizer has its origins in those very *Relations* of the Jesuits that are the source of the film, which, taking the narrative model of the *Acta sanctorum*, posited the Amerindians as objects of a discourse of salvation, allowing the Jesuits "to retain from the Other only those aspects which not only found difference or inferiority but constitute an essence."[23] In the film, the Jesuits' problems of identity as new inhabitants of Canada are mediated through another mediation, that is, the represented imaginary Indian or "Indien du discours."[24] Thus the elements of syncretism in the Jesuits' approach to the Amerindians, their scrupulous study of language and custom, go without mention.[25]

The clues to the film's agenda lie in the conventions of the historical costume drama and the political and social context of the early 1960s. As we saw with *Maria Chapdelaine*, the textual instability of the costume drama permits the finite nature of the nation and its internal difference or differences to be addressed: the past is both the Same (an origin, French language, not the Indians) and Other (a Catholicism unable to cope with difference, or the Huron culture), and both the Indians *and* the Jesuits are "other" to "our" present. In addition, in *Le Festin des morts*, that elaboration of new national hegemonic cultures and beliefs is unusually still in the process of historical construction, and it is difficult to formulate it in terms other than "modern" scepticism. But even the latter phrase implies a certain subjectivity, which, as P. Berthiaume points out, is incompatible with that either of "l'Indien du discours" or the Jesuits themselves:

The journey to the end of night, like the spiritual exercises which required meditating over hagiographic texts, opens up a Truth – or rather the Truth – by yielding up to be read a metaphysics as much of the silent body of the Other, of "the absent" ... of the Amerindian as of that of the missionary, as similar as he is. This is an ethnography of alterity but also of oneself, hollowed out, through a game of mirrors commanded by a cultural instance which displaces the subject of the discourse and reduces it in its turn, like the Amerindian, to something through which the Word speaks.[26]

If, in different ways, *Le Festin des morts* therefore renders as past "Other" both Huron and Jesuit, its "doubt" requires a full, secular subjectivity such as that collectively being elaborated during the Quiet Revolution, a process not yet clearly structured during the film's conception and production. The internal Others addressed in the film's reception are varied but do not deal with the Amerindians, let alone, of course, the contradictions between Quebec nationalism and First Nations' autonomy demands expressed in the 1980s and 1990s. In the mid-1960s, emphasis is placed on death and therefore survival in a secular age, a question relevant in relation both to the harshness of nature and to interhuman and therefore political, Anglo-French questions;[27] on the *occidental/oriental* binary opposition, as currently evinced in Indo-China;[28] or, according to Alec Pelletier, on generational conflict in Quebec ("It's the opposition between a generation clinging to values it knows to be out of date, and another younger generation which is finding it difficult to act and is impatiently seeking an outlet for its action.")[29] The native issue surfaces mainly when correspondents complain of historical inaccuracies or negative portrayal.[30] When shown on Radio Canada in 1965, the film was the first to show bare breasts on North American television, a source of further lively reaction and an example of the greater sexual licence accorded to representations of the native peoples, as well as of the libidinal investment in the Other's image.

It is useful briefly to contrast Bruce Beresford's *Black Robe* of 1991. Not *stricto sensu* a "Québécois" film, co-produced on a large budget in English for the international market by companies in Toronto and New South Wales, it offers intriguing resemblances and differences. Paradoxically, since *Dances with Wolves*, subtitles for Indian languages are acceptable in the international film market but not for French or any "modern" language other than English, an interesting comment on the relationship between, on the one hand, the indigenous Other and attendant cultural agenda, and, on the other, the place created for that figure in the world cultural system. For his novel and screenplay, Brian Moore used the Jesuits' *Relations* and is therefore stuck in "l'Indien du discours" and its (mis)representations. The dream beliefs of the Amerindians are at least given some credence in the way they propose a seemingly unmediated relationship with nature in a pre-Enlightenment, epistemic culture based on cyclical rather than linear time. The Jesuits' skilful syncretism is ignored; from the film's

twentieth-century, sexy, ecological point of view or subject of enunciation, they are clueless. The film concentrates on the journey from
Quebec to Huronia and therefore intertextualizes colonial narratives
such as Conrad's 1902 novella *Heart of Darkness*, as well as permitting
shots of the natural scene which breathtakingly (for a contemporary,
white tourist gaze) interrupt the narrative. The Otherness of the
Jesuits and Indians in the historical costume-drama genre is tempered
by the liberal distinction between "good" (Algonquin) and "bad"
(Iroquois) Indians, and especially by the way in which the heterosexual couple of Frenchman Daniel (Aden Young) and Algonquin
Annuka (Sandrine Holt) is formed, contrasting with the celibate, self-
flagellating Laforgue (Lothaire Bluteau). The Laforgue/Daniel opposition (for it is the latter who embodies the attainable and acceptable
elements of the Amerindians, echoing the *coureur de bois* at the beginning of the film who has gone native and is posited as Other to the
Jesuits) is played out largely in terms of the body (and therefore
"nature") across the oppositions: planning/the moment, afterlife/
life, cathedral/forest, celibacy/sex, purity/complexity. The couple
that is formed is thus hybrid, mobile, sexually glamorous, at ease with
"nature": a fittingly postmodern ecological creation, exemplary of a
film that is a world rather than national text, with the Amerindians
and the landscape taking roles analogous to those played by the
aborigines and Australia in *Until the End of the World*.

The intricate links between racial alterity and sexual anxieties are
already in evidence in these two films, but they are concealed by the
fact that the historical costume drama to an extent posits all its protagonists as "Other." Homi Bhabha has argued that the "stereotype" in
colonial discourse generates its own logic of, and is constructed by, a
disavowal of difference. Just as in Freudian psychoanalysis, where the
fetish embodies an object of desire devoid of the castration threat supposedly embodied by the figure/body of "woman" in the patriarchal
unconscious, so can the racial "Other" come to figure an anxiety associated with lack and difference for a colonial subject that seeks to
ascribe "pure" origin while being constantly threatened by division.
The Other racial body, in fact object of both desire and derision, suggestive of both order and disorder, must therefore be "fixed" as "stereotype": "The stereotype impedes the circulation and articulation of
the signifier of 'race' as anything other than its fixity as racism." The
stereotype/fetish, in its play of knowledge and disavowal, mastery and
defence, pleasure and unpleasure, both masks absence and difference
(in metaphor, narcissistically) and registers lack (in metonymy, aggres-
sively): "The process by which the metaphoric 'masking' is inscribed
on a lack which must then be concealed gives the stereotype both its

fixity and its phantasmatic quality."[31] As well as granting an extra-fantasmatic charge to Todorov's categories of *égalité-identité* (narcissism) and *différence-inégalité* (aggression), these ambiguities are central to our next two films, *Red* and *Visage pâle*, for what they articulate both about the possibly hybrid nature of Québécois "identity" (the Other as the Same) and the specific anxieties associated with masculinity. In postcolonial Quebec, disavowal and fetishism centre on the nation's internal others.

Red (Gilles Carle, 1969; released March 1970) is the story of Red/Reginald Mackenzie (Daniel Pilon), half-Algonquin on his mother's side, half Franco-Québécois by his father. Through shoplifting and then by burgling the car showroom of Frédéric Barnabé (Gratien Gélinas), married to his white half-sister Elizabeth (Fernande Giroux), he acquires wealth and status which he displays to his mother in Kahnawake, to his three white working-class half-brothers, and to a succession of women, notably Géorgette (Geneviève Deloir). But when Elizabeth is killed by his own shotgun, Red has to go on the run with Géorgette, ending up in a remote lakeside Amerindian reservation. Realizing that Frédéric had in fact murdered Elizabeth, Red returns to Montreal to shoot him while he is speaking at a car show, but he is himself shot dead by his half-brothers who believe him to be the killer.

The contradictions of the tale can be pieced together by looking at the film's intertexts. First, the film comes in the period of the "érotico-mélo" genre associated with Fournier and Héroux but also impelled by Carle.[32] With some (female) nudity, a handsome leading man, an action-packed script laced with gratuitous cinematic spectacle (one thinks of the James Bond formula as well as the otiose car chases of *Red*), this rather dated-looking movie nonetheless marks an important stage in the development of the construction of the "popular" in Quebec film and of its frequent coexistence with auteurist and/or social-critical emphases and tendencies. In a sense these strands come together in the road-movie genre, as in *Easy Rider* (Hopper, 1969) and films by Wim Wenders, with their combination of simple and accessible narrative form, cinematic spectacle, male narcissism, and hints of counter-cultural social critique. In the case of *Red*, the road movie lends itself to metaphors of displacement and marginality, to comments on modernity in the frequent sequences on the freeway or in the final scenes in the Montreal Metro and the place Bonaventure. In addition, typically for a Carle film, it denounces social exploitation and commodification even as it colludes with them. Carle himself, born at Maniwaki near a reservation and himself the great-grandson of an Indian, is impenitent about this in an interview on the film's release: "I'm simultaneously a film-maker who wants to influence people, change reality and change the system and simultaneously [sic] a film-maker who profits from the system," adding, "I tell myself: my situation is not to be this or that but to be both at the same time. So I'm a half-breed [*métis*]."[33]

The problem is that, in *Red*, the metonym (the racial hatred against Red) and the metaphor (as displacement, alienation) of racial difference is used to express any hybridity other than that pertaining to the problematic of Québécois national identity vis-à-vis the Amerindians. In the film, Red and Elizabeth jokingly re-enact a cowboy and Indian scenario which comments on the Americanization (in the sense of the United States) of Quebec society's myths (Red's James Bond syndrome can be read in the same way). In addition, for Carle, "Quebec is the most culturally hybrid country I know"[34] – but the examples he gives are the coexistence of French cheeses, Gide, hippies, and American TV commercials. In fact the Other with which the film and Carle are dealing is the *Anglais*, conquest by whom has resulted in the "historical frustration" lived by the Québécois, who is "a hybrid man that is a man who lives in a sub-culture, in an incredibly syncretized civilization ... And the long repressed violence will spring forth from that feeling of being torn [*écartèlement*]."[35] Thus the presence of anglophone businessmen and the English language in the film comes to occupy a space in which the hybridity and internal otherness of the Quebec nation are disavowed in favour of the fullness of identity offered by the Self/Other, French/English binary (to which Red falls victim).

That disavowal and that fullness are also, of course, sexual, for the figure and indeed the body-on-the-screen of Red himself are more centred than the text would have us believe. The (literal) vehicles of his displacements are the sports cars he steals, so that no position, political or otherwise, outside consumerism seems possible in this individuated narrative of revolt. This is, of course, the argument of the film, since Red is killed in a veritable temple of consumerism, with General Motors looking on. The back-to-nature sequence on the Indian reservation similarly demonstrates how the lives of the indigenous peoples have been definitively altered by consumerism, for the men have become, as well as hunters, the recyclers and repairers of modern detritus. (This approach is signalled by the joke shot which tracks a pair of Algonquin hunters to the site of Red's sports car in the middle of the forest.) But, moreover, the potential otherness within is disavowed and defused by the heavily virilized persona of Red and the playing of Pilon. The sexiness of the hybrid is something both desired and dangerous, here desire being used to compensate for the danger in the same way that fetishism (guns, cars) wards off the castration threat.

Red is thus figured vis-à-vis other men and within masculine groups, and he comes out positively: Frédéric is a feminized killer who has sold out to the anglophones; with his brothers Red figures as degree-zero masculinity, to coin a phrase used of Jean Gabin,[36] not too fat, old, or virginal, neither alcoholic nor misogynistic, devoid, of course, of the hints of racism against their "sauvage" sibling. He similarly proves himself worthy of his Indian fellows (among whom figure Daniel Pilon's own brother Donald). In *Red*, the pessimistic social comment of the auteur Gilles Carle means that hybridity is physically eliminated, but in reality it is the twin plenitudes of nationalism and of heterosexual masculinity which create the untenable contradictions that kill Red. When Red proclaims to his mother, "Whites, Indians, it's all the same now," he is wrong in that he proves to be a victim of particular marginalization through race, but right in that, metaphorically, that marginalization, the atomization of modernity, extends across the whole society of which he is a representative.

The connection between masculinity and the difference of the indigenous Other is developed further in Claude Gagnon's *Visage pâle* of 1985, when questions of homosexuality and the homoerotic rear their head. Claude Hébert (Luc Matte), blonde *sportif* and hockey trainer, leaves the city to spend some time camping near a lake farther north. He is harassed during his stay by three unemployed white Québécois men. This include a scene when one of their number, Richard (Guy Thauvette), seemingly attempts to seduce Claude as he swims naked, only then to deny the homosexual possibility. Later, the three attempt to rape Claude, but the latter is rescued by an Amerindian, Peter (Denis Lacroix). Returning to the bar frequented by the three *voyous*, a fight breaks out in which Claude kills one of them with a blow to the head. He and Peter are forced to flee, but the latter drowns as they swim across a lake. Claude makes contact with Peter's family, who send him to a cabin in the forest with Peter's sister Marie (Allison Odjig). Initially hostile because of the death of her brother as well as the history of the white oppression of her people, she begins a sexual relationship with Claude which ends with the winter and Claude's decision to return home and give himself up, leaving Marie in the north.

As Gilles Thérien points out,[37] the film raises questions of Québécois identity without resolving them. Oppositions between city/country, white/Indian are in fact maintained: the male-male friendship is cut short by death, Marie does not follow Claude to the south. The film's liberal discourse not only posits Claude as the "good" Québécois in relation to the three rural louts, it figures him as at ease equally in city and "nature," as embodying a well-balanced ecological virility in fact superior to that of the drowned and failed Indian. In contrast, the three rural Québécois represent a nature out of control, violent, atavistic, disruptive of Claude's gender identity as they threaten to turn him into sexual object. Equilibrium is restored when Claude goes deeper into nature and forms the heterosexual couple. There is a learning process, but it is limited to individual maturing rather than social awareness: while Claude ceases his resentment of the "jeux de sauvage/savage's games" that for him characterized Peter producing a knife in the bar or Marie's initial aggressiveness, he confesses his love for Marie and that the real lesson he has learned is that of his own vulnerability. The recurring motif is that of the hockey game, which, played in the southern city, frames the whole film but also punctuates the stay in the cabin and marks the point where Claude decides to return "home" and face the workings of the Law. A hockey puck momentarily lost in the snow heavy-handedly signals the need to stop "playing." The status of the modern, unified masculine subject is assured as centred with the maintenance of the boundaries policed by the film.

Elsewhere, however, it has been argued that the homosexual theme in *Visage pâle* relates to a recurring pattern in Quebec films of the 1980s, after the referendum defeat which highlighted and exacerbated Quebec's identity problems.[38] In a complex and convoluted argument that draws on Jacques Lavigne's essay of 1971, *L'Objectivité: ses conditions instinctuelles et affectives*, Gilles Thérien claims that Claude's refusal to acknowledge and to establish relations with others, except for the brief and inconclusive tryst with Marie, is emblematic of Quebec's own failure to attain nationhood. Claude, in refusing, for example, the homosexual invitation, stresses the fact that he is not like the villagers and that his own cult of his physical body is not already homoerotic narcissism ("a perversion," according to Thérien). But the price he pays for maintaining his virtue is disastrous: two deaths, exile in nature, probable imprisonment. This reading depends on certain conceptual distinctions. First, "symbolic homosexuality" is the good and inevitable phase whereby in the pre-Oedipal stage the infant identifies with and eroticizes the parent of the same sex. However, these desires are integrated into the emerging young identity as it sets off on to the royal road to heterosexuality. "Real homosexuality" marks the failure of this integration, and the reign of the "false-feminine," an impasse or identity blockage exacerbated in the past by the disempowering and repressive "false fathers" of the Catholic clergy. This "real homosexuality" means that the Other cannot be interpellated, and that the self remains stuck in the domain of *parenté* or family, associated with reproduction, rather than progressing to the domain of sociality, associated with relations of domination. For Thérien, homosexuality ("real" rather than "symbolic") in films of the 1980s represents a post-referendum flaccid and uneasy compromise between the two, in which neither retreat into the family or oneself nor combat in the world are possible. This is all because no national father is there with which to identify, merely fathers that are absent, colonial. Thus in *Visage pâle*, the uneasiness of the compromise is visible as Claude refuses a homosexual identity, but its supposed equivalent, death, still prevails.

We discussed in chapter 5 the blind spots of Thérien's arguments on homosexuality and *Pouvoir intime*. Here again, the obvious objections are to the assumption of homosexuality as a problem, as something outside the nation, as always bound up with the desire for the Self rather than Other, as possessing no autonomy but always symptomatic of something else; to the false homogenization of gender and sexual identity; and, moreover, to the suppression of the possibility of these films having gay spectators and thus alternative readings to that posited by Thérien for "the nation." What is clear is that *Visage pâle* is constantly seeking to achieve "balance," and that the attempted gay seduction and rape is part of a homosocial logic which the figure of Claude does not surpass. In other words, Claude's unproblematized heterosexual male identity is typically predicated on macho physical activities and social contact with other men (hockey) from which women, as well as the possibility of homosexual activity and desire, are rigorously excluded. The rural village is marginal to Claude's home landscapes, that is, the southern city with its middle-class comforts, and is therefore a site of dangerous avowal of desire and violence and of an unstable homosociality, displaced here onto white Québécois perpetrators. As in *Red*, anxieties concerning difference are elided, compensated for, via the male protagonist and his body. Claude himself comes to embody some of the fantasms of colonialism that are usually attributed to the colonized (Peter on the three when they harass Claude: "I know their way of having fun"). He becomes the victim of aggression based on perceived class difference, and lack, in that he embodies the temptation of same-sex desire which disrupts the polarizations of the Self/Other, masculine/feminine binaries of sexual difference. These factors are amalgamated with racial difference by the three aggressors, as they complain of the bar being frequented by "sauvages et tapettes." The attempted rape of Claude is in fact based on the repression and *disavowal* of homosexuality on the part of Richard, a point missed by Thérien: the attempted violent penetration of Claude positions him as "female," preserving the sex-gender system, subjugating both the victim and the internalized but disavowed femininity of the aggressor.

The fatal fight in the bar is provoked by Claude's revelation that Richard had come to see him at the lake alone.

Deepest nature and the figure of Marie (though impressively portrayed by Allison Odjig) are in fact the sites of his empowerment as *coureur de bois* or hybrid *canadien*. However, the charming and "taming" of the rebellious Marie, the persistent echo of the hockey game, and the decision to reintegrate the Law and society mean that this *coureur de bois* figure eschews the hybrid possibilities of the liminal, of *identité-mouvance*, of the transcultural, to retain only the virile sexiness and with it the plenitude of fixed and full liberal subjectivity. And Claude's predicament in nature, as well as his physical attributes and indeed narcissism, metaphorically mask the difference between himself and the Indians. Historical and political issues are displaced, not untypically for commercial mainstream cinema, onto issues of individual heroism and growth.

L'Automne sauvage of 1992, directed by Gabriel Pelletier and the first Québécois feature in the aftermath of Oka to deal with the native question, encapsulates within genre cinema some of the identity dead ends described above. Charlie Minton (Serge Dupire) returns to Coeur d'Indien after an eleven-year absence on receiving a telegram asking for help for his childhood Indian friend Régis (Raoul Trujillo), who has been arrested for the murder of a white *planteur*. Minton is the scion of the family who owns the sawmill on which the town's livelihood depends and which is run by Charlie's irascible anglophone grandfather Eddy Minton (Leslie Yeo) and his sister Hélène (Marie-Josée Gauthier). The mill is currently in financial trouble, but Eddy is unwilling to sell out to the Japanese firm Kinobishi, represented by Eve Duchesneau (Anne Létourneau), and wants Charlie to take over. As Charlie investigates both the provenance of the telegram and the murder, getting sexually involved with Eve, Régis is allowed to escape from custody by the sinister police chief Laviolette (Raymond Bouchard). Charlie finds him in the forest with his warrior companions and is united with him spiritually in a ritual ceremony. Returning to the town and breaking into Laviolette's house, Charlie discovers the truth while Laviolette is shot dead by another intruder. Laviolette, a homosexual involved in drug trafficking with the young *planteurs* from Montreal, was responsible for the murder in the forest. The Minton land had been expropriated from the Indians through a massacre seventy years earlier in which the young Eddy participated: Charlie leads the provincial police to these killing fields. Hélène Minton had been paying blackmail to Laviolette, and then she shot him because he did not protect her lover, Régis. Régis is killed in a confrontation in the forest between the warriors and the police. Finally, Charlie and Eve reach an agreement by which the Indians regain their ancestral lands, with Kinobishi retaining felling rights. Eddy Minton, victim of a stroke, signs everything over to Hélène and recognizes Indian title to the land, and Charlie leaves Coeur d'Indien having humiliated Eve, who had sent the original telegram and told the police about Régis's hideout.

The ideological work of this concoction is mediated first of all through modes of melodrama, notably Hollywood melodrama, in a drama of patriarchal right which betokens a crisis of social legitimacy. The Minton house recalls *Giant, Written on the Wind,* and *Dallas.* The only visible "father," Eddy Minton, is a corrupt and immoral failure. Charlie's own father, a pilot, had been shot down in Vietnam, while his mother, a francophone, had left him for a millworker. Moreover, the melodrama is overlaid with the discourse of Quebec nationalism, with the francophobic Eddy speaking subtitled English, and Charlie insisting of French, "C'est ma langue/it's my language," and replying to Eddy's description of his mother as "not one of us" with "c'est pour ça que je l'aimais/that's why I loved her." This Quebec national melodrama thus exemplifies a generational and Oedipal conflict, with Charlie Minton rising unproblematically to the occasion. At the end of the film, Eddy is symbolically castrated in a wheelchair, his pet falcon flown away; the phallic metaphor of flight is again embodied in Charlie, at the controls over the vagina-like Saguenay fjord. The "false feminine," in the form of the *tapettes* Laviolette or the boys from Montreal (their penknife easily overcome by Charlie), is eliminated. In addition, the enigmatic, desirable but/and therefore potentially castrating figure of Eve, who belongs to the male investigative and action narrative in the mode of film noir, is eliminated, humiliated by the phallic power of the plane when Charlie momentarily hands her the controls.

But what of the native peoples? Charlie's centred Québécois male heterosexual identity means first of all that the film's narrative is always conducted from his point of view: Régis's militancy is a problem *for him.* As centred, he can also mediate, by rejecting the colonialism and genocide of the grandfather but also by refusing to embrace Régis and the radical difference his militancy represents, other than through the homosocial bond, the *fratriarcat* formed between them. In the end, the film's liberal discourse is not surpassed: there are good policemen and bad, the natives are basically happy with their lot (as evinced in the visit to the community to the north, presided over by its chief, played by the former Huron leader Max Gros-Louis), crimes against them are located in the distant past and associated with the Anglos anyway, and Quebec is happy to participate in the global economy as represented by the Japanese, as this is at least preferable to Anglo economic domination. Once again, the sexy male figure mediating between the white and Indian worlds is put to use in a discourse of unanimity rather than hybridity, full identity rather than difference. However, the film's balancing act is probably unable to contain all the contradictions it sets in motion. A consensus is not reached via the formation of a heterosexual couple, and the militancy and shooting of Régis are too excessive and too contemporaneous to be closed off by the Anglos' guilt or by Charlie's protestations about the democratic nature of the Quebec state.

The sheer adjacency of the native peoples vis-à-vis the received notion of a fully constituted and unified Québécois identity and culture underlines the amount of ideological work necessary to prevent their "Otherness" slipping into the Same and disrupting the oppositional categories. In the films we have examined, the problematic is dealt with by narcissistically figuring natives as projections of Québécois anxieties concerning the lack of fixed identity, be it national, racial, or sexual. The fullness of the national/sexual body is predicated on a series of displacements which fail to give authoritative voice or point of view either to the First Nations peoples or to women. However, there are a cluster of films in which this evasion – the *coureur de bois* figure as sexy and mediating – is avoided.

Jean Pierre Lefebvre's *Les Maudits Sauvages* of 1970 is subtitled "1670 – 1970, ou l'eau de vie ou de mort." In the seventeenth century, a young, betrothed Indian couple are separated by the arrival of white men bearing alcohol and (twentieth-century) technology. Thomas Hébert (Pierre Dufresne), a *coureur de bois*, takes the young woman, Tékacouita (Rachel Cailhier) away with him to the city, twentieth-century Montreal, and "domesticates" her, although he is already married, to Jeanne-Mance (Nicole Filion). While Thomas is being interrogated by police, Tékacouita stabs a history-book salesman who had called round to the house and tried to assault her sexually. With Jeanne-Mance returned to France, Tékacouita resigns herself to her existence and is forced by Thomas to dance in a bar while he is away seeking furs: her betrothed comes to the bar and stabs both her and himself. The film ends with Thomas, apparently shot at an Indian camp, reviving to join with a group of hippies in sitting, whooping, and smoking dope.

Les Maudits Sauvages must be seen in the context of Lefebvre's other work in the second half of the 1960s: a deconstruction of myths and media images, hooked on to the "authenticity" of a heterosexual romance, in this case the lost love of the native couple. As a Quiet Revolution text, it looks at the church-inspired narratives of Quebec history and finds them wanting: the church, represented by l'abbé Frelaté

(Luc Granger), is indifferent to Tékacouita's fate and complicit with the natives' exploitation; "Jeanne Mance," named after one of those who founded Montreal in 1642, says that the country should never have been colonized; Marcel Sabourin plays Jean Talon, *intendant* and instigator of the colony's expansion after 1660, being interviewed on television like any mediocre politician. However, Lefebvre also casts his analytical eye on contemporary orthodoxies, on the continuities of power across different epochs, and on the counter-cultural fashion for all things Indian. Tékacouita is not silent; her voice-over and still photographs periodically interrupt the narrative and comment on her fate. The slogan with which her dance show is sold at the bar – "an authentic exotic beauty from right here [*de chez nous*]" – neatly encapsulates the oxymoronic uses to which the "native" is put, although arguably the film is unable to hoist the native issue away from Franco-Québécois identity interrogations and therefore risks also fetishizing the *belle sauvagesse*.

Arthur Lamothe (b. 1928) is a Gascon from southwest France who emigrated to Quebec in 1953. His mainly documentary output has made him the leading film-maker of the native peoples of Quebec, his work of the 1970s and 1980s making a significant contribution, well before the collapse of Meech Lake and the events at Oka, to putting native issues on the agenda of Quebec nationalism. *Mémoire battante* (1983) is an investigation of the cultural issues raised by the encounter between native peoples and Western modernity, in particular that of the Montagnais communities around the old mining town of Scheffer-ville in Labrador. Lamothe combines here several techniques. Somewhat like Perrault in *Pour la suite du monde* but unlike the white-centred procedure of *Le Goût de la farine*, Lamothe gives voice to the natives. Alexander McKenzie and Mathieu André speak at length to camera about Montagnais legends. At another level, there are dramatized segments of Gabriel Arcand as Father Lejeune, the seventeenth century Jesuit priest whose *Relations* struggle to come to terms with the rituals of Montagnais shamanism. Finally, Lamothe is also an important presence in his own film, his voice-over narration providing analysis, often over footage of his previous films such as *Le Train du Labrador* (1967), and he himself appears on camera to explain how the documentary has been confected.

The effect of these techniques is to create a multilevelled text. On the one hand, there is the socially committed realist documentary film-maker, describing the economy of the region and the Quiet Revolution "myth of infinite progress" which has led to this disruption and impoverishment. Lamothe's encounter with the native peoples is always closely linked to a critique of capitalism and an adjacency with the exploitation of the white working class, as in his earlier *Bûcherons de la Manouane* and *Le Mépris n'aura qu'un temps* (1969). Lamothe's universalism ("By investigating Indian man in his specific environment, I discovered universal man")[39] is thus in part a universalism of the exploited and economically marginalized, be they workers, peasants, or hunter-gatherers, hence his quotation from Camus on the impoverishment of the Kabyles. On the other hand, Lamothe is interested in wider, "civilizational" issues. The natives are interesting in this respect, not because of what they have to say about Quebec identity or hybridity, but because their disruption of the master Quiet Revolution narrative ("The Indians are the first Québécois"[40]) is a disruption of all narratives of modernity. He quotes Michel Foucault in the voice-over of empty shots of the rectilinear architecture of institutions and schools imposed on the Indians to underscore the irreducibility of one culture to another.

It is in this sense that the slippage in Lamothe from social realism to cultural analysis reproduces the tendency noted earlier to construct indigenous peoples as a kind of last bulwark against the logic of capitalism and the commodification of the whole of life and culture. This reaches its apogee in the famous *scapulomancie* scene in *Mémoire battante*, when a caribou bone is placed in a fire and then "read" to reveal the location of a herd. The next day, the natives and crew fly off and indeed find the herd in that location. This raises the question of the relationship between those filming and those filmed, the complexity of which Lamothe is well aware, hence the presence of different levels of representation in his film. As in the direct cinema practised by Perrault in *Pour la suite du monde*, Lamothe lets his protagonists speak, act, take the initiative, *fabulate*, while at the same time these activities are provoked by the camera and the presence of the crew. However, while Perrault was filming fellow Québécois, so that a double becoming was possible in that fabulation and the relationship to which it gave rise, Lamothe is well aware that he and his crew are not Montagnais. The natives' freedom to enact their traditions does not lead to a becoming-other. Rather, the narrative of the film is interrupted, just as that of instrumental modernity is disrupted at this point, so that Lamothe and his crew can take stock of the event and recount their own experience of it, an experience that was disorientating and productive of speculation but not identity-transforming because of the irreducibility of the cultures represented. The world has been re-enchanted, but only as spectacle.

Lamothe was invited by the Montagnais of the Natashquan area to film *La Conquête de l'Amérique*, 1990 and 1991, about the struggle over salmon fishing rights, with a former band council chief acting as intercessor. Here again several levels operate: voice-over narration that includes the voices of native peoples as well as actors, the "provoked reality" of the community enacting a night-time fishing ritual in a part of the river now open to them, and history lessons with the anthropologist Rémi Savard explaining the fundamental illegality of the confiscation of native land, backed up by dramatized re-enactments of British men in suits in the eighteenth century.[41] Lamothe's first fictional feature on the native issue, *Le Silence des fusils* of 1996, returns to the territory of *La Conquête de l'Amérique,* closely following the real-life mystery of the death, supposedly by drowning, of two young Innu men on the north shore of the St Lawrence in 1977.

In the film, a co-production between Rock Demers's Productions La Fête and the third French television channel, Jacques Perrin plays Jean-Pierre Lafond, a French biologist, settled in Montreal for decades, who discovers one of the bodies. Along with the sister of one of the men, Roxane (Michèle Audette), with whom he has an affair, and other helpers including the local Catholic priest, Lafond discovers the "truth" of the murders in the context of a society segregated on racial grounds and the tensions associated with the white salmon-fishing club appropriating fishing rights. The film is effective in portraying the colonized space in which the Innu lived (it is set in 1984 before much self-organization in the community) and the liberal alibis of the white inhabitants (fishing rights for the Innu would mean "special" rights based on "date of arrival" in Quebec), but it is itself marred by its construction of a liberal consensus. Catholicism is "modernized," the local priest and the Catholic funeral of one of the victims making up for Roxane's account of having to "unlearn" what the nuns had taught her about the *saints martyrs canadiens.* Despite the powerful presence of Audette, the conventional narrative has the French male hero embodying the "truth" through his active, sexual persona, the *difference* from the Innu superseded by the end because of his action ("My brother, now you're like us," says Mike [Marco Bacon] in the prison cell). It is as if the co-production circumstances had sent the *coureur de bois* back to France, redomesticated and ecologically aware (father and son listening to whales).

Windigo (Robert Morin, 1994) is a transposition of both *Heart of Darkness* and the Oka crisis. When news comes that Eddy Laroche (Donald Morin) has declared the independence of lands in Abitibi claimed by the Algonquin but given over to a lumber company, a motley crew sets off up river to investigate and negotiate, including Jean Fontaine (Guy Nadon), a journalist, and his cameraman; Christine Bastien (Nathalie Coupal), who had worked with Laroche and the native communities; Yves St Hilaire (Michel Laperrière), from the

Canadian prime minister's office and an army agent; Rogatien Côté (Yvon Leroux) from the "Ministry of Native Affairs"; and a "moderate" chief from the nearby reservation, Conrad Volant (Richard Kistabish). The menace of the river journey is (literally) mediated by the presence on board of news reporters and cameramen. On arrival, the group are taken prisoner, but they kidnap the terminally ill Laroche in order to prevent his followers participating in a massacre to defend him.

The very deliberate evocations of *Heart of Darkness* represent a high-risk strategy, in that Conrad's novella, despite its condemnation of European injustices in the Congo, partakes of an othering of "Africa" as the past, the infantile, and the barbaric. However, because of the media presence that is represented, *Windigo* (the title of which refers to the river, the Indian legend of a monster devouring souls, and the mass media) succeeds in "making strange" "the Same" that is, "our" Quebec identity through its portrayal of the native protests, and in emphasizing white people's perceptions of native peoples rather any (colonial) "truth" about the latter. Unlike the Oedipal narrative of *L'Automne sauvage*, here the variety of partial views works against the idea that there is a "truth" to be learned about the native peoples. In this, *Windigo* is perfectly consistent with Morin's procedure in his 1990s features. The many screens featured in the film include a TV news report which refers to the character Régis from *Requiem pour un beau sans-coeur*, and an image from a remote-controlled bulldozer sent to crush native barricades. During the river journey, each character is allowed his or her point of view on Laroche, narrated in flashback. For the two journalists on board, the narrative is one of apprenticeship in responsibility and commitment, since they actively participate in events at the end. Fontaine in particular evolves from a glib, toupeed media hack to someone who realizes that his experience cannot be summarized in a three-minute news report. The "truth" of this apprenticeship is that there is no totalizing "truth." This is perhaps why Morin described the film as "politically incorrect," in that it refuses a positive, heroic role for the natives (or for anyone) even as it explains the reasons for Laroche's nihilistic revolt and articulates the *negativity* of his protest.[42] Laroche's death-bed TV confession, which obviously has its own will-to-truth, is one that refuses the appropriation of native peoples by whites, including the "gang" of ecologists who see them as savers of the planet. Laroche is lucid both about the media as "stealer of souls" ("Windigo") and about his own implication in white society's fantasies even as he tries to escape them.

No director of native origin has yet made a fictional feature in Quebec. However, there is a leading native documentary film-maker, Alanis Obomsawin. Born in 1932 to an Abenaki community, she was brought up in French but has worked mainly in English for the NFB since the early 1970s. She is also a singer and storyteller. Her one full-length film, *Kanesatake, 270 Years of Resistance*, is the definitive film statement from the native point of view on the Oka crisis, but it has to be located in relation to antecedents such as the short *Incident at Resti-gouche* (1984), about a fishing dispute involving Micmac natives on the Quebec/New Brunswick border, and short spin-off films such as *My Name is Kahentiiosta* (1996), about one of the Mohawk women mil-itants at Oka, and *Spudwrench* (1997), about Mohawk construction workers.

Obomsawin's work shows little interest in formal innovation and has few stylistic flourishes. Indeed, her practice could be seen to be consis-tent with a certain NFB pedagogical tradition. However, as Jerry White has argued, this aspect of her work represents a subtle hijacking of the Griersonian project, because instead of "showing Canada to Canadi-ans," "Canada" (and "Quebec") are profoundly called into question.[43] This is because of the films' profound commitment in relation to on-going struggles, their combination of affect and knowledge, their project of eliciting reaction rather than passivity (often outside theatri-cal modes of consumption), and their construction of a (national, na-tive) "we" rather than a silent or exotic Other. Obomsawin's own voice and even body are present in her films, which do not pretend to an exnominated "objectivity." She often leads the voice-over narration, and the films frequently depend on interviews with participants whose contribution to the film is active. They often speak at length, while at the same time Obomsawin intervenes, in frame. The most notable example of this is her interview with the Quebec fisheries minister in *Incident at Restigouche*, in which she admonishes him with the history of white exploitation of natives. The most ambitious work, *Kanesatake*, not only narrates the very beginning and end of the Oka crisis, it is at pains to include a lengthy historical digression placing the crisis in the context of a 270-year-long dispute. The digression includes his-torical prints, paintings, contemporary drawings, Mohawk family pho-tographs, and a dramatized exchange between a nineteenth-century chief and a representative of the Sulpician order who had taken Mohawk land.[44]

Writing about "performative documentary," Bill Nichols argues that "the sense of the local, specific, and embodied as a vital locus of social subjectivity ... gives figuration to and evokes dimensions of the politi-cal unconscious that remain suspended between an immediate here and now and a utopian alternative."[45] This reminder of the utopian element in the political unconscious, present in the political aspira-tions of Obomsawin but also co-existent with commodification, in the communities of popular cinema, forces us to look for utopian yearnings that would include the Other and render the Self/Other binary inoperative. However, it is fair to say that no Quebec film has yet articulated the full symbolic and narrative potential that lies within the relationship between native peoples and *Canadiens*/Québécois (and that might sidestep the conflicts between federal Canada and the natives). This is, crudely, a "reflection" of the cultural if not geographical distance that currently lies between them, a *métissage* to be rediscovered. The question arises, then, as to whether the relationships of lack, plenitude, and production of something new fare better in relation to the immigrant Other.

10 The Immigrant Other

At first sight, if the native peoples problematize Quebec identity through reference to its past, immigrants problematize the future. Multiculturalism, cruelly described as "the masochistic celebration of Canadian nothingness,"[1] is a central social reality of Canada, but it is also a voluntarist governmental policy and indeed an official ideology of the Canadian state. It was instituted by Trudeau in 1971 and enshrined in the 1982 version of the constitution, the influx of non-British immigrants after the Second World War having eventually challenged the cultural hegemony of the country's Anglo-Celtic élites. Originally an extension, therefore, of Canada's new bilingualism, it enlarged the "two founding peoples" notion to that of a "community of communities," as expressed in the Charlottetown constitutional accord – subsequently rejected in a referendum – of 1992. Federal Canada, it is argued, possesses a weak, under-symbolized culture, bereft of the founding myths of the United States, a culture in the anthropological (with distinct politics and policies) but not integrated sense.[2] The Trudeau vision was thus of a potential decoupling of polity and culture. Most ethnic groups integrate well into Canadian society, conserving at home or in their communities their own symbols or affective ethnicity.

The successes of Canadian multiculturalism can thus also conceal problems. Multiculturalism often elides the historical inequalities attendant upon the postcolonial era, renders all groups equivalent and therefore homogeneous, perpetuates majority/minority relationships, and fails to address notions of cultural hybridity (witness the city of Toronto, still run in the main by its Anglo-Celtic élites, with the ethnic groups that give the city its staggering diversity relating vertically to that power but by and large not horizontally to and with each other). Such evaluations may coincide with positions urgently concerned in Quebec to wrestle with the tension between fixed and fluctuating identities, as when Jean-Michel Lacroix writes anxiously of Canada, "The respect of the Other in a society characterized by a 'soft' consensus and founded on tolerance pushed to the extreme could lead to a conglomeration of sub-cultures."[3] As Abdul JanMohamed and David Lloyd write of minority discourse, "The pathos of hegemony is frequently matched by its interested celebration of differences, but only of differences in the aestheticized form of recreations."[4] Quebec nationalists have been wary of the mosaic or salad-bowl vision, since French language and culture in both Canada at large and in Quebec thus run the risk of becoming just another ingredient, with the old threat of disappearance and assimilation to an overwhelmingly Anglo-Saxon North America not far off. The Québécois's reluctance to become another ethnic group recalls the ambivalent relationship with native cultures, in that the blurred boundaries of Self and Other are often denied because of the projection onto the Other of a possible unwanted destiny of the Self. In the case of immigrants, this is one of assimilation, a fear doubled if allophones (those whose first language is neither English nor French) turn to English (and also bound up with the past, in the memory of nearly one million Québécois who emigrated to the United States, often to the factories of New England, and became anglicized):[5] "A minority among minorities, the writer of immigrant origin is in the uncomfortable position of mirroring the terrors of a feared deculturation."[6] And so in fact, like the native peoples, immigrants challenge not only perceptions of destiny and the future but also received Québécois notions of identity such as origin, history, what continent they belong to, and the notion of "belonging" itself. The question of the immigrant Other thus goes to the heart of the Quebec national-allegorical tension and represents the biggest challenge to the nationalist project (in the 95 per cent "no" vote in 1995 among allophones and anglophones).

The discourses of Quebec nationalism in the 1960s emphasized territory and its oneness with the vision of an integrated national culture. Thus "Québécois" supplanted "French-Canadian," Quebec identity coming to be seen as discontinuous with francophone identities outside the territory. At the same time, national emancipation was often couched in terms of Third World nationalist theory, as we have seen. It is interesting to confront this with the actions of nationalists in power from 1976 to 1985, by which time a francophone bourgeoisie had fully emerged and the analogy between Quebec and the Third

World had become difficult to make. The PQ government, torn between its radical credentials and the economic realities and shifting hegemonies of the 1980s, had also to reconcile its largely integrational vision of the nation inherited from the 1960s with the new demographics of especially the city of Montreal. Immigration laws in Canada were changed in 1962 to remove discriminatory criteria, and in the 1980s one in twelve Montrealers had Third World antecedents, one in ten southern European, and a fifth were neither French nor British in origin.[7] These postcolonial realities were mediated by an additional complicating factor, that is, Quebec and the French language's minority situation within Canada and North America and the potential for the allophones to adopt English as their language of work and home. In other words, the situation of the Québécois, shared only with the Afrikaners, of a white European settler population conquered by another, had produced a double majority/minority structure, English/French in Canada, French/English and allophone in Quebec. Already in 1968–69 the Italian community in St-Léonard had confronted the provincial government over compulsory attendance at French schools. Culturally, then, the tendency had been to construct the Other as *L'Anglais.*

One of the first steps for the PQ government was to decouple "allophone" and "*Anglais,*" and this in fact is one of the effects and intentions of Law 101: "It cancels, in Quebec, any equivalence between the so-called founding culture and the French language."[8] This was a potentially enormous step for the development of definitions of "Quebec," for if belonging to the national community entailed merely proficiency in French rather than initiation into cultural references and historical memory, then "Quebec" became a mobile rather than fixed, open rather than closed, notion. At the same time as the law enshrined French as the official language of Quebec, far from ostracizing other cultures it officialized respect for cultural differences and enacted a *programme d'enseignement des langues d'origine* (PELO). In 1981 the Ministère de l'Immigration became the Ministère des Communautés Culturelles et de l'Immigration, and in 1986 the Liberal government produced a *Déclaration sur les relations interethniques et interraciales,* with new equality programs. Faced with the declining birth rate in Quebec, the new immigration policy announced in December 1990 emphasized, rather than the mosaic or the reproduction of ethnic institutions, measures to integrate and *franciser* immigrants. Fernand Harvey summarizes thus the interrelating differences between the policies of Quebec and Canada in this domain: "The Quebec model relies on quite a strongly structured identity. The question is to widen this identity by introducing new cultural parameters. As for the Canadian model, it seeks to reinforce an uncertain but real identity by relying on cultural diversity. In both cases the relationship between the nation and civil society is posed by the mediation of the State."9 These political and social developments have major consequences for cultural expression in Quebec. What cultural forms have emerged in response to the juxtaposition of cultural difference and the peculiar context of Quebec and its national project, and in particular what twists do they give to the notion of Quebec national cinema? Have opportunities for producing new "minor" cultural spaces, undoing fixity and mastery, been grasped, and how do they relate to the "major" or "molar" side of Quebec's unique cultural politics?

There are those Franco-Québécois who suggest that Quebec is uniquely placed to be the site of a reconceptualization of cultural identities via the post-colonial immigrations, at least better placed than old, centralized, former imperial powers such as France (this is another point scored for the Americanness of Quebec as opposed to the modernizing quasi-Gaullist model of the Quiet Revolution). The work of Pierre Monette represents one end of this argument, in that it opts for abandoning the quest for a Quebec nation based on the reference to France and instead favours a "becoming-immigrant" and "becoming-American," a recognition of the "outsider [*étranger*] inside us all,"10 of the immigrant origin and hybrid identity (the word he chooses is *partance* – instead of van Schendel's *mouvance* – as opposed to *appartenance*) of everyone in Quebec. But also Lise Bissonnette has written of "the capacity of a host [*de souche*] minority culture to enter into osmosis with other immigrant cultural minorities, and so to produce and create in ways freed from the whiff of cultural colonialism which still dominates artistic life."11 "Osmosis" implies movement and *déplacement*, and thus one may be justified in employing the terms centre and periphery rather than the inert binary majority and minority, which, as is suggested by the Haitian writer Jean Jonassaint, founder of the journal *Dérives*, are words that "demonstrate that you're always at the centre of some things and on the periphery of others." Thus there are no longer "two single possible positions where one is a function of the other, but variable positions, on the part of the minority as well as the majority, which escape the mosaic and the melting-pot [*fusion*]. In other words, movements [*déplacements*], not only from the Self to the Other, but within one's own array of cultures, identities and memories."12 These arguments are compatible not only with Deleuze and Guattari but also with Julia Kristeva's analysis of the constitutive heterogeneity of Western thought and thus the paradoxical character of communities, be they host or immigrant.13 However, it is important not to drown the lived material reality of economic and other inequalities in a joyous cosmopolitanism which risks flattening out very different experiences. It is salutary to recall the context of the world system and global inequality, and that while "nation" and its redefinitions are part of the jostling for position and accommodation within the "centre" *or* periphery, the seme/category of "race" (and therefore the phenomenon of racism) is one that historically finds its context in struggles between the centre (to which Quebec definitely belongs) and periphery of that system (Haiti).

Élite opinion in Quebec is broadly divided between seeing the French language as simply the vehicle of expression of a francophone collectivity to which everyone belongs, and viewing it as the prime signifier of a given ethno-historical community with its narratives, filiations, and memory. Various cultural movements and theorists, writing in French and often from immigrant backgrounds, have from the early 1980s argued for the francophone but "in-between" and "minor" realities of Quebec culture: Marco Micone on *mixité* from an Italophone perspective; the linking of feminism and immigration in the review *La Parole métèque*. But it is particularly *Vice versa*, founded by Lamberto Tassinari and Fulvio Caccia, which was at the forefront of the theorizing and practice (its Latin title, its trilingualism) of heterogeneity, as opposed to the homogenizing of the melting pot or the inert particles of multiculturalism. The key term used is "transcultural," based on the Cuban Fernando Ortiz's term "transculturation" to express the hybridity of Cuban identity, and the way in which a constant process of reciprocal exchange and acquisition takes place between cultures when they meet through conquest and/or migration. Its address extending beyond the Italo-Québécois intelligentsia, the magazine made a significant contribution to debates on identity. However, the eclecticism of its intellectual inspiration (Deleuze and Guattari, Scarpetta on the postmodern *impur*) points to the minefield of theories of cultural (and political) identity which lies in wait.

Régine Robin, from a Parisian and Jewish background, is one of the most articulate exponents of these "in-between," transcultural positions, in essays and in her 1983 novel, *La Québécoite*. One of the planks of her theory is that of a *dialectic* between "objective" identity (name, passport, the cultural sediment of our biography, a certain opacity *at first*) and "imaginary" identity, the desire to avoid the fixed point, the will to be porous. In her contribution to the *Métamorphoses d'une utopie* volume, "Sortir de l'ethnicité/Leaving Ethnicity,"[14] Robin seeks to weave between on the one hand the "trop plein/too full," "identity contraction," absolutization of differences of racism, nationalism, ethnic retreat, and religious fundamentalism; and the "trop vide/too empty," the "pulverization" of identity represented by American mass culture,

the reign of the image, and the postmodern erasure of history. The solution lies for Robin in a reinvocation of French republican discourse,
in which cultural identity and identities are the domain of the private
and *la vie associative* ("civil society"), while public life is the domain of
equal and free individual citizens ("civic society"). Society is not a *body*;
in modernity it has always been about managing division. There has to
be some *vide* because, in an argument reminiscent of that of Régis
Debray, there has to be distance between the citizen and the site of politics for there to be democratic "play." There are some contradictions
here. The invocation of French republican citizenship, and of a dialectic, sits uneasily with the Deleuze-inspired notion of "becoming" and
"becoming-other." The United States is posited as villain for its military
and cultural imperialism (p.33), but its assimilation of immigrants this
century is viewed as positive in a manner distinct from but analogous to
that of France (p.31). It should also be stressed that the homogenizing
rampage of the post-1945 United States takes place with a constitution
and a discourse of rights and citizenship not totally dissimilar to that of
France, with both countries possessing records of failure as well as success in the encounter with certain forms of Otherness (Blacks, North
Africans). As Robin herself admits, the democratic state that-does-
not-coincide-with-itself often threatens to solidify its (empty) symbols
into something more authoritarian (p.29). If the French Revolution's
emancipation of the Jews is a model (p.32), then what about Marx's
distinction in *On the Jewish Question* between political and human emancipation, and the fact that the former promises merely an unreal universality in the fiction of citizens equal in theory but not in fact? If
Fanon and Senghor had their uses, so that the meaning and assessment
of difference depend on their context (p.36), then can this not be applied to current "ethnic" claims in North America? Is it sufficiently
clear that the universalism Robin is favouring is not, unlike in colonial
times, a"conquering universalism"? All the more so because the Enlightenment and republican tradition does imply an important ethnocentric
idea, namely, that what is superior is what is individualistic. Paradoxically, this is one of the traits of the world system, interested more in the
techno-political selection of individuals than in traditional and historical
cultural categories. So republican individualism can be seen to connect
with a certain aspect of the postmodern. Nonetheless, Robin creates a
valuable space "in-between" a Trudeauesque federalism marred by the
blind spots of an exnominating (in fact dominant) L/liberal cosmopolitan individualism (risk of too much *vide* coupled with panoptic and
physical power), and a Quebec nationalism perpetually threatening an
essentializing *trop plein* (unless "Quebec" simply = "francophone," but
Régine Robin is sceptical about that too).

Quebec culture is, of course, full of hybridity. Indeed, as with the contribution of native peoples in the colonial period, many founding figures of the modern period are in fact the product of immigration and intermarriage. Both the "national poet" Émile Nelligan and the iconic vaudeville singer La Bolduc (Mary Travers), a key figure in the history of Quebec popular music, had Irish fathers. We have already seen examples of Quebec's ethnic minorities playing important roles in films. But, while one of Gilles Groulx's seminal NFB shorts, *Golden Gloves* of 1961, had included a black anglophone boxer in the newly emerging "direct" images of Quebec society, other films, such as *Le Chat dans le sac* and later *Léolo*, had used ethnic otherness as a sounding-board for the exploration of "Québécois" identity. In retrospect, one of the distinguishing strengths of Jutra's *À tout prendre* in relation to many other Quebec films lies in its treatment of ethnicity and the way in which it is articulated with the film's other national, gender, sexual, and cultural discourses. It remains perhaps the best illustration of Quebec's identity complexity and, moreover, the political dilemmas it generates. That complexity is well summarized by Ella Shohat: "The intersection of ethnicity with race, class and gender discourses involves a shifting, relational social and discursive positioning, whereby one group can simultaneously constitute 'norm' and 'periphery.' A given community can in a single context exist in a relation of domination toward another."[15]

In much of Quebec cinema, however, the white francophone Québécois position constitutes the exnominated horizon of the film,[16] a fact that is particularly striking in the films set, as most Quebec films are, in Montreal. This is largely a result of the industry's location there, but it means that the "national cinema" and the images it generates are centred on a place that is highly problematic for representations of cultural identity. A total of 92 per cent of Quebec's of allophones live in the Montreal area and form 12.2 per cent of the population (figures from the 1996 census). The feature films we shall now examine are either directed by Franco-Québécois, sometimes with ethnic minority scriptwriters, and take ethnic and cultural difference as their central themes, or directed by "néo-Québécois." But bearing in mind Jonassaint and Shohat's arguments about the mutability of power relations, the latter corpus is also open to scrutiny for the challenges it might offer not only to totalizing views of "Quebec" but also to its own positions, from the point of view of fixed versus finished, major versus minor identities, and the workings of gender, familial, and sexual discourses.

The most high-profile film to deal with ethnic minorities in Montreal is still probably *The Apprenticeship of Duddy Kravitz*, adapted by

Mordecai Richler, with Lionel Chetwynd, from his own novel. Its engagement with Quebec society is virtually non-existent, however, despite Duddy's affair with a Québécoise, for it chooses to concentrate on Jewish upward mobility in "America." Most film-making in Quebec by ethnic-minority directors takes the form of documentary, although in some cases this has led to features. Tahani Rached, born in Cairo in 1947, made one of the first full-length documentaries on the immigrant experience in Montreal, *Les Voleurs de job*, in 1980, and concentrated on one ethnic group in *Haïti-Québec* (1985). Her *Au chic resto pop* (1990) is one of the most accomplished socially engaged documentaries of the decade, dealing with impoverished and marginalized white francophone Québécois in a poor district of Montreal. Marilú Mallet, born in 1944 in Santiago, Chile, has made several documentaries with immigration as the central theme, notably *Les "Borges"* (1978) and *Chère Amérique* (1990). *Journal inachevé* (1982) articulates the personal and public, political and gender alienation in a plural, non-authoritative form which mixes direct cinema, improvized conversations, most notably and tensely with her Australian-born husband, brutal archive footage of Pinochet's putsch, and the director's voice narrating her diary.[17] *Xénofolies*, directed in 1991 by Michel Moreau (born in 1931 in France), is one of the most sustained reflections in Quebec documentary on the relations between Québécois *de souche* and those from immigrant backgrounds. In a Montreal high school, Moreau interviews two sixteen-year-old girls, one Québécoise *de souche* and one from an Italian background, and provokes discussion and debate between the polarized groups of teenagers. What is striking, however, is how "Québécoise" the Italian girl seems, and would seem to an audience outside Quebec. Her command of (Québécois) French but refusal of the Quebec cultural symbols, such as the hunt, which her counterpart holds so dear, places her in an intercultural position which the film's binary oppositions fail to address, and increases the pressure on the Québécois to invent a "supplement of particularity"[18] beyond language.

Michel Brault has directed two films, initially for television, which deal centrally with immigration and ethnic diversity. *Les Noces de papier* (1989) formed part of a series of ten television films made for Radio Québec by the NFB, Productions du Verseau, and Productions T.V. Films associés, shot on a $846,000 budget on 16 mm. over twenty days. Shown to some acclaim at the Berlin Film Festival in 1990, it gained a theatrical release in several countries and obtained $100,000 in box-office receipts in France. Its televisual origins, as well as the heritage of documentary realism and *le direct*, are the source of its simplicity and economy; the presence and the nuanced performance of its star, Geneviève Bujold, help to explain its ability to find audiences.[19]

Pablo (Manuel Aranguiz) is a Chilean political refugee living illegally and precariously in Montreal in the Latin-American community, pursued by immigration officials, notably the zealous Bouchard (Gilbert Sicotte). Claire (Bujold) is a university teacher of literature, unmarried but carrying on an affair with the married Milosh (Théo Spychalski). Her mother (Monique Lepage), the owner of a bridalshop, is trying to marry her off. Her sister and social activist lawyer Annie (Dorothée Berryman) suggests she marry her client Pablo to allow him resident status, and she eventually agrees. The ceremony takes place in full church regalia, arranged by the mother, after immigration officials chase them out of city hall. When the latter find her in bed with Milosh and no sign of Pablo, the couple decide to live together, the better to pass the immigration test. After a difficult start the beginnings of a relationship develop, via the mutual reminiscences of childhood, her discovery of his torture scars, and her attendance at his community's *fiesta*. Their separate interviews at immigration convince the authorities of the validity of their marriage, and Pablo moves out of the apartment. Missing him, she goes to find him at the Latin American club.

The film primarily belongs to the romance genre, with particular spin-offs for the idea of the nation. As Lapsley and Westlake have argued via Lacan, the sexual relation is basically impossible, since there is no psychic position in which self and other can coincide.[20] The romance genre, however, promises a making good of lack and a complementariness of the sexes not always evident in heterosexual relations, but this promise is constituted by narratives of obstacles to love and the deferral of rapport, as here. Cinema promises to answer the desire it constitutes through the scenario it enacts. Spectators are not so much seeking to possess a lost object as to become the subjects who in the imaginary of the text can possess the lost object it constructs. Such scenarios are relevant to nation-building not only because of the material need for reproduction and the symbolic need to organize gender identities into social roles, but also because of their narrative surpassing of the lack at the heart of national identity.

The national romance refused by *Kamouraska* is here offered for the contemporary age. First, there is the specificity of Claire herself. Like one of the characters in *Le Déclin de l'empire américain* (to be discussed in the next chapter), she inhabits a post-traditional world, bereft even of the glue of a social project. A sexually emancipated career woman, she had rejected the masquerade and asymmetry of a marriage in which men demand particular roles, but she is also dissatisfied with the role of *maîtresse*. In romance fiction, all problems are resolved by displacing them into the one issue of sexual rapport, but there is also the fantasy of sacrificing nothing in exchange for that rapport. Claire loses nothing except "order" which she had chosen over "life." This presents a neat way of dealing, via the miraculous, with the division (of the individual subject), but also a way for the society and nation to reconcile sexuality, social organization, and the symbolic.

The trajectory of the romance narrative is to make the subject "complete" in psychoanalytic terms, but because Claire/Bujold is also located in a story about identities in a secularized, post-traditional Quebec, and in an intertextual network of stories around her star persona, this individuated narrative also has collective repercussions. The relationship with Pablo is initially mapped out in terms of territories and territorialization, namely, her apartment (connoting solitude, privacy) and the spaces of his community, notably the fiesta. The completing gaze of the romantic/sexual Other contributes to a dialectical narrative in which new "truths" and identities can be created and (provisionally) inhabited. The romance narrative becomes one of the coincidence of the legal and the "real," the Law and authenticity, an authenticity that brings Pablo fully "inside" Quebec at the same time as it offers Claire the chance to renew herself. Otherwise, the differences between Pablo and Claire are not particularly marked as bound up with Quebec nationhood. The international art-movie circuit beckons to the film's universalism, with few Quebec accents, an exnominated middle-class point of view, and psychological ambiguity. The contemporariness of the film for Western audiences lies in the identification of Claire and of audiences who do not believe in romance but want to, hence the use of irony and distance. At the same time, the arousal of sentiment in the film depends not on nature or tradition but on the effects of power, as the couple invent narratives of their courtship, and a metaphor of policing prevails: "On nous surveille/ They're watching us." (This recalls – witness Bouchard's search of the apartment in this film – Brault's tendency in *Les Ordres* to create an abstract, generalizable account of events as well as a particular, national one.) Claire and Pablo develop forms and strategies of resistance while they are simultaneously held within bureaucratic power, and are aware of being so. These "adult" ambiguities (romantic love as bounded by myths, traditions, discourses, and apparatuses) are ultimately dependent on Bujold's performance; the prevailing shot patterns are closeups of her reactions – to his torture scars, to his announced departure – that is, of her being looked at.

Les Noces de papier's box-office chances in the United States were scuppered by the near simultaneous release there of *Green Card* (Peter Weir, 1990). While both films share a narrative of obstacles to romance and of an evolution from "false" to "authentic" via the transition for the woman from "order" to "life" provided by the Other, there are crucial differences. In *Green Card* the American woman, Brontë

(Andie MacDowell), does not need the hegemonies around her national "we" to be reworked. The landscapes of "America" are naturalized, because they are familiar to the spectator from the United States audio-visual industry. The "false" images are those in which Georges (Gérard Depardieu) buys into American cultural spaces and motifs through the photographs supposedly taken at "Aspen" and in "California," with the Beach Boys playing on the soundtrack. The paradox, of course, is that that "naturalization" – including the uses of the New York cityscapes – takes place according to the terms of the cultural industries, and this is central to the role of consumerism in the film. Brontë is an upper-middle-class New Yorker. The Frenchman in the film is not, therefore, coded as "posh" and sophisticated à la Louis Jourdan but embodies to the hilt the physical, hedonistic, and expansive side of Depardieu's persona. The eruption of love is therefore here unambiguously "natural" and "authentic." The host country's view of itself is not being reworked by contact with the Other; rather, the Other is in fact the Same and the one who educates Brontë to be a more authentic American: not uptight, and happy to consume.

Michel Brault's second feature on immigrant communities is the 1992 television film *Shabbat Shalom*, which is based on real conflicts in the 1980s between the middle-class francophones of Outremont and the Hassidic community residing in it. Transposing the events to the suburbs of Montreal, it portrays the difficult relationship between the town's mayor, Jean-Marie Guérin (Gilbert Sicotte), and his teenage son Simon (Robert Brouillette) in the emotional aftermath of the wife and mother's suicide several years previously. Simon makes contact with the Hassidic neighbours and also falls in love with a non-Hassidic Jewish girl, Barbara (Françoise Robertson: her diegetic name is possibly a reminiscence of *Le Chat dans le sac*). He supports the Hassidics' planning request for a synagogue, to which Guérin eventually agrees.

As Sherry Simon and Jean Sébastien Dubé have pointed out, the seemingly radically Other Hassidic Jews are in fact here corralled into a Quebec identity narrative.[21] Seen at a distance, they are always the object of the gaze from the initial encounter Simon has at a cashpoint. At best, they are part of a discourse of tolerance, as when Guérin articulates his median, reconciling role in the film by berating his assistant Brisebois (Michel Daigle) for racism and by making the link with the Québécois at the council meeting: "The Québécois, as a minority, have struggled enough to keep their language and culture to be able to understand that the Jews also have the right to preserve their traditions." The problem is that the Québécois have ceased to share collective ideals and traditions such as the family, as evidenced when Guérin makes his wretched microwave dinner and looks through the window at the warmth of his neighbours' gathering. The Hassidic Jews are co-opted not only to this problematic but also to the family romance. Simon in fact comes to realize that his supposed engagement with Otherness is to do with the relationship with his father. The sexualization of the Other is mediated by the relationship with Barbara, the object of his gaze in class immediately following the cashpoint scene. The fantasy of being Jewish means that there is no "becoming-Jewish" in the film, a fact seemingly exemplified at one point by the disturbing comedy of the skull-capped Simon swaying in prayer, but rather an adjusted, reconciled set of identifications in which both father and son happily embark on the social and sexual roles assigned by society.

Questions of sexuality and the family also play crucial, but distinctive roles in films with a significant creative input from Quebec's minorities. *Comment faire l'amour avec un nègre sans se fatiguer* (Jacques Benoît, 1989), based on the Montreal Haitian writer Dany Laferrière's 1985 novel of the same name, is the story of two black men living in the plateau district of Montreal. Vieux (Isaach de Bankolé) is an aspiring writer and composes the title novel of the same name as the film progresses, while bedding a succession of beautiful anglophone young women, most regularly Miz Littérature (Roberta Weiss). Mouba (Maka Kotto) is a Moslem, owns an iguana, listens to jazz, reads Freud, and acts as "counsellor" to a variety of neurotic francophone women, notably Miz Suicide (Myriam Cyr). Three local thugs perceive these black men as potential rivals in their drug trade, and their harassment reaches a climax when Miz Suicide and a friend, who owe them money, are seen leaving the apartment. The drug-pushers set the building on fire, but Vieux manages to save his manuscript.

A thin narrative line is here structured around the rhythm of a porn film, boys' talk alternating with episodic sexual encounters with women. Voice-over, point-of-view shots of the women, and direct address to camera all conspire to construct an authoritative masculinity. On one level, the film can be seen to be in the same lineage as *Valérie* and its aftermath, but with a trendy racial edge and the role of sex object transferred from *la Québécoise* to Westmount girls. The film can be seen to address not questions of Quebec or other national/local identities but rather an international community of heterosexual men, in which black as Other becomes a variation of the Same, bearing out the shifting and multiple nature of the relations between centre and periphery. This view is supported by the film's status as co-production: France financed 20 per cent of the $2.5 m. budget and insisted on the presence of de Bankolé, the now bankable star of *Black Mic-Mac* (Thomas Gilou, 1986) and *Chocolat* (Claire Denis, 1988). The specificity of Quebec is not particularly marked: apart from the references to Westmount, which might otherwise stand in for "America," the film might have been set in any cosmopolitan (francophone) city: the Carré St-Louis resembles a Paris square, and the cross on the Mount, while it plays a role in the novel as a metonym of Quebec Catholicism, functions merely as a backdrop here (seen from the roof in the arson scene). In a particularly distasteful scene in a post office, a racist "feminist" intervenes as Vieux chats up a young woman, which provokes an altercation when members of the queue join in to discuss the relative malevolence of *la drague* ("cruising," "picking up") and the slave trade. The scene reproduces the film's structure of playing women off against black men, and of countering racism with misogyny. The only black women in the film are shot, silently, from behind, in a disco. In a general evacuation of politics and history (as well as of the more distressing signs of poverty), we never learn Vieux and Mouba's country of origin, and the status quo of the white man/white woman/black man/black woman hierarchy (no one brings the latter to orgasm) is perceived as inert, merely functioning as an explanation for the attraction of white women to black men. The absence of a dialogic dimension means that women who disagree are dumped or humiliated. What polyphony there is consists of Vieux aspiring to integration into Western society even as he mocks it, while Mouba the outsider, does not.

The pretext for this procedure is the exposure of white myths. The use of the term "negro," and the reference to large penises in the poster, meant that ads for the film were refused by the *New York Times* and the *Toronto Star*. Of course, the film has it both ways with these myths, not only because of Vieux's manipulation of them for sexual conquest, but because (black) masculinity and prowess are perceived as audience hooks and as "solutions" the characters adopt to the complexities of identity and power. In the novel, a degree of internalized satire and self-irony through Vieux's first-person narration and associative prose generated a certain carnivalesque element which pitched the work into a more pluralist mode, revealing the absence of a "coherent cultural fund from which the narrator [could] draw the sustenance of identity."[22] The emphatic schema of a black *mind* and white *bodies* had greater mileage in written form. Laferrière's own "intentions" are set out as follows in the Aska Films press kit: "My dream is for someone to come out of the film, walk along the street and on seeing a Black man, say to himself: I'm looking at this Black man but I know that he's looking at me too; and that the way the Black man sees me depends on his culture, his history and his own personality." Aside from the elusiveness of the "history" and "culture" being referred to here (and its placing in the singular), the layers of analysis in the film are greatly reduced: the role of the drug-pushers is to represent an externalized white Québécois racism, and Vieux's exposure of myths is limited, for example, to white women's surprise to see a black man reading. The black men's white flatmate François (Antoine Durand) plays a mediating role and ensures that the homosociality is multiracial. Not in the novel is a racist McGill literature professor, who boasts, "Je vais faire hennir ma blanche comme un nègre/I'll make my white woman whinny like a Black man does," but who, in a rather ridiculous overdetermination, is also coded as gay. Although black men here possess both a voice and the gaze, and form the metadiscourse of the film, the lack of engagement with the Quebec context and the transcendence of the phallus mean that it represents a missed opportunity, as the briefest of comparison with the work of Spike Lee would illustrate (the role of the women in *She's Gotta Have It* [1986] and *Jungle Fever* [1991] permits an interrogation of, and rings the changes on, black masculinities).

The one element that might destabilize some of the inert structures of *Comment faire l'amour avec un nègre* is the display of Vieux's body (he is usually stripped to the waist or dressed in a singlet). This homoeroticism, despite the male heterosexual address of the film, raises several questions, or rather reveals several embedded historical and cultural layers: the emphasis on black male physicality dominant in Western cultures since slavery; a hook, as old as feature film-making, for heterosexual female spectators but now consistent with changing sexual roles and the increased circulation of homoerotic imagery; the aestheticization of social life and relations in contemporary society, consistent with Vieux's musings on success, and with the idealization in late 1980s Quebec and elsewhere of the efficient manager with connotations of the sportsman and seducer. The film also points to the increasingly central role of the city (generic or specifically Montreal) in these histories and cultures, with here transracial *drague* offering a contemporary or postmodern equivalent of the *flâneur*; witness the montage of Vieux in the streets, and also of Vieux and François at the jazz festival in rue Prince-Arthur.

Manuel le fils emprunté, directed by François Labonté, was produced in 1989 by the NFB and two private production companies, Cléo 24 and Productions EGM. The co-scriptwriters were the Québécois novelist Monique Proulx and the producer, Nardo Castillo, himself the son of Spanish immigrants. In the present-day plateau district of Montreal, near the Boulevard Saint-Laurent, Manuel Entrada (Nuno da Costa) is twelve and in frequent confrontation with his Portuguese baker father Vasco (Luis Saraviva) for indiscipline and failure at school. Sleeping away from home, Manuel is enticed into petty crime with some older francophone boys and is befriended by a local cobbler, Juan Alvarez (Francisco Rabal), an old Spanish anarchist from 1930s Barcelona who pretends to the police he is Manuel's grandfather. He teaches Manuel improved reading skills via books on the Spanish Civil War and anarchism. After further crime, however, Manuel is arrested by the police and is counselled by a social worker; Alvarez and Manuel's father confront each other in her office. Alvarez is given temporary custody of Manuel, to some disquiet on the part of his wife, Rosa (Kim Yaroshevskaya). Manuel takes anarchist precepts to heart, and uses them to justify shoplifting and organizing a strike of pupils at school against the imposition of a uniform. When Alvarez fails to back him up in front of the principal, Manuel is resentful, but they become close again when they read together about the anarchists in 1930s Spain.

The modest realism of the piece belies a complex structure that makes it a truly Bakhtinian film. The work of Robert Stam is valuable for its use of Bakhtin and the study of ethnic and racial representations in film, in that Bakhtin offers ways of talking about relational, incomplete identity positions rather than the impasses of "true" versus "false" images.[23] *Manuel le fils emprunté* is replete with a variety of untotalizable voices which combine individuated narrative with a spectrum of ideologemes from the wider social and historical world. None of the four adult viewpoints is invalidated by the end, but instead each is held in dialogue with the others. Alvarez's anarchism is the means by which Manuel becomes empowered and acquires a value system, and his tradition is "movingly" and nostalgically evoked in the final scene. Vasco Entrada's traditional patriarchical authoritarianism emerges negatively in confrontation with his son and daughter, but not his dreams of "success" and a house in the suburbs, which during a visit to Manuel (for which a right has been granted) is posited as the revolutionary tradition, that "social justice so that everyone can live better"; the first confrontation between Alvarez and Vasco, as they caricature each other with the terms "fascist" and "communist," is followed by a more gentle scene on a park bench, as, framed in long shot together, they share bread. Alvarez's politics are challenged by Rosa as she criticizes his authority in the home and her domestic labour as inconsistent with theories of equality: at one point, taking off her apron, she proclaims her desire to go off and read Bakunin and Marx, or better still, "a good Harlequin novel," so that he can do the cooking. She tells Manuel that Alvarez's politics are fraught with unconscious, sexual desires like the passion for a woman, and she urges him even to become a managing director: "Above all don't waste your life for a dream." Even the social worker has her *mot à dire*: to Alvarez's refusal to fill in the adoption papers, she replies, "The universe is full of compromises." The film presents the different narratives via which people make sense of their lives, instead of a master narrative, and places them in dialogue.

Any "solution" to these conflicting ideologemes is posited in terms of "Quebec" or "Canada" or "North America" (the ambiguity is significant and inevitable) versus "Europe," but it precisely figures that first half of the binary, and thus Manuel and his apprenticeship, as a relatively open text. While certainly a representation of a post-traditional society (hence the critique of patriarchy), it nonetheless does not imply any *a priori* interpretation of the free/freedom seme as represented either by Manuel's sister Estelle (Isabel Serra) (sexual freedom, consumerism, and pleasure: Vasco complains about her wearing a crucifix with her outfit – shades of the early Madonna) or by Alvarez. If anything, the film simply emphasizes the need not to forget the European revolutionary tradition (at least the anarchist one), while at the same time seeking to surpass it. Post-traditional, post-industrial, multiethnic Quebec/Canada need not imply historical forgetting, hence the extensive invocation of *memory*, including the flashbacks of the Spanish Civil War via newsreel footage and the traumatic moment, revealed near the end of the film, when Alvarez saw before him a young boy's throat cut by Nationalists. Even if one narrative of Montreal in the film can be read spatially (from the Boulevard Saint-Laurent to the suburbs), the sense of time is not lost, and here it is useful to invoke another Bakhtinian term, that of the chronotope, to describe the film's articulation of space-time. The chronotope is a "unit of analysis for studying texts according to the ratio and nature of the temporal and spatial categories represented ... The chronotope is an optic for reading texts as x-rays of the forces at work in the culture system from which they spring."[24] Martin Allor, drawing on the work of Doreen Massey, has written of the Boulevard Saint-Laurent in these terms, as a "place," in fact many "places," not bounded but an articulation or set of articulations of social relations in space and time.[25] Thus "memory" is in the film an ongoing site of struggle and questioning: whose memory is operating for whom?

This lack of closure is, of course, also confirmed by the role of "fatherhood." Labonté's previous two features, *Henri* (1986) and *Gaspard et fil$* (1988) both represented Oedipal narratives of pursuit, of filling the lack, the telos being that of union or reconciliation with the father. *Manuel le fils emprunté* is still largely a boy's story, but the boy's future cultural (and sexual) identity or rather identities are left open. The film thus departs from the standard Quebec Oedipal narrative while intriguingly and tantalizingly referring to the family romance through the encounter with the substitute father, who does not present a comment on some complex cultural relation between Spain and Portugal (and nothing is done with his specifically Catalan origins) but whose role offers the possibility of departing from the Oedipal logic altogether. The only Québécois *de souche* in the film are the social worker and the teenage thugs, a moral polarity consistent with the pluralism of the film and the absence of a Quebec national metadiscourse. Of course, the film is about Manuel's insertion into society, but at the same time its narrative structure is dialogic and non-teleological rather than dialectic, since that insertion is to do with hybridity and non-completion rather than fixity. This tension is illustrated by the motif of the paperweight that circulates from Manuel's theft of it in the first scene in Alvarez's cobbler shop, to his retrieving it after he has left home, looking through it in his conversation with Rosa, smashing it when Alvarez lets him down at school. It is metonymically associated with reading and thought, with looking, and, of course, castration: the smashing of it, of the purloined masculine identity, signals the process of Manuel's acquisition of a mature (masculine) position, but the point is that the object *circulates* from one "parental" home and from one ideologeme to another, and so comes to embody pluralism and contradiction. In contrast, the circulations in *Shabbat Shalom*, those associated with the dead fox terrier and its replacement, and with the Jewish grandfather's pendent, are linked to an axis of truth and falsehood which is resolved in the end, along with the son's sexual, familial, and national affiliations.

Despite these factors, the reach of *Manuel le fils emprunté* is limited by its televisual realism and its masculinist bias. A more sustained vision and bigger budget are evident in Paul Tana's *La Sarrasine* (1992). Tana (b. 1947) came to Quebec from Italy at the age of eleven, and the scripts of his films dealing with the Italian community – as well as *La Sarrasine*, the drama documentary *Caffè Italia Montréal* (1985) on the experience of immigration since the turn of the century, and the family melodrama *La Déroute* (1998) – have all been written with the historian Bruno Ramirez and star Tony Nardi, another *Montréalais* who came from Italy as a child. *La Sarrasine* was produced by ACPAV and funded in part by Multiculturalisme et citoyenneté Canada. Set in Montreal at the turn of the century and based on true events, *La Sarrasine* tells the story of the tailor, Giuseppe Moschella (Nardi), a close friend of the Québécois *de souche* Alphonse Lamoureux (Jean Lapointe). Moschella's desire to pay tribute to Lamoureux at his wedding turns sour when two of his Italian lodgers mistime their entrance and serenade, and this produces an altercation with Lamoureux's son-in-law Théo (Gilbert Sicotte). Conflict flares up again a few days later when Théo and his drunken friends taunt the Italians outside the tailor shop cum lodging-house: in the ensuing confrontation, Giuseppe shoots Théo dead. At the trial, he is condemned to death. At the moment of the murder, however, Giuseppe's wife, Ninetta (Enrica Maria Modugno), begins to take an active role and campaigns successfully with a lawyer and with Celi (Nelson Villagra), the leader of the Italian community in the city, for the sentence to be commuted. Giuseppe and his elder brother Salvatore (Biagio Pelligra) pressure her to return to Italy, but she refuses. A final private meeting in the prison ends in Giuseppe slapping her. Ninetta decides to go into hiding instead of returning to Italy with Salvatore, and with the help of one of the lodgers she takes refuge in the abandoned shop Lamoureux had given to Théo. Meanwhile, Théo's widow Félicité (Johanne-Marie Tremblay) has herself taken the initiative to return to Montreal and start running the shop, and discovers Ninetta, forcing her to flee. Salvatore has, however, returned to Italy without her; Ninetta learns that Giuseppe has committed suicide in prison.

The title of the film refers to the puppet show that takes place at the start of the film at Moschella's shop, Lamoureux joining the Italian audience when he comes to collect his suit. The show represents the scene from Tasso's *Gerusalemme liberata* when the crusader Tancredo kills his enemy but discovers that it is his Turkish lover, Clorinda, dressed as a man. As Simon and Dubé point out,[26] this intertext has many connotations relevant to the film. The puppet show is revealing of the intercultural heritage of southern Italy, the blurred boundaries of victory and defeat, Self and Other, the historical turnarounds evident in the context of Tasso's fifteenth-century Italy when the Turks were making inroads in the south. Moreover, the mistaken identity in the scene can be extended to the film's narrative as a whole, where the tragic events are set in motion by cultural ignorance and the absence of common codes (rather like the eponymous hero of Balzac's short story *Sarrasine*, whose "national mistake" in believing a *castrato* to be a woman leads to his death "from a gap in knowledge ... from a blank in the discourse of others," in other words in the encyclopedia of the cultural code).[27] At the end of the film, Ninetta gives the puppets to Lamoureux in a symbolic intercultural exchange which "consacrates the process of cultural hybridation in which the two communities are henceforth engaged."[28]

One of the strengths of the film is the lack of homogeneity and completeness in both the Italian and Franco-Québécois communities. The Italians speak a Sicilian dialect but also a standard Tuscan Italian (Celi) and are marked by class differences; moreover, the communities are divided on gender lines. It is Ninetta who steps (literally) into the foreground after her husband's imprisonment, not as bearer of the look, but, from the moment of the murder, as the one to be looked at because of the symbolic weight she bears. Despite the violent hostility she feels towards her husband's killer, Félicité also experiences an apprenticeship of empowerment which runs counter to the patriarchy of both Italian and Franco-Québécois societies, when she reads Ninetta's diary. That apprenticeship implies both gender ambiguity within that society, as in the Sarrasine puppet, and an ambivalence of identity within Quebec, as a final shot of Ninetta is of the disjunction of her black-clad figure shot against the snow, but also of the belonging and territorializing implied by her urinating.

However, there are some limits to these hybrid exchanges. *La Sarrasine* partly belongs to that strand of Quebec "quality" filmmaking since *J.A. Martin photographe*, that of the historical costume drama with a woman at the centre that raises questions of origin and performativity across the gap between *énonciation* and *énoncé* and the caesura of the Quiet Revolution. The passage from orality to literacy, having originated in the lessons given by Giuseppe Moschella, is one shared with the Sicilians by the Franco-Québécois decades earlier, and by extension can be seen to be part of a teleological narrative of modernization entirely consistent with a post-Quiet Revolution optic. Félicité is faced with the hostility of the priest when she wishes to return to the city: "You're asking me to be the accomplice of your perdition … Montreal is becoming a sewer attracting all the dregs of the Earth. All these foreigners act as if they were at home [*chez eux*], or even worse, and they get away with it."[29] Fulvio Caccia's description of immigrant culture as that of "those who are changing, of those who have changed" is in fact harnessed to this more general post-Quiet Revolution narrative in which education, *bildung*, literacy, and progress are seen as the forces that shape, and are shaped by, intercultural exchange. This film's own status and its implied audience are part of that process, with extensive use of subtitling for the Italian dialogue (but no subtitling of the French). (However, Ninetta's process of acculturation does not mean deculturation; she does not lose her "Italianness" or "Sicilianness.") A liberal aspect of the film, with an exnominating view of the "norm," runs counter to the demystification of that norm set in motion by the repetition of rituals and the massive presence of the Italian community. This is most clear in the figure of Alphonse, the "good" Québécois, father and husband, italophile, and admirer of Garibaldi, but who cannot speak a word of Italian and whose own wife Margie (Murielle Dutil) is silent, her story unknown.

The Italians are an interesting and representative group in Quebec society, for they are proximate and adjacent to the *Québécois de souche*, through their Catholicism, Latin origins, and narratives of modernization. They are distinct despite and because of the "minor" differences, but they also offer a dialectical overcoming, as Caccia points out: "Italy allows the Québécois to 'confront' their own (latin) origin in order to assert their Americanness; and in doing so bypassing the conflict with the mother-culture: France."[30]

Apart from Tana, the only other "minority" film-maker in Quebec (if we except Léa Pool) to have made a fictional feature is Michka Saäl, who had also directed a series of shorts, notably *Loin d'où?* (1989) and *L'Arbre qui dort rêve à ses racines* (1991). A co-production with France, *La Position de l'escargot* (1998) tells the story of Myriam (Mirella Tomassini), a young woman of Tunisian-Jewish origin who works as an interpreter for the immigration services in Montreal. The film's examination of the relationships between fixity and flow, *appartenance*, and *partance* are structured around the unexpected return of Myriam's father Dédé (Victor Lanoux), who had left his family twenty years before. His presence provokes a highly personal (the film is dedicated to the director's father) reflection on the past, its loss (the dead mother) and its nostalgias (the house by the Mediterranean). But the past co-exists with the tumultuous present, with its kaleidoscope of cultures and images (jazz, *À tout prendre*), its sexual departures (Myriam's affair with a Jamaican marginal, Lou [Judes-Antoine Jarda]), its transitional spaces (the port of Montreal, the streets and stairwell in which the first confrontations with Dédé take place, Lou's squat, the friend's apartment where Myriam temporarily stays). The film's title thus refers not only to lovemaking but also to the snail carrying its home on its back, a tension point between roots and nomadism. In the end, however, when the atmosphere of the North African house, garden, and fountain seem to be reproduced, the pull of origin threatens to unbalance the film, since the spectator fails to invest in the father-figure with quite the same intensity as the director.

This overview of "immigrants" in Quebec cinema has pointed to the way this theme is in fact part of a much broader problematic. In this way it can be seen to be always present, implicit even if unspoken, in the national-allegorical tension of Quebec cinema. The role of the city of Montreal in Quebec cinema means that the subject is unavoidable. For example, the popular comedy *Karmina*(Gabriel Pelletier, 1996), about a group of vampires from Transylvania, can be seen to be an allegory of immigration, assimilation, and difference, but from the point of view of the Franco-Québécois "norm." In order to avoid the marriage her parents have arranged with Vlad (Yves Pelletier), a successful businessman who might help them ward off American promoters eyeing their castle, Karmina (Isabelle Cyr) flees to Montreal to stay with her aunt Esmeralda (France Castel), who uses her potion to enable her to live like a "human." Karmina must learn how to fit into the society and falls in love with a nice Québécois boy, Philippe (Robert Brouillette). Meanwhile, Vlad has followed her and turned a customs official (played by Gildor Roy) into a vampire. Matters are resolved with the arrival of Karmina's parents and the transformation of Philippe. It should be noted that much of the film's humour is unexportable, very "Québécois" in its use of language and juxtaposition of familiar icons (faces and places) with the supernatural Other.

These overspills of immigrant and ethnic themes into wider genres and co-productions suggest that, as with the native peoples, Quebec national cinema here threatens or promises to generate "world texts" and to unravel the "national" altogether. A remarkable example of such a film is *Clandestins* (Denis Chouinard and Nicolas Wadimoff, 1997). This Quebec-Swiss-Belgian-French co-production, directed by a Québécois and a Swiss and with French dialogue, tells the story of six stowaways – Arab, Gypsy, and East European – bound for Canada. Set almost entirely in the claustrophobic container of a cargo ship, the film communicates the physical hardships and psychological pressure with the kind of documentary realism associated with Canadian cinema (the directors-writers based their account on testimonies). But the film also denounces both the desperation that provokes such migrations and the injustices of the immigration system: because Canada fines ships $5,000 per illegal immigrant, on discovering them the captain puts them off the ship into an open boat (but the gypsy teenager remains at liberty with the little girl, a promise of renewal).

This cinema at the fringes of nation and identity, in terms of both content and production, is, like those films representing the indigenous Other, part of a developing transnational genre[31] (which partly reiterates the transnational nature of cinema since its origins, partly points to something new). But it also takes the analysis beyond the tidy idea of "the representation of immigrants" into an examination of those global forces wrenching apart and churning around compartmentalized industrial practices and cultural identities. The world system is more interested in the techno-political selection of individuals and spaces than in given historical cultural categories, but, as Etienne Balibar and Immanuel Wallerstein have argued, the relationship is complex. Non-economic social relations also react against those destructurations that the logic and expansion of profit and value bring, and by aiming to restore perceived lost unities they can actually contribute to the system's stability. The play of these forces corresponds to the national-allegorical tension: "The flexibility of claiming a link with the boundaries of the past combined with the constant redrawing of these boundaries in the present takes the form of the creation and constant re-creation of racial and/or ethno-national-religious groups or communities."[32] What might be emphasized here is the productivity of that tension and its capacity for creating the new, what Lawrence Grossberg calls "the becoming[s] of time and space."[33] The cultural periodizations made feasible by contemporary, absolute globalized capital are the subject of our final chapter.

11 Modernity and Postmodernity

Denys Arcand's *Le Déclin de l'empire américain* (1986) and *Jésus de Montréal* (1989) are significant not only for their domestic and international success (*Le Déclin* grossed more than any other film in Quebec in its year of release, and remains the biggest-grossing Quebec film of all time in the world market), and for the fillip they provided for the Quebec film industry, reoriented towards an emphasis on lucrative auteur cinema. They also inaugurated, at the end of the 1980s, a cinema preoccupied less by national self-definition, assertion, and creation than by the awareness of a Quebec inserted in global flows of culture and communication. The decade following the failed sovereignty referendum had also, of course, seen an economic recession that blighted Montreal's older industries, the relative eclipse of working-class movements, the signing of the North American Free Trade agreement, the acceleration of technological change and the information society, and the fall of communism in Eastern Europe. These "world" developments and their accompanying cultural shifts would remain on the agenda despite the resurgence of Quebec nationalism after the collapse of the Meech Lake Accord in 1990. The 1995 referendum took place in a context coloured by the increasing prominence over the previous fifteen years of issues of ethnic pluralism and native rights, and also by the new confidence on the part of sections of the Quebec bourgeoisie that a sovereign nation could function effectively in terms of its economy and (linguistically cushioned) culture in a free-trading North America.

It is tempting to see the whole of this book as teleologically organized so that its final chapter marks the culmination of that fragmentation of and challenge to notions of unified, fixed, and finished national identity that it has traced. However, the reverse is true. Those challenges are and were always already there in the Quebec national project, indeed in any national project. Politically, they do not necessarily invalidate it. Culturally, the national-allegorical tension continues in the 1980s and 1990s, but in changing circumstances and a context altered from the 1960s. This chapter is not called simply "Postmodernity," as if an end point had been reached and the cultural epoch had assumed a new totality, created a new narrative of "before" and "after." Old and new, residual and emergent cultural discourses always coexist. As with the national-allegorical tension, it is the relationship between forces that is important rather than a finished state of wholeness or dissolution. For this reason we can happily explore and hypothesize around the two terms without getting too bogged down in their validity (for example, Anthony Giddens favours the expression "late modernity" over "postmodernity," since he sees contemporary society as characterized by the acceleration and intensification of processes instigated in the late eighteenth century).[1]

In chapter 3, we saw that the hegemonic project of the "modernization" of Quebec society was itself always incomplete. Nevertheless, it founded certain narratives of, and conflicts around, Quebec identity and the national project. The "modernization" of Quebec would deliver the benefits, but also dilemmas, of "modernity": the replacement of tradition, the creation of a secular society based on free individual citizens and consumers, the idea of the nation and its participation on the world stage, and above all a society and existence marked by perpetual change. The relationship between "modernity" and "postmodernity" usefully forces two questions that in turn compel a relationship between the temporal and spatial: what is different and specific about the 1980s and 1990s compared with what went before; and what is different and specific (or not, given the globalizing impetus of the epoch) about Quebec. At the very least, the term "postmodernity" allows some sort of purchase on the experience of living in this particular, seemingly all-conquering phase of capitalism.

That experience, as evoked by commentators such as David Harvey and Fredric Jameson, can be distilled as follows. The extension of commodification to the whole of culture has produced a crisis of the "depth models" associated with that earlier artistic response to modernity, namely, modernism.[2] The alienation and anguish associated with Munch and Van Gogh were replaced, for example, by the multiplying surfaces and signifiers of Warhol, taking his cue from commodity culture, since the "truth claims" needed to assert what we are alienated *from* have also unravelled, as Jean-François Lyotard argues in *The Post-modern Condition* of 1979. The "grand narratives" of the Enlightenment such as progressivism (the emergence of the adult liberal subject as explored in the nineteenth-century *bildungsroman*), Marxism, and even nationalism have lost their founding thrust, their content thrown into crisis by the commodification and circulation of "bits" of information, so that only local language games are left. In the post-war era, while Fordism and Keynesianism were "based on massive fixed capital investments in mass production, agglomeration in industrial regions, strong labor unions and state management of national business cycles,"[3] contemporary "post-Fordism" and "post-Keynesianism" are characterized by flexible accumulation, rapid technological change, accelerated reformation of tastes, speed-ups in the turnover of capital, a retreat of the state, and an unfixing of centralized corporate forms in favour of dispersed and fragmented production and employment. The speed and range of capitalist activity are now unsurpassed, and the creation of a world economy and market more or less complete.

One received opinion in the 1990s is that Canada is the first "postmodern state."[4] For some commentators, this permits a refreshing decoupling of polity and culture, so that "Canada" can be defined as an agreed-on set of distinctive policies and institutional arrangements, on health care, for example, and can dispense with the usual founding and binding accoutrements of a unified national identity.[5] For others, there is on the other hand a real crisis and risk of fragmentation, partly because the retreat of Keynesian economics (which would include the provision of health care, for example) renders extremely fragile the whole socio-political contract between subject and state which in turn depended on the recognition processes of nationhood, and partly because the rise of identity politics attendant upon the Canadian Charter of Human Rights and Freedoms, created by the 1982 patriation of the constitution, generates a disconnection between personal action and collective existence. Within this purview, the national demands of Quebec can be seen as another of those centrifugal forces threatening the cohesion of Canada, or, more locally, as an inappropriately retrograde strategy of reinventing a nineteenth-century nation-state.

The strength of Quebec culture, however, is that, perhaps even more than the greater solidity possessed by its national symbols and narratives, the making explicit of buffetings of identity, of the relationship between identity and becoming something else, between existing and disappearing, are nothing new. (It is sometimes forgotten that Lyotard's *La Condition postmoderne* was in fact commissioned as a "report on knowledge" by the Conseil des Universités of the government of Quebec.) This suggests that Quebec is not only spectacularly touched by the flows of postmodernity but also possesses the cultural resources to carve out distinctive spaces within them. The specificity of Quebec postmodernity is about this duality, the coexistence of a national project and the long-held knowledge, and reality, of its aspirant and incomplete nature. The 1980s and 1990s throw up new challenges, new transformations and intensifications of these dilemmas:

1) the crisis of the technocratic progressivism of the Quiet Revolution, a period that, as we have seen, was already an "interregnum";
2) the magnification in importance of the relationship with the United States, and particularly its cultural commodities and images;
3) connected with this, the effects of globalization on minorities (native peoples, lesbians and gay men, but in the latter national loyalties are not distinct from those of the wider population), cultural consumers, and Québécois business and political elites, who become inscribed within a public and media space whose frontiers do not coincide with the national territory;
4) in turn, the effects of globalization on not only cultural identifications but also space-time itself, given that temporal and spatial issues are crucial to national identity construction and its cinematic images, and that postmodern society is said to flatten out history into a perpetual present (the spatial supplants the temporal, "space" is separated from "place"); and
5) the penetration of the commodity form into every aspect of the culture, including and especially the image.

The "always already there" aspect of Quebec identity construction means that many of the cultural and specifically filmic modalities of these questions have already been addressed in this study. Binary oppositions, such as self/other and high/low culture, were always already problematized by the specificities of Quebec history, and we have seen, in the chapters on popular cinema, immigration, and native peoples, how Quebec cinema has attempted to negotiate them or displace them. Despite the overwhelming presence of American mass culture in the audiovisual cultural practices of the Québécois, its 75 per cent share of the CD market (this includes British and other anglophone pop music) and 84 per cent share of movie attendance, francophone television in Quebec enjoys an 88 per cent viewing share.[6] While much of the Quebec film industry is a branch plant for anglophone Canadian and American productions (two-thirds of films shot there in 1997, for example, were in English), this both enables "national" cinema production to take place and creates new solidities, new repatriations, within the flows of capital. The clearest example of this is Montreal's recent spatial reconfiguration within the multimedia industry, which is due partly to technical and industrial factors (the branch-plant phenomenon, the animation tradition) and partly to cultural ones (Montreal as linguistically rich and as located between European and North American culture). Daniel Langlois (b. 1957), founder of Softimage, which provided animation software for *Jurassic Park* (Spielberg, 1993) and *Toy Story* (Lasseter, 1995), has invested in the Festival of New Cinema and New Media and sponsored the new $16-million cinema complex on the Boulevard Saint-Laurent devoted to experimental and auteur cinema.[7] Meanwhile, that old state mono-lith the NFB has suffered several years of budget cuts, from $82 million in 1994–95 to $55 million in 1998–99, and has withdrawn, probably definitively, from fictional features to concentrate on documentary and animation and to diversify its distribution (video, internet, the cinerobotheque in Montreal). The budgets for Quebec films made in the private sector have stagnated at the levels of the late 1980s (at approximately $2 million). It is tempting to read François Girard's *The Red Violin* (1998) – the epitome of the big-budget ($14 million) inter-national art movie – as containing an allegory of these territorializing and deterritorializing movements. Girard (b. 1963) has not made a feature film in Quebec since *Cargo* (1990). The enigma of the globe-trotting violin is solved and the "truth" revealed – a kind of textual homecoming in the final sequence in the Montreal auction house, but, with another twist of the spiral, by an African-American.

The corpus of films examined in this chapter points to four varia-tions of the modernity/postmodernity problematic: diagnostic, pas-tiche, the city, and memory. Arcand's major two films clearly belong to the first category. The scenario of *Le Déclin de l'empire américain* is well known: through parallel editing, the lives and attitudes of male and female members of the intellectual élite are scrutinized. The women are working out in a gym: Dominique (Dominique Michel), head of a university history department and author of a work articulating the thesis of the film's title; Diane (Louise Portal), another, less senior academic; a naive wife and mother, Louise (Dorothée Berryman); and a graduate student, Danielle (Geneviève Rioux). The men are prepar-ing a meal in a chalet in the Eastern Townships. Among them are three university lecturers – Claude (Yves Jacques), the chalet's gay owner; Pierre (Pierre Curzi), lover of Danielle; Rémi (Rémy Girard), philandering husband of Louise – and a young graduate student, Alain (Daniel Brière). Both groups talk mainly about sex. Their meal and weekend together are disrupted first by the arrival of Diane's Montreal-rough lover Mario (Gabriel Arcand), with whom she enjoys sado-masochistic sex, and then by Louise's discovery of Rémi's serial infidelity with Dominique, Diane, her own sister, and many others.

The most obvious point to be made in this film *de constat* is its satire of these members of a highly protected segment of society. Apart from Louise, the older characters are depicted as motivated by hedonism, individualism, and instant gratification, while the younger ones are in no position to offer any alternative (Alain ends up sleeping with Dominique, Danielle is ensconced with Pierre). This is a post-traditional society, in which there is no longer a moral centre (the past has ceased to be the source of exnominated belief) or a collective social or political project. The diagnosis, made by conservative and left-wing commentators alike, is of an absence or void where historical memory and "truth," in traditional society or even modernity, were once located. (It also recalls the analyses of Herbert Marcuse in *One-Dimensional Man* on "repressive desublimation.") This void is epitomized at the end of the film, when, after the traumas of the night before, life and conversation begin again in cyclical fashion, and Pierre summarizes the uncertainty around a colleague's sexual dalliances with the statement, "I think we'll never know the truth of the matter." The narrative has contained no structure of *bildung*, no teleology of emerging consciousness or truth.

In addition, there is, of course, the dimension of Quebec specificity. The protagonists are the baby-boomers who benefited from the educational reforms of the Quiet Revolution and who lived through the political effervescence of the 1960s and 1970s in Quebec. The casting of Dominique Michel as one of the academics is startling for being against type, worlds away from the populist heroines of the 1970s, but makes sense because it underlines what that set of discourses has come to. This post-referendum film analyses the "comfort and indifference" that characterizes the Quebec intelligentsia. In the history book that Mario rather incongruously presents to Diane, Michel Brunet's *Notre passé, le présent et nous*, published in 1976, we read the following words: "When a collectivity chooses to ignore its past, it means it is refusing to confront the challenges of the present and lacks the courage to build a future."[8] As Fulvio Caccia has pointed out, not only does the film appropriately take sex and sexuality as the touchstones of contemporary upheaval, it deftly links the general and the particular, the Western world and this corner of it: "The crisis of the uprootings [*déracinements*] of modernity coincide with that of a minority society confronted with the failure of its national project."[9] This is announced in the pre-credit scene, when Rémi expounds to his class his theory of numbers deciding historical outcomes, an argument advantageous to black South Africans but not to black Americans (nor by implication to the

Québécois; the opening shot is a close-up of a Vietnamese student; Rémi will later expound at the chalet on the sexual "flavour" of that nationality).

Here, however, lies the ambiguity of the film, in its view of history and its positioning of the spectator. Much of the considerable debate it generated concerned precisely what the "truth" of the film might be, that is, the relationship between the discourse of the protagonists and that of the film's "author." This relationship is summarized by the two most striking shots of the film. The first is the long tracking shot, over the title credits, through a hallway of the University of Montreal that finally homes in on Diane and Dominique, when the latter first expounds the views in her book on the decline of civilizations being based on the quest for individual pleasure and happiness. Here the film pins down its protagonists like laboratory animals, observed from a distant, omniscient narrative position. The second is the first encounter between the men and women in the film as the latter arrive at the chalet. The editing has the two groups approaching each other suspiciously and apprehensively like at a western shoot-out, and then a shot is briefly held of empty space which the two sides then fill with smiles and embraces. As Denis Bellemare has suggested, this interval encapsulates the spectatorial space of criticism, knowledge, and distance that has been prepared by the previous sequences of parallel editing contrasting the men and women's discourse, and it also lays the ground for the confrontations and dramas to come beneath the civility.[10] But, while the spectator is permitted to differentiate truth and falsehood in relation to the protagonists's words and deeds, the relation between their beliefs and "the truth of the film," if it exists, is elusive.

It is not surprising, for example, that the film leaves itself open to denunciations of sexism and homophobia. The feminist writer Louky Bersianik wrote a devastating critique of *Le Déclin* in *Le Devoir*, accusing Arcand of misogyny in his portrayal of women who are masochistic (Diane) or servile to men (Danielle and Louise), and taking as "the truth of the film" the men's disgust in relation to the female body, a disgust not "balanced" by the women's repartee, because they criticize individuals, not all men, and in any case seem to be "size queens," placing the phallus at the centre.[11] While Bersianik is clearly neglecting the critical distance vis-à-vis its characters the film sets up,[12] such an attitude is comprehensible because any reading of the film has to confront the central dilemma of whether to take seriously or not the thesis propounded by Dominique, which after all is reproduced in the title. Her argument had partly attributed decline to women attaining power in societies and empires (a highly dubious proposition, as Bersianik points out). Thus the comfort and indifference of the characters would have them living out the decline of Western civilization in its periphery, safely observing the nuclear explosions that might take place over the border at the Plattsburgh air base (the Cold War conditions of the 1980s should not be forgotten when contextualizing the film). Of course, one reading of the film is that the characters project their own tawdriness and parochialism onto grand transhistorical narratives.

This dilemma of reading can be addressed, not by attributing an all-knowing auteurism to Arcand, but by locating his own position in history and in the political economy of the industry to which he belongs. This reveals uncertainties in relation to the innovations, the despair *but also possibilities* of the current age,[13] and here the representation of the gay character is symptomatic. Claude does indeed present a "heterosexual vision of homosexuality," as Denise Pérusse points out,[14] since he is a source of emotional comfort for Louise, and of some envy for the straight men, in the complete decoupling he represents of sex and any social functions. Robert Schwartzwald has effectively dealt with the shortcomings of this representation, relating it to the homophobia and sexism of Arcand's 1960s *Parti pris* phase.[15] Thus Claude's pissing of blood renders him analogous to women, whose menstrual blood so disturbs the straight men. The incoherences of Arcand's current position have no small part to play here: Claude has to be portrayed as secretly ill in order to counterbalance, not only the "positive" characteristics he embodies, the combination of freedom and empathy, but also the impossibility of heterosexual relationships that the film has relentlessly and devastatingly portrayed. Parallel editing in *Gina* had established different histories, different constructions in history which could inform each other. What the parallel editing between the men and women in *Le Déclin* reveals is the historical constructedness of heterosexuality itself, and how, given the unravelling of tradition, the differences between masculinity and femininity are exposed, and the similarities reduced, for this class fraction, to a common comfort and indifference. Unable to know what to do with some of the more radical consequences of his *constat*, the corrections to the games of falsity portrayed in the film have to be located in myths of "the natural" and "the spontaneous": Louise's naivety in fact provides the only challenge to Dominique's thesis; the latter responds in kind by dropping the intellectual mask and taking an emotional revenge. Louise is also the one who momentarily allies herself with Mario in critical distance vis-à-vis the intellectuals. And the drama unfolds in a natural setting, "beautifully" photographed by Jacques Leduc, to which the characters are mostly indifferent.

These incoherences in *Le Déclin* relate to the secrets of its success. An arthouse audience watches variations of itself talking about sex in an "international" French (which Mario dramatically punctuates). (Considerable research needs to be done on the differences as well as similarities within the Québécois audience response, and the processes of recognition – "us" and "not us" – variously inscribed according to social position.) The film titillates and at the same time absolves the guilt of that titillation through the convenience of its irony. This is another way in which it tips into something unexpected or inadmissible to itself. Knowledges, that of the protagonists, that of the ironically distant audience, are played with in the film, traded off according to a marketing game of flattery and indulgence.[16] Arcand's pessimism, his refusal to explore counter-discourses to the *constat*, and his irony that refuses to comment on its own construction through a severing of the realist illusion, all in fact make him complicit with the very forces of cultural commodification that flatten out and undermine claims to truth.

Arcand's "solution" in *Jésus de Montréal* is to return to the main origin of Western and Quebec society's "truth" and confront it with the contemporary age. The structure of the film is transformative as well as diagnostic. An actor, Daniel (Lothaire Bluteau), is recruited by Father Leclerc (Gilles Pelletier) to take over the annual open-air performance on Mont-Royal of the Passion of Christ. He surrounds himself with his team: Martin (Rémy Girard), who is dubbing porn movies; René (Robert Lepage), recruited at the planetarium where he is narrating the "big bang" theory of the universe's origin; Constance (Johanne-Marie Tremblay), who is having an affair with Leclerc; and Mireille (Catherine Wilkening), who is rescued from degrading performances for the advertising industry. The actors' production meets with critical and public success, but its radical interpretation of the Gospels based on the latest archaeological evidence and "Christology" (Christ's "resurrection" is but a misrecognition some years later by his followers of someone resembling him) brings it into conflict with Leclerc and the church authorities. In a scuffle during one production, Daniel suffers a head injury after his cross falls to the ground, and eventually dies, his organs being used to bring sight and life to patients around the world.

As this *dénouement* illustrates, the film reworks the Gospels not only in the *mise en abyme* of the actors' production, but through the contemporary diegesis, in which many Biblical scenes are echoed. One of Mireille's shoots for a perfume ad has her walking on water. Daniel's anger has him wrecking one of her auditions, recalling Christ's fury at the money-changers in the Temple: the destruction of the electronic equipment, cables and all, evokes the whips and floggings before the crucifixion. Daniel is judged for his crime by a Pontius Pilate figure played by Arcand himself. An opportunistic lawyer, Cardinal (Yves Jacques), tempts Daniel like the devil, promising successful conquest of the city and its media. Daniel's actor friend, Pascal Berger (Cédric Noël), who is first seen performing in an adaptation of Dostoyevsky's *The Brothers Karamazov* (which, of course, explores the moral consequences of a non-existent God), ends up being the "face" of a new advertising campaign, his "head" symbolically severed like St John the Baptist's and adorning the corridors of the Metro in which Daniel utters his final delirium.[17]

The relationship between the film and play-within-the-film enables Arcand to rework his technique of parallel editing. The *longue durée* (what can we do with a Christian legacy which can neither be believed nor exorcized) is effectively cast into new, more prosaic but still meaningful moulds. At the same time, a whole history of Quebec is also encapsulated, its rapid entry into modernity tracked, from the disillusioned and pragmatic priest through to yet another scene in the Metro, that contemporary space of speed, urban crowds, and consumerism now taking on the role of underground antechamber to death. As with *Le Déclin*, the film's success can partly be explained in the fruitful relationship it constructs between particular and universal, or, as I would prefer to call it, with "world," or "geopolitical," an attempt to refashion national allegory into a conceptual instrument for grasping our new being-in-the-world.[18]

However, there are limits to Arcand's approach. Two evaluations are possible here. On the one hand, *Jésus de Montréal* grasps the postmodern recycling of history and stories, and the flattening out of signifiers this entails, and therefore reacts with a subtle play of grounding (the story of the Passion) and recasting which enables at least an ethical or even aesthetic purchase on contemporary life and a start at constructing positivities to counter the nihilism and despair of the characters of *Le Déclin*. (Thus the decline of a collective project produces the disastrous state of the health service: Daniel is eventually taken to an anglophone Jewish hospital, and dies in English.) The audiovisual media can be so ruthlessly and hilariously satirized, because Arcand has created a new myth permitting a standpoint from which they can be judged. On the other hand, while the film joyfully proclaims again a belief in the world, Arcand seems unable to articulate, or to be able to account for, the emergence of anything new. The end of the film is a reworking of an old myth, not an exploration of new cultural hybridities or ways of being. His next film, *Love and Human Remains* (1993), was his first in English and his first not based on his own screenplay (it was adapted from the Brad Fraser play, *Unidentified Human Remains and the True Nature of Love*). The familiar "particular" side of his dialectic is lost, the film being located in a kind of "no-place" (non-linguistically-marked corners of Montreal). The protagonists are like characters in *Le Déclin*, but in their twenties.[19]

Jésus de Montréal is one of a group of films made at the end of the 1980s which make use of the natural sciences to comment on the contemporary unfixing of personal identity, belief, and community. In *Portion d'éternité* (Robert Favreau, 1989), the struggle of a married couple to have children is juxtaposed with a documentary-like investigation of the abuses and possibilities of embryo research. In a rather more complex movie, Jacques Leduc's *Trois pommes à côté du sommeil* of 1988, the scientist Hubert Reeves plays himself and is the nearest to a father-figure for the unnamed *Lui* (Normand Chouinard). The film takes place during one day, the latter's fortieth birthday. The events of that day (lunch with former lover and nationalist militant Madeleine [Paule Baillargeon], floral tribute at the lake in which a companion had drowned twenty years previously, a surprise dinner party with friends) are punctuated with numerous flashbacks of former lovers, conversations with Reeves in the forest, and the funeral of René Lévesque in 1987. The film's form thus succeeds in interpenetrating the personal and political, individual and collective: the films of Leduc (b. 1941), a former contributor to *Objectif*, have mostly been documentaries, but tend to articulate, as well as realism, the "poetic" and the "everyday" (*Trois pommes* was only his third fictional work, after *On est loin du soleil*, 1970, and *Tendresse ordinaire*, 1973). However, his procedure risks allegorizing *Lui*, who currently has no fixed abode, keeps all his possessions in his car, and whose life is blank and purposeless apart from the freelance articles he writes vulgarizing science. Meaning is located in nature and the naturalistic: the "apples" of the title refer to the three former lovers, and metaphorically to discord, but especially to Robert Frost and the poem "After Apple-Picking" (1914), with the trope of the continuities between landscape and human existence ("I am over-tired of the great harvest I myself desired").[20] In *Trois pommes à côté du sommeil*, this continuity is established through the metaphor of water (which in liquid form is essential for all life, as Reeves points out) and time and the cosmos (there is a scene at the planetarium, as in *Jésus de Montréal*). Disjunctions of sound and image, notably the Polish language recited from a former lover, contribute to the richness of the film. Links are made between the fragmentary former presents of the flashbacks, and the film is partly about "feelings" that plunge into the past and even communicate with each other. However, unlike, say, in the films of Alain Resnais, "psychology" is not surpassed in favour of suprapersonal memories, sentiments, histories. Even though he is located in a broad historical and geographical canvas, there is a "centre" to the film. Even if *Lui* is a void, he is a void aching to be filled, missing not being so. *Lui* seems to promise not the new and different, but repetition (the final coupling in the motel). Through its formal play, the film partly revels in the "in-betweenness" of not only Quebec (the "pays de passage/transitory country" because of the St Lawrence) but also human life, and it and its main protagonist are unwilling fully to embrace the minor over the molar.

As well as these diagnostic films, there are the films of pastiche. As Jameson argues, "pastiche" must be distinguished from "parody" because it is "blank," a neutral imitation that comes from nowhere, is disengaged, that simply quotes.[21] However, pastiche is not a very developed approach in Quebec cinema, for reasons to do with cinema history and insertion into the global film industry. In France, 1980s films such as *Diva* and *Subway* inaugurated what might be termed a "Forum des Halles" cinema (after the central Paris shopping mall inhabited by rootless *banlieue* youth) or "cinema of the look" which in ludic fashion raided past cinematic forms and broke with the sociological, vaguely committed cinema of some 1970s output. While Quebec, like France, also has an advertising and rock-video industry which might serve as a training ground for such a cinema, it does not have the same history of indigenous genre cinema to rework. (*Diva*, for example, invoked the *Fantômas* and *Judex* silent adventure serials.) On the contrary, the documentary tradition still weighs strongly, influencing films as diverse as *Portion d'éternité* and *L'Homme idéal* (the investigation through fiction and comedy of new social realities). This means that a Quebec cinema of pastiche is always inevitably bound up with the relationship with American mass culture and is swiftly swept back into that general problematic. This is well illustrated by Jacques Godbout's *IXE-13*, which never leaves the realms of parody (of the "federalist" "as des espions canadiens"), with the help of the comedy troupe Les Cyniques, famed in the 1960s for their mockery of the old clerical establishment. This chimes well with Godbout's hostility to American mass culture, but, as a member of Quebec's intellectual élite fearful of the restratification that may bring, arguably makes him miss interesting gender issues in the spy series.[22]

Selling out to Hollywood values was a criticism levelled against *Dans le ventre du dragon* (Yves Simoneau, 1989),[23] which is one of the few examples (along with *Jusqu'au coeur*, possibly, and *Le Martien de Noël*) of a Quebec science-fiction film. Made in comic mode, it tells of two Montreal leaflet deliverers, Bozo and Steve (Michel Côté and Rémy Girard), who rescue their young colleague Lou (David La Haye) from a pharmaceutical company which is using him as a human guinea pig.

While not as effective a reworking of genre cinema for Quebec as *Pouvoir intime*, it nonetheless puts its finger on some of the problematics of the so-called postmodern. Montreal working-class culture and language are combined with a science-fiction rescue narrative, but the film hovers undecidedly between a belief in "authenticity" faced with the anonymity of high-tech capitalism (Steve has an anarchist past) and the performance of that "authenticity" as pastiche and camp. This duality is reproduced in the scene in the tenement back street when the citizens quarrel in lively fashion as to whether they want circulars delivered. It is in fact the same duality that structures Michel Tremblay's portrayals of that milieu. The film combines an understanding that capitalism is accelerating out of control (Lou: "La machine est rendue trop grosse/the machine has become too big") with an abandonment of a belief in linear progress. As in *Blade Runner* (Ridley Scott, 1982), the sets (of the factory/laboratory) present a dingy mishmash, in different time-scales, of decay and high-tech. Simoneau has since left for anglophone cinema in Toronto (*Perfectly Normal*, 1990) and Hollywood (*Mother's Boys*, 1993).

In *Jésus de Montréal*, Montreal itself was cast as a generalized *Cité*, a place of sin, corruption, modest heroics, shot either from above and at a distance (the mountain) or in interiors. However, the question of the representation of Quebec's *métropole* is crucial to an understanding of the relationship between modernity and postmodernity. We saw in the previous chapter how the ethnic diversity of Montreal, its permeability to the "world," collided with its central role in the Quebec national film industry and the emphasis on its function in the construction of the "national-popular." Under the category of "the postmodern," we would expect to see an intensification of the city's fragmentation, transformations of space provoked by the contradictory pulls of globalization, and surprising remappings not conditioned by its traditional boundaries, divisions, and hierarchies.

A considerable corpus of cultural criticism exists which places the relationships between city, modernity, and cinema at the centre of its analysis. As David B. Clarke points out, "the spectacle of the cinema both drew upon and contributed to the increased pace of modern city life, whilst also helping to normalize and cathect the frantic, disadjusted rhythms of the city ... reflected and helped to mould the novel forms of social relations that developed in the crowded yet anonymous city streets; and both documented and helped to transform the social and physical space that the modern city represented."[24] However, the specificity of Quebec means that Montreal's insertion into such a narrative, and the developments that follow, is both problematic and revealing. Certainly, Montreal partook of that general Western and

North American process of rural exodus, immigration, technological change, and industrial/urban development at the turn of the century, with a new leisure industry such as the cinema taking its place within the new dispositions of capital flow, urban space, and audience patterns, as well as constructing, through shock, montage, and its "virtual presence," the kinds of subjectivity appropriate to the new culture. Walter Benjamin wrote: "Technology has subjected the human sensorium to a complex kind of training. There came a day when a new and urgent need for stimuli was met by the film. In a film, perception in the form of shocks was established as a formal principle."[25] Thus the first film screening in Canada took place in Montreal in June 1896; by 1912 the city had seventy cinemas attracting a quarter of the city's population on Sundays. Indeed, although this Sunday cinema-going was virulently opposed by the Catholic hierarchy, Montreal remained for the first decades of the century the only North American city where it took place.[26]

And yet Montreal's position within Quebec/Canada meant that a special inflection was given to the notions of "strangeness" that accompanied modernity. According to this argument, the "intimately related, lived totality"[27] of traditional society was replaced by an abstract space of physical proximity and social distance, so that in the modern city strangers experienced a world populated by strangers. It thus seems odd that a "modernist" depiction of Montreal is so rare in Quebec culture and cinema. *Le Sourd dans la ville* is an exception, but here it is no accident that the "alienation" is very specifically lived by a bourgeois middle-aged woman who has lost the moorings tying her to a conventional and functional mapping of the city and is using high-cultural references to grasp her new reality. We saw how the extraordinary opening of *Being at Home with Claude* was obliged to lay its alienation on thick in order to support its romantic narrative and to counteract the urban postmodern pleasures it had represented. However, quite apart from the clerical-nationalist hegemony and the subordination of high culture to France at the turn of the century, there lies a political reality. For the "French-Canadians" of the rural exodus just as for the immigrants (as in *La Sarrasine*), Montreal was literally "strange," dominated as it was by the large Anglo population, by Anglo capitalism, and by the English language. In other words, the internalization of the "strangeness" of modernity could at least in part be avoided through displacement onto the Other, and all sorts of appropriations and resistances could be constructed in order to perpetuate a notion of "home": these could take a conservative form such as the role of the church, but could also be found in the formation of francophone communities, their outside decks, landings, and courtyards reproducing the communality of village life. Whereas Kafka depicted a Prague at whose centre lay the castle, centre of a system of power and surveillance in which his heroes were both implicated and estranged, and whereas Joyce figured a Dublin both peripheral and central within the British imperial system, for the francophone *Montréalais* a (provisional) notion of autonomy, of "home," could persist. The city thus intensifies, and gives a national-identity twist to, Kevin Robins's observation of the "productive tension" that has been at the heart of urban development, "the city as container and the city as flow," settlement and movement, the bounded and the boundless.[28]

Montreal is at the heart of the national-allegorical tension in Quebec culture, for the "modernizing" force of cinema was always already implicated in that relationship between identity and the flows which would undo it: until the 1940s, "the cinema" meant either Hollywood films in English (the vast majority) or films from France. (This is why the films of the 1960s, from *À tout prendre* onwards, are so crucial in the reappropriation of Montreal for a specifically francophone modernizing vision that combines the city and the cinematic.) The election of the first PQ government in 1976 and with it the enactment of language laws making French the language of work and of commercial signage marked the end of a narrative pitting the "strangeness" of Anglo culture against the francophone "home." This was replaced by a new emphasis on the ethnic minorities as either "strange" or as sources of new hybrid identities. However, Montreal as "home" was, typically for Quebec culture, always relational, in transformation, becoming something else. Not only were there rival and competing models for modernization and urban development, namely American and French, but the ambivalences of the construction of "home" itself could not be suppressed. These ambivalences are at the heart of Michel Tremblay's work, in which notions of "home" and "identity" (Germaine Lauzon or Hosanna in *Il était une fois dans l'est*) coexist precariously with alienation and inauthenticity, to the point of overcoming that binary opposition in a rather postmodern way: everything becomes a play of ungrounded signifiers, performances, provisional masquerades.

If the postmodern marks "the triumph of flow,"[29] in which places no longer have boundaries but "can be imagined as articulated movements in networks of social relations and understandings,"[30] and public space is now forever marked by its *non*-coincidence with "what you are," then what are the implications for Quebec cultural identity and cinematic representations of Montreal? On the one hand, this non-coincidence is not new: Montreal as colonized space is present even in the appropriations of 1960s cinema (one thinks of the English signs prominent in scenes in *Il ne faut pas mourir pour ça*). The variation on this is its masquerade, outside Quebec cinema, as New York, Paris, even Vienna (*Hotel New Hampshire*, dir. Tony Richardson, 1984) or as futuristic "no-place" (Robert Altman's use of the old Expo '67 site for *Quintet*, 1979). As we have seen, for a European art movie director "exiled" in Montreal and working within the Quebec film industry, the city can in turn become a Deleuzean "any-space-whatever" accompanying the wanderings, disintegrations, and reconstructions of her heroes (Pierre's photography of the city in Pool's *À corps perdu*).

On the other hand, certain "city films" of the 1990s have taken on board and attempted to negotiate the new state of affairs, which both unbalances that old tension between place and space, container and flow, and creates new possibilities as well as exclusions. The portmanteau film made for Montreal's 350th anniversary, *Montréal vu par* (1992), can be seen to inaugurate this sequence. All six short films are in fact very oblique, either figuring the city as elsewhere, or, in their narratives of encounters and combinations, favouring the transversal over the panoptic, the *parcours* over the *carte*. (In Michel de Certeau's work on everyday life, the *parcours* is associated with "the microbe-like, singular and plural practices which an urbanistic system [associated with the *carte*] was supposed to administer or suppress, but which have outlived its decay.")[31]

The most conventional film is in a sense Jacques Leduc's *La Toile du temps*, which uses theatrical devices such as back projection to trace the story of a portrait of Jacques Viger (Montreal's first mayor, played by Jean-Louis Millette) from 1850 through various facets of the city's social history, until in 1992 its blanked-out canvas serves as a prop for the very film we have been watching. The painting's circulation does, however, recall the fantastic itinerary in Raul Ruiz's *L'Hypothèse du tableau volé* (1978). In Denys Arcand's *Vue d'ailleurs*, the *mondanités* of a Quebec diplomat's reception somewhere in Central America, with the accompanying comic chit-chat misapprehensions of Montreal, are hijacked, even, in the situationists' sense, *détournées*, by a wife's recollection of a passionate sexual encounter with an unnamed man of Amerindian appearance in the city in 1963. The lengthy flashback inserts this event, contradictorily, in the international flows in which the city is located (both protagonists were delegates at an international conference), its linguistic boundaries (they are staying in Westmount), and its frontline nationalist struggle (the climactic FLQ bomb in a letterbox), as well as in the narrator's imagination and memory-image. In Michel Brault's *La Dernière Partie*, space is dramatically gendered. A wife (Hélène Loiselle) announces to her husband (Jean Mathieu) that she is leaving him, this in the recesses of the Forum, where he has dragged her to the Saturday night hockey match. The yellows and browns of the home where she has prepared her departure give way to the grey space of the stadium, a liminal place of transition in a space overwhelmingly coded as masculine, dotted with television screens displaying the match which distract the husband even at this time. In the end, he is swallowed up by the departing crowd and wakes up alone at home in front of the television. The codifications of space are seen no longer to be operating, as this desperate but now empowered middle-aged woman chooses to pitch herself into displacement and the abandonment of "home."

Léa Pool's *Rispondetemi* relates inner and outer worlds, as a young woman, victim of a car accident with her female lover, is transported by ambulance to hospital. The flashbacks of her past life are juxtaposed with the view of the city from a moving horizontal position, as she "sees" through the ambulance roof, underlining cinema's vocation as here, literally, the vehicle of a mobility that is virtual rather than actual, and creating a non-place and time which blurs and renders problematic both the notions of destination (will the hospital be reached and does it matter?) and speed (the slowed-down temporality of her experience). That moving film image is at opposite poles from the panopticism that characterizes, say, the Canadian tradition of envisioning an east-west line from which to survey the country (CBC/SRC's animated close-down sequence of a gull's flight from the Pacific to the Atlantic).

The other two films are by English-Canadian directors, and their re-enchantment of the city via the mediations of representation, distance and information is foregrounded in signs and language. In what is almost a film without dialogue, Atom Egoyan's *En passant* casts Maury Chakin as a silent visitor to Montreal attending a snazzy conference of obscure purpose. He is bombarded with the pictographs of contemporary urban life, at the airport and hotel, in the street. Taking a commented walking tour of the city by Walkman, his ordered itinerary shifts into the fantastic, as the voice-over begins to address him directly, leading him through the partly troubling, partly arousing crowd to an encounter with the customs inspector at the airport (Arsinée Khanjian) who collects the baggage labels of travellers and whose work and domestic routines have been represented in parallel to his: a classic narrative transformation of *carte* into *parcours*. This process is taken further in Patricia Rozema's *Desperanto*, in which Sheila McCarthy reprises her role as a cute, organizationally challenged woman from the director's debut feature *I've Heard the Mermaids Singing* (1987), this time playing Ann Stewart, a Toronto housewife holidaying in Montreal. She, too, visits the tourist sites, in a tourist bus. Enticed by the sexual licence of *Le Déclin de l'empire américain*, which she re-views in her hotel room, she decides to make the most of her last night, dresses in a gauche

white dress, and crashes a "sophisticated" francophone party. Her unsuccessful attempts at picking up a man lead to misunderstandings, a
squashed strawberry which makes her seem to be menstruating or experiencing some haemorrhage, and a fainting which produces the
dream/fantasy sequence that closes the film. Her virtual self is also in
white but has a fairy queen high collar; she is able to stop time with a
remote control in order to flick through her dictionary to translate
conversations; the English subtitles become part of the diegesis as she
stands between them and the cinema spectator, reading them and
appropriating them physically. Even when midnight strikes and the
Cinderella fantasy ends, Ann finds herself tended to by ambulance personnel Denys Arcand and Geneviève Rioux, whom she recognizes from
Le Déclin and who waft her away to a euphoric dance in the air above
Montreal.

All but one film places a female protagonist at or near the centre.
This is significant because, for example, that central modernist figure
of the *flâneur*, that detached wanderer playfully and transversally
enthralled by the stimuli, the *virtuality*, of the city, has been so overwhelmingly coded as masculine,[32] and its feminization, if that is the
case, would raise important questions for the relationship between
modernity and postmodernity. The gendered nature of urban space
goes to the heart of debates about modernity and its development into
the contemporary postmodern. Against Janet Wolff, Elizabeth Wilson
has argued that the figure of the *flâneur*, rather than a bastion of male
privilege, marked a crisis of masculinity, "a shifting projection of angst
rather than a solid embodiment of male bourgeois power."[33] This conglomeration of pleasure ("the *flâneur* appears as the ultimate ironic,
detached observer, skimming across the surface of the city and tasting
all its pleasures with curiosity and interest"),[34] shopping, and anxiety
(because unfixed and nostalgic) has ultimately transmuted itself into
new forms which are consistent with the generalized fragmentation
and "sensations without consequence"[35] of contemporary consumer
society, what David Clarke calls "the *systemic* appropriation of the
flâneur's originally *anti-systemic* existence."[36]

Montreal can currently be seen as not only a generalized example of
that curious representation in the urban scene of a *simultaneous* utopia
and dystopia, but also as a particular space in which European nostalgia, melancholy, and alienation coexist with a North American utopianism bound up with the pluralism of consumer lifestyles. The prime
emblems for these ambivalences are women and youth, who are precisely the main protagonists of *Eldorado* (Binamé, 1995), *Cosmos* (Jennifer Alleyn, Manon Briand, Marie-Julie Dallaire, Arto Paragamian,
André Turpin, Denis Villeneuve, 1996), and *2 Secondes* (Briand, 1998).

This inflection is not surprising, given the ambivalences both "home" and "outside" or "the street" acquire for women in terms of their assessment of confinement and freedom, safety, and danger; and for "youth" who, in the mobile churning of their lifestyle, are also an embodiment (and object) of anxiety in Quebec society, in that this current generation is bearing the full brunt of contemporary instabilities and unfixings (including unemployment or precarious employment) that the baby-boomer generation growing up under Fordism and the Quiet Revolution lacked. All three films also pivot round an emblem of movement.

Eldorado renews to an extent the tradition of *le direct* in Quebec cinema, in its relatively small budget ($1.5 million), use of natural decor and lighting, improvisational dialogues, and the ambition to capture *sur le vif* the lives of its young urban protagonists. On the other hand, it relies a lot on a carefully composed soundtrack of urban noise and rock music and on montage. Pascale Bussières, twelve years on from *Sonatine*, plays the pivotal figure of Rita, a roller-blading drug-taking marginal still mourning the death of a friend in a suicide pact she survived. She connects briefly with the lives of Henriette (Pascale Montpetit: this casting reunites the star duo from the phenomenally successful *téleroman, Blanche*, which provides a past, authenticating and founding narrative for Quebec[37]), a lonely neurotic attending psychotherapy, and with Roxan (Isabel Richer), a generous benefactor, daughter of bourgeois, whose apartment is wrecked by Rita's drug suppliers. Henriette's neighbour, who she comes on to ungraciously and unsuccessfully in the supermarket is Lloyd (James Hyndman), a radio shockjock who has a brief sexual encounter in the toilets of the post-punk bar Les Foufounes électriques with the barmaid Loulou (Macha Limonchik), whose live-in relationship with Marc (Robert Brouillette), an employee at the Société des alcools du Québec, is in difficulty.

The film, however, leans towards a modernist dystopia rather than a postmodern utopia, and its sexual politics are ultimately rather conventional, despite or because of the character of Rita, mobile but nostalgic. Rita at one point hijacks Lloyd's car to break into an open-air swimming pool at night, this, and her involvement with drugselling, emblematic of that destabilizing "agoraphobic space" of the city, tempting "the individual who staggers across it to do anything and everything."[38] However, it is clear that, while this urban society lacks roadmaps, the characters, bereft of "love," are still looking back for some, in particular those that lead to heterosexual couple formation. The frequent shots of aerial telephone lines connote these attempts to connect, to remap the film sentimentally. Astonishingly for a film purporting to be a portrait of contemporary Montreal, there are no characters who are gay or members of ethnic minorities. The comparison with Almodóvar's Madrid is telling. In films like *Law of Desire* (1987), the Madrid of the post-Franco *movida* is remythologized into a new set of social and sexual realignments which rework the previous order (the family, Catholicism, representatives of authority such as the police) to create a new urban utopia of desire.[39] The reasons for the absence of such motifs in recent Quebec urban cinema are various: the "transition" from authoritarian, isolationist Catholicism in Quebec took place earlier, under the signs of modernity rather than postmodernity, and the national question impelled, as we have seen, a certain degree of homophobia because Quebec phallic plenitude had never been achieved, according to the *Parti pris* theorists; and the economic situation in the late 1980s/early 1990s in the two countries is very different, with an economic boom in Spain (despite consistently high unemployment, but Almodóvar is interested in myth not social realism) providing at least a sense of social mobility which accompanies the physical movement of Almodóvar's cinema. In contrast, the mobility of Rita and other characters in *Eldorado* is, if anything, downward both financially and emotionally, with forever the risk of being barred from the urban spectacle.

Cosmos, a showcase for young directors put together by Roger Frappier at Max Films, does, however, feature ethnicity (the eponymous Greek taxi driver who links the segments, his black colleague who helps him chase his stolen cab and waxes philosophic about the origins of cities in the last sequence, *Cosmos et Agriculture*, directed by Arto Paragamian). It also carries the fragmentation of the previous film further, its portmanteau fabrication reinforcing the idea of the city as an assemblage of distinct and separate subjects. This structure recalls Walter Benjamin's notion of the metropolis as labyrinth, in which "we observe bits of the 'stories' men and women carry with them, but never learn their conclusions; life ceases to form itself into epic or narrative, becoming instead a short story, dreamlike, insubstantial or ambiguous."[40] The film produces, within the twenty-four-hour unity of time, notions of simultaneity that are reminiscent of the role of the novel and newspaper in Benedict Anderson's account of nation-building, but with no overall viewpoint that would allow a position of mastery, and any collective identity that emerges is both provisional and fading. Cosmos himself is a conduit in the literal and figurative senses, the prime connector of this rhizomatic network of relations: an unconsummated sexual re-encounter (André Turpin's *Jules et Fanny*); "transversal" friendships between a woman and a gay man nervous about obtaining the result of his HIV test (Manon Briand's *Boost*); a romance between a nineteen-year-old budding actress and a wise elderly gentleman (Jennifer Alleyn's *Aurore et Crépuscule*); the rapid montage of a nervous young film director bombarded with screen images as he faces an interview and a compulsory make-over for an internet channel (Denis Villeneuve's *Le Technétium*); and, lurking in the city's labyrinthine depths (echoed in Turpin's hotel corridors), the serial killer, the *M* or Minotaur, first glimpsed and tracked as one of the anonymous crowd in the Metro, the camera alighting on him as if arbitrarily, as less coded as "strange" than another (a cameo from André Forcier), and then following him to his next victim (Marie-Julie Dallaire's *L'Individu*).

Manon Briand's first feature after her contribution to *Cosmos*, *2 Secondes*, casts Charlotte Laurier as Laurie, a champion cyclist who hesitates at the start of a race, loses, and returns to Montreal to be a bicycle courier. The regulations of this work create a *carte* for the city which Laurie sidesteps to create her own *parcours* both in space and in time. Her brother is a theoretical physicist interested in relativity; her mother has Alzheimer's and has regressed to childhood; her substitute father-figure is an eccentric Italian bicycle-repair man (Dino Tavarone) whose shop is almost in a time warp outside history and commerce but whose body bears the marks of his long professional cycling career. The woman photographer with whom Laurie eventually forms a sexual relationship is the double of the repair man's dream girl, whom he left behind to win a race in France decades ago, in a conceit that echoes the account of Einstein and differential aging given by the brother. Above all, the film sets up the bicycle as a supremely cinematic machine, in its echo of the cinematic apparatus, its movement, and the rapid, flickering vision of the city it provides.

If the contemporary cultural epoch is to be understood as distinctly postmodern, then it is necessary to ask in what ways the new emphasis on space, the perpetual present, and the loss of historical grand narratives might be transforming cinema's representation of memory and the past. The question is particularly moot for Quebec cinema, which needs to retain a sense of the past if it is to conserve the distinctiveness of its own national-allegorical tension. But what past and what kind of relationship with identity? The work of Robert Lepage (b. 1957) is a response to these questions. Two films are adapted from his work in the theatre. *Le Polygraphe* (1996) questions the nature of truth via the motif of the lie detector, uses Hitchcockian devices to depict a murder mystery, and makes links with the political divisions of Germany (Peter Stormare as a pathologist former refugee from the East). *Nô* (1998), an adaptation of one of *The Seven Streams of the River Ota*, Lepage's epic investigation of the post-war era which uses the bombing of Hiroshima as its starting-point, juxtaposes the (farcical, in all senses) visit of a

Quebec theatre troupe to the World's Fair in Osaka and the misadventures of a group of amateur revolutionaries in Montreal in October 1970. (October as "nothing," as "zero," if we recall the arguments of chapter 2: the film's title is a reference both to Japanese theatre and to the 1980 referendum vote featured in a coda.) However, Lepage's cinematic reputation rests for the moment on his first film.

The closing scene of *Le Confessionnal* (1995) has Pierre Lamontagne (Lothaire Bluteau) carrying a child on his shoulders as they walk precariously along the parapet of the Pont de Québec, the steel-girder bridge across the St Lawrence at Quebec City. The child is the product of the liaison of his adoptive brother Marc (Patrick Goyette), a prostitute, and a striptease artist, Manon (Anne-Marie Cadieux), and is the third generation of a family afflicted by diabetes. It is the realization of the hereditary nature of this disease that has revealed the central enigma of the film, the identity of Marc's father. His mother, Rachel (Suzanne Clément), had given birth to this illegitimate child in 1953 at the age of sixteen and then committed suicide by throwing herself off the same bridge. In the film's two time frames of 1952 and 1989, suspicion had fallen on the priest, Massicotte (Normand Daneau), who had then lost his position and by 1989 become a diplomat/politician (Jean-Louis Millette) and the lover/client of Marc. True paternity lay with Pierre's recently deceased father, Paul-Émile Lamontagne (François Papineau), who had had sex with Rachel while she lived in the family home they shared with his wife and her sister Françoise (Marie Gignac).

Since Lepage's film is all about time (and space), it has seemed appropriate to summarize its *fabula* via the kind of distortions of chronological time (beginning at the end) that characterize its *syuzhet* (discourse). The final scene also encapsulates some of the film's main preoccupations. The Pont de Québec has an originary and foundational connotation, since it is at this point where the river narrows enough for this first bridge to be constructed, one of the reasons (as well as its defensible site) that it became the heart of the new French settlement in 1608 (even the word in Algonquin means "where the river narrows"). (Significantly, the other bridge here bears the name of another "origin" – if we recall the arguments of chapter 2 – the Pont Pierre-Laporte). The film purports also to have something to say about Quebec nationhood and its inscriptions in time and space. The relationship between "now" and "then" takes place across the caesura of the Quiet Revolution, with the priest-ridden, pious, but hypocritical society of the early 1950s replaced by the commercialism, hedonism, and moral fragmentation of the 1980s and 1990s. This, and economic and cultural globalization, bring Pierre back from studying art in

China, send Marc and Massicotte on business to Japan, and confront the characters with television (news) images that are the outcome of the development Pierre notes in his first voice-over: 1952 as the year of the start of television in Quebec, as well as Hitchcock's arrival in the city to film *I Confess* (but also the re-election of Maurice Duplessis as premier). The bridge functions, too, as a space of transition and as an opening out from the closed, indeed walled city (a feature put to use in *Le Polygraphe*), a line linking the film's enclosed, archaic spaces (especially the Lamontagne family kitchen, the dysfunctional relations it stages echoing but subverting the agreeable ambivalent populism of les Plouffe) with the tawdry modernity of the suburban strip-club and beyond it a world of difference (Japan, the shot of the bullet train below Mount Fuji). Quebec City is also "not Montreal." Not really a city of immigration, nor a "North American" city in terms of capital flows, nor a city structured by a business or cultural élite, it provides a "local" space connecting with "the world" by leapfrogging over its larger and more cosmopolitan counterpart. Distinctively, Lepage's whole (theatrical) career summarizes and dramatizes a continuum traced between these spaces of contraction and expansion,[41] not least the place of Oriental, mainly Japanese culture in his theatre but also in *Le Confessionnal*, as, for example, the ritual and detail of Massicotte's game of chess with glasses of alcohol which he uses to confront Pierre.

The bridge, metonymically, also summarizes all the connotations of "Quebec City" in the film, its temporal but also spatial meaning as city of secrets and mystery, an official and tourist city where menace lies beneath, a city of power, here represented as entirely in the hands of older men, in which younger or female denizens (and not only in 1952) struggle to find their place. (The huge young and student population of the contemporary city is entirely absent from the film.) As we have noted, the vast majority of Quebec films have been set either in Montreal or in rural areas. The relatively rare representation of Quebec City in film, apart from *Les Plouffe*, has tended also to emphasize menace (Yves Simoneau's 1982 film, *Les Yeux rouges ou les vérités accidentelles*, about a murderer of women) or conspiracy (*Liste noire*). The *hommages* in the film to Hitchcock, including his Gothic representations of, among other sites, the Chateau Frontenac (distorted angle shot of its tower from *I Confess*, its staircase shot from above as in the final scene of *Vertigo*), are dovetailed into this approach, as are the preponderance of night shots in those scenes away from the family home.

The lattice of girders had also formed part of a series of images in the film connoting the confessional itself, used in the Hitchcock extract and by the two sisters in 1952, reflected in the sunroof of Massicotte's car, referred to in the netting of the gay sauna in which Pierre had first sought out Marc after the father's funeral, and metaphorized in the cubicles of the Charny strip joint. Clearly, the image underlines the secularization of Quebec since the 1950s, but its reverberations are more profound. As Michel Foucault has argued, the Catholic confession was the prototype of the modern construction of the subject. With the increase in the frequency and in the detail of the confession decided by the Counter-Reformation and practised from the seventeenth century onwards, the body and its multiple erotic workings were put into discourse: "The confession was, and still remains, the general standard governing the production of the true discourse on sex."[42] By the nineteenth and twentieth centuries, this practice became disseminated in pedagogy, law, medicine, autobiography, and finally science. The invention of "sexuality" is the way in which the workings of power impose a grid of interpretation, demarcations of licit and illicit, normal and abnormal, on the heterogeneous possibilities of the body. In *Le Confessionnal*, the strictly Catholic confessions (the scene from *I Confess*, Rachel confessing her suicidal thoughts, Françoise her miscarriage) have given way to the sexual spaces of sauna and strip joint, but all raise the fundamental question of truth and identity. Not only "who am I?" and "what is the truth?" with regard to the central enigma of the film, but a more fundamental problematization of the grounds on which we can both ask these questions and receive a remotely satisfactory response in terms of any solidity, fixity, or finality. This is the case for both personal and collective (Quebec) identity.

It is hardly surprising, then, that Pierre walks a tightrope at the end, indeed a tightrope between life and death, an ending as open as that of *The Birds*, as Lepage argues.[43] This spectator prefers to see the life-affirming continuity in the transversal, transgenerational post-nuclear family which is being created. After all, Pierre promises that they are nearly "home": the Charny motel, perhaps, or is it perpetually, not only a transitional space, but the tightrope? The child, of course, more than anything brings the notion of time to centre stage: "Dans la ville où je suis né, le passé porte le présent comme un enfant sur ses épaules/in the city in which I was born, the past carries the present like a child on its shoulders." I wish to link this idea of "dancing on the edge" with some of the ideas about time, and techniques for representing it, to be found in *Le Confessionnal*. For it is also a film that deploys both the "movement-image" and the "time-image."

To recapitulate: following Bergson, Deleuze emphasizes the fact that past, present, and future are not separate events that can be isolated as within the spatial divisions of a clock face. Time in fact has two arrows, one that perpetually moves into the future ("the present which passes"), and one that drops away into the past ("the preserved past"). What we call "the present" always consists of an actual image and its contemporary past: "Since the past is constituted not after the present that it was but at the same time, time has to split itself in two at each moment as present and past, which differ from each other in nature, or, what amounts to the same thing, it has to split the present in two heterogeneous directions, one of which is launched towards the future while the other falls into the past."[44] One key procedure in *Le Confessionnal* is to create between past and present a relationship of exchange in which they are both distinct and indiscernible. For Lepage, this is profoundly cinematic, or rather is fertile ground for the hybrid practices of both his cinematic and theatrical work. Consistent with the manipulations of theatrical space, montage in Lepage's cinema can be organized within the image or shot itself, the favoured technique in *Le Confessionnal* being that inspired by Alain Resnais, namely, the tracking shot. The camera tracks from right to left, for example, in the early scene at the father's funeral in 1989, along the (empty) church pews (also a quotation from early in *Mon oncle Antoine*) to reach the (packed) congregation of 1952, or from the mother's miscarriage in the bathroom in 1952 to Pierre reorganizing the flat in 1989. All are examples of the "irrational cut" and "aberrant movement" which, for Deleuze, marks a cinema emancipating itself from the present and affording a direct representation of time. Moreover, *Le Confessionnal* provides further examples of the "virtual image" constantly accompanying the "actual image," in what Deleuze analyses in terms of a crystal, a "bifacial" image with interchangeable facets: "The two related terms differ in nature, and yet 'run after each other,' refer to each other, reflect each other, without it being possible to say which is first, and tend *ultimately* to become confused by slipping into the same point of indiscernibility."[45] This "crystal-image" can be represented by the tiniest circuit of exchange, those contracted moments of the film which are a crucial counterweight to the vast, dilated circuits that take it beyond the boundaries of the city and to and from the Far East. As well as through the tracking shot, these are achieved through editing: red going down the plughole immediately after a 1952 scene in which Rachel gazes at a razor turns out to be Pierre rinsing his paintbrush in 1989, but it also announces the future suicide of Marc; a girl auditioning for a part in *I Confess* in 1952 in fact reads the news of the massacre at Tian an men Square recounted in the television image that follows. Cause and effect between past, present, and future begin to break down. The film-within-the-film also, of course, plays a crucial role in establishing the mirrorings and reflections characteristic of the crystal-image.

Whereas Deleuze is reticent about ascribing a greater "truth" to the time-image over the movement-image,[46] it is the case that the ways of looking implied by the former allow us to cut through habitual and automatic, indeed hegemonic, modes of perception. Drawing on Bergson's distinction, Deleuze sees the movement-image as dependent on a perception based on use and which remains in the same plane, whereas the time-image is dependent on a perception which is "attentive": "My movements – which are more subtle and of another kind – revert to the object, return to the object, so as to emphasize certain contours and to take 'a few characteristic features' from it."[47] The same object thus passes through different planes. Whereas in movement-image cinema the emphasis is on a pragmatic vision which accepts anything bound up in the system of actions and reactions, in time-image cinema "the purely optical and sound situation gives rise to a seeing function, at once fantasy and report, criticism and compassion."[48] better able to grasp the mutations and transformations of the world. Lothaire Bluteau's performance as Pierre combines passivity and transformation: he is not a political actor (there is no reaction to the news from China despite his recent trip there) but one who sees and changes. Moreover, the version of masculinity he embodies is a feminized, fallible, and chastened one, far from notions of phallic mastery with its "denial of embodiedness, of time and of mortality,"[49] indeed quite the contrary.

In recent discussions of cinema and memory, commentators have emphasized the uses of Walter Benjamin for injecting a political dimension. In an article examining *Cinema Paradiso* (Tornatore, 1988) and *The Long Day Closes* (Davies, 1992) from the points of view of feminism and postmodernism, Susannah Radstone reads Benjamin's concept of *Erfrahrung*, that lost auratic formulation of experience aligned with memory rather than the shocks of modernity, as offering a recollection of the past bound up neither with the pastiche of the nostalgia film nor with unquestioned Oedipal masculinity. Laura U. Marks notes how Benjamin criticized Bergson's denial of the historical determination of his own philosophy, which was a reaction after all to "the inhospitable, blinding age of big-scale industrialism,"[50] and argues that Deleuze's notion of the time-image needs Benjamin's notion of ritual, of "the association of images with history, of individual with community experience," to form part of the "shock" that peels away the accretions of habit and official memory "to create a flow of experience."[51] However, because of the 'minor' Quebec context, this family drama is always already bound up with collective memory, as the opening voice-over makes clear, and as the to-ing and fro-ing, the communication, between the characters' inner crises and the wider city emphasize. We have seen that representations of the Quebec past tend to construct not founding plenitudes but a highly problematic play of similarity and difference between "now" and "then." *Le Confessionnal* goes further, for it emphasizes the simultaneity of "now" and "then" without subordinating one to the other or reconciling them in some new "resolved" totalization. This is what marks it as more radical than a film like *Les Portes tournantes* (Mankiewicz, 1988), which similarly refers to an earlier cinematic moment (the silent films for which Céleste, played by Monique Spaziani, played the piano) but which subordinates its flashbacks to the fixed point of her voice-over narration in the late 1980s, so that the "former presents" are organized around the grandson's quest narrative which unites him with her in the final shot of the film.[52]

The ambiguous ending of *Le Confessionnal*, in contrast, shows how "we" are contemporaneous with the child, just as Quebec is swollen with its past. Deleuze uses Charles Peguy's notion of the "in-ternal" [*internel*] (as opposed to "eternal") to designate those vertical lines which bisect the horizontal succession of "presents," linking each one to the past of all the other "presents," constituting with them a single coexistence and contemporaneity.[53] Pierre and the child not only form a vertical line perched on the bridge and over the flowing but unseen river, punctuating the passage of the present, they also form one continuous human figure, adult and child: what if Pierre's dictum could be reversed, with the present carrying the past on its shoulders, the past of the adult as child? As Deleuze puts it, "people and things occupy a place in time which is incommensurable with the one they have in space."[54] All these possibilities form a potentially new conception of nation-time, not the homogeneous empty time described by Benedict Anderson, with its tendency to construct teleologies and totalizations, nor a throwback to the vertical relationship with God which enabled a simultaneity of all instants from His viewpoint, but a time that enables a revitalization and problematization of "our" perception of the present, reinstating the child, making visible the historical sedimentation, emphasizing connectedness. Both Deleuze and Lepage use the word "tectonic" to describe this kind of image and artistic practice.[55] In addition, the final scene on the bridge can be seen in terms of a bifurcation point, a term associated both with Borges (the short story "The Garden of Forking Paths") and with physics, in which a system either descends into chaos or makes an unpredictable leap forward into something more complex. The present opens on to a future that is contingent and open.

The film clearly does not propose a complete dissolution of the self or even of the collective in time, in some kind of transhistorical stream of particles of which the diabetes gene would be an example. Centres and points in the present are maintained, "sense" is made and found. *Le Confessionnal* proposes a deterritorializing *mémoire-monde*, but at the same time this process is always in relation to a "territory," namely, Quebec. This ambivalence plays itself through the dance it performs along the border between, on the one hand, a time-image, and on the other, a movement-image taken to its limit. It proposes an investigative narrative, sensory-motor activity takes place, and a "truth" is revealed, guilt and innocence established as in a Hitchcock film. (Indeed, Deleuze takes Hitchcock as his example of a film-maker who took the movement-image to its limit, creating, through "suspense" and the mental activity of the spectator's knowledge and interpretation, a "mental image" within the film that establishes the chain of its relations.) The plot of *Le Confessionnal* is a whodunnit without suspense, and to that extent un-Hitchcockian. On the other hand, it depicts characters caught in networks of relations that are not of their own making, that are put into disequilibrium by the father's death and the return of Pierre to Quebec, and that reach a new equilbrium of both loss and renewal by the end. In this way, the motif of Greek tragedy, of destiny and nemesis playing themselves out through the generations, is particularly apt. Memory is not within us as individuals; rather, we are within memory, of the nation and of the world. *Le Confessionnal* plays on that tension between destiny and choice, past sediments and an open future.

Notes

PREFACE

1 For more on the animation tradition in Quebec and Canada, see Jean, *Le Langage des lignes,* and *Pierre Hébert, L'Homme animé.*

2 Seymour, *La Nation en question,* chapter 8. Unlike Seymour, however, I would like to conserve, via the categories of major and minor, the cultural spanner in the works represented by minorities in relation to some of the claims of the "national majority" culture. Many Quebec anglophones enjoy this "minor" status in relation both to Canada *and* Quebec and to the English *and* French languages.

CHAPTER ONE

1 My emphasis.

2 Jameson, "Third-World Literature in the Era of Multinational Capitalism," 69.

3 Ahmand, "Jameson's Rhetoric of Otherness and the National Allegory," 3–25.

4 Jameson (1986), 73.

5 A note on terminology. I shall use "Québécois," as opposed to the ugly "Quebecker," to denote the population of Quebec and its distinctly francophone character. If I wish to differentiate the francophone majority from the rest of the population, I shall use "Franco-Québécois."

6 *The Dialogic Imagination,* 270–2.

7 "National cinemas can be seen as a response to the internationalization of the cinema. They are not alternatives to internationalization, they are one of its manifestations. National cinemas ... are from inception vehicles for international integration": O'Regan, *Australian National Cinema*, 50.

8 My use of this term is a general development from Jean-Pierre Jeancolas's piece, "The Inexportable: The Case of French Cinema and Radio in the 1950s," in Dyer and Vincendeau, eds., *Popular European Cinema*, 141: "I would describe such films as inexportable, because they were too insignificant and/or unintelligible to be appreciated by spectators outside a given popular cultural area, which was at once uncouth, coded and based on recognition."

9 Anderson, *Imagined Communities*, 15.

10 Dumont, *Genèse de la société québécoise.*

11 Althusser, *Lenin and Philosophy*, 127–86.

12 Taylor, "The Politics of Recognition," in *Philosophical Arguments*, 231.

13 *Reconciling the Solitudes: Essays on Canadian Federalism and Nationalism.*

14 "The Politics of Recognition," 252.

15 See, for example, *L'Actualité*, 15 May 1996, 37–48.

16 A classic example of this can be found in René Lévesque, writing in July 1976 just a few months before his first election victory: "It is quite possible that a separatist [*indépendantiste*] government will soon be elected in Québec ... its success would very simply be the result of a long and laborious national evolution. The clear outline of a nation existed in that conquered little French colony"; *René Lévesque: textes et entrevues*, 160.

17 Anderson, 31.

18 Bhabha, "DissemiNation," in *Nation and Narration*, 297.

19 In Moi, ed., *The Kristeva Reader.*

20 Hall, "Cultural Identity and Cinematic Representation," 69.

21 Ibid., 70. The latter is my emphasis.

22 Deleuze and Guattari, *A Thousand Plateaus*, 272.

23 Ibid., 37.

24 Ibid., 67.

25 Deleuze and Guattari, *Kafka: Toward a Minor Literature*, 16.

26 *A Thousand Plateaus*, 79–80.

27 Ibid., 24.

28 *A Thousand Plateaus*, 104.

29 Ibid., 134.

30 Régine Robin has argued that certain uses of the word "minor" run the risk of falling back into discourses of identity (for her, Kafka retained the nostalgia for a lost, supportive community): "À propos de la notion kafkaïenne de 'littérature mineure.'" I am emphasizing its potential for creating tension and disruption in relation to its internal and external differences.

31 Deleuze, *The Time-Image*, 217.

32 Higson, "The Concept of National Cinema," 37. My emphasis. We shall see that many commentaries on Quebec cinema fall into these homogenizing traps. Two examples out of many: "Erotic or even pornographic works correspond to the liberations of collective sexual tensions" (Baby, "Interprétation historique, interprétation sociétale: le cinéma québécois," Aumont, et al., eds., *L'Histoire du cinéma: nouvelles approches*, 166); "film can be an effective mirror of a society, and the *québécois* cinema is no exception to that principle. Through film we may observe the broadest manifestations of a culture, and its minutest icons ... material items that reflect the language and the values of a given people" (Pallister, *The Cinema of Québec*, 229).

33 *A Thousand Plateaus*, section 7.

34 For further details on this episode, see Pendakur, *Canadian Dreams and American Control*, 258–64.

35 Jean, *Le Cinéma québécois*, 40.

36 Winston, *Claiming the Real*, 6.

37 Quoted in Evans, *In the National Interest*, 17. My emphasis. Similar vocabulary is to be found in the conclusion to the executive summary of the Feature Film Advisory Board's report to the federal minister of Canadian Heritage in 1999: "Canadians deserve to see themselves, their history, their geography and their dramas interpreted in films": www.pch.gc.ca/culture/cult_ind/filmpol/pubs/advcomm/members.html.

38 See the comments by the director Fernand Dansereau: "La Leçon du direct," 80, in *Image et son*, 336.

39 Marsolais, *L'Aventure du cinéma direct*, 22.

40 Bakhtin, *Rabelais and His World*.

41 See Barthes, "The Reality Effect", in *The Rustle of Language*, 141–8.

42 Marsolais, 123. My emphasis.

43 Lever, *Le Cinéma de la révolution tranquille*, 33–4.

44 Comolli, "Le détour par le direct I," 51. Emphasis in original.

45 "Le détour par le direct II," 41.

CHAPTER TWO

1 Perraton, "Usages des techniques et représentation cinématographique dans le cinéma du vécu de Pierre Perrault," in *Du simple au double*, 101.

2 Ibid., 103.

3 *La Grande Allure*, 389.

4 Perrault, *Pour la suite du monde*, 279.

5 *Dialectic of Enlightenment*, 198.

6 Lever, *Le Cinéma de la révolution tranquille*, 29.

7 Barthes, "Rhetoric of the image," in *Image Music Text*, 32–51.

8 *Pour la suite du monde*, 156–7.

9 Rodowick, *Gilles Deleuze's Time Machine*, 16.

10 *The Time-Image*, 154–5.

11 Ibid., 150.

12 Ibid., 152.

13 "1440: The Smooth and the Striated," in *A Thousand Plateaus*, 475–500. I would differ with Perraton and Desautels's description of the New York sequence (Cahiers du Gerse, 128) as presenting the shock of the vertical. Such dramatic "striations" are partly, but problematically, prepared by the *harts* sequence.

14 *Cahiers du gerse*, 163.

15 Ibid., 180.

16 Uzel, "Nietzsche ou comment la suite du monde devint fable," in *Cahiers du Gerse*, 79.

17 See Lever, *Le Cinéma de la révolution tranquille*, 77. Lever himself shares this assessment of "the complete irrelevance [*décrochage*] to the Quebec collective real," 78.

18 *The Time-Image*, 250. "Series are the expressions of forces through which the body transforms itself and through which I becomes other ... the series takes up the body in an image where disparate spaces overlap without resolving into a totality or whole" (Rodowick, 168).

19 Arcand, "Cinéma et sexualité," *Parti pris*.

20 Leach, *Claude Jutra Filmmaker*, 86–97.

21 *Cinéastes du Québec 4: Claude Jutra*, 17.

22 See chapter 5 for a fuller discussion of sexualities and national identity. Tom Waugh underlines the fact that *A tout prendre* was made "six years before Stonewall": "Nègres blancs, tapettes et 'butch.'"

23 Brady, "*À tout prendre*: fragments du corps spéculaire."

24 Hocquenghem, *Homosexual Desire*.

25 See my discussion of *Les Nuits fauves* in Alderson and Anderson.

26 Rodowick, 155.

27 *Du Canada au Québec*, epilogue.

28 Debray, *Critique of Political Reason*, especially 169–83. See also Létourneau, *Les Années sans guide*, for an analysis of the Québécois predilection for "rebellion" rather than "revolution": "Rebellion [one figure of which is the *coureur de bois*] is marked ineluctably by incompleteness [*incomplétude*]. It is a failed, unfinished act" (118).

29 Žižek, *For They Know Not What They Do*, 105.

30 For an overview, see Lever, "Octobre 70 dans le cinéma québécois," and Véronneau, "Les Événements d'Octobre au cinéma."

31 Vallières, "*Bingo* sur une foire de confusion."

32 Véronneau (1990–91), 35.

33 *L'Aventure du cinéma direct revisitée*, 295–7.

34 Vallières, "Brault a manqué son coup."

35 Žižek, *For They Know Not What They Do*, 107. Author's emphasis.
36 "A man died. It's awful. It's horrible. We don't have the right in such a beautiful country to make films about such dirty subjects," quoted in Falardeau, *La Liberté n'est pas une marque de yogourt*, 157. For Falardeau's responses to and accounts of the obstacles he faced, see also 146–63 and the interview published as an annexe to one of the last versions of the script: *Octobre*, 177–91.
37 The actual quotation is "nécessaire et inexcusable": Camus, *L'Homme révolté*, 205.
38 "*Octobre* de Pierre Falardeau. Un film nécessaire?"
39 Bordwell, "The Art Cinema as a Mode of Film Practice."
40 *Octobre*, 190.

CHAPTER THREE

1 "La Saga du Québec moderne en images"; "Le 'Québec moderne': un chapitre du grand récit collectif des Québécois."
2 Lever, *Le Cinéma de la révolution tranquille*, 675–6.
3 Ibid., 641.
4 Marx and Engels, *The Communist Manifesto*, 83.
5 Létourneau, 1992, 69.
6 Ross, *Fast Cars, Clean Bodies: Decolonization and the Reordering of French Culture.*
7 "The Modern Prince," in Gramsci, *Selections from the Prison Notebooks*, 181–2.
8 Ibid., 276.
9 "The Study of Philosophy," ibid., 324.
10 Williams, "Base and Superstructure in Marxist Cultural Theory," in *Problems in Materialism and Culture*, 31–49.
11 Gramsci, 324.
12 Landy, *Film, Politics and Gramsci*, 30.
13 To be discussed in chapter 9.
14 See Evans, *In The National Interest*, 160.
15 Quoted in Pendakur, *Canadian Dreams and American Control*, 148.
16 Daudelin, *Vingt ans de cinéma au Canada français*, 23. My emphasis.
17 "Gilles Groulx: *Le Chat dans le sac*," 56–9.
18 Ross, *Fast Cars, Clean Bodies*, 11.
19 "Their manner of thinking is dialectical, because, living on borderlines of nations and religions, they see society in a state of flux. They conceive reality as being dynamic, not static. Those who are shut in within one society, one nation, or one religion, tend to imagine that their way of life and their way of thought have absolute and unchanging validity and that all that contradicts their standards is somehow 'unnatural,' inferior, or evil. Those, on

the other hand, who live on the borderlines of various civilizations compre-
hend more clearly the great movement and the great contradictoriness of
nature and society"; Deutscher, *The Non-Jewish Jew and Other Essays*, 35.

20 Lever, *Le Cinéma de la révolution tranquille*, 144.

21 A 1989 article suggests that the binary oppositions suggested by Groulx's
aesthetic avant-gardism and political vanguardism may not be quite so
polarized: "No national cinema can deprive itself from facing its iminority
cinema, which is an indispensable propulsive force," Beauchamp,
"Aujourd'hui Gilles Groulx," 78–81.

22 Barrowclough, *Jean Pierre Lefebvre*, 13.

23 Interview with Lefebvre, ibid., 27.

24 Quoted in Lefebvre, *Sage comme une image*, 111.

25 "Petit éloge des grandeurs et des misères de la colonie française de l'Office
national du film," 11.

26 Ibid. Also quoted in *Sage comme une image*, 80.

27 Barrowclough, *Jean Pierre Lefebvre*, 15.

28 Lever, *Le Cinéma de la révolution tranquille*, 460.

29 Benjamin, "On Some Motifs in Baudelaire," in *Illuminations*, 195.

30 Ibid., 177.

31 These processes of sanitization, reconciliation, and "balance" in the film
can be likened to the ways in which the female nude in art has been used to
frame, contain, and unify what is perceived in bourgeois and patriarchal
societies to be the threateningly messy reality of the "naked," the female
body, and femininity itself: see Nead, *The Female Nude*.

32 Quoted by Lever, *Le Cinéma de la révolution tranquille*, in a 1966 interview in
Objectif, 464.

33 *Cinéastes du Québec 2: Gille Carle*, 33.

34 Gramsci, "Problems of Marxism," in *Selections from the Prison Notebooks*, 418.

35 Marx, *Capital*, 1003. Author's emphasis.

36 Freud, "Fetishism (1927)," in *The Penguin Freud Library*, vol. 7, *On Sexuality*,
345–57; L. Mulvey, "Visual Pleasure and Narrative Cinema," in Mast and
Cohen, eds., *Film Theory and Criticism*, 803–16.

37 Perrault, *Pour la suite du monde*, 74.

38 Lever, *Le Cinéma de la révolution tranquille*, 198.

CHAPTER FOUR

1 See Simard, *Mythe et reflet de la France*.

2 Arriving by ship from Saint-Pierre-et-Miquelon, he landed at l'Anse au
Foulon (where Wolfe had landed in 1759) in Quebec City, and proceeded
through the towns and villages along the *chemin du Roy* until he made his
famous declaration from the balcony of Montreal's *hôtel de ville* on 24 July.

He thus deliberately (and, from the point of view of protocol, unusually) avoided arriving first in the capital – Ottawa – of the "nation" – Canada – to which he was making a state visit.

3 One group participating in the demonstration against the unveiling of a statue to de Gaulle in Quebec City to commemorate the thirtieth anniversary of his visit was that of the war veterans, who recalled the Canadian troops who fell for France in the twentieth century. For the debates surrounding this occasion, see *Le Devoir,* 24 July 1997, as well as Chartier, "De Gaulle n'a pas improvisé," *Le Devoir,* 22 July 1997.

4 Chartier, "De Gaulle s'était adressé aux Québécois dès 1940," *Le Devoir,* 22 July 1997.

5 Thérien, "L'Empire et les barbares."

6 Pinto, "The Atlantic Influence and the Mellowing of French Identity," in Howorth and Ross, eds., *Contemporary France: A Review of Interdisciplinary Studies,* 116–33.

7 Barrowclough, *Jean-Pierre Lefebvre,* 18.

8 See interview with Jacques Rancière, *Radical Philosophy.*

9 Lovell, "Sociology of Aesthetic Structures and Contextualism," in McQuail, ed., *Sociology of Mass Communications,* 329–49.

10 The question of the political meaning of the emerging *nouvelle vague* in 1956–62 is a complex one. Co-opted for national cultural marketing by the culture minister, André Malraux, the movement can be read as more conservative, more interested in cinematic form and in ideologies of individualism, either than the Left Bank group around Alain Resnais and Agnès Varda or the writings of the rival magazine to *Cahiers du cinéma, Positif.*

11 Vincendeau, "France 1945–65 and Hollywood: The *Policier* as International Text."

12 Quoted in Letendre, "La mise en marché du cinéma québecois: connaître le marché et la perception du public," Larouche, 51–71.

13 Bachand, "Figures de spectateurs. Approche exploratoire du public du Festival du cinéma québécois de Blois," in Larouche, *L'Aventure du cinéma,* 85–106.

14 Source: Larouche (1996), 252. Figures for the five most successful French films in Quebec in recent years are: *Indochine* (Wargnier, 1992), with 251,066 tickets sold and $1,359,888 in box-office receipts; *La Reine Margot* (Chéreau, 1994), 133,465 and $766,173; *Les Visiteurs* (Poiré, 1993), 126,671 and $695,577; *Tous les matins du monde* (Corneau, 1991), 107,048 and $574,857; and *La Crise* (Serreau, 1992), 106,446 and $560,798. Why these films should come out top would make an interesting research project in itself. A story of romance and colonialism/globalization with the major French female star; two historical costume dramas set before 1759; a modern story of domestic upheaval and masculine crisis; and a time-travel

comedy with significant implications for French national identity which does well, but far less well than in France, where it is the third-highest grossing film of all time.

15 Gauthier, "Petite histoire subjective du direct québécois vu des rivages orientaux de la mer Atlantique."

16 Bachand, "La Réception des films québécois en France."

17 "La vie heureuse, ou la vraie nature de Gilles Carle," in Larouche, *L'Aventure du cinéma*, 159–80.

18 In 1998 Aviva Distribution spent $650,000 on the promotion of *Les Boys II*, which was given the biggest release of any Quebec film in France, but to no avail.

19 See Deslandes, "L'éternelle question du doublage français: 'tannés' de se faire doubler?"

20 A portmanteau film, *La Fleur de l'âge* (1965), made with France, Italy, and Japan, the Canadian section of which, *Geneviève*, was directed by Michel Brault; *Coup de grâce* (J. Cayrol, 1965), shot entirely in France with mainly French personnel.

21 Coulombe and Jean, eds., *Le Dictionnaire du cinéma québécois*, 120.

22 Dorland, "Quest for Equality: Canada and Coproductions: A Retrospective (1963–1983)," 16.

23 "The possibility de looking at oneself at the same time as one is seen": Nadeau, "Américanité ou americanisation: l'exemple de la coproduction au Québec," 66.

24 Frow, John, "Intertextuality and Ontology," in Still and Worton, eds., *Intertextuality: Theories and Practices*, 45–55 (46–7).

25 Simard, *Mythe et reflet de la France*, 315. See Todorov, *On Human Diversity: Nationalism, Racism and Exoticism in French Thought*, for a history of, among other structures, the utopias constructed in *l'Amérique* in the French imagination; and the title of, for example, a recent transatlantic volume on ethnic diversity, Lacroix and Caccia, *Métamorphoses d'une utopie*, for its (knowing) persistence.

26 See Gérols, *Le Roman québécois en France*, and contemporary interviews with players in the French film and television industry, for exemple, Larouche, 68–9.

27 Deschamps et al., eds., *Le Mythe de Maria Chapdelaine*, 29.

28 Ibid., 218.

29 Sommer, "Irresistible Romance: The Foundational Fictions of Latin America," in Bhabha, ed., *Nation and Narration*, 76.

30 Ibid., 85.

31 Hémon, *Maria Chapdelaine*, trans. W.H. Blake, 157–8.

32 Ibid., 159–60.

33 For another discussion of these versions, see Paquette, "Maria sous trois regards."

34 See Sorlin, "The Fanciful Empire: French Feature Films of the Colonies in the 1930s," 135–51.

35 *La Presse*, 13 July 1934. Quoted in Fortier, "Maria Chapdelaine à l'écran," 20.

36 The two French-Canadian actors in the film are Fred Barry as Nazaire Larouche and Jacques Langevin as Edwige Légaré.

37 Nora, "Between Memory and History," in Nora, *Realms of Memory*, 2.

38 Noiseux, *Les Nouveaux Rapports: Film-Télévision*.

39 Bhabha, *Nation and Narration*, 295.

40 Ibid., 297.

CHAPTER FIVE

1 Anderson, *Imagined Communities*, 131.

2 Ibid., 140. My emphasis.

3 *The Penguin Freud Library*, vol. 7, *On Sexuality*, 217–25.

4 Robert, *Origins of the Novel*.

5 Freud's account is based on the little girl's acceptance of castration as something that has already befallen her, her underestimation of the clitoris, separation from amounting to identification with the mother as love object of the father, with a baby as substitute penis: Freud (1977), "The Dissolution of the Oedipus Complex," 321–31. ("It must be admitted, however, that in general our insight into these developmental processes in girls is unsatisfactory, incomplete and vague.")

6 See, for example, Bergstrom, "Alternation, Segmentation, Hypnosis: Interview with Raymond Bellour."

7 Maheu, "L'Oedipe colonial."

8 Schwartzwald, "Fear of Federasty: Québec's Inverted Fictions" in Spillers, *Comparative American Idention*, 175–95.

9 Marsolais, "Le temps d'un échec: un jeu de mort," in *Le Temps d'une chasse*, 13.

10 Sedgwick, *Between Men*.

11 Vincendeau, "Community, Nostalgia and Masculinity."

12 Lockerbie, "Les Bons débarras ou l'état d'une nation." Also: "Quebec Cinema as an Allegory of Nationhood," in *Image and Identity*.

13 Weinmann, *Cinéma de l'imaginaire québécois*, 99–102.

14 Leduc-Park, *Réjean Ducharme*.

15 Weinmann, *Cinéma de l'imaginaire québécois*, 116.

16 This is reminiscent of one of Schwartzwald's quotations from the joke page "Vulgarités" of *Parti pris*: "Il y aurait, semble-t-il, un million de pédales au Canada. La confédéra(s)tion est bien en selle" (*Spillers*, 1991, 179 and 192).

17 Schwartzwald (1991), 178.

18 Weinmann, *Cinéma de l'imaginaire québécois*, 118.

19 "Entretien avec Jean-Claude Lauzon," 10.

20 The company has diversified into mainstream production (such as Micheline Lanctôt's *La Vie d'un héros*, 1994), and it also made for Channel Four the second series of Armistead Maupin's books (*More Tales of the City*) in Montreal in 1998.

21 This was co-scripted by Roger Cantin, whose subsequent film-making career has partly specialized in children's films, such as the time-travel pirate series *Matusalem* (1993) and *Matusalem II* (1997).

22 Quoted in Pratley, "Tribute to Rock Demers: 'Tales For All,' " in Cowie, *Variety International Film Guide*, 107–16.

23 Ariès, *Centuries of Childhood.*

24 *Co-ire.*

25 Rose, *The Case of Peter Pan or the Impossibility of Children's Fiction*, 2.

26 Ibid., 141.

27 "The fairy-tale is future-oriented and guides the child ... to relinquish his infantile dependency wishes and achieve a more satisfying independent existence": Bettelheim, *The Uses of Enchantment*, 8. Bettelheim recognized the historical context in which such meanings were extracted, notably the decline of communities and extended families, and this recognition can be extended to the modern transformations of intimacy, including the high divorce rate, which have manifested themselves in Quebec as elsewhere and perhaps more intensely. For a summary of these readings of *E.T.*, see Krohn, "L'été de E.T.," and Narboni, "Peut-on être et avoir E.T.?"

28 *A Thousand Plateaus*, 239.

29 It is instructive, therefore, to see how a Fournier comedy deals with these issues a quarter-century on. *J'en suis* (1997) casts Roy Dupuis as Dominique, an architect and family man fallen on hard times, who pretends to be gay in order to get a job with a middle-aged antiquarian, Etienne (Albert Millaire). On one level, the anxieties around masculinity are, in a 1990s way, connected with yuppiedom, individualism, and fear of falling/failing rather than the nation. However, national discourses enter into the film because of its (failed) attempt to appeal to metropolitan French audiences with the casting of Arielle Dombasle as a visiting Parisian interior decorator who "cures" Dominique of his sexual anxieties as his "act" threatens to take over and the homosocial/homosexual boundary collapses: he wins her over by giving her an animatronic doll of de Gaulle repeating his 1967 Montreal speech. Ambiguities are thus dealt with by equating "homosexuality" with impotence (with women), and, in typical 1960s fashion, by blaming the phallic mother (France Castel) for the man's sexual dysfunction. Homosexuality thus continues to be Othered, and the references to gay politics, consumerism (the look Dominique adopts), and art all suggest the existence of a separate gay Mafia running organizations such as the an-

tiques industry and the Quebec Ministry of Culture (homosexuality as molar or major position vis-à-vis a supposedly still precarious Quebec male heterosexuality). In the end, the family is reconstituted, the "progress" since the 1970s being that Etienne is "included" on its terms only (allowed to play with the children and act as honorary grandfather).

30 "Nègres blancs, tapettes et 'butch.' "

31 Sedgwick, "Nationalisms and Sexualities in the Age of Wilde," in Parker, et al., eds., *Nationalisms and Sexualities*, 241.

32 Sedgwick, *Epistemology of the Closet*, 1.

33 Quoted in Stychin, "Queer Nations: Nationalism, Sexuality and the Discourse of Rights in Quebec," 6.

34 *Les Belles-soeurs, Hosanna, La Duchesse de Langeais, À toi, pour toujours, ta Marie-Lou, En pièces détachées*, and *Demain matin, Montréal m'attend*.

35 Butler, *Gender Trouble*, 136.

36 Radway, *Reading the Romance*.

37 For a (sometimes confused) discussion of this, in which is to be found yet again the old chestnut of homosexuality being about the Same, see *Théâtre et homosexualité*, 54. A useful overview is: Rocheleau, "Gay Theater in Quebec: The Search for an Identity."

38 Burston, Review of *Being at Home with Claude*, 67.

39 Foucault, *The Will to Knowledge*, 63.

40 "I felt no difference between him and me": Dubois, *Being at Home with Claude*, 103.

41 Lavoie, "Le lieu du crime."

42 Thérien, "Cinéma québécois: la difficile conquête de l'altérité."

43 Schwartzwald, "(Homo)sexualité et problématique identitaire," in Simon, *Fictions de l'identitaire au Québec*, 115–50. For a discussion of the 1991 film biography of the poet Émile Nelligan and Jean Larose's reading of him as a colonized subject characterized by a false plenitude associated with France and the phallic mother, see my contribution, "National Allegory in Francophone Canada," to Forbes and Kelly, eds., *French Cultural Studies*, 273–8, which is indebted to Schwartzwald's work.

44 "Subversive Discourse in Yves Simoneau's *Pouvoir intime*."

45 Larose, "Images pressées."

46 Kafka: *Toward a Minor Literature*, 70.

47 Some of these ideas can be found in Hocquenghem, *Homosexual Desire*, especially 109.

CHAPTER SIX

1 "De Gérard Pelletier à Francis Fox," *Le Devoir*; "Francis Fox's Silent Film Policy," *Cinema Canada*, 21.

2 Quoted in Lever, *Cinéma et société québécoise*, 435.

3 *Les 50 Ans de l'ONF,* 147.

4 Arcand, "Cinéma et sexualité."

5 Jean, *Le Cinéma québécois,* 94.

6 "Regarder la mort en face."

7 "La mise en intrigue. Configuration historico-linguistique d'une grève célébrée: Asbestos, P.Q., 1949."

8 *The Time-Image,* 54–5.

9 Bhabha, *Nation and Narration,* 307–8.

10 Sartre's play, however, evokes a situation in which the characters, being dead, are no longer able to make choices, to alter the choices they made, or, because of their interrelations, establish systems of denial.

11 In *The Time-Image,* 60–4, Deleuze, following Alain Masson's work on the musical (*La Comédie musicale*), analyses the transition from narrative to the spectacular or "implied dream" with the possibility of return, but he also points out that such a transition can call into question the concreteness of the "normal" narrative world, so that we go from the "spectacular" to the "spectacle," the "dream" element enveloping both or all worlds. This latter view is consistent with the strange temporal and narrative relations of Jutra's film, but here, of course, the musical sequence is an extension of the misery containing it, not something giving life back to the everyday.

12 Lever, *Histoire du Cinéma au Québec,* 325.

13 See Coulombe, *Denys Arcand: la vraie nature du cinéaste,* 118. In an interview in 1987, Arcand goes into more detail about his silent and distant father, whose dismissal of cinema as an art form (and of Quebec folk culture, unlike the higher-class and urban Brault and Perrault) was a part of the socially aspiring, religious, petit-bourgeois habitus of the family at Deschambault: see *Copie Zéro,* 34–5, 4–12.

14 *24 Images,* 44–5:51.

15 Coulombe, *Denys Arcand,* 106.

16 For more on these first three shorts, see Jean, "L'Éternel retour."

17 See Evans, *In the National Interest,* 180–4.

18 *Copie Zéro,* 34–5:6.

19 Coulombe, *Denys Arcand,* 25.

20 *24 Images,* 44–5:52.

21 Interview in *Le Monde,* 8 December 1973, 25. Reprinted in Lévesque, ed., *Réjeanne Padovani,* 10–11.

22 "A Cinema of Radical Incompatibilities: Arcand's Early Fiction Films," in Loiselle and B.McIlroy, eds., *Auteur/provocateur,* 52–68.

23 "L'Espace politique," in *Le Regard et la voix,* 125–31.

24 Bellemare, "La mélancolie et le banal," *Dérives,* 20.

25 Testa, "Denys Arcand's Sarcasm: A Reading of *Gina,*" in Véronneau et al., eds., *Dialogue: Canadian and Quebec Cinema,* 208.

26 See, for example, MacCabe, "Realism and the Cinema: Notes on Some Brechtian Theses," in Bennett et al., eds., *Popular Television and Film*, 216–35.

27 "If comparison is an historical procedure, it is also an absolutely cinematographic procedure. It is montage as defined by Eisenstein. You take a sequence which in itself has no meaning, you add a second which gives it one, then a third which permits everything that's been seen previously to acquire a new meaning, and so on": *24 Images*, 44–5:47. What he is describing sounds more like Griffith.

28 Testa, "Denys Arcand's Sarcasm," 211.

29 Testa in Loiselle and McIlroy, *Auteur/provocateur*, 94.

30 Jean, "L'histoire chez Denys Arcand: la marque du passé sur les temps présents," in *Copie Zéro*.

31 Lise Bissonnette in *Le Devoir*, 30 January 1982.

32 "Le miroir de Narcisse," *Virus*, February 1982.

33 *24 Images*, nos. 44–5:50.

34 *Sage comme une image*, 172.

35 *Cinéma Québec* 3, no. 4 (December 1973–January 1974), 23.

36 See *Dialogue: cinéma canadien et québécois*, 92.

37 *Sage comme une image*, 157–8.

38 Ibid., 157–9, on the length (152 minutes) of *Les Fleurs sauvages*, and Deleuze, *The Time-Image*, 77–8, on "time as money" in cinema.

39 As opposed to representing a "deviation from the real, the better to restore belief in it," Rodowick, *Gilles Deleuze's Time Machine*, 91.

40 *The Time-Image*, 254–5.

41 *Sage comme une image*, 43.

42 Coulombe, *Entretiens avec Gilles Carle*, 81.

43 "What is interesting is to have a fertile, multiple idea which bursts out in all directions. A sort of mini Big Bang!"; ibid., 197.

44 "We tried to tune into their songs on the radio, at home, on the only available country radio station: Chicago. We sometimes succeeded, but usually Roy Rogers's voice got mixed up with the family rosary on the Montreal station": ibid., 19.

45 Ibid., 21.

46 Carle, interview, *Cinéma Québec* 1, no. 9 (May–June 1972), 18–21.

47 Pallister, *The Cinema of Québec*, 75.

48 Interview with Forcier, *Copie Zéro* 19 (January 1984), 4.

49 "La Mise en scène du trompe-l'oeil: Gilles Carle et André Forcier," *Dérives*, 52 (1986), 89–100.

50 Bazin, *Baroque and Rococo*, 6–7.

51 Carle: "I create … a strangeness, in other words I won't try to recreate the real but to recreate the idea of the real. That's why it's a fable and it isn't

realist. But the fable is an important moment in our general reality";
Forcier: "My work is the poetry of realism." Quoted in Bonneville, *Le
Cinéma québécois par ceux qui le font*, 183 and 334.

52 *Signatures of the Visible*, 138–9.

53 The exceptions are Carle's "historical" films, notably *Maria Chapdelaine*
and *Les Plouffe* (1981), which are adaptations from other works and display
a variation on the idea of embeddedness in the present.

54 Ibid., 149.

55 Interview with Robert Morin, *24 Images*, 91 (spring 1998), 32–3.

56 Nicks, "Sex, Lies and Landscape."

57 Nora, *Realms of Memory*.

58 Benjamin, *Charles Baudelaire: A Lyric Poet in the Era of High Capitalism*, 149.

59 "A Certain Tendency of French Cinema," in Nichols, ed., *Movies and
Methods* 224–7.

CHAPTER SEVEN

1 Hobsbawm, *Nations and Nationalism in Europe since 1780*, especially
chapter 2, "Popular Proto-nationalism."

2 Hall, "Notes on Deconstructing 'The Popular,'" in Samuel, ed., *People's
History and Socialist Theory*, 233.

3 Frith, "Hearing Secret Harmonies," in MacCabe, ed., *High Theory/Low
Culture*, 55.

4 Hall, "Notes," 234.

5 Bourdieu, *Distinction*.

6 Major, *Le Cinéma québécois à la recherche de son public*, 153.

7 "Reification and Utopia in Mass Culture," 140.

8 See Jameson, "Euphorias of Substitution: Hubert Aquin and the Political
Novel in Quebec."

9 For example, Yves Lever on *Deux femmes en or*: "To do aesthetic criticism
on it for fun would be to waste one's energy with the risk of sinking into
insignificance": *Cinéma et société québécoise*, 151–2. But see Loiselle, "Subtly
Subversive or Simply Stupid: Notes on Popular Quebec Cinema."

10 "La place du sexe et la fonction du rire dans le film *Deux femmes en or*," in
Chabot and Pérusse, eds., *Cinéma et sexualité*, 101–16.

11 None of this was spotted at the start of its release in France. Like Carle's *Les
Mâles*, it was first shown in a porn cinema in Paris (on the Boulevard Bonne
Nouvelle) with the title *Deux filles perverties*.

12 Lever, *Histoire générale du cinéma au Québec*, 287. Léo Bonneville called *Bingo*
"un mélange effervescent de *Z*, de *Réjeanne Padovani*, des *Belles-soeurs*":
review, *Séquences*, 19, no. 76 (April 1974), 34.

13 *Cinéma Québec*, 3, no. 3 (November–December 1973), 16–18.

14 Shek, "Lemelin sur film: entre réalisme et mélodrame," in *Littérature québécoise et cinéma*, 43–56.

15 See Probyn, *Outside Belongings*, 3–15 ("Approximating Belonging") for this aspect of Quebec social and domestic space.

16 For a discussion of this adaptation of the Gabrielle Roy novel, see Shek, "*Bonheur d'occasion* à l'écran: fidélité ou trahison?" Also: Brosseau, *Le Cinéma d'une guerre oubliée*.

17 Brooks, *The Melodramatic Imagination*.

18 "Minnelli and Melodrama," in Gledhill, ed., *Home Is Where the Heart Is*, 73.

19 Larose, *La Petite Noirceur*, 79.

20 La Rochelle, *Cinéma en rouge et noir*, 97–9.

21 "La Nouvelle forme identitaire du Québécois." One critic described *Le Matou* as tracing the portrait of a Quebec "integrated into the North American capitalist universe": Summers, "La réception critique du *Matou*," 385.

22 See Bouchard et al., *Le Phénomène IXE–13*.

23 Guérif, *Le Cinéma policier français*; Tchernia, *80 Grands Succès du cinéma policier français*.

24 See my "National Identity and the *Film Policier*: The moment of 1981."

25 See Jameson, "Reflection and Utopia in Mass Culture," 282–3, on the first two *Godfather* films.

26 Bérubé and Magnan, "La distribution des films québécois aux États-Unis," 51.

27 Lavoie, "La petite noirceur," 43.

28 "Signes d'overdose," *Le Devoir*, 21 July 1997, A1.

29 Lipovetsky, *L'Ère du vide*.

30 Horton, ed., *Comedy/Cinema/Theory*.

31 Ibid., 5.

32 *Insight and Outlook*.

33 *The Logic of the Absurd*.

34 Freud, "Humour" (1927).

35 Neale and Krutnik, *Popular Film and Television Comedy*, 77.

36 For more on this, see Jenkins, *Textual Poachers*.

37 Colpron, *Les Anglicismes au Québec*, 132–3.

38 Pierre Maheu discusses these ambivalences around what he calls "tipop" in connection with Lefebvre's film *Patricia et Jean-Baptiste: Un Parti pris révolutionnaire*, 43–6.

39 "Entretien avec Roger Frappier."

40 "Assumer son américanité."

41 Dyer, *Stars*; *Heavenly Bodies*.

42 In the mid-1960s Bujold made films in France (*La Guerre est finie*, dir. Alain Resnais 1965; *Le Voleur*, dir. Louis Malle 1966) before returning to Quebec for *Entre la mer et l'eau douce* and the first of a trilogy directed by her

anglophone partner Paul Almond (*Isabel*, 1968). Her Oscar nomination for *Anne of the Thousand Days* (Jarrot, 1969) laid the basis for her extensive Hollywood work.

43 Ellis, *Visible Fictions*, 106.

44 For more on this point, see Jean, "Qui est la star?"

45 *24 Images*, 38:10.

46 Gauthier, "Trois Heures enchantées," 2.

47 "Les scénaristcs ont la parole: Gilles Richer et la comédie québécoise," 9.

48 One commentator points out how she is never involved in scandal of any kind: "Dodo ne se prend pas pour une autre/Dodo doesn't take herself for another" (Lemay, "Simple comme Dodo," 3).

49 Lemery, "Donner au rire une tournure bien féminine." An article in *Écho-Vedettes* (29 October 1994, 38) underlined the link between personal and national authenticity by publishing her genealogy, which can be traced back to the beginning of New France in the person of Nicolas Sylvestre, a soldier from Champagne posted to Quebec.

50 Dyer, "Don't Look Now."

51 Blanchard, "Le retour de l'enfant prodigue."

52 "I've got a wild side. I've never been someone very social": Nuovo, "Roy Dupuis: la traversée des apparences," 9; "He's the product of a hostile climate and an imposing natural scene [*nature*]": Bois, "Roy Dupuis nature," 30–2.

53 The other famous Ti-Guy in Quebec cinema is the mentally handicapped brother in *Les Bons Débarras*, one reading of whom is that of a failed Quebec.

54 This casting reiterates the point made earlier about the repertoire of (interchangeable) celebrity faces that is crucial to Quebec national cinema. One reviewer, sceptical about the film, missed the point when stating, "Imagine a team consisting of players-actors we didn't know at all, say Finns or Italians, the film probably wouldn't have the same success": Martel, "Pour public partisan!"

55 This is the joke of the film about the Jamaican bobsleigh team, *Cool Runnings* (Turteltaub, 1993).

CHAPTER EIGHT

1 Micheline Lanctôt: "I don't see what is feminine about a film or what's masculine about a film … I don't make feminist films. I don't believe in 'feminism' as such. I'm an anarchist. It's my voice. I don't want to grow as a woman. I want to grow as a person. Then I'm a woman. Then I'm a Quebecker. Then I'm 36. Then I'm a mother. I'm myself. They can bunch me up with the mothers because I'm a mother. They can say I make mother's

films. But, honestly, I can't think of a worse label than 'Quebec woman filmmaker.' How many minorities can you possibly bunch up in one sentence?" Quoted by Tadros, "*Sonatine*: 'Film maudit,' " 8. Anne Claire Poirier has said of the difference for the industry between male and female filmmakers: "They're 'pure' film-makers" [*cinéastes à l'état pur*], we're just women film-makers, a subcategory, a little bit like the Third World of the profession." *Copie Zéro*, 6 (1980), 18–19. Léa Pool is similarly resistant: she agrees that there are social differences between men and women but none of "sensibility": "We absolutely must smash this whole idea of women's films," *24 Images*, 56–7 (autumn 1991), 49.

2 "The Origins of the Women's Movement in Quebec," in Backhouse and Flaherty, eds., *Challenging Times*, 72–89.

3 See Walby, *Theorizing Patriarchy*.

4 Backhouse and Flaherty, *Challenging Times*, 89. See also: de Sève, "The Perspectives of Quebec Feminists," ibid., 110–16.

5 A documentary short was made on the tragedy by Catherine Fol: *Au-delà du 6 décembre* (1991).

6 Smart, *Écrire dans la maison du père*, 23 (no equivalent in English version).

7 Johnstone, "Women's Cinema as Counter-Cinema," in Nichols, ed., *Movies and Methods*, 208–17; Mulvey, "Visual Pleasure and Narrative Cinema."

8 "Feminism and Culture – the Movie."

9 Johnstone, "Women's Cinema," 214.

10 Lovell, *Pictures of Reality*.

11 Kaplan, *Women and Film*, 86.

12 Braidotti, *Patterns of Dissonance*.

13 *A Thousand Plateaus*, 242.

14 Ibid., 277.

15 Ibid., 275–6.

16 Lacroix, *Septième art et discrimination*. See also, for the period to 1970, Denault, *Dans l'ombre des projecteurs*.

17 *Copie Zéro*, 23 (February 1985), 23.

18 For an account of Studio D, see Anderson's chapter, "Studio D's Imagined Community: From Development (1974) to Realignment (1986–1990)," in Armatage, et al., *Gendering the Nation*, 41–61.

19 1971 text reprinted in *Copie Zéro*, 23 (February 1985), 23.

20 From a 1973 text by Poirier, "La 'femme,' une réalité en devenir": reprinted in *Copie Zéro*, 23 (February 1985), 10. The same reason was given for not adopting humour as a strategy: "You've got to be pretty liberated to be able to look at yourself with humour!"

21 Kandiyoti, "Identity and Its Discontents," 434.

22 Bersianik, "Tout ça c'est du cinéma," *Copie Zéro*, 23 (February 1985), 33–4.

23 *Copie Zéro*, 23 (February 1985), 6.

24 *Copie Zéro*, 23 (February 1985), 15. For an interesting reading of the film which sees a duality and interaction between counter-cinema and melodrama, see Loiselle, "Despair as Empowerment."

25 Haskell, *From Reverence to Rape.*

26 Sloniowski, *The Cinema of Cruelty*, 224–55.

27 Caverni, "Réflexions en vrac d'une spectatrice," in Carrière, *Femmes et cinéma québécois*, (1983), 133–40.

28 Zucker, "Les oeuvres récentes d'Anne Claire Poirier et Paule Baillargeon."

29 Nicks, "Aesthetic Memory in *Mourir à tue-tête*: Fragments from *Screens from Silence*," in Allan et al., eds., *Responses: In Honour of Peter Harcourt*, 168–82 (178).

30 *Copie Zéro*, 23 (February 1985), 6.

31 Quoted in Coulombe and Jean, eds., *Le Dictionnaire du cinéma québécois*, 1.

32 From an interview with Dansereau: "Mireille Dansereau: ' *La Vie rêvée*,' " in Feldman and J. Nelson, eds., *Canadian Film Reader*, 250–8.

33 Carrière, *Femmes et cinéma québécois*, 165.

34 Smart, *Writing in the Father's House*, 8.

35 In Feldman and Nelson, *Canadian Film Reader*, 251.

36 Deleuze, *The Movement-Image*, 87.

37 Pérusse, *Micheline Lanctôt: La Vie d'une héroïne*, 116–18.

38 This is as far as I would go in allegorizing this film, other than its general comment about (Quebec) modernity. For a more sustained attempt, with the bus ride as "the times of the pioneers" and the night boat as "la grande noirceur," see Deléas, "La quête du père dans le film *Sonatine* de Micheline Lanctôt."

39 Donohoe, "*Sonatine* in Context: A Neglected Film of Micheline Lanctôt," in Donohoe, ed., *Essays on Quebec Cinema*, 164–5.

40 Chambers, "A Miniature History of the Walkman."

41 Pérusse *Micheline Lanctôt*, (1995), 114.

42 White, "To Act Is To Be: Identity in Recent Quebec Cinema."

43 Deleuze discusses this as Pasolini's favoured view of subjectivity in cinema in general: *The Movement-Image*, 72–6. See also the discussion of *style indirect libre* as the way we speak in nations/communities with their "order-words" (*mots d'ordre*): "Indirect discourse is not explained by the distinction between subjects; rather, it is the assemblage, as it freely appears in this discourse, that explains all the voices present within a single voice"; *A Thousand Plateaus*, 80.

44 See, for example, an excellent piece by Longfellow: "The Search for Voice: *La Femme de l'hôtel*," in Véronneau et al., eds., *Dialogue: Cinéma canadien et québécois*, 269–81.

45 "Women in French-Quebec Cinema: The Space of Socio-Sexual (In)difference," 14.

46 See also Nadeau, "Les Femmes frappées de disparition" and "La Représentation de la femme comme autre."

47 "Léa Pool's Gynefilms," in Donohoe, ed., *Essays on Quebec Cinema*, 111–34.

48 Stacey, "Desperately Seeking Difference." As Stacey herself notes, however, Seidelman's film also addresses differences between women across class and subcultural boundaries, a strategy avoided by Pool's abstractions. See also Mulvey, "New Wave Interchanges: *Céline and Julie* and *Desperately Seeking Susan*," in Nowell-Smith and Ricci, eds., *Hollywood and Europe*: 119–28.

49 Quoted in Kaplan, *Women and Film*, 93.

50 *The Time-Image*, 19.

51 Longfellow, "The Melodramatic Imagination," 273.

52 *The Movement-Image*, 120. "The fact is that, in Europe, the post-war period has greatly increased the situations which we no longer know how to react to, in spaces which we no longer know how to describe. These were 'any-spaces-whatever,' deserted but inhabited, disused warehouses, waste ground, cities in the course of demolition or reconstruction. And in these any-spaces-whatever a new race of characters was stirring, kind of mutant: they saw rather than acted, they were seers": *The Time-Image*, xi.

53 *The Movement-Image*, 84.

54 "Cinéma québécois à l'ombre de la mélancolie."

55 *L'Ame atomique.*

CHAPTER NINE

1 The issue was complicated by the fact that, because of seventeenth-century alliances, the Mohawk's second language is English rather than French. Cinematic records of the conflict can be found in documentary form in *Acts of Defiance* (Alec McLeod/NFB, 1992); *Kanesatake*, by the leading native film-maker, Alanis Obomsawin (1993); and *Okanada: Behind the Lines at Oka* (Catherine Bainbridge/Albert Nerenberg, 1992).

2 See, for example, the riposte from a *souverainiste* point of view: Philpot, *Oka: dernier alibi du Canada anglais.*

3 Prepared by Brad Morse, a University of Ottawa law professor, for the Native Council of Canada on "Comparative Assessments of Indigenous Peoples in Quebec, Canada and Abroad" (45–6, 49).

4 Axtell, *The Invasion Within: The Contest of Cultures in Colonial North America*; Dickason, *The Myth of the Savage and the Beginnings of French Colonialism in the Americas.* Denys Delâge's account of unequal exchange from the start – *Le Pays renversé* – nonetheless argues for the hybridity of the *Canadiens*/Québécois, or at least the considerable interaction with the Indians.

5 Perrault, "La Question amérindienne," in *Caméramages*, 80.

6 Ibid., 112.

7 For the continuing political and discursive controversies of that situation, see Cohen, "Technological Colonialism and the Politics of Water."

8 Chaloupka and Cawley, "The Great Wild Hope: Nature, Environmentalism and the Open Secret," in Bennett and Chaloupka, eds., *In the Nature of Things*, 3–23 (5).

9 Wilson, *The Culture of Nature: North American Landscape from Disney to the Exxon Valdez*, 12.

10 To take a few examples: *Dances with Wolves* (Costner, 1991, in which heterosexual masculinity and the homosocial play a central mediating role); *Clear Cut* (Bugajski, 1991); *The Dark Wind* (Morris, 1994); *The Emerald Forest* (Boorman, 1985); *Thunderheart* (Apted, 1992); *Where the Green Ants Dream* (Herzog, 1984).

11 Todorov, *The Conquest of America*, 5.

12 Ibid., 97.

13 Ibid., 42.

14 Todorov, *On Human Diversity*.

15 *Conquest of America*, 249.

16 Ibid., 250. However, Todorov's text is also a process of doubling and mirroring with regard to the Other, a process sometimes consciously acknowledged, sometimes not. The whole theme of alterity that embraces the Spanish/Mexican encounter encapsulates certain characteristics of Todorov's status as exile. But the book as a whole is in part a response to the new multicultural world and France of the 1980s, in which period the shock of the Iranian revolution and resurgence of a fundamentalist Islam, as well as the visibility of non-European ethnic minorities in France (and this before the electoral successes of the *Front national*), had granted a certain urgency and topicality to the whole mechanism of the relation with the the extra-European Other. And while Todorov describes reactions to the loss of communication with "the world" or nature such as the *Club Méditerranée*, "hippies," and religious fundamentalism, he fails fully to acknowledge the way in which his own bemoaning of that loss is located in a post-1968 "ecological" discourse which to an extent puts non-European, pre-capitalist indigenous cultures to European use. Most of all, the granting of the status as subject (as opposed to object) to the Other, inevitably destabilizing Eurocentrism or the notion of cultural homogeneity, is sensed by the mandarin Todorov as a danger, the codeword for which is "eclecticism." So Todorov still identifies with a relatively homogeneous notion of what a "culture" (in dialogue or not) might be and desires a "hard" identification with it.

17 Dollimore, *Sexual Dissidence*, 254.

18 Bhabha, "The Other Question – the Stereotype and Colonial Discourse."

19 Van Schendel, "L'Identité métisse ou l'histoire oubliée de la canadianité," in Létourneau, ed., *La Question identitaire au Canada francophone*, 101–21.

20 Morisset, *L'Identité usurpée*.

21 For example, Julien, "Ne sommes-nous pas tous des Amérindiens?"

22 Thérien, "L'Indien du discours," in *Les Figures de l'Indien*, 365.

23 Berthiaume, "Les *Relations* des Jésuites: nouvel avatar de *La Légende dorée*," in ibid.

24 Lefebvre, "*Le Festin des morts* et les *Relations des Jésuites*: Histoire et écriture," in *Cinéma et histoire*, 41–9.

25 Axtell, 286; "The Jesuits achieved the conversions as they did by a judicious accommodation and adaptation to the ways of the people among whom they were working. They recognized perhaps as clearly as anyone of their time that too much was made of the distinction between 'savage' and 'civilized'; that the Amerindians possessed a viable culture which, while it did not always correspond to the French way, still had its own logic that worked very well": Dickason, *The Myth of the Savage*, 267.

26 Berthiaume in *Les Figures de l'Indien*, 134.

27 Interview with Dansereau, *Le Devoir*, 29 May 1965.

28 Dansereau quoted in Daigneault, "Alimenter *notre* cinéma à *notre* histoire" (my emphasis).

29 Daigneault, "Alec Pelletier, une femme à la mesure de notre éveil." Alec Pelletier had been in the Jeunesse Étudiante Catholique in the 1940s and might be described as a "modernizing Catholic."

30 Nadeau, "Jean-Paul Nolet [an Abenaki correspondent] fait une *violente* sortie contre *Le Festin des morts*" (my emphasis).

31 Bhabha, "The Other Question," 28–9.

32 The term is from Lever, *Histoire générale du cinéma au Québec*, 282.

33 *La Presse*, 28 March 1970.

34 *La Tribune*, 18 July 1970.

35 *Le Devoir*, 21 March 1970.

36 Vincendeau, "Community, Nostalgia, and the Spectacle of Masculinity."

37 "Les Indiens de celluloïd."

38 Thérien, "Cinéma québécois; la difficile conquête de l'altérité."

39 Bonneville, *Le Cinéma québécois*, 520.

40 Ibid., 520.

41 For more on Lamothe's documentary work, see Baril, *Les Amérindiens du Québec dans le cinéma documentaire*.

42 *Séquences*, 175 (November-December 1994), 13.

43 White, "Alanis Obomsawin, Documentary Form and the Canadian Nation(s)."

44 For more on Obomsawin, see Pick, "Storytelling and Resistance: The Documentary Practice of Alanis Obomsawin," in Armatage et al., eds., *Gendering the Nation*, 76–93. For more on native film-making, see Aklil, "Le septième art de la première nation."

45 Quoted by Pick. Nichols, *Blurred Boundaries: Questions of Meaning in Contemporary Culture*, 106.

CHAPTER TEN

1 G. Horowitz quoted in Tétu, "L'Opposition hybridité/métissage et patrie/ nation dans le contexte pluriculturel du Canada", in Lacroix and Caccia, eds., *Métamorphoses d'une utopie*, 158. A high-profile critique of Canadian multiculturalism, from an "immigrant" point of view, can be found in Neil Bissoondath's *Selling Illusions*, which argues for a common Canadian public culture rather than the cultivation of superficial differences which deny the major ones. The denial of the existence of more than one nation within Canada is also why Bissoondath's book was received favourably in Quebec, where Lise Bissonnette, the then editor of the nationalist daily, *Le Devoir*, wrote a preface for the French edition.

2 Collins, *Television Policy and Culture*, especially 217–20.

3 Lacroix, "Quel avenir pour le multiculturalisme? Nation et communautés en France et au Canada," in *Métamorphoses d'une utopie*, 213.

4 *The Nature and Context of Minority Discourse*, 5.

5 This is the theme of the historical drama *Les Tisserands du pouvoir* (Claude Fournier, 1988).

6 Caccia, "Le Roman francophone de l'immigration en Amérique du Nord et en Europe: une perspective transculturelle," in *Métamorphoses d'une utopie*, 93.

7 Ledoyen, *Montréal au pluriel*.

8 Helly, *L'Immigration pour quoi faire?* 14.

9 Harvey, "Les Communautés culturelles et le multiculturalisme: une comparaison des politiques québécoise et canadienne," in *Métamorphoses d'une utopie*, 170.

10 Monette, "Nous sommes tous des immigrants." See also his *Pour en finir avec les intégristes de la culture*.

11 "La Transculture, entre l'art et la politique," *Métamorphoses d'une utopie*, 312.

12 L'Hérault, "Pour une cartographie de l'hétérogène: Dérives identitaires des années 1980," in Simon, et al., eds., *Fictions de l'identitaire au Québec*, 75.

13 *Strangers to Ourselves*.

14 *Métamorphoses d'une utopie*, 25–41.

15 Chapter 8, "Ethnicities-in-Relation: Toward a Multicultural Reading of American Cinema," in Friedman, ed., *Unspeakable Images*, 216.

16 According to Roland Barthes, the bourgeoisie "exnominates" its rule since it is defined as "the social class which does not want to be named" and is thus "naturalized": *Mythologies*, 138.

17 For an interesting discussion that links this film to the work of that other "exile," Léa Pool, see Longfellow, "L'Écriture féministe de *Journal inachevé* et *Strass café*."

18 Balibar and Wallerstein, *Race, Nation, Class*, 59.

19 For a discussion of the film's production history, see Posner, *Canadian Dreams*, 79–93.

20 Lapsley and Westlake, "From *Casablanca* to *Pretty Woman*: The Politics of Romance."

21 *L'Autre intime*, 9–12.

22 Simon, "The Geopolitics of Sex, or Signs of Culture in the Quebec Novel."

23 For example, Chapter 9, "Bakhtin, Polyphony and Ethnic/Racial Representation," in Friedman, *Unspeakable Images*.

24 *The Dialogic Imagination*, 188.

25 Allor, "Locating Cultural Activity: The 'Main' as Chronotope and Heterotopia." Allor uses Foucault's concept of "heterotopia" to take the argument further, in that the "Main" can be seen to produce all sorts of different and incommensurable spatio-temporal relations that transform their referents and "origins."

26 Simon and Dubé, *L'Autre intime*, 13–22.

27 Barthes, *S/Z*, 185.

28 Simon and Dubé, *L'Autre intime*, 19.

29 Ramirez and Tana, *La Sarrasine*, 137. This speech is reminiscent of a speech made by the bishop of Montreal, Monseigneur Gauthier, in the 1930s: "Our great cities are becoming heterogeneous. The Jew is taking possession of them with the gold hidden in his rags, the Southern European with his dagger in his breast, the entertainer with his filthy theatre, the atheist with his subversive principles, the sectarian with his ferocious hatred"; quoted in Lacoursière, *Épopée en Amérique: Une Histoire populaire du Québec* (Télé-Québec, dir. Gilles Carle, 1997), episode 11, "Enfin la guerre."

30 Simon and Dubé, *L'Autre intime*, 80.

31 To give but a few examples: *Happy Together* (Wong-Kar-Wai, Hong Kong, 1997); *Journey of Hope* (Xavier Koller, Switzerland, 1990); *Mississippi Masala* (Mira Nair, United States, 1992); *Time of the Gypsies* (Emir Kusturica, Yugoslavia, 1989).

32 Balibar and Wallerstein, *Race, Nation, Class*, 34.

33 Grossberg, "The Space of Culture, the Power of Space," in Chambers and Curti, eds., *The Post-Colonial Question*, 177.

CHAPTER ELEVEN

1 Giddens, *The Consequences of Modernity*.

2 Arguably, "modernism," understood in its high cultural sense of a response to commodification and reification through the problematization of language, de-centring of consciousness and proclamation of alienation, has existed only sporadically in Canada, for historical and social reasons (an urban life and élite cultural structure different from and peripheral to the

experience of Berlin, New York, Paris and Vienna in the first three decades of the century).

3 Friedland and Boden, eds., *Nowhere: Space, Time and Modernity*, 31.

4 In *The Canadian Postmodern*, Linda Hutcheon argues that Canada's unstable cultural identity calls into question "the possibility of a centred, coherent subjectivity" (174–5). Quebec's own national-allegorical tension is partly about the relationship between that pole and the "modernist" project of nation-building.

5 Collins, *Culture, Communication, and National Identity*.

6 Nguyên-Duy, "Frontières: l'influence américaine sur la télévision et la culture québécoises."

7 For more on this general topic, see Bellemare Brière, "Montréal capitale multimédia." Langlois has written an optimitsic preface for the 1999 edition of the *Dictionnaire du cinéma québécois*. Montreal has the highest per-capita concentration of high-technology jobs of any major North American city (speech by Richard Guay, delegate general of Quebec in London, 28 October 1999).

8 Brunet, *Notre présent, le passé et nous*, 11. Quoted in Shek, "History as a Unifying Structure in *Le Déclin de l'empire américain*."

9 Caccia, "La vérité perdue," in *Copie Zéro*, 34–5.

10 Bellemare, "Retournement et duplicité," in ibid.

11 Bersianik, "L'empire du statu quo," *Le Devoir*, 9 August 1986.

12 Among other replies to Bersianik, see that of the political scientist Anne Légaré in *Le Devoir*, 23 August 1986, C2.

13 Arcand was criticized in *Le Devoir* by a group of young correspondents for failing to understand the current generation: Fournier et al., "Déclin d'un empire ou échec d'une génération?"

14 Pérusse, "*Le Déclin*: une stratégie filmique oscillant entre le cliché et l'ironie."

15 Schwartzwald in Spillers; Arcand, "Cinéma et sexualité."

16 Peter Wilkins writes: "In Arcand's filmic irony, however, the perspective renders everything at once 'flat' and unstable; no clues will correct the irony for us and make us feel sure that we are perceiving the message in the right way": Loiselle and McIlroy, eds., *Auteur/provocateur*, 130.

17 Heinz Weinmann in *Cinéma de l'imaginaire québécois* makes much of this *rapprochement* with Quebec's patron saint, arguing that the whole film marks the new maturity of Quebec identity and its ability to engage with the Other.

18 See Jameson, *The Geopolitical Aesthetic*.

19 Arcand's most recent feature, *Joyeux Calvaire* (1996), is a fairly impersonal film about two down-and-outs in Montreal.

20 *Selected Poems*, 68–9.

21 Jameson, "Postmodernism, or the Cultural Logic of Late Capitalism."

22 See Baby et al., "Jacques Godbout rencontre IXE-13 ou du texte au film: quelles transformations?"

23 See Paul Warren's article on *Dans le ventre du dragon*: "Américanisation."

24 Clarke, ed., *The Cinematic City*, 3.

25 "On Some Motifs in Baudelaire," in *Illuminations*, 177.

26 See Lacasse, "Le Dimanche, Montréal va aux vues *ou* la ville aux vues s'anime," in Véronneau, ed., *Montréal ville de cinéma*, 5–11. For more on this period and the cross-cultural fertilization which took place, see Lascasse, "American Film in Quebec Theater."

27 Clarke, *The Cinematic City*, 4.

28 Robins, "Prisoners of the City: Whatever Could a Postmodern City Be?" 11.

29 Ibid., 13.

30 Massey, "A Global Sense of Place."

31 "Walking in the City," in During, ed., *The Cultural Studies Reader*, 156.

32 See Wolff, "The Artist and the *Flâneur*: Rodin, Rilke and Gwen John in Paris," chapter 6 of *Resident Alien: Feminist Cultural Criticism*, 88–114.

33 Wilson, "The Invisible Flâneur," 109.

34 Ibid., 97.

35 Clarke, *The Cinematic City*, 7.

36 Ibid., 6.

37 See my "Récits du passé et identité nationale: La télésérie *Les Filles de Caleb*," in Jewsiewicki and Létourneau, eds., *L'Histoire en partage*, 45–69.

38 Wilson, "The Invisible Flâneur," 109.

39 D'Lugo, "Almodóvar's City of Desire."

40 Wilson, "The Invisible Flâneur," 107.

41 See, for example, his evocation of the enrichment provided and "horizons" opened up by his work with Peter Brook, Peter Gabriel, the National Theatre in London, and Dramaten in Stockholm, their relationship with the "petit centre" at Quebec City, and his work which remains "profondément québécois": Charest, *Robert Lepage Quelques zones de liberté*, 56.

42 Foucault, *The Will to Knowledge*, 63.

43 "La première confession de Robert Lepage," 27.

44 *The Time-Image*, 81.

45 Ibid, 46.

46 Ibid, 40.

47 Ibid, 44.

48 Ibid, 19.

49 Radstone, "Cinema/memory/history," 35.

50 Benjamin, *Illuminations*, 159.

51 Marks, "A Deleuzian politics of hybrid cinema," 258.

52 This is not to underestimate the interest of Mankiewicz's film, in the use of Céleste's composition "You Don't Shoot the Piano Player" to organize the past/present relationship, and the skipping of generations involved in the

grandmother/grandson contact. Co-production obliges, however, a portrait of the Blaudelle family into which Céleste married in the 1920s as indistinguishable from the French bourgeoisie which has formed the butt of so many French films.

53 *The Time-Image*, 91.

54 Ibid., 39.

55 Ibid., 243 and 246. See also Lepage's play *Tectonic Plates* (adapted for television in Britain in 1993, directed by Peter Mettler).

Bibliography

24 Images, 38 (summer 1988), on star system.

24 Images 39–40 (autumn 1988), on Montreal.

24 Images 56–7 (autumn 1991), on Léa Pool.

Adorno, Theodore W. *Aesthetic Theory*, translated by R. Hullot-Kentor. Minneapolis: University of Minnesota Press 1997.

Ahmand, Aijaz. "Jameson's Rhetoric of Otherness and the 'National Allegory.'" *Social Text* 17 (fall 1987). 3–25.

Aklil, Myriam. "Le Septième art de la Première nation." *L'Initial* (June 1991): 19.

Alderson, David and Linda Anderson. *Territories of Desire.* Manchester, U.K.: Manchester University Press 2000.

Alfred, Gerald R. "From Bad to Worse: Internal Politics in the 1990 Crisis at Kahnawake." *Northeast Indian Quarterly* 8, no. 1 (spring 1991): 23–31.

Allan, Blaine et al., eds. *Responses: In Honour of Peter Harcourt.* Kingston, Ont.: Responsibility Press 1992.

Allor, Martin. "Cultural *métissage*: National Formations and Productive Discourse in Quebec Cinema and Television." *Screen* 34, no. 1 (spring 1993): 69–75.

– "Locating Cultural Activity: The 'Main' as Chronotope and Heterotopia." *Topia* 1 (1997): 42–54.

Althusser, Louis. *Lenin and Philosophy*, translated by B. Brewster. London: NLB 1971.

Anderson, Benedict. *Imagined Communities: Reflections on the Origin and Spread of Nationalism.* London: Verso 1983.

Amin, Samir. *Eurocentrism*, translated by R. Moore. New York: Monthly Review Press 1989.

Arcand, Denys. "Cinéma et sexualité." *Parti pris* 9–11 (summer 1964): 90–7.

– *Le Déclin de l'empire américain*. Montreal: Boréal 1986.

– *Jésus de Montréal*. Montreal: Boréal 1989.

Ariès, Philippe. *Centuries of Childhood*, translated by R. Baldick. London: Peregrine Books 1962.

Armatage, Kay, Kass Banning, Brenda Longfellow, and Janine Marchessault, eds. *Gendering the Nation: Canadian Women's Cinema*. Toronto: University of Toronto Press 1999.

Atwood, Margaret. *Survival: A Thematic Guide to Canadian Literature*. Toronto: Anansi 1972.

Aumont, Jacques et al., eds. *L'Histoire du cinéma, nouvelles approches*. Paris: Publications de la Sorbonne 1989.

Axtell, James. *The Invasion Within: The Contest of Cultures in Colonial North America*. Oxford, U.K.: Oxford University Press 1985.

Baby, François et al. "Jacques Godbout rencontre *IXE-13* ou du texte au film: quelles transformations?" *Études littéraires* 12, no. 2 (1979): 285–302.

Bachand, Denis. "Le *Nouvel âge* québécois. " *Possibles* 8, no. 4 (summer 1984): 147–58.

– "La Réception des films québécois en France." *Québec Studies* 9 (1989/90): 69–78.

– "Regards sur la nature canadienne au cinéma." *Cultures du Canada français* 4 (autumn 1987): 5–13.

Backhouse, Christine and David H. Flaherty, eds. *Challenging Times: The Women's Movement in Canada and the United States*. Montreal: McGill-Queen's University Press 1992.

Bakhtin, Mikhail. *The Dialogic Imagination*, translated by M. Holquist. Austin: University of Texas Press 1981.

– *Rabelais and His World*, translated by H. Iswolsky. Cambridge, Mass: MIT Press 1968.

Balibar, Étienne and Immanuel Wallerstein. *Race, Nation, Class: Ambiguous Identities*, Balibar translated by C. Turner. London: Verso 1991.

Baril, Gérard. *Les Amérindiens du Québec dans le cinéma documentaire*. MA thesis: Université Laval 1984.

Barrowclough, Susan, ed. *Jean Pierre Lefebvre: The Quebec Connection*. London: British Film Institute 1981.

Barthes, Roland. *Image, Music, Text*, translated by S. Heath. London: Fontana 1977.

– *Mythologies*, translated by A. Lavers. London: Jonathan Cape 1972.

– *The Rustle of Language*, translated by R. Howard. Oxford, U.K.: Blackwells 1986.

– *S/Z*, translated by R. Muller. London: Jonathan Cape 1975.

Bataille, Georges. *Literature and Evil*, translated by A. Hamilton. London: Marion Boyars 1997.

Bazin, Germain. *Baroque and Rococo,* translated by J. Griffin. London: Thames and Hudson 1964.

Beauchamp, M. "Aujourd'hui Gilles Groulx." *24 Images* 44–5 (autumn 1989): 78–81.

Beauchemin, Yves. *Le Matou.* Montreal: Québec/Amérique 1981.

Bellemare, Denis. "La Mélancolie et le banal." *Dérives* 52 (1986): 7–24.

Bellemare Brière, V. "Montréal capitale multimédia." *Séquences* 197 (July–August 1998): 54.

Benjamin, Walter. *Charles Baudelaire: A Lyric Poet in the Era of High Capitalism,* translated by H. Zohn. London: NLB 1973.

– *Illuminations,* translated by H. Zohn. London: Fontana/Collins 1972.

Bennett, Jane and William Chaloupka, eds. *In the Nature of Things: Language, Politics and the Environment.* Minneapolis: University of Minnesota Press 1993.

Bennett, Tony et al., eds. *Popular Television and Film.* London: British Film Institute 1981.

Benvenuto, Bice and Roger Kennedy. *The Works of Jacques Lacan: An Introduction.* New York: St Martin's Press 1986.

Bergstrom, Janet. "Alternation, Segmentation, Hypnosis: Interview with Raymond Bellour." *Camera Obscura* 3–4 (1979): 71–103.

Bersianik, Louky. "L'Empire du statu quo." *Le Devoir* (9 August 1986): C1, C6.

Bérubé, Bernard and Richard Magnan. "La distribution des films québécois aux États-Unis." *Cinémas* 7, no. 3 (spring 1997): 31–59.

Bettelheim, Bruno. *The Uses of Enchantment: The Meaning and Importance of Fairy Tales.* London: Peregrine Books 1978.

Bhabha, Homi, ed. *Nation and Narration.* London: Routledge 1990.

– "The Other Question – the Stereotype and Colonial Discourse." *Screen* 24, no. 6 (November–December 1983): 18–36.

Bissoondath, Neil. *Selling Illusions: The Cult of Multiculturalism in Canada.* London: Penguin Books 1994.

Blais, Marie-Claire. *Le Sourd dans la ville.* Montreal: Stanké 1975.

Blanchard, S. "Le Retour de l'enfant prodigue." *Le Devoir* (21 October 1995): B1–B2.

Bois, Anne. "Roy Dupuis nature." *Clin d'oeil* (October 1994): 30–2.

Bonitzer, Pascal. *Le Regard et la voix.* Paris: UGE 1976.

Bonneville, Léo, ed. *Le Cinéma québécois par ceux qui le font.* Montreal: Paulines and ADE 1979.

– Review of *Bingo. Séquences* 19, no. 76 (April 1974): 34.

Bordwell, David. "The Art Cinema as a Mode of Film Practice." *Film Criticism* 4, no. 1 (1979): 56–64.

Bouchard, Guy et al. *Le Phénomène IXE-13.* Sainte-Foy: Presses de l'Université Laval 1984.

Bourdeau, Roger. "L'utilisation du montage comme langage cinématographique dans l'oeuvre de Gilles Groulx." *24 Images* 5 (May 1980): 54–60.

Bourdieu, Pierre. *Distinction: A Social Critique of the Judgement of Taste*, translated by R. Nice. London: Routledge 1984.

Brady, James. "*À tout prendre*: fragments du corps spéculaire." *Copie Zéro* 37 (October 1988): 23–6.

Braidotti, Rosi. *Patterns of Dissonance: A Study of Women in Contemporary Philosophy*, translated by E. Wild. Cambridge, U.K.: Polity Press 1991.

Brault, François. "Manifeste pour un cinéma vraiment national." *Possibles* 7, no. 1 (1982): 83–7.

Brontë, Emily. *Wuthering Heights*. Harmondsworth, U.K.: Penguin 1985.

Brooks, Peter. *The Melodramatic Imagination: Balzac, Henry James, Melodrama and the Mode of Excess*. New Haven, Conn.: Yale University Press 1976.

Brosseau, Louis. *Le Cinéma d'une guerre oubliée*. Montreal: VLB 1998.

Brunet, Michel. *Notre présent, le passé et nous*. Montreal: FIDES 1976.

Burston, Paul. Review of *Being at Home with Claude*. *Time Out* (26 May 1992): 67.

Butler, Judith. *Gender Trouble: Feminism and the Subversion of Identity*. London: Routledge 1990.

Caccia, Fulvio. "Le miroir de Narcisse." *Virus* (February 1982).

Camus, Albert. *L'Homme révolté*. Paris: Gallimard 1951.

Carle, Gilles. Interview. *Cinéma Québec* 1, no. 9 (May–June 1982).

– *La Vraie Nature de Bernadette*. *L'Avant-scène cinéma* 130 (November 1972).

Carrière, Daniel. *Claude Jutra*. Montreal: Lidec 1993.

Carrière, Louise. "Assumer son américanité." *Ciné-Bulles* 14, no. 4 (winter 1995): 27–31.

– , ed. "Aujourd'hui le cinéma québécois." *CinémAction* 40 (1986).

– , ed. *Femmes et cinéma québécois*. Montreal: Boréal 1983.

Cartmill, Matt. *A View to a Death in the Morning: Hunting and Nature through History*. Cambridge, Mass.: Harvard University Press 1993.

Cayouette, Pierre. "Signes d'overdose." *Le Devoir* (21 July 1997): A1.

Chabot, Claude and Denise Pérusse, eds. *Cinéma et sexualité*. Quebec City: Prospec 1988.

Chabot, Claude et al. *Le Cinéma québécois des années 80*. Montreal: Cinémathèque québécoise 1989.

Chambers, Iain. "A Miniature History of the Walkman." *New Formations*, 11 (summer 1990): 1–4.

– *The Post-Colonial Question: Common Skies, Divided Horizons*. London: Routledge 1996.

Charest, Robert. *Robert Lepage Quelques zones de liberté*. Quebec City: L'Instant même/Ex machina 1995.

Chartier, J. "De Gaulle n'a pas improvisé." *Le Devoir* (22 July 1997): A1 and A8.

– "De Gaulle s'était adressé aux Québécois dès 1940." *Le Devoir* (22 July 1997): A2.

Chevallier, Jacques. *Kids: 51 films autour de l'enfance*. Paris: Centre national de documentation pédagogique 1988.

Cinéastes du Québec 2: Gilles Carle. Montreal: Conseil québécois pour la diffusion du cinéma 1976.

Cinéastes du Québec 4: Claude Jutra. Montreal: Conseil québécois pour la diffusion du cinéma 1970.

Cinéma et histoire: Bilan des études en cinéma dans les universités québécoises. Montreal: Colloque de l'Association québécoise des études cinématographiques 1986.

Clandfield, David. *Canadian Film.* Toronto: Oxford University Press 1987.

– "Dialectical Interpretation: The case of *cinéma direct* and Pierre Perrault. *Cineaction* 16 (May 1989): 20–4.

Clarke, David B., ed. *The Cinematic City.* London: Routledge 1997.

Cohen, Barry. "Technological Colonialism and the Politics of Water." *Cultural Studies* 8, no. 1 (January 1994): 32–55.

Collectif CLIO. *L'Histoire des femmes au Québec depuis quatre siècles.* Montreal: Le Jour 1992.

Collins, Richard. "Between Two Broadcasting Acts: Canadian Broadcasting Policy and the Public Sector from 1968 to 1991 ". *British Journal of Canadian Studies* 6, no. 2 (1991): 319–38.

– *Culture, Communication, and National Identity: The Case of Canadian Television.* Toronto: University of Toronto Press 1990.

– *Television Policy and Culture.* London: Unwin Hyman 1990.

Colpron, Gilles. *Les Anglicismes au Québec.* Montreal: Beauchemin 1970.

Comolli, Jean-Louis. "Le détour par le direct I." *Cahiers du cinéma* 209 (February 1969): 48–53.

"Le détour par le direct II." *Cahiers du cinéma* 211 (April 1969): 40–5.

Copie Zéro 19 (January 1984), on André Forcier.

Copie Zéro 23 (February 1985), on Anne Claire Poirier.

Copie Zéro 31 (March 1987), on André Melançon.

Copie Zéro 33 (September 1987), on Claude Jutra.

Copie Zéro 34–5 (December 1987–March 1988), on Denys Arcand.

Coulombe, Michel. *Denys Arcand: la vraie nature du cinéaste.* Montreal: Boréal 1993.

– "Entretien avec Michel Poulette." *Ciné-Bulles* 13, no. 3 (summer 1994): 16–19.

– *Entretiens avec Gilles Carle: le chemin secret du cinéma.* Montreal: Liber 1995.

Coulombe, Michel and Marcel Jean, eds. *Le Dictionnaire du cinéma québécois.* Montreal: Boréal, 1991.

Cousineau, Louise. "On a ri aux larmes en voyant *Dodo,* mais Dodo et Denise se sont mises à pleurer." *La Presse,* 25 February 1992.

Cowie, Peter, ed. *Variety International Film Guide.* London: André Deutsch 1991.

Daigneault, C. "Alec Pelletier, une femme à la mesure de notre éveil." *Le Soleil* (29 May 1965).

D'Apollonia, François. "Gilles Carle: *Les Plouffe.*" *24 Images* 9 (May–June 1981): 77–81.

Daudelin, Robert. *Vingt ans de cinéma au Canada français.* Quebec City: Ministère des affaires culturelles 1967.

Debray, Régis. *Critique of Political Reason,* translated by D. Macey. London: Verso 1983.

Delâge, Denys. "Les Amérindiens dans l'imaginaire québécois," three parts, *Le Devoir* 12–14 September 1991: 15, 13, B14.

– *Le Pays renversé.* Montreal: Boréal 1985.

Deléas, Josette. "La quête du père dans le film *Sonatine* de Micheline Lanctôt." *Cinémas* 8, nos. 1–2 (fall 1997): 187–99.

Deleuze, Gilles. *Cinema 1: The Movement-Image,* translated by H. Tomlinson and B. Habberjam. London: Athlone Press 1986.

– *Cinema 2: The Time-Image,* translated by H. Tomlinson and R. Galeta. London: Athlone Press 1989.

Deleuze, Gilles and Félix Guattari. *Kafka: Toward a Minor Literature,* translated by D. Polan. Minneapolis: University of Minnesota Press 1986.

– *A Thousand Plateaus: Capitalism and Schizophrenia,* translated by B. Massumi. London: Athlone Press 1988.

Denault, Jocelyne. "Le cinéma féminin au Québec." *Copie Zéro* 11 (1981): 36–44.

– *Dans l'ombre des projecteurs: les Québécoises et le cinéma.* Sainte-Foy: Presses de l'Université du Québec 1996.

Desaulniers, Jean-Pierre. *De* La Famille Plouffe *à* La Petite Vie*: Les Québécois et leurs téléromans.* Quebec City: Musée de la civilisation/FIDES 1996.

Deschamps, Nicole et al., eds. *Le Mythe de Maria Chapdelaine.* Montreal: Presses de l'Université de Montréal 1980.

Deschênes, Jocelyn. "La mise en scène du trompe-l'oeil: Gilles Carle et André Forcier." *Dérives* 52 (1986): 89–100.

Deutscher, Isaac. *The Non-Jewish Jew and Other Essays.* Oxford, U.K.: Oxford University Press 1968.

Dickason, Olive P. *The Myth of the Savage and the Beginnings of French Colonialism in the Americas.* Edmonton: University of Alberta Press 1984.

D'Lugo, Marvin. "Almodóvar's City of Desire." *Quarterly Review of Film and Video* 13, no. 4 (1991): 47–65.

"Dodo: voici sa généalogie." *Échos-Vedettes* (29 October 1994): 38.

Dollimore, Jonathan. *Sexual Dissidence: Augustine to Wilde, Freud and Foucault.* Oxford, U.K.: Oxford University Press 1991.

Donohoe, Joseph, ed. *Essays on Quebec Cinema.* East Lansing: Michigan State University Press 1991.

Dorland, Michael. "Quest for Equality. Canada and Co-productions: A Retrospective (1963–1983)." *Cinema Canada* (October 1983): 13–19.

Dubois, René-Daniel. *Being at Home with Claude*. Ottawa: Leméac 1986.

Dumont, Fernand. *Genèse de la société québécoise*. Montreal: Boréal 1993.

During, Simon, ed. *The Cultural Studies Reader*. London: Routledge 1993.

Dyer, Richard. "Don't Look Now." *Screen* 23, nos. 3–4 (September–October 1982): 61–73.

– *Heavenly Bodies: Film Stars and Society*. London: Macmillan 1986.

– *Stars*. London: British Film Institute 1979.

Dyer, Richard and Ginette Vincendeau, eds. *Popular European Cinema*. London: Routledge 1992.

Ellis, John. *Visible Fictions: Cinema Television Video*. London: Routledge 1982, 1992.

"Entretien avec Gilles Carle." *Séquences* 113 (July 1983): 24–8.

"Entretien avec Jean-Claude Lauzon." *24 Images* 61 (summer 1992): 10.

"Entretien avec Roger Frappier." *24 Images* 52 (November–December 1990): 4–11.

"Entretiens avec Denys [sic] Héroux." *Séquences* 71 (January 1973): 4–10.

Evans, Gary. *In the National Interest: A Chronicle of the National Film Board of Canada from 1949 to 1989*. Toronto: University of Toronto Press 1991.

Falardeau, Pierre. *La Liberté n'est pas une marque de yogourt*. Montreal: Stanké 1995.

– *Octobre*. Montreal: Stanké 1994.

Feldman, Seth, ed. *Take Two: A Tribute to Film in Canada*. Toronto: Irwin Publishing 1984.

Feldman, Seth and J. Nelson, eds. *Canadian Film Reader*. Toronto: Peter Martin Associates 1977.

Fetherling, Douglas, ed. *Documents in Canadian Film*. Peterborough, Ont.: Broadview Press 1988.

Forbes, Jill and Michael Kelly, eds. *French Cultural Studies: An Introduction*. Oxford, U.K.: Oxford University Press 1995.

Fortier, André. "Maria Chapdelaine à l'écran." *Séquences* 104 (April 1981): 17–30.

Foucault, Michel. *Discipline and Punish*, translated by Alan Sheridan. London: Allen Lane 1977.

– *The Will to Knowledge: The History of Sexuality*, vol. 1, translated by R. Hurley. Harmondsworth, U.K.: Penguin 1981.

Fournier, F. et al. "Déclin d'un empire ou échec d'une génération?" *Le Devoir* (25 August 1986).

Freud, Sigmund. "Contributions to the Psychology of Love I and II," in Gay, Peter, *The Freud Reader*. London: W.W. Norton 1989.

Freud, Sigmund. "Family Romances" (1909), "The Dissolution of the Oedipus Complex" (1924), and "Fetishism" (1927). *The Penguin Freud Library*, vol. 7, *On Sexuality*. Harmondsworth, U.K.: Penguin 1977: 217–25, 313–22, and 345–57.

– "Humour" (1927). *Standard Edition of the Complete Psychological Works*, vol. 21 (London: Hogarth Press 1961): 159–66.

– "The Uncanny" (1919). *Standard Edition*, vol. 17, translated by J. Strachey (London: Hogarth Press 1959): 217–52.

Friedland, Roger and Deirdre Boden. *Nowhere: Space, Time and Modernity*. Berkeley: University of California Press 1994.

Friedman, Lester D. *Unspeakable Images: Ethnicity and the American Cinema*. Champaign-Urbana: University of Illinois Press 1991.

Frost, Robert. *Selected Poems*. Harmondsworth, U.K.: Penguin 1973.

Frow, John. "The Concept of the Popular." *New Formations* 18 (winter 1992): 255–38.

Fuss, Diana. *Inside/Out: Lesbian Theories, Gay Theories*. London: Routledge 1991.

Gagné, Jean-Pierre and Carmen Strano. *Regardez, c'est votre histoire*. Montreal: Saint-Martin 1992.

Gagnon, Alain and Mary Beth Montcalm. *Quebec beyond the Quiet Revolution*. Scarborough, Ont.: Nelson Canada 1989.

Garel, Sylvain and André Pâquet, eds. *Les Cinémas du Canada*. Paris: Centre Georges Pompidou 1992.

Garneau, Michèle. "Dépolitisation et féminisme pépère." *24 Images* 55 (summer 1991): 24–9.

Garrity, Henry. "Subversive Discourse in Yves Simoneau's *Pouvoir intime*." *Québec Studies* 9 (1989–90): 29–37.

– "True Lies: Autobiography, Fiction and Politics in Jean-Claude Lauzon's *Léolo*." *Québec Studies* 20 (spring-summer 1995): 80–5.

Gauthier, Guy. "Petite histoire subjective du direct québécois vu des rivages orientaux de la mer Atlantique." *CinémAction* 40 (1986): 126–37.

Gauthier, Suzanne. "Trois heures enchantées." *Télé-horaire* 7–13 March 1992: 2.

Gay, Richard, ed. *Les 50 ans de l'ONF.* Saint-Martin: Radio-Canada 1989.

Gérols, Jacqueline. *Le Roman québécois en France*. Montreal: Hurtubise 1984.

Giddens, Anthony. *The Consequences of Modernity*. Cambridge, U.K.: Polity Press 1991.

Gilbert, Sandra M. and Susan Gubar. *The Madwoman in the Attic: The Woman Writer and the Nineteenth-Century Literary Imagination*, New Haven, Conn.: Yale University Press 1979.

"Gilles Groulx: *Le Chat dans le sac*." *Cahiers du cinéma* 168 (July 1965): 56–9.

Gledhill, Christine, ed. *Home Is Where the Heart Is: Studies in Melodrama and the Woman's Film*. London: British Film Institute 1987,

Godbout, Jacques. "Francis Fox's Silent Film Policy." *Cinema Canada* 109 (July–August 1984), 21.

– "De Gérard Pelletier à Francis Fox." *Le Devoir* (22 October 1983).

– *Le Murmure marchand 1976–1984*. Montreal: Boréal 1984.

Gourdeau, Gabrielle. *Maria Chapdelaine ou le paradis retrouvé*. Montreal: Quinze 1992.

Gramsci, Antonio. *Selections from the Prison Notebooks*, edited and translated by Q. Hoare and G. Nowell-Smith. London: Lawrence and Wishart 1971.

Green, Mary Jean. "Léa Pool's *La Femme de l'hôtel* and Women's Film in Québec." *Québec Studies* 9 (fall 1989–winter 1990): 49–62.

Grugeau, G. "*Le Sourd dans la ville.*" *24 Images* 36 (spring 1988): 60–1.

Guérif, François. *Le Cinéma policier français.* Paris: Henri Veyrier 1981.

Hall, Stuart. "Cultural Identity and Cinematic Representation." *Framework* 36 (1989): 68–81.

Harcourt, Peter. *Jean Pierre Lefebvre.* Ottawa: Canadian Film Institute 1981.

Haskell, Molly. *From Reverence to Rape: The Treatment of Women in the Movies.* London: New English Library 1975.

Hébert, Anne. *Kamouraska.* Paris: Seuil 1970.

Helly, Denise. *L'Immigration pour quoi faire?* Montreal: Institut québécois de recherche sur la culture 1992.

Hémon, Louis. *Maria Chapdelaine*, translated by W.H. Blake. Toronto: Macmillan 1965.

Higson, Andrew. "The Concept of National Cinema." *Screen* 30, no. 4 (autumn 1989): 36–46.

Hobsbawm, Eric. *Nations and Nationalism in Europe since 1780.* Cambridge, U.K.: Cambridge University Press 1990.

Hocquenghem, Guy. *Homosexual Desire*, translated by D. Dangoor. Durham, N.C.: Duke University Press 1993.

Hocquenghem, Guy and René Schérer. *L'Âme atomique: pour une esthétique d'ère nucléaire.* Paris: Albin Michel 1986.

– *Co-ire: album systématique de l'enfance.* Paris: Recherches 22 (1976).

Hollows, Joanne and Mark Jancovich, eds. *Approaches to Popular Film.* Manchester, U.K.: Manchester University Press 1995.

hooks, bell. *Black Looks: Race and Representation.* Toronto: Between the Lines 1992.

Horton, Andrew. *Comedy/Cinema/Theory.* Berkeley: University of California Press 1991.

Hirsch, Marianne. *The Mother/Daughter Plot: Narrative, Psychoanalysis, Feminism.* Indianopolis: Indiana University Press 1989.

Hobsbawm, Éric. *Nations and Nationalism in Europe since 1780.* Cambridge, U.K.: Cambridge University Press 1990.

Horkheimer, Max and Theodor Adorno. *Dialectic of Enlightenment*, translated by J. Cumming. London: Allen Lane 1973.

Howorth, Jolyon and George Ross, eds. *Contemporary France: A Review of Interdisciplinary Studies.* London: Pinter 1988.

Image et son 336 (February 1979).

Hutcheon, Linda. *The Canadian Postmodern: A Study of Contemporary English-Canadian Fiction.* Toronto: Oxford University Press 1988.

Jameson, Fredric. "Euphorias of Substitution: Hubert Aquin and the Political Novel in Quebec." *Yale French Studies* 65 (1983): 214–23.

– *The Geopolitical Aesthetic: Cinema and Space in the World System.* London: British Film Institute 1992.
– "Postmodernism, or the Cultural Logic of Late Capitalism." *New Left Review* 146 (July–August 1984): 53–92.
– "Reification and Utopia in Mass Culture." *Social Text* 1 (1979): 130–48.
– *Signatures of the Visible.* London: Routledge 1992.
– "Third-World Literature in the Era of Multinational Capitalism." *Social Text* 15 (fall 1986): 65–88.
JanMohamed, Abdul R. and David Lloyd, eds. *The Nature and Context of Minority Discourse.* Oxford, U.K.: Oxford University Press 1990.
Jean, Marcel. *Le Cinéma québécois.* Montreal: Boréal 1991.
– "L'Éternel retour." *24 Images* 44–5 (fall 1989): 62–3.
– *Le Langage des lignes.* Laval: Les 400 coups 1995.
– *Pierre Hébert. L'Homme animé.* Laval: Les 400 coups 1996.
– "Qui est la star?" *24 Images* 38 (summer 1988): 5–7.
Jenkins, Henry. *Textual Poachers: Television Fans and Participatory Culture.* New York: Routledge 1992.
Jewsiecki, Bogumil and Jocelyn Létourneau, eds. *L'Histoire en partage: usages et mises en discours du passé.* Paris: L'Harmattan 1996.
Johnstone, Frederick. "Quebeckers, Mohawks and Zulus: Liberal Federalism and Fair Trade." *Telos* 93 (fall 1992): 2–20.
Julien, P.-A. "Ne sommes-nous pas tous des Amérindiens?" *Le Devoir,* 5 August 1992: 13.
Jutra, Claude. *Mon Oncle Antoine.* Montreal: Art Global 1979.
Kandiyoti, Deniz. "Identity and its Discontents: Women and the Nation." *Millennium: Journal of International Studies* 20, no. 3 (1991): 429–43.
Kaplan, E. Ann: *Women and Film: Both Sides of the Camera.* London: Methuen 1983.
Koestler, Arthur. *Insight and Outlook: An Inquiry into the Common Foundations of Science, Art and Social Ethics.* London: Macmillan 1949.
Kristeva, Julia. *Strangers to Ourselves,* translated by L.S. Roudiez. London: Harvester Wheatsheaf 1991.
Krohn, Bill. "L'été de E.T.." *Cahiers du cinéma* 342 (December 1982): 16–24.
Lacasse, Germain. "American Film in Quebec Theater." *Cinema Journal* 38, no. 2 (winter 1999): 98–110.
Lacoursière, Jacques. *Épopée en Amérique: une Histoire populaire du Québec, épisode 11 Enfin la guerre.* Montreal: Télé-Québec 1997.
Lacroix, Jean-Guy. *Septième art et discrimination: le cas des réalisatrices.* Montreal: VLB 1992.
Lacroix, Jean-Michel and Fulvio Caccia, eds. *Métamorphoses d'une utopie.* Paris: Presses de la Sorbonne nouvelle 1992.
Laferrière, Dany. *Comment faire l'amour avec un nègre sans se fatiguer.* Montreal: VLB 1985.

Lafond, Jean-Daniel. "Le Choc du réel." *Dérives* 52 (1986): 25–40.

Lamonde, Yvan and Pierre-François Hébert. *Le Cinéma au Québec: Essai de statistique historique (1896 à nos jours)*. Montreal: Institut québécois de recherche sur la culture 1981.

Landy, Marcia. *Film, Politics and Gramsci*. Minneapolis: University of Minnesota Press 1994.

Lapsley, Robert and Michael Westlake. "From *Casablanca* to *Pretty Woman*: The politics of romance." *Screen* 33, no. 1 (spring 1992): 27–49.

La Rochelle, Réal. "Un Cinéma de défense des autochtones." *Copie Zéro* 11 (1981): 60–6.

– "Le cinéma québécois, en voie d'assimilation ou de métissage," in Baillargeon, Jean-Paul, ed. *Les Pratiques culturelles des Québécois*. Montreal: Institut québécois de recherche sur la culture 1986: 215–32.

– *Cinéma en rouge et noir*. Montreal: Triptyque 1994.

– "Gilles Groulx: 'collager' politiquement le culturel québécois." *Copie Zéro* 20 (1984): 4–5.

Larose, Jean. "*Chez Denise.*" *Liberté* 141 (May–June 1982): 36–47.

– "Images pressées." *Revue belge du cinéma* 27 (autumn 1989): 25–8.

– *Le Mythe de Nelligan*. Montreal: Quinze 1981.

– *La Petite Noirceur*. Montreal: Boréal 1987.

Larouche, Michel, ed. *L'Aventure du cinéma québécois en France*. Montreal: XYZ 1996.

– , ed. *Le Cinéma aujourd'hui: films, théories, nouvelles approches*. Montreal: Guernica 1988.

"Godard et les Québécois." *CinemAction* 52 (July 1989): 158–64.

Latour, Pierre. *Gina*. Montreal: l'Aurore 1976.

– , ed. *La Maudite Galette*. Montreal: le Cinématographe 1979.

Lauret, Maria. "Feminism and Culture – the Movie: A Critical Overview of Writing on Women and Cinema." *Women: A Cultural Review* 2, no. 1 (spring 1991): 52–69.

Laverdière, Suzanne. "Maria Chapdelaine: personnage symbolique ou fin d'époque?" *24 Images* 17 (June 1983): 36–7.

Lavigne, Jacques. *L'Objectivité: ses conditions instinctuelles et affectives*. Montreal: Leméac 1971.

Lavoie, André. "Le lieu du crime." *Ciné-Bulles* 11, no. 2 (December 1991–January 1992): 50–3.

– "La petite noirceur." *Ciné-Bulles* 14, no. 4 (winter 1995): 43.

Leach, Jim. *Claude Jutra Filmmaker*. Montreal: McGill-Queen's University Press 1999.

Ledoyen, Alberte. *Montréal au pluriel: huit communautés ethno-culturelles de la région montréalaise*. Montreal: Institut québécois de recherche sur la culture 1992.

Leduc-Park, René. *Réjean Ducharme: Nietzsche et Dionysos*. Sainte-Foy: Presses de l'Université Laval 1982.

Lefebvre, Jean Pierre. "Petit éloge des grandeurs et des misères de la colonie française de l'Office national du film." *Objectif* 28 (August–September 1964).

– *Sage comme une image: essai biographique sur le cinéma et autres images d'ici et d'ailleurs.* Outremont: Isabelle Hbert 1993.

Lemay, Daniel. "Simple comme *Dodo.*" *Télé* + (7–14 March 1992): 3.

Lemery, M. "Donner au rire une tournure bien féminine." *Le Droit* (15 March 1980).

Létourneau, Jocelyn. *Les Années sans guide: le Canada à l'ère de l'économie migrante.* Montreal: Boréal 1996.

– "La mise en intrigue. Configuration historico-linguistique d'une grève célébrée: Asbestos, P.Q., 1949." *Recherches sémiotiques* 1–2 (1992): 53–71.

– "La Nouvelle Forme identitaire du Québécois: essai sur la dimension symbolique d'un consensus social en voie d'émergence." *British Journal of Canadian Studies* 6, no. 1 (1991): 17–32.

– "Québec d'après-guerre et mémoire collective de la technocratie." *Cahiers internationaux de sociologie* 90 (1991): 67–87.

– "Le 'Québec moderne': un chapitre du grand récit collectif des Québécois." *Discours social* 4 (winter–spring 1992): 63–88.

– , ed. *La Question identitaire au Canada francophone: récits, parcours, enjeux, hors-lieux.* Sainte-Foy: Presses de l'Université Laval 1994.

– "La saga du Québec moderne en images." *Genèses* 4 (May 1991): 44–71.

Lever, Yves. *Les 100 Films québécois qu'il faut voir.* Quebec City: Nuit blanche 1995.

– *Le Cinéma de la révolution tranquille de Panoramique à Valérie.* Montreal: Yves Lever 1991.

– *Cinéma et société québécoise.* Montreal: le Jour 1972.

– *Histoire générale du cinéma au Québec.* Montreal: Boréal 1988.

– "Octobre 70 dans le cinéma québécois." *Cinéma Québec* 4, no. 5 (1975): 10–15.

– "*Octobre* de Pierre Falardeau. Un film nécessaire?" *Ciné-Bulles* 13, no. 4 (autumn 1994): 50–2.

– "*Robe noire* ou l'impossible rencontre." *Relations* (December 1991): 313–15.

Lévesque, René. *René Lévesque: textes et entrevues 1960–1987.* Montreal: Presses de l'Université du Québec, 1991

Lévesque, Robert, ed. *Réjeanne Padovani.* Montreal: l'Aurore 1975.

Linteau, Paul-André et al. *Histoire du Québec contemporain: I De la confédération à la crise (1867–1929).* Montreal: Boréal 1989.

– *Histoire du Québec contemporain: II Le Québec depuis 1930.* Montreal: Boréal 1989.

Lipovetsky, Gilles. *L'Ère du vide: essais sur l'individualisme contemporain.* Paris: Gallimard 1983.

Littérature québécoise et cinéma: Revue d'histoire littéraire du Québec et du Canada français 11. Ottawa: Éditions de l'Université d'Ottawa 1986.

Lloyd, David. *Nationalism and Minor Literature: James Clarence Morgan and the Emergence of Irish Cultural Nationalism.* Berkeley: University of California Press 1987.

Lockerbie, Ian. "Les Bons débarras ou l'état d'une nation." *Ciné-Bulles* 14, no. 1 (winter-spring 1995): 36–40.

– "Regarder la mort en face." *Ciné-Bulles* 15, no. 2 (summer 1996): 44–9.

– , ed. *Image and Identity: Theatre and Cinema in Scotland and Quebec.* Stirling, U.K.: John Grierson Archive 1988.

Loiselle, André. "Cinema, Theater and Red Gushing Blood in Jean Beaudin's *Being at Home with Claude.*" *Canadian Journal of Film Studies* 5, no. 2 (fall 1996): 17–34.

– "Despair as Empowerment: Melodrama and Counter-Cinema in Anne Claire Poirier's *Mourir à tue-tête.*". *Canadian Journal of Film Studies* 8, no. 2 (fall 1999): 21–43.

– *The Function of André Brassard's Film* Il était une fois dans l'est *in the Context of Michel Tremblay's "Cycle des Belles-Soeurs."* MA thesis, University of British Columbia 1989.

– "Subtly Subversive or Simply Stupid: Notes on Popular Quebec Cinema". *Post Script* 18, no. 2 (winter 1999): 75–83.

Loiselle, André and Brian McIlroy, eds. *Auteur/provocateur: The Films of Denys Arcand.* Trowbridge, U.K.: Flicks Books 1995.

Loiselle, Marie-Claire. "Au-delà du vrai et du faux." *24 Images* 70 (December 1993–January 1994): 4–5.

Longfellow, Brenda. "L'Écriture féministe de *Journal inachevé* et *Strass café.*" *Dérives* 52 (1986): 101–16.

– "The Melodramatic Imagination in Quebec and Canadian Women's Feature Films." *Cineaction* 28 (spring 1992): 4–15.

Lovell, Terry. *Pictures of Reality: Aesthetics, Politics and Pleasure.* London: British Film Institute 1980.

MacCabe, Colin, ed. *High Theory/Low Culture: Analysing Popular Television and Film.* Manchester, U.K.: Manchester University Press 1986.

McQuail, Denis, ed. *Sociology of Mass Communications.* Harmondsworth, U.K.: Penguin 1972.

Magder, Ted. *Canada's Hollywood: The Canadian State and Feature Films.* Toronto: University of Toronto Press 1993.

Maheu, Pierre. "L'Oedipe colonial." *Parti pris* 9–11 (summer 1964): 19–29.

– *Un Parti pris révolutionnaire.* Montreal: Parti Pris 1983.

Major, Ginette. *Le Cinéma québécois à la recherche de son public: bilan d'une décennie.* Montreal: Presses de l'Université de Montréal 1982.

Marcuse, Herbert. *One-Dimensional Man: Studies in the Ideology of Advanced Industrial Society.* London: Routledge and Kegan Paul 1964.

"*Maria Chapdelaine*: Carle versus Louis Hémon." *Cinema Canada* 97 (June 1983): 17–19.

Marks, Laura U. "Deterritorialized Filmmaking: A Deleuzian politics of hybrid cinema." *Screen* 35, no. 3 (autumn 1994): 244–64.

Marshall, Bill. "National Identity and the *Film Policier*: The Moment of 1981."
  French Cultural Studies 3, no. 7 (1992): 31–42.

Marsolais, Gilles. *L'Aventure du cinéma direct revisitée*. Laval, Qué.: Les 400 coups
  1997.

– , ed. *Le Temps d'une chasse*. Montreal: Le Cinématographe 1978.

Martel, D. "Pour public partisan!" *Journal de Québec* (13 December 1997):
  we 11.

Martineau, Richard. "Through a Stranger's Eyes: Gilles Carle and the Image of
  Quebec." *Cinema Canada* 97 (June 1983): 15–16.

Marx, Karl. *Capital: a Critique of Political Economy*, vol. 1, translated by B. Fowkes.
  Harmondsworth, U.K.: Penguin 1976.

Marx, Karl and Friedrich Engels. *The Communist Manifesto*, translated by
  S. Moore. Harmondsworth, U.K.: Penguin 1967.

Massey, Doreen. "A Global Sense of Space." *Marxism Today* (June 1991): 28.

Masson, Alain. *La Comédie musicale*. Paris: Stock 1981.

Mast, Gerald and Marshall Cohen, eds. *Film Theory and Criticism*. Oxford, U.K.:
  Oxford University Press 1985.

Miron, Gaston. *L'Homme rapaillé*. Montreal: Presses de l'Université de Montréal
  1970.

Moffat, Alain-Napoléon. *À tout prendre* de Claude Jutra: une rhétorique de l'homosexualité Montreal: Cinémathèque québécoise/Association québécoise
  des études cinématographiques Série Regarder Voir 1991.

Moi, Toril, ed. *The Kristeva Reader*. Oxford, U.K.: Blackwell 1986.

Monette, Pierre. "Nous sommes tous des immigrants." *Le Devoir* (10 July
  1992): B8.

– *Pour en finir avec les intégristes de la culture*. Montreal: Boréal 1996.

Morisset, Jean. *L'Identité usurpée: I L'Amérique écartée*. Montreal: Nouvelle optique
  1985.

Morse, Brad. *Comparative Assessments of Indigenous Peoples in Quebec, Canada and
  Abroad*. Ottawa: Native Council of Canada 1992.

Murat, Pierre. "Geneviève Bujold: la meilleure façon de marcher." *Télérama*
  1849 (19 June 1985): 10–11.

Nadeau, Chantal. "Américanité ou américanisation: l'exemple de la coproduction au Québec." *Cinémas* 1, nos. 1–2 (autumn 1990): 61–71.

– "Les Femmes frappées de disparition." *24 Images* 56–7 (autumn 1991): 60–3.

– "La Représentation de la femme comme autre: l'ambiguïté de Léa Pool pour
  une position féministe." *Québec Studies* 17 (fall 1993–winter 1994): 83–96.

– "Women in French-Quebec Cinema: The Space of Socio-Sexual (In)differ-
  ence." *Cineaction* 28 (spring 1992): 4–15.

Nadeau, M. "Jean-Paul Nolet fait une violente sortie contre *Le Festin des morts*."
  Télé Radiomonde (3 July 1965).

Narboni, Jean. "Peut-on être et avoir E.T.?" *Cahiers du cinéma* 342 (December
  1982): 25–9.

Nead, Lynda. *The Female Nude: Art, Obscenity and Sexuality*. London: Routledge 1992.

Neale, Steve and Frank Krutnik. *Popular Film and Television Comedy*. London: Routledge 1990.

Nguyên-Duy, Véronique. "Frontières: l'influence américaine sur la télévision et la culture québécoises." *Québec français* 98 (summer 1995): 77–98.

Nichols, Bill. *Blurred Boundaries: Questions of Meaning in Contemporary Culture*. Bloomington: Indiana University Press 1994.

– *Ideology and the Image: Social Representation in the Cinema and Other Media*. Bloomington: Indiana University Press 1981.

– , ed. *Movies and Methods: An Anthology*. Berkeley: University of California Press 1976.

Nicks, Joan. "Sex, Lies and Landscape: Meditations on Vertical Tableaux in *The Far Shore* and *J.A. Martin photographe*." *Canadian Journal of Film Studies* 2, nos. 2–3 (1993): 81–93.

Noguez, Dominique. *Essais sur le cinéma québécois*. Montreal: Le Jour 1970.

Noiseux, Lise. *Les Nouveaux Rapports: Film-Télévision*. MA thesis, Université de Montréal 1987.

Nora, Pierre, ed. *Realms of Memory: The Construction of the French Past.*, vol. 1, *Conflicts and Divisions*, translated by A. Goldhammer. New York: Columbia University Press 1996.

Nowell-Smith, Geoffrey, ed. *Oxford History of World Cinema*. Oxford, U.K.: Oxford University Press 1996.

Nowell-Smith, Geoffrey and Steven Ricci, eds. *Hollywood and Europe: Economics, Culture, National Identity 1945–95*. London: British Film Institute 1998.

Nuovo, F. "Roy Dupuis: la traversée des apparences." *Weekend* 5, no. 15 (9 January 1993): 9.

O'Regan, Tom. *Australian National Cinema*. London: Routledge 1996.

Parker, Andrew et al., eds. *Nationalisms and Sexualities*. London: Routledge 1992.

Pallister, Janis L. *The Cinema of Québec: Masters in Their Own House*. Madison, Wis.: Fairleigh Dickinson University Press 1995.

Palmer, Jerry *The Logic of the Absurd*. London: British Film Institute 1987.

Pendakur, Manjunath. *Canadian Dreams and American Control: The Political Economy of the Canadian Film Industry*. Toronto: Garamond Press 1990.

Penley, Constance, ed. *Feminism and Film Theory*. London: British Film Institute 1988.

Perraton, Charles, ed. *Du simple au double: approches sémio-pragmatiques de* Metropolis *et* Pour la suite du monde. Montreal: Cahiers du Gerse 1 1995.

Perrault, Pierre. *Caméramages*. Paris: Edilig 1983.

– *La Grande Allure*. Montreal: l'Hexagone 1989.

– *De la parole aux actes: essais*. Montreal: l'Hexagone 1985.

– *Pour la suite du monde: récit*. Montreal: l'Hexagone 1992.

Pérusse, Denise. *Micheline Lanctôt: la vie d'une héroïne*. Montreal: l'Hexagone 1995.

– *La Mise en espace-temps des femmes dans le cinéma québécois de 1976 à 1986.* PHD thesis, Université Laval 1989.

Petrowksi, Nathalie. "La Renaissance de l'empire québécois." *Le Devoir* (31 May 1986): D1, D12.

Philpot, Robin. *Oka: dernier alibi du Canada anglais.* Montreal: VLB 1991.

Posner, Michael. *Canadian Dreams: The Making and Marketing of Independent Films.* Vancouver: Douglas and McIntyre 1993.

"La première confession de Robert Lepage." *Séquences* 180 (September–October 1995): 24–9.

Probyn, Elspeth. *Outside Belongings.* London: Routledge 1996.

Radstone, Susannah. "Cinema/memory/history." *Screen* 36, no. 1 (spring 1995): 34–47.

Radway, Janice. *Reading the Romance: Women, Patriarchy and Popular Literature.* Chapel Hill, N.C.: University of North Carolina Press 1984.

Ramirez, Bruno and Paul Tana. *La Sarrasine.* Montreal: Boréal 1992.

Rancière, Jacques. Interview. *Radical Philosophy* 82 (March–April 1997): 33.

Richard, Pierre. *25 ans de télévision au Québec.* Montreal: Quebecor 1986.

Rioux, Daniel. "Dodo qui pleure Dodo qui rit." *Le Journal de Montréal* (25 February 1992).

Robert, Marthe. *Origins of the Novel,* translated by S. Rabinovitch. Brighton, U.K.: Harvester 1980.

Robin, Régine. "À propos de la notion kafkaïenne de 'littérature mineure': quelques questions posées à la littérature québécoise." *Paragraphes* 2 (1989): 5–14.

– "Notre américanité." *Vice versa* 21 (November 1987): 9.

– *Le Roman mémoriel.* Longueil: Préambule 1989.

Robin, Régine et al. *Montréal: l'invention juive.* Montreal: département d'études françaises de l'UQAM 1991.

Robins, Kevin. "Prisoners of the City: Whatever Could a Postmodern City Be?" *New Formations* 15 (winter 1991): 1–22.

Rocheleau, Alain-Michel. "Gay Theater in Quebec: The Search for an Identity." *Yale French Studies* 90 (1996): 115–36.

Rodowick, D.N. *Gilles Deleuze's Time Machine.* Durham, N.C.: Duke University Press 1997.

Rose, Jacqueline. *The Case of Peter Pan or the Impossibility of Children's Fiction.* London: Methuen 1984.

Ross, Andrew. *No Respect: Intellectuals and Popular Culture.* London: Routledge 1989.

Ross, Kristin. *Fast Cars, Clean Bodies: Decolonization and the Reordering of French Culture.* Cambridge, Mass.: MIT Press 1995.

Rouillé, Lyne. "Roy Dupuis: portrait intime d'un homme secret." *Le Lundi* (17 September 1994): 8–14.

Rousseau, Yves. "La Comédie, ce n'est pas notre genre." *24 Images* 68–9 (September–October 1993): 20–4.
– "Dérives urbaines." *24 Images* 77 (summer 1995): 50–1.
"Roy Dupuis." *24 Images* 65 (February–March 1993): 12–13.
Rutherford, Jonathan. *Identity: Community, Culture, Difference.* London: Lawrence and Wishart 1990
Said, Edward. *Orientalism.* New York: Vintage Books 1979.
Sainte-Marie, Gilles. "L'Année des retombées." *Études françaises* 3, no. 2 (1972): 214–23.
Samuel, Raphael, ed.: *People's History and Socialist Theory.* London: Routledge 1981.
Scarpetta, Guy. *L'Impureté.* Paris: Grasset 1985.
"Les scénaristes ont la parole: Gilles Richer et la comédie québécoise." *Cinéma Québec* 2, nos. 6–7 (March–April 1973): 9.
Schwartzwald, Robert. "From Authenticity to Ambivalence: Michel Tremblay's *Hosanna.*" *American Review of Canadian Studies* 22 (1992): 499–510.
– "L'Essai littéraire au Québec: entre l'histoire revue et l'avenir abordé." *International Journal of Canadian Studies* 6 (fall 1992): 161–72.
Sedgwick, Eve Kosofsky. *Epistemology of the Closet.* Berkeley: University of California Press 1990.
– *Between Men: English Literature and Male Homosocial Desire.* New York: Columbia University Press 1985.
Séguin, Maurice. *Histoire de deux nationalismes au Canada.* Montreal: Guérin 1997.
Seymour, Michel. *La Nation en question.* Montreal: l'Hexagone 1999.
Shek, Ben-Z. "*Bonheur d'occasion* à l'écran: fidelité ou trahison?" *Etudes littéraires* 17, no. 3 (1984): 481–97.
– "History as a Unifying Structure in *Le Déclin de l'empire américain.*" *Québec Studies* 9 (winter 1989–90): 9–15.
Simard, Sylvain. *Mythe et reflet de la France: l'image du Canada en France 1850–1914.* Ottawa: Presses de l'Université d'Ottawa 1987.
Simon, Sherry et al. *Fictions de l'identitaire au Québec.* Montreal: XYZ 1991.
– "The Geopolitics of Sex, or Signs of Culture in the Quebec Novel." *Essays on Canadian Writing* 40 (spring 1990): 44–9.
– and Jean-Sébastien Dubé. *L'Autre intime: représentations de la diversité culturelle dans le cinéma et la vidéo québécois.* Montreal: Groupe de recherche sur la citoyenneté culturelle/Concordia University 1997.
Sloniowski, J. *The Cinema of Cruelty: Affective Rhetoric in the Cinema.* PHD thesis, University of Toronto 1992.
Smart, Patricia. *Écrire dans la maison du père: l'émergence du féminin dans la tradition littéraire du Québec.* Montreal: Québec-Amérique: 1988.
– *Writing in the Father's House: The Emergence of the Feminine in the Quebec Literary Tradition.* Toronto: University of Toronto Press 1991.

Sorlin, Pierre. "The Fanciful Empire: French feature films of the Colonies in the 1930s." *French Cultural Studies* 2, no. 5 (June 1991): 135–151.

Spillers, Hortense J. *Comparative American Identities: Race, Sex and Nationality in the Modern Text.* London: Routledge 1991.

Stacey, Jackie. "Desperately Seeking Difference." *Screen* 28, no. 1 (winter 1987): 48–61.

Stam, Robert and Louise Spence. "Colonialism, Racism and Representation." *Screen* 24, no. 2 (March–April 1983): 2–20.

Stern, Megan. "Making the Old Myth New: The Frontier in *The Last of the Mohicans* and *Dances With Wolves.*" *Wasifiri* 17 (spring 1993): 49–53.

Still, Judith and Michael Worton, eds. *Intertextuality: Theories and Practices.* Manchester, U.K.: Manchester University Press 1990.

Stychin, Carl F. "Queer Nations: Nationalism, Sexuality and the Discourse of Rights in Quebec." *Feminist Legal Studies* 5 no. 1 (1997): 3–34.

Summers, Frances J. "La réception critique du *Matou.*" *Voix et Images* 36 (spring 1987): 383–92.

Tadros, C. "*Sonatine*: 'Film maudit': A conversation with Micheline Lanctôt." *Cinema Canada* 110 (September 1984): 7–11.

Taylor, Charles. *Philosophical Arguments.* Cambridge, Mass.: Harvard University Press 1995.

– *Reconciling the Solitudes: Essays on Canadian Federalism and Nationalism.* Montreal: McGill-Queen's University Press 1993.

Taylor, Helen. *Scarlett's Women:* Gone with the Wind *and Its Female Fans.* London: Virago 1989.

Tchernia, Pierre. *80 grands succès du cinéma policier français.* Paris: Casterman 1989.

Théâtre et homosexualité. Cahiers de théâtre Jeu 54 (1990).

Thérien, Gilles. "Cinéma québécois: la difficile conquête de l'altérité." *Littérature* 66 (May 1987): 101–14.

– "Cinématographie des Québécois: Voyageries à 24 images/secondes." *Voix et images* 1 (autumn 1979): 133–41.

– "L'Empire et les barbares." *Cinémas* 1, nos. 1–2 (1990): 9–19.

–, ed. *Les Figures de l'Indien.* Montreal: département d'études littéraires de l'UQAM 1988.

– *L'Indien imaginaire: matériaux pour une recherche.* Montreal: Groupe de recherches sur la lecture/UQAM 1991.

Todorov, Tzvetan. *The Conquest of America: The Question of the Other,* translated by R. Howard. New York: Harper Perennial 1992.

– *On Human Diversity: Nationalism, Racism and Exoticism in French Thought,* translated by C. Porter. Cambridge, Mass.: Harvard University Press 1993.

Torgovnick, Marianna. *Gone Primitive: Savage Intellects, Modern Lives.* Chicago: University of Chicago Press 1990.

Tremblay, Michel. *Les Belles-Soeurs.* Ottawa: Leméac 1972.

– *Hosanna; La duchesse de Langeais.* Ottawa: Leméac 1984.

Turner, Frederick. *Beyond Geography: The Western Spirit against the Wilderness.* New Jersey: Rutgers University Press 1983.

Usmiani, Renate. *Michel Tremblay.* Vancouver: Douglas and McIntyre 1982.

Vallières, Pierre. "*Bingo* sur une foire de confusion." *Cinéma Québec* 3, nos. 6–7 (1974): 31–3.

– "Brault a manqué son coup." *Cinéma Québec* 4, no. 1 (1975): 18–20.

– *Nègres blancs d'Amérique.* Montreal: Parti pris 1968.

Véronneau, Pierre. "*Le Chat dans le sac*: un film emblématique." *CinémAction* 65 (September 1992): 161–8.

– , ed. *Les Cinémas canadiens.* Montreal: Cinémathèque québécoise/Paris: Lherminier 1978.

Véronneau, Pierre et al. *Dialogue: Cinéma canadien et québécois/Canadian and Quebec Cinema.* Montreal: Mediatexte/Cinémathèque québécoise 1987.

– "Les Evénements d'octobre au cinéma." *Québec Studies* 11 (1990–91): 29–36.

– , ed. *Montréal ville de cinéma.* Montreal: Cinémathèque québécoise 1992.

Vincendeau, Ginette. "Community, Nostalgia, and the Spectacle of Masculinity." *Screen* 26, no. 7 (November–December 1985): 18–38.

– "France 1945–65 and Hollywood: The *policier* as international text." *Screen* 33, no. 1 (spring 1992): 50–80.

Viswanathan, J. "Approche pédagogique d'un classique du cinéma québécois: *Mon Oncle Antoine.*" *French Review* 63, no. 5 (1990): 849–58.

Walby, Sylvia. *Theorizing Patriarchy.* Oxford, U.K.: Blackwells 1990.

Warren, Paul. "Américanisation." *Revue de la cinémathèque* 1 (May–June 1989): 18.

Warwick, Jack. *The Long Journey. Literary Themes of French Canada.* Toronto: University of Toronto Press 1968.

Waugh, Tom. "Nègres blancs, tapettes et 'butch.'" *Copie Zéro* 11 (1981): 12–29.

Weinmann, Heinz. *Du Canada au Québec: généalogie d'une histoire.* Montreal: l'Hexagone 1987.

– *Cinéma de l'imaginaire québécois: de La Petite Aurore à Jésus de Montréal.* Montreal: l'Hexagone 1990.

– "Cinéma québécois à l'ombre de la mélancolie." *Cinémas* 8, nos. 1–2 (fall 1997): 35–46.

White, Jerry. "Alanis Obomsawin, Documentary Form and the Canadian Nation(s)." *Cineaction* 49 (1999): 26–36.

– "To Act Is To Be: Identity in Recent Quebec Cinema." *Cineaction* 45 (1996): 18–26.

Williams, Raymond. *Problems in Materialism and Culture.* London: Verso 1980.

Wilson, Alexander. *The Culture of Nature: North American Landscape from Disney to the Exxon Valdez.* Oxford, U.K.: Blackwells 1992.

Wilson, Elizabeth. "The Invisible Flâneur." *New Left Review* 191 (January–February 1992): 90–110.

Winston, Brian. *Claiming the Real: The Documentary Film Revisited.* London: British Film Institute 1995.

Wolff, Janet. *Resident Alien: Feminist Cultural Criticism.* Cambridge, U.K.: Polity Press 1995.

Žižek, Slavoj. *For They Know Not What They Do: Enjoyment as a Political Factor.* London: Verso 1991.

Zucker, Carol. "Les oeuvres récentes d'Anne Claire Poirier et Paule Baillargeon." *Copie Zéro* 11 (1980): 52–5.

Index